D1364077

THE OCCULT ROOTS
OF NAZISM

Secret Aryan Cults and Their
Influence on Nazi Ideology

NICHOLAS GOODRICK-CLARKE

With a foreword by Rohan Butler
and a new preface by the author

NEW YORK UNIVERSITY PRESS
Washington Square, New York

Nicholas Goodrick-Clarke is a specialist on Nazi ideology and currently Research Fellow in the Western Esoteric Tradition, University of Wales, Lampeter.

Published in the U.S.A. in 2004 by
NEW YORK UNIVERSITY PRESS
Washington Square
New York, NY 10003
www.nyupress.org

Published by arrangement with I.B.Tauris & Co, Ltd, London

Library of Congress Cataloging-in-Publication Data
Goodrick-Clarke, Nicholas.
The occult roots of Nazism: secret Aryan cults and their
influence on Nazi ideology: the Ariosophists of Austria and Germany,
1890-1935 / Nicholas Goodrick-Clarke : with a foreword by Rohan
Butler.
p. cm.
Includes bibliographical references and index.
ISBN 0-8147-3054-X (cloth : alk. paper)
ISBN 0-8147-3060-4 (paper : alk. paper)
1. National socialism and occultism.   2. List, Guido, 1848-1919.
3. Lanz-Liebenfels, Jörg, 1874-1954.   4. Racism—Austria—History.
6. Nationalism—Germany—History.   7. Nationalism—Austria—History.
I. Title.   II. Title:
Ariosophists of Austria and Germany, 1890-1935.
DD256.5.029   1992   92-26668
320.5'33'0943—dc20   CIP

Printed and bound in Great Britain by MPG Books Ltd, Bodmin

Contents

Acknowledgements

SEVERAL individuals were kind enough to help me gather the rare sources of Ariosophy and also offered valuable encouragement. Here I would like to thank especially Mr Ellic Howe, Pastor Ekkehard Hieronimus, Dr Armin Mohler, Professor Dr Helmut Möller, the late Herr Rudolf J. Mund, Dr Reginald H. Phelps, and Dr Wilfried Daim. Meetings and correspondence with Herren Hermann Gilbhard, Gerhard Kurtz, Eckehard Lenthe, Arthur Lorber, Adolf Schleipfer, Karlheinz Schwecht, Dr Johannes Kopf, and Dr Johannes von Müllern-Schönhausen also furthered my quest in Germany and Austria.

An earlier version of this work was submitted as a thesis for the degree of Doctor of Philosophy in the University of Oxford and I therefore wish to record my gratitude to my successive supervisors who gave constructive criticism and support: Professor Norman Cohn, Dr Bryan Wilson, and Professor Peter Pulzer. I am also grateful to the German Historical Institute, London, for the award of a travelling bursary in 1978.

I owe thanks to the libraries and staffs of the British Museum; the Bodleian Library, Oxford; the Warburg Institute, University of London; the Wiener Library, London; the Bundesarchiv, Koblenz; the Bayerische Staatsbibliothek, Munich; the Berlin Document Center, and the Österreichische Nationalbibliothek, Vienna.

I am finally grateful to Mr Leonard Baker for assisting me in the correction of the proofs.

Illustrations

between pages 150 and 151

Author's Preface to 2004 Edition

As WE witness the renewed growth of the far right across Europe, America and the former East Bloc, *The Occult Roots of Nazism* helps illuminate its ideological foundations. By examining the occult ideas that played midwife to the Hitler movement, the most destructive rightwing ideology in history, we can better understand their implications today.

When the book first appeared, popular literature on the link between Hitler, Nazi ideology, occultism and Tibetan mysteries had proliferated since the 1960s and Nazi "black magic" was regarded as a topic for sensational authors in pursuit of strong sales. The very existence of this sort of literature tended to inhibit serious historical enquiry into the religious and occult aspects of German National Socialism.

Before the 1980s only a few serious writers, including Raymond Aron, Albert Camus, Romano Guardini, Denis de Rougemeont, Eric Voegelin, George Mosse, Klaus Vondung and Friedrich Heer had alluded to the religious aspects of National Socialism. This neglect was all the more surprising since commentators during the Third Reich had already noted its cultic appeal. A wider understanding of Nazi religiosity awaited the scholarly examination of the pre-Nazi *völkisch* ideology.

The Occult Roots of Nazism documents the lives, doctrines and cult activities of the Ariosophists of Vienna and their successors in Germany, who combined *völkisch* German nationalism and Aryan racial theories with occultism. They articulated a defensive ideology of German identity and illiberalism, since they were especially concerned with the political emergence of the subject nationalities of multi-ethnic Austria-Hungary after 1900. Since their ideas in respect of ancient Aryan homelands (Hyperborea and Atlantis), suppressed pagan priesthoods, Germanic religion and runic wisdom later filtered through to

Heinrich Himmler and his SS research departments, Ariosophy provided a model case-study in Nazi religiosity. The continuity of such beliefs through the Third Reich, with its eschatological vision of genocide, clearly demonstrated the irrelevance of a Marxist analysis based on a critique of capitalism, economic factors and class interest. Only religious beliefs and myth could explain the success of an ideology concerned with special racial and esoteric knowledge, the belief in a nefarious world-conspiracy of scheming Jews and other racial inferiors, and the apocalyptic promise of group salvation in a millenarian apotheosis of the German nation. These ideas all derived from pre-rational and pre-modern traditions.

The first publication of *The Occult Roots of Nazism* stimulated a wider scholarly appreciation of the religious and cultic aspects of National Socialism. Several German books were subsequently published on the *völkisch* movement, now with special reference to the Ariosophists; British and American historians gave increased attention to the importance of religious and millenarian elements in Nazi ideology.

But there is a further compelling reason why *The Occult Roots of Nazism* is increasingly read and noted. The widening scholarly awareness and treatment of Nazism as a political religion is in part a response to the growing role of religion in politics today. The end of the Cold War also concluded the twentieth-century "ideological wars" of fascism, liberalism and communism. Idealistic visions of political order have given way to ideologies of cultural identity, in which religion plays a major part. The rapid growth and impact of Islamic militancy, Hindu nationalism and Christian fundamentalism in the 1990s have sharply reminded us that beliefs and myths can provide a dynamic and often destructive form of political expression. The re-emergence of these forms of political religiosity makes it much easier to understand the extraordinary appeal of myth, religious imagery and political idealism that animated Nazism in its own era.

Meanwhile, the radical right itself has resurfaced in the Western democracies. From the mid-1980s onwards, Western countries witnessed the rise of the radical right, pushing for political space on the margins of liberal society. By the early 1990s, the increasing numbers and political assertion of immigrant and ethnic minorities in advanced industrial states, led the United States, Britain and other states still with predominantly white populations to embrace the idea of a multicultural society. The end of the Soviet empire and its erstwhile impermeable borders across central and eastern Europe then unleashed a further movement of economic migrants, refugees and so-called asylum-seekers across Asia. By the early 2000s Europe and North America had become the favoured destination for migrant population flows from the developing world, often placing an unsustainable burden on local housing, education and health services. Skyrocketing immigration figures, coupled with liberal demands for multi-culturalism, have recreated similar political circumstances to those which gave rise to far-right neo-Nazi parties in the United States and Britain in the 1960s, in response to civil rights legislation and non-white immigration. Once again, far right parties have re-emerged, with the British National Party winning a number of local council ward seats in urban areas of mixed ethnic settlement. Fuelled by these issues, populist parties have achieved a high profile in other European states.

However, the expression of right-wing radicalism is by no means limited to the populist parties that seek electoral success in Britain, France, Austria, Germany, Holland and Denmark. Racial nationalism escalates in numerous underground groupuscules, which communicate through small magazines available from PO box addresses or on the internet, through white power rock music groups and concerts. In this 'cultic milieu' one discovers the ideological heirs of the pre-Nazi *völkisch* movement. This milieu and its mentors are examined in my successor volume *Black Sun: Aryan Cults, Esoteric Nazism and the Politics of Identity*. Such groupuscules coin esoteric symbols of white racial identity, facilitate discourses of resistance to the coloured invasion of the West, and embrace a rich plethora of conspiracy theories and occult ideas involving the mystique of the blood, Nazi-Tibetan connections and even Nazi-manned UFOs. The names of the Ariosophists, Guido von List, Jörg Lanz von Liebenfels, Rudolf John Gorsleben and Karl Maria Wiligut ('Himmler's Rasputin') have themselves become current in this milieu, thereby underlining the direct line of descent between Ariosophy in the 1920s and 1930s and the re-emergence of a cultic far right today.

This new edition of *The Occult Roots of Nazism* appears at a time when the cultic far right has increased its range and impact further by focusing resentment against big government and the growth of regulatory bureaucracy, affirmative action and the race relations industry, and massive increases in third-world immigration. It is highly significant that today's multi-culturalism also recapitulates the special circumstances in multi-ethnic Austria-Hungary before 1914. The example of the Ariosophists, definitively documented in this volume, resonates no less strongly today in the context of globalization, mass immigration and religious nationalism.

Foreword

I HAVE no claim to be an occultist but I welcome this opportunity to write a word at the inception of Dr Nicholas Goodrick-Clarke's telling study of the occult roots of national socialism. When I wrote *The Roots of National Socialism* Adolf Hitler was in power. At that time it had become the fashion, in England certainly, to regard the Nazis as hardly more than a bunch of gangsters who had by some economic or propogandist trick won the following of the liberal-minded bulk of the German people. I wrote to suggest that a deeper explanation might be sought in a German tradition of political thought which was liable to promote an outlook on society in some sympathy with aspects of national socialism. Thus, my book proved to be initially controversial.

As the Second World War progressed, however, it became increasingly evident that something more, even, than fear had been needed to keep a large majority of the German people loyal to the Nazi Third Reich through thick and thin, displaying remarkable courage and endurance almost to the bitter end. After the war this was recognized by the Rhineland statesman who began to lead the Germans of the Federal Republic into the light again and into the great combination of the western nations in defence of freedom. Dr Konrad Adenauer wrote: 'National socialism could not have come to power in Germany if it had not found, in broad strata of the population, soil prepared for its sowing of poison. I stress, in broad strata of the population. It is not accurate to say that the high military or the great industrialists alone bear the guilt . . . Broad strata of the people, of the peasants, middle classes, workers and intellectuals did not have the right intellectual attitude.'

Since the publication of my book (now reprinted in the United States) a formidable amount of further research into the ideology and practice of national socialism, much of it untranslated from the German, has added to our stock of facts and theories. I have sometimes wondered whether the gain in fresh insights has been commensurate. No such doubt arose in reading *The Occult Roots of Nazism*.

Dr Goodrick-Clarke describes his study as an unusual and underground history in exploration of a 'netherworld of fantasy'. In the romantic amalgam of fact and make-believe characteristic of the steamy subculture of Ariosophy, of supposedly occult wisdom concerning the Aryans, the two leading exponents here presented are Guido von List and Jörg Lanz von Liebenfels, both of Vienna in the early days there of Adolf Hitler.

In my own survey, less concentrated in theme and treatment, I considered areas of German political thought liable to predispose many educated Germans towards Nazi ideology, while remarking that the Nazi leaders themselves were mostly men of small education who seized hold of the ideas and prejudices which came most naturally to them, as to others. I also referred to a German interplay of nihilism and mysticism and to a 'deficient German grip upon reality' so that Germans, for all their technical mastery, might find it difficult in times of stress to distinguish the heroic from the trumpery. This suggestion is richly illustrated in the present book, starting from the stress experienced by those of German stock in the face of the Slav resurgence towards the close of the Austro-Hungarian empire, succeeded by the shock of defeat in the First World War.

In examining those thinkers, or dreamers, who most probably did actually influence Hitler and his intellectual peers Dr Goodrick-Clarke validates extensive research by scholarly evaluation. One may notice, for instance, his caution in assessing the influence of Lanz von Liebenfels, assumed by Joachim Fest in his biography of Hitler to have dominated his early years. There is no doubt about the Nazi connections of Rudolf von Sebottendorff of the Thule Society or of Karl Maria Wiligut, the magus who was promoted SS-Brigadeführer by Himmler, more addicted than Hitler to the pagan cult of nordic mythology. Harking back to primitive myths, propagating that of the subhuman *Untermensch*, the Nazis in the twentieth century evolved with great efficiency a political dispensation so innovative and so cruel that it still exerts a horrid fascination.

Dr Goodrick-Clarke concludes that the Nazi leaders were obsessed by 'semi-religious beliefs in a race of Aryan god-men, the needful extermination of inferiors, and a wonderful millennial future of German world-domination . . . a hellish vision . . . Auschwitz, Sobibor, and Treblinka are the terrible museums of twentieth-century Nazi apocalyptic.' Those fierce names were as yet hardly known when I wrote my study. One knows now. And this book further helps one to understand.

ROHAN BUTLER
June 1985

Introduction

THIS is an unusual history. Although it presents an account of past events relating to the origins and ideology of National Socialism in Germany, its proper subject is not the parties, policies and organizations through which men rationally express their interests in a social and political context. Rather, it is an underground history, concerned with the myths, symbols and fantasies that bear on the development of reactionary, authoritarian, and Nazi styles of thinking. It is also a marginal history, since its principal characters were mystics, seers and sectarians who had little to do with the outer realities of politics and administration. But such men had the imagination and opportunity to describe a dream-world that often underlay the sentiments and actions of more worldly men in positions of power and responsibility. Indeed, their abstruse ideas and weird cults anticipated the political doctrines and institutions of the Third Reich.

For historians trained exclusively in the evaluation of concrete events, causes, and rational purposes, this netherworld of fantasy may seem delusive. They would argue that politics and historical change are driven only by real material interests. However, fantasies can achieve a causal status once they have been institutionalized in beliefs, values, and social groups. Fantasies are also an important symptom of impending cultural changes and political action. The particular fantasies discussed in this book were generated within an extreme right-wing movement concerned with the creation of a superman élite, the extermination of lesser beings, and the establishment of a new world-order. The nature of this movement has set it quite apart from the mainstream of rational politics in the twentieth century and demands answers relating to its deeper inspiration. An analysis of the fantasies underlying such a movement can provide new answers to old questions.

1

The following study traces these fantasies by presenting an historical account of the lives, doctrines and cult activities of the Ariosophists,[1] namely Guido von List (1848–1919) and Jörg Lanz von Liebenfels (1874–1954) and their followers in Austria and Germany. The Ariosophists, initially active in Vienna before the First World War, combined German *völkisch* nationalism and racism with occult notions borrowed from the theosophy of Helena Petrovna Blavatsky, in order to prophesy and vindicate a coming era of German world rule. Their writings described a prehistoric golden age, when wise gnostic priesthoods had expounded occult-racist doctrines and ruled over a superior and racially pure society. They claimed that an evil conspiracy of anti-German interests (variously identified as the non-Aryan races, the Jews, or even the early Church) had sought to ruin this ideal Germanic world by emancipating the non-German inferiors in the name of a spurious egalitarianism. The resulting racial confusion was said to have heralded the historical world with its wars, economic hardship, political uncertainty and the frustration of German world power. In order to counter this modern world, the Ariosophists founded secret religious orders dedicated to the revival of the lost esoteric knowledge and racial virtue of the ancient Germans, and the corresponding creation of a new pan-German empire.

The Ariosophists were cultural pessimists. An obvious link exists between their fantasies and the grievances of German nationalists in the Habsburg empire of Austria-Hungary towards the end of the nineteenth century. Such factors as Catholicism, the rapid urban and industrial changes in society, the conflict of Slav and German interests in a multi-national state, the rise of the Austrian Pan-German movement under Georg von Schönerer, and the vogue of Social Darwinism and its racist precepts were also crucial influences upon their thinking. The role and importance of occultism in their doctrines is principally explicable as a sacred form of legitimation for their profound reaction to the present and their extreme political attitudes. The fantasies of the Ariosophists concerned élitism and purity, a sense of mission in the face of conspiracies, and millenarian visions of a felicitous national future.

This introduction is intended to set the scene for a detailed examination of Ariosophy. The background against which Ariosophy arose was that of the contemporary nineteenth-century ideas of nationalism, anti-liberalism, cultural pessimism, and racism. Our point of departure will be the *völkisch* movement which combined these concepts into a coherent ideological system. In his study of the *völkisch* ideology, George L. Mosse has commented on the spiritual connotations of the word '*Volk*'. During the nineteenth century this term signified much more than its straightforward translation 'people' to contemporary Germans: it denoted rather the national collectivity inspired by a common creative energy, feelings and sense of individuality. These metaphysical qualities were supposed to define the unique cultural essence of the German people. An ideological preoccupation with the *Volk* arose for two reasons: firstly, this cultural orientation was the result of the delayed political unification of Germany; secondly, it was closely related to a widespread romantic reaction to modernity.[2]

The disunity of Germany had been graphically illustrated by the mosaic of small particularist kingdoms, principalities and duchies which, together with the larger states of Prussia and Austria, constituted the Holy Roman Empire of the German Nation until its formal dissolution in 1806. After the defeat of Napoleon this state of affairs was barely changed by the creation of a loose German Confederation that left the member states free to pursue their separate paths. If the results of the Congress of Vienna had disappointed German nationalists in 1815, their hopes were again frustrated after the revolutions of 1848. As a result of this slow progress towards political unification, Germans increasingly came to conceive of national unity in cultural terms. This tendency had begun in the late eighteenth century, when writers of the pre-romantic *Sturm und Drang* movement had expressed the common identity of all Germans in folk-songs, customs, and literature. An idealized image of medieval Germany was invoked to prove her claim to spiritual unity, even if there had never been political unity. This emphasis on the past and traditions conferred a strongly mythological character upon the cause of unification.[3]

When Bismarck proclaimed the Prussian king the German Kaiser of a new Second Reich in 1871, national unity seemed won at last. But the new state proved a disappointment to many Germans. The idealistic anticipation of unity had nurtured utopian and messianic expectations, which could not be fulfilled by the prosaic realities of public administration. Quasi-religious sentiments could find no outlet in the ordinary business of government and diplomacy. It was widely felt that political unification under Prussia had not brought with it that exalted sense of. national self-awareness implicit in its expectation. Moreover, the new Reich was feverishly occupied in building up industry and the cities, a process which seemed merely materialistic and which was destroying the old rural Germany, an essential idyll in the romantic celebration of German identity. The mock-medieval Kaiser, his modern battleships and the contemporary *Gründerstil* architecture, have all been cited as symbols of this tension between the old and new in the Second Reich. Behind the extravagance of royal pageantry and pompous street façades lay the secular realities of a rapid industrial revolution.

The exclusion of Austria from the new Prussian-dominated Reich had left disappointed nationalists in both countries. Hopes for a Greater Germany had been dashed in 1866, when Bismarck consolidated the ascendancy of Prussia through the military defeat of Austria, forcing her withdrawal from German affairs. The position of German nationalists in Austria-Hungary was henceforth problematic. In 1867 the Hungarians were granted political independence within a dual state. The growth of the Pan-German movement in Austria in the following decades reflected the dilemma of Austrian Germans within a state of mixed German and Slav nationalities. Their programme proposed the secession of the German-settled provinces of Austria from the polyglot Habsburg empire and their incorporation in the new Second Reich across the border. Such an arrangement was ultimately realized by the *Anschluss* of Austria into the Third Reich in 1938.

The *völkisch* ideology also embraced a general reaction to modernity. Both Germany and Austria-Hungary had been late developers in comparison with the western economies. The survival of pre-capitalist attitudes and institutions in these countries meant that modernization imposed a particular strain upon individuals who still identified with a traditional, rural social order. Many people despised modernization because the growing towns and mushrooming industries uprooted established communities and disturbed their sense of security and status. Liberalism and rationalism were also rejected because they tended to demystify time-honoured institutions and to discredit accepted beliefs and authorities. This anti-modernist discontent has been analysed in the writings of three important German nationalist prophets: Paul de Lagarde, Julius Langbehn, and Moeller van den Bruck.[4]

Racism and élitism also had their place in the *völkisch* ideology. The fact of racial differences was exploited to lend validity to claims of national distinction and superiority. Once anthropology and linguistics had offered empirical standards for the classification of races, these became a staple in *völkisch* eulogies of the German race. A set of inner moral qualities was related to the external characteristics of racial types: while the Aryans (and thus the Germans) were blue-eyed, blond-haired, tall and well-proportioned, they were also noble, honest, and courageous. The Darwinist idea of evolution through struggle was also taken up in order to prove that the superior pure races would prevail over the mixed inferior ones. Racial thinking facilitated the rise of political anti-Semitism, itself so closely linked to the strains of modernization. Feelings of conservative anger at the disruptive consequences of economic change could find release in the vilification of the Jews, who were blamed for the collapse of traditional values and institutions. Racism indicated that the Jews were not just a religious community but biologically different from other races.[5]

The Ariosophists had their political roots in the late nineteenth-century *völkisch* ideology and the Pan-German movement in Austria. Their reactionary response to the nationality problem and modernity led to a vision of a pan-German empire, in which the non-German nationalities and the lower classes would be denied all claims to emancipation or representation. Theories of Aryan-German racial excellence, anti-liberalism, and anxiety about social and economic changes typify their *völkisch* concerns, but their occultism was an original contribution. Occultism was invoked to endorse the enduring validity of an obsolescent and precarious social order. The ideas and symbols of ancient theocracies, secret societies, and the mystical gnosis of Rosicrucianism, Cabbalism, and Freemasonry were woven into the *völkisch* ideology, in order to prove that the modern world was based on false and evil principles and to describe the values and institutions of the ideal world. This reliance on semi-religious materials for their legitimation demonstrated the need of the Ario-sophists for absolute beliefs about the proper arrangement of human society: it was also an index of their profound disenchantment with the contemporary world.

As romantic reactionaries and millenarians, the Ariosophists stood on the margin of practical politics, but their ideas and symbols filtered through to several anti-Semitic and nationalist groups in late Wilhelmian Germany, from which the early Nazi Party emerged in Munich after the First World War. This study traces that survival of Ariosophy through personal contacts and literary influences. The possibility that List and Lanz von Liebenfels may have already had an influence on Adolf Hitler in his pre-war Vienna days is also investigated. Ariosophy continued to be fostered in the 1920s by small coteries that propagated racist mystery-religions during the Weimar Republic in the hope of a national revival. At least two Ariosophists were closely involved with

Reichsführer-SS Heinrich Himmler in the 1930s, contributing to his projects in prehistory, SS order ceremonial, and even to his visionary plans for the Greater Germanic Reich in the third millennium. In this account of their succession, it is shown how the fantasies of Ariosophy, besides being symptoms of anxiety and cultural nostalgia, illuminate the ultimate dream-world of the Third Reich.

PART 1

The Background

1

The Pan-German Vision

THE Austrian state in which both List and Lanz came of age and first formulated their ideas was the product of three major political changes at the end of the 1860s. These changes consisted in the exclusion of Austria from the German Confederation, the administrative separation of Hungary from Austria, and the establishment of a constitutional monarchy in the 'Austrian' or western half of the empire. The constitutional changes of 1867 ended absolutism and introduced representative government and fulfilled the demands of the classical liberals, and the emperor henceforth shared his power with a bicameral legislature, elected by a restricted four-class franchise under which about 6 per cent of the population voted. Because liberalism encouraged free thought and a questioning attitude towards institutions, the democratic thesis of liberalism increasingly challenged its early oligarchic form. A measure of its appeal is seen in the decline of the parliamentary strength of parties committed to traditional liberalism and the rise of parties dedicated to radical democracy and nationalism, a tendency that was reinforced by the widening of the franchise with a fifth voter class in 1896. This development certainly favoured the emergence of Pan-Germanism as an extremist parliamentary force.

The other political changes in Austria concerned its territorial and ethnic composition. Separated from both Germany and Hungary, the lands of the Austrian half of the empire formed a crescent-shaped territory extending from Dalmatia on the Adriatic coast through the hereditary Habsburg lands of Carniola, Carinthia, Styria, Austria, Bohemia, and Moravia to the eastern provinces of Galicia and Bukovina. The somewhat incongruous geographical arrangement of this territory was compounded by the settlement of ten different nationalities within its frontiers. Nationality in Austria was defined by the preferred language of the individual. Most of the Germans—about 10 million in 1910—lived in the western provinces of the state and constituted about 35 per cent of its 28 million inhabitants. In addition to Germans, Austria contained 6,400,000 Czechs (23 per cent of the total population), 5,000,000 Poles (18 per cent), 3,500,000 Ruthenes or Ukrainians (13 per cent), 1,200,000 Slovenes (5 per cent), 780,000 Serbo-Croats (3per cent), 770,000 Italians (3 per cent), and and 275,000 Romanians (1 per cent). The population and nationality figures for the provinces of the state indicate more dramatically the complexity of ethnic relationships: not only did the relative strength of the peoples vary from one province to another, but within the boundaries of some of the provinces the Germans were a clear majority, while in others they found themselves confronting a single united majority race, and in still others they were one nationality among several.[1]

After the Prussian–Austrian war of 1866, the Austrian Germans were barred from union with their co-nationals outside Austria, and were compelled to exist as one people among many in the Habsburg empire. Against the background of democratization, some Austrian Germans began to fear that the supremacy of German language and culture in the empire, a legacy of rationalization procedures dating from the late eighteenth century, would be challenged by the non-German nationalities of the state. This conflict of loyalties between German nationality and Austrian citizenship, often locally sharpened by anxieties about Slav or Latin submergence, led to the emergence of two distinct, although practically related, currents of German national-ism. *Völkisch*-cultural nationalism concerned itself with raising national consciousness among Germans, especially in the large conurbations and provinces of mixed nationality, through the foundation of educational and defence leagues (*Vereine*) to foster German culture and identity within the empire. Pan-Germanism was more overtly political, concerned with transforming the political context, rather than defending German interests. It began as the creed of the small minority of Germans in Austria who refused to accept as permanent their separation from the rest of Germany after 1866, and who determined to repair this breach of German unity by the only means possible after Bismarck's definitive military victory over France in 1870: the *Anschluss* of what they called German-Austria—those provinces that had formed part of the German Confederation from 1815 to 1866—to the Bismarckian Reich, even though that union meant the destruction of the Habsburg monarchy. This idea of making German-Austria a province of the German Reich was called *kleindeutsch* (little German) nationalism, in contrast to *grossdeutsch* (greater German) unity under Vienna, a concept that had declined in credibility after 1866.

By 1885 a considerable number of *völkisch*-cultural *Vereine* were operating in the provinces and Vienna. They occupied themselves with the discussion and commemoration of figures and events in German history, literature and mythology, while investing such communal activities as choral singing, gymnastics, sport and mountain-climbing with *völkisch* ritual. In 1886 a federation of these *Vereine*, the *Germanenbund*, was founded at Salzburg by Anton Langgassner. Member *Vereine* of the federation held Germanic festivals, instituted a Germanic calendar, and appealed to all classes to unite in a common Germanic *Volkstum* (nationhood). Their chief social bases lay in the provincial intelligentsia and youth. The government regarded such nationalism with wariness and actually had the *Germanenbund* dissolved in 1889; it was later re-founded in 1894 as the *Bund der Germanen*.

In 1900 more than 160 *Vereine* of this kind belonged to the federation, distributed throughout Vienna, Lower Austria, Styria and Carinthia, Bohemia and Moravia.[2] Given that there was an equal number of unaffiliated *Vereine*, it is probable that between 100,000 and 150,000 people were influenced by their propaganda.[3] List formed his ideas and political attitudes almost exclusively within this *völkisch*-cultural milieu. During the 1870s and 1880s he wrote for the journals of the movement; he attended the *Verein 'Deutsche Geschichte'*, the *Deutscher Turnverein* and the rowing club *Donauhort* at Vienna, and the *Verein 'Deutsches Haus'* at Brno; and he was actively involved in the festivals of the *Bund der Germanen* in the 1890s. It is against this ongoing mission of the *völkisch*-cultural *Vereine* in the latter decades of the century that one may understand the inspiration and appeal of his nationalist novels and plays in the pre-occult phase of his literary output between 1880 and 1900.

The Pan-German movement originated as an expression of youthful ideals among the student fraternities of Vienna, Graz, and Prague during the 1860s. Initially formed in the 1840s, these Austrian fraternities were modelled on the German *Burschenschaften* (student clubs) of the *Vormärz* period (the conservative era between 1815 and the bourgeois liberal revolution of March 1848), which had developed a tradition of radical nationalism, romantic ritual and secrecy, while drawing inspiration from the teachings of Friedrich Ludwig Jahn (1778–1850), the *völkisch* prophet of athleticism, German identity, and

9

national unity. Certain fraternities, agitated by the problem of German nationality in the Austrian state after 1866, began to advocate *kleindeutsch* nationalism; that is, incorporation of German-Austria into the German Reich. They glorified Bismarck, praised the Prussian army and Kaiser Wilhelm I, wore blue cornflowers (supposed to be Bismarck's favourite flower) and sang *'Die Wacht am Rhein'* at their mass meetings and banquets. This cult of Prussophilia led to a worship of force and a contempt for humanitarian law and justice.

Georg von Schönerer (1842–1921) first associated himself with this movement when he joined a federation of *kleindeutsch* fraternities in 1876 at Vienna.[4] Without the leadership of Schönerer, Pan-Germanism would have remained an amorphous 'tendency' among politically naïve student, *völkisch*, and working-class groups. His ideas, his temperament, and his talent as an agitator, shaped the character and destiny of Austrian Pan-Germanism, thereby creating a revolutionary movement that embraced populist anti-capitalism, anti-liberalism, anti-Semitism and prussophile German nationalism. Having first secured election to the *Reichsrat* in 1873, Schönerer pursued a radical democratic line in parliament in common with other progressives of the Left until about 1878. By then he had begun to demand the economic and political union of German-Austria with the German Reich, and from 1883 he published a virulently nationalist newspaper, *Unverfälschte Deutsche Worte* [*Unadulterated German Words*], to proclaim his views. The essence of Schönererite Pan-Germanism was not its demand for national unity, political democracy, and social reform (aspects of its programme which it shared with the conventional radical nationalists in parliament), but its racism—that is, the idea that blood was the sole criterion of all civic rights.

The Pan-German movement had become a minor force in Austrian politics in the mid-1880s but then languished after the conviction of Schönerer in 1888 for assault; deprived of his political rights for five years, he was effectively removed from parliamentary activity. Not until the late 1890s did Pan-Germanism again attain the status of a popular movement in response to several overt challenges to German interests within the empire. It was a shock for those who took German cultural predominance for granted when the government ruled in 1895 that Slovene classes should be introduced in the exclusively German school at Celje in Carniola. This minor controversy assumed a symbolical significance among German nationalists out of all proportion to its local implications. Then in April 1897 the Austrian premier, Count Casimir Badeni, introduced his controversial language decrees, which ruled that all officials in Bohemia and Moravia should be able to speak both Czech and German, a qualification that would have clearly discriminated against Germans. These decrees provoked a nationalist furore throughout the empire. The democratic German parties and the Pan-Germans, unable to force the government to cancel the language legislation, obstructed all parliamentary business, a practice which continued until 1900. When successive premiers resorted to rule by decree, the disorder overflowed from parliament onto the streets of the major cities. During the summer of 1897 bloody conflicts between rioting mobs and the police and even the army threatened to plunge the country into civil war. Hundreds of German *Vereine* were dissolved by the police as a threat to public order. It is in this background of events involving parliamentary breakdown, public disorder, rampant German chauvinism, and the electoral gains of the Pan-Germans in 1901, that one may find the roots of a new rancorous nationalist mood among Germans in the decade that witnessed the emergence of Ariosophy.[5]

The underlying theme of these varied political protests was the attempt on the part of many Austrian Germans to fight a rearguard action against Slav demands for political and national expression and unity within the increasingly anachronistic multi-national Habsburg empire. Not all Pan-German voters expressly wanted the economic and political union of German-Austria with the German Reich as proposed by Schönerer's programme. Their reasons for supporting the party often amounted to little more than the electoral expression of a desire to bolster German national interests *within* the empire, in common with the myriad *völkisch*-cultural *Vereine*. For wherever they looked in the course of the past decade, Austrian Germans could perceive a steadily mounting Slav challenge to the traditional pre-dominance of German cultural and political interests: the Celje school controversy, the Badeni language ordinances and the menacing implications of universal male suffrage (finally introduced in 1907) represented climaxes in this continuing and unresolved issue. Many Austrian Germans regarded this political challenge as an insult to their major owning, tax-paying and investment role in the economy and the theme of the German *Besitzstand* (property-owning class) in the empire was generally current at the turn of the century. Lanz's early *Ostara* issues and other articles addressed themselves to the problems of universal suffrage and the German *Besitzstand*. Both List and Lanz condemned all parliamentary politics and called for the subjection of all the nationalities in the empire to German rule. The concerns of

Ariosophy were clearly related to this late nineteenth-century German-Slav conflict in Austria.

The strident anti-Catholicism of Ariosophy may also be traced to the influence of the Pan-German movement. Although predisposed towards the *völkisch* paganism of the *Germanenbund*, Schönerer had begun by 1890 to think of a denominational policy by which he might counter the Catholic Church, which he regarded as alien to Germandom and a powerful electoral force. The episcopate advised the emperor, the parish priests formed a network of effective propagandists in the country, and the Christian Social party had deprived him of his earlier strongholds among the rural and semi-urban populations of Lower Austria and Vienna. He thought that a Protestant conversion movement could help to emphasize in the mind of the German public the association of Slavdom—after 1897 hated and feared by millions—with Catholicism, the dynasty, and the Austrian state. The conservative-clerical-slavophile governments since 1879 had indeed made the emergence of a populistic and anti-Catholic German reaction plausible and perhaps inevitable. Many Germans thought that the Catholic hierarchy was anti-German, and in Bohemia there was resentment at the number of Czech priests who had been given German parishes. In order to exploit these feelings, Schönerer launched his *Los von Rom* (break with Rome) campaign in 1898.[6]

Having liaised with Protestant missionary societies in Germany, Schönerer publicly associated the Pan-German movement with a new Lutheran movement, which accounted for about 30,000 Protestant conversions in Bohemia, Styria, Carinthia, and Vienna between 1899 and 1910. The alliance remained uneasy: most of the *völkisch* leagues were strongly opposed to the movement, while other Pan-Germans denounced the *Los von Rom* campaign as a variation of old-time clericalism. For their part, the missionary pastors complained that the political implications of conversion alienated many religious people who sought a new form of Christian faith, while those who were politically motivated did not really care about religion. The rate of annual conversions began to decline in 1902, and by 1910 had returned to the figure at which it had stood before the movement began. Although a movement of the ethnic borderlands, its social bases were principally defined by the professional and commercial middle classes. The greatest success of the *Los von Rom* movement therefore coincided chronologically and geographically with the prestige of the Pan-German party: the campaign neither widened the appeal of Pan-Germanism nor significantly weakened the Catholic Church.[7]

Although the *Los vom Rom* movement was a political failure, it highlights the anti-Catholic sentiment that prevailed among many Austrian Germans during the 1900s. This mood was an essential element of Ariosophy. List cast the Catholic Church in the role of principal antagonist in his account of the Armanist dispensation in the mythological Germanic past.[8] He also conflated the clericalism, the conservatism and the Slav interests of the Austrian governments since 1879 into the hateful adversary of Germanism—the Great International Party. This wholly imaginary organization was held responsible for all political developments contrary to German nationalist interests in Austria and impugned as a Catholic conspiracy.[9] Lanz also appears to have been caught up in this current of feeling. He abandoned his Cistercian novitiate in a profoundly anti-Catholic mood in 1899, joined the Pan-German movement, and is said to have converted briefly to Protestantism.[10] Although going *los von Rom* was but a short intermediate stage in his evolution towards his own race cult of Ariosophy, this step indicates the signal importance of Pan-Germanism in his ideological development.

Racism was a vital element in the Ariosophists' account of national conflict and the virtue of the Germans. An early classic on the superiority of the Nordic-Aryan race and a pessimistic prediction of its submergence by non-Aryan peoples was Arthur de Gobineau's essay.[11] Although this work evoked no immediate response, its notions were echoed and its conclusions reversed by numerous propagandists for the superiority of Germandom towards the end of the century. When the Social Darwinists invoked the inevitability of biological struggle in human life, it was proposed that the Aryans (or really the Germans) need not succumb to the fate of deterioration, but could prevail against the threats of decline and contamination by maintaining their racial purity. This shrill imperative to crude struggle between the races and eugenic reform found broad acceptance in Germany around the turn of the century: the principal works of Ernst Krause, Otto Ammon, Ludwig Wilser, and Ludwig Woltmann, all Social Darwinists, were all published between the early 1890s and 1910.[12]

Ernst Haeckel, the eminent zoologist, warned repeatedly against the mixing of races and founded the Monist League in 1906 in order to popularize this racist version of Social Darwinism among Germans.[13] These scientific formulations of racism in the context of physical anthropology and zoology lent conviction to *völkisch* nationalist prejudice in both Germany and Austria. List borrowed stock racist notions from this movement, while Lanz contributed to *Das freie Wort* [*The Free Word*, est. 1901], a semi-official journal of the Monist League, and to Woltmann's *Politisch-Anthropologische Revue* [*Political-Anthropological Review*, est. 1902]. The central importance of 'Aryan' racism in Ariosophy, albeit compounded by occult notions deriving from theosophy, may be traced to the racial concerns of Social Darwinism in Germany.

If some aspects of Ariosophy can be related to the problems of German nationalism in the multi-national Habsburg empire at the end of the nineteenth century, others have a more local source in Vienna. Unlike the ethnic borderlands, Vienna was traditionally a German city, the commercial and cultural centre of the Austrian state. However, by 1900, rapid urbanization of its environs, coupled with the immigration of non-German peoples, was transforming its physical appearance and, in some central districts, its ethnic composition. Old photographs bear an eloquent testimony to the rapid transformation of the traditional face of Vienna at the end of the nineteenth century. During the 1850s the old star-shaped glacis of Prince Eugene was demolished to make way for the new Ringstrasse, with its splendid new *palais* and public buildings. A comparison of views before and after the development indicates the loss of the intimate, aesthetic atmosphere of a royal residence amid spacious parkland in favour of a brash and monumental metropolitanism. It may be that List rejected urban culture and celebrated rural-medieval idylls as a reaction to the new Vienna.

Between 1860 and 1900 the population of the city had increased nearly threefold, resulting in a severe housing shortage. By 1900 no less than 43 per cent of the population were living in dwellings of two rooms or less, while homelessness and destitution were widespread.[14] Parallel with this process of overcrowding and slum creation was the large immigration of Jews from Galicia. In 1857 only some 6,000 Jews had resided in the capital, but by 1910 this number had risen to 175,000, which was more than 8 per cent of the total city population; in certain districts they accounted for 20 per cent of the local residents.[15] These eastern Jews wore traditional costume and made a scant living as poor tradesmen or pedlars. Germans with *völkisch* attitudes would have certainly regarded this new influx as a serious threat to the ethnic character of the capital. An example of this reaction is found in Hitler's description of his first encounter with such Jews in the Inner City.[16] Given the Ariosophists' preoccupation with the growing predominance of non-German nationalities in Austria, such local changes would have furnished palpable evidence of the problem.

It remains to be asked if Ariosophy's assimilation of occult notions deriving from theosophy also had a local source in Vienna. Although a Theosophical Society had been established there in 1886, no German translation of the movement's basic text, *The Secret Doctrine*, was published until 1901. The 1900s subsequently witnessed a wave of German theosophical publishing. But while the date of the ariosophical texts (from 1907 onwards) relates to the contemporary vogue of the theosophical movement in Central Europe, it is not easy to ascribe a specifically Austrian quality to the *völkisch*-theosophical phenomenon. Mystical and religious speculations also jostled with quasi-scientific forms (e.g. Social Darwinism, Monism) of *völkisch* ideology in Germany. It is furthermore significant that several important ariosophical writers and many List Society supporters lived outside Austria.[17] It is thus correct to say that, while the *völkisch* racism, the anti-Catholicism, and the anti-modernity of Ariosophy relate to specifically Austrian factors, its involvement with theosophy indicates a more general phenomenon. Given the large number of *völkisch* leagues in Vienna, it is not so remarkable that a small coterie should have exploited the materials of a new sectarian doctrine as fresh 'proof' for their theories of Aryan-German superiority. The particular appropriateness of theosophy for a vindication of élitism and racism is reserved for a later discussion.[18]

To conclude: the origins of Ariosophy in Vienna may be related to the problems of modernity and nationalism in the Habsburg empire at the beginning of the century. Although still outwardly brilliant and prosperous, Vienna had become embedded in the past. In the modernizing process, that 'old, cosmopolitan, feudal and peasant Europe'—which had anachronistically survived in the territory of the empire—was swiftly disappearing. Some bourgeois and petty bourgeois in particular felt threatened by progress, by the abnormal growth of the cities, and by economic concentration. These anxieties were compounded by the increasingly bitter quarrels among the nations of the empire which were, in their turn, eroding the precarious balance of the multi-national state. Such fears gave rise to defensive ideologies, offered by their advocates as panaceas for a threatened world. That some individuals sought a sense of status and security in doctrines of German identity and racial virtue may be seen as reaction to the medley of nationalities at the heart of the empire. Writing of his feelings towards non-Germans in contemporary Vienna, Hitler had written:

> *Widerwärtig war mir das Rassenkonglomerat, das die Reichshauptstadt zeigte, widerwärtig dieses ganze Völkergemisch von Tschechen, Polen, Ungarn, Ruthenen, Serben und Kroaten . . . Mir erschien die Riesenstadt als die Verkörperung der Blutschande.*[19]

> [I found the racial conglomeration of the Imperial capital disgusting, this whole medley of Czechs, Poles, Hungarians, Ruthenians, Serbs and Croats was disgusting . . . The city seemed the very embodiment of racial infamy.]

It is a tragic paradox that the colourful variety of peoples in the Habsburg empire, a direct legacy of its dynastic supra-national past, should have nurtured the germination of genocidal racist doctrines in a new age of nationalism and social change.

2

The Modern German Occult Revival
1880–1910

OCCULTISM has its basis in a religious way of thinking, the roots of which stretch back into antiquity and which may be described as the Western esoteric tradition. Its principal ingredients have been identified as Gnosticism, the Hermetic treatises on alchemy and magic, Neo-Platonism, and the Cabbala, all originating in the eastern Mediterranean area during the first few centuries AD. Gnosticism properly refers to the beliefs of certain heretical sects among the early Christians that claimed to posses *gnosis*, or special esoteric knowledge of spiritual matters. Although their various doctrines differed in many respects, two common Gnostic themes exist: first, an oriental (Persian) dualism, according to which the two realms of Good and Evil, Light and Darkness, order and chaos are viewed as independent battling principles; and second, the conviction that this material world is utterly evil, so that man can be saved only by attaining the gnosis of the higher realm. The Gnostic sects disappeared in the fourth century, but their ideas inspired the dualistic Manichaean religion of the second century and also the *Hermetica*. These Greek texts were composed in Egypt between the third and fifth centuries and developed a synthesis of Gnostic ideas, Neoplatonism and cabbalistic theosophy. Since these mystical doctrines arose against a background of cultural and social change, a correlation has been noted between the proliferation of the sects and the breakdown of the stable agricultural order of the late Roman Empire.[1]

When the basic assumptions of the medieval world were shaken by new modes of enquiry and geographical discoveries in the fifteenth century, Gnostic and Hermetic ideas enjoyed a brief revival. Prominent humanists and scholar magicians edited the old classical texts during the Renaissance and thus created a modern corpus of occult specu-lation. But after the triumph of empiricism in the seventeenth-century scientific revolution, such ideas became the preserve of only a few antiquarians and mystics. By the eighteenth century these unorthodox religious and philosophical concerns were well defined as 'occult', inasmuch as they lay on the outermost fringe of accepted forms of knowledge and discourse. However, a reaction to the rationalist Enlightenment, taking the form of a quickening romantic temper, an interest in the Middle Ages and a desire for mystery, encouraged a revival of occultism in Europe from about 1770.

Germany boasted several renowned scholar magicians in the Renaissance, and a number of secret societies devoted to Rosicrucianism, theosophy, and alchemy also flourished there from the seventeenth to the nineteenth centuries. However, the impetus for the neo-romantic occult revival of the nineteenth century did not arise in Germany. It is attributable rather to the reaction against the reign of materialist, rationalist and positivist ideas in the utilitarian and industrial cultures of America and England. The modern German occult revival owes its inception to the popularity of theosophy in the Anglo-Saxon world during the 1880s. Here theosophy refers to the international sectarian movement deriving from the activities and writings of the Russian adventuress and occultist, Helena Petrovna Blavatsky (1831–91). Her colourful life and travels in the 1850s and 1860s, her clairvoyant powers and penchant for supernatural phenomena, her interest in American spiritualism during the 1870s, followed by her foundation of the Theosophical Society at New York in 1875 and the subsequent removal of its operations to India between 1879 and 1885, have all been fully documented in several biographies.[2] Here the essentials of theosophy as a doctrine will be summarized before tracing its penetration of Central Europe.

Madame Blavatsky's first book, *Isis Unveiled* (1877), was less an outline of her new religion than a rambling tirade against the rationalist and materialistic culture of modern Western civilization. Her use of traditional esoteric sources to discredit present-day beliefs showed clearly how much she hankered after ancient religious truths in defiance of contemporary agnosticism and modern science. In this enterprise she drew upon a range of secondary sources treating of pagan mythology and mystery religions, Gnosticism, the *Hermetica*, and the arcane lore of the Renaissance scholars, the Rosicrucians and other secret fraternities. W. E. Coleman has shown that her work comprises a sustained and frequent plagiarism of about one hundred contemporary texts, chiefly relating to ancient and exotic religions, demonology, Freemasonry and the case for spiritualism.[3] Behind these diverse traditions, Madame Blavatsky discerned the unique source of their inspiration: the occult lore of ancient Egypt. Her fascination with Egypt as the fount of all wisdom arose from her enthusiastic reading of the English author Sir Edward Bulwer-Lytton. His novel *The Last Days of Pompeii* (1834) had been conceived of as a narrative of the impact of the Isis cult in Rome during the first century AD. His later works, *Zanoni* (1842), *A Strange Story* (1862), and *The Coming Race* (1871), also dwelt on esoteric initiation and secret fraternities dedicated to occult knowledge in a way which exercised an extraordinary fascination on the romantic mind of the nineteenth century. It is ironical that early theosophy should have been principally inspired by English occult fiction, a fact made abundantly clear by Liljegren's comparative textual studies.[4]

Only after Madame Blavatsky and her followers moved to India in 1879 did theosophy receive a more systematic formulation. At the new headquarters of the Theosophical Society in Madras she wrote *The Secret Doctrine* (1888). This work betrayed her plagiarism again but now her sources were mainly contemporary works on Hinduism and modern science.[5] Her new book was presented as a commentary on a secret text called the 'Stanzas of Dzyan', which she claimed to have seen in a subterranean Himalayan monastery. This new interest in Indian lore may reflect her sensitivity to changes in the direction of scholarship: witness the contemporary importance of Sanskrit as a basis for the comparative study of so-called Aryan languages under Franz Bopp and Max Müller. Now the East rather than Egypt was seen as the source of ancient wisdom. Later theosophical doctrine consequently displays a marked similarity to the religious tenets of Hinduism.

The Secret Doctrine claimed to describe the activities of God from the beginning of one period of universal creation until its end, a cyclical process which continues indefinitely over and over again. The story related how the present universe was born, whence it emanated, what powers fashion it, whither it is progressing, and what it all means. The first volume (Cosmogenesis) outlined the scheme according to which the primal unity of an unmanifest divine being differentiates itself into a multiformity of consciously evolving beings that gradually fill the universe. The divine being manifested itself initially through an emanation and three subsequent Logoi: these cosmic phases created time, space, and matter, and were symbolized by a series of sacred Hindu sigils $\bigcirc \, \odot \, \oplus \, \ominus \, \oplus$. All subsequent creation occurred in conformity with the divine plan, passing through seven 'rounds' or evolutionary cycles. In the first round the universe was characterized by the predominance of fire, in the second by air, in the third by water, in the fourth by earth, and in the others by ether. This sequence reflected the cyclical fall of the universe from divine grace over the first four rounds and its following redemption over the next three, before everything contracted once more to the point of primal unity for the start of a new major cycle. Madame Blavatsky illustrated the stages of the cosmic cycle with a variety of esoteric symbols, including triangles, triskelions, and swastikas. So extensive was her use of this latter Eastern sign of fortune and fertility that she included it in her design for the seal of the Theosophical Society. The executive agent of the entire cosmic enterprise was called Fohat, 'a universal agent employed by the Sons of God to create and uphold our world'. The manifestations of this force were, according to Blavatsky, electricity and solar energy, and 'the objectivised thought of the gods'. This electro-spiritual force was in tune with contemporary vitalist and scientific thought.

The second volume (Anthropogenesis) attempted to relate man to this grandiose vision of the cosmos. Not only was humanity assigned an age of far greater antiquity than that conceded by science, but it was also integrated into a scheme of cosmic, physical, and spiritual evolution. These theories were partly derived from late nineteenth-century scholarship concerning palaeontology, inasmuch as Blavatsky adopted a racial theory of human evolution. She extended her cyclical doctrine with the assertion that each round witnessed the rise and fall of seven consecutive root-races, which descended on the scale of spiritual development from the first to the fourth, becoming increasingly enmeshed in the material world (the Gnostic notion of a Fall from Light into Darkness was quite explicit), before ascending through progressively superior root-races from the fifth to the seventh. According to Blavatsky, present humanity constituted the fifth root-race upon a planet that was passing through the fourth cosmic round, so that a process of spiritual advance lay before the species. The fifth root-race was called the Aryan race and had been preceded by the fourth root-race of the Atlanteans, which had largely perished in a flood that submerged their mid-Atlantic continent. The Atlanteans had wielded psychic forces with which our race was not familiar, their gigantism enabled them to build cyclopean structures, and they possessed a superior technology based upon the successful exploitation of Fohat. The three earlier races of the present planetary round were proto-human, consisting of the first Astral root-race which arose in an invisible, imperishable and sacred land and the second Hyperborean root-race which had dwelt on a vanished polar continent. The third Lemurian root-race flourished on a continent which had lain in the Indian Ocean. It was probably due to this race's position at or near the spiritual nadir of the evolutionary racial cycle that Blavatsky charged the Lemurians with racial miscegenation entailing a kind of Fall and the breeding of monsters.[6]

A further important theosophical tenet was the belief in reincarnation and karma, also taken from Hinduism. The individual human ego was regarded as a tiny fragment of the divine being. Through reincarnation each ego pursued a cosmic journey through the rounds and the root-races which led it towards eventual reunion with the divine being whence it had originally issued. This path of countless rebirths also recorded a story of cyclical redemption: the initial debasement of the ego was followed by its gradual sublimation to the point of identity with God. The process of reincarnation was fulfilled according to the principle of karma, whereby good acts earned their performer a superior reincarnation and bad acts an inferior reincarnation. This belief not only provided for everyone's participation in the fantastic worlds of remote prehistory in the root-race scheme, but also enabled one to conceive of salvation through reincarnation in the ultimate root-races which represented the supreme state of spiritual evolution: 'we men shall in the future take our places in the skies as Lords of planets, Regents of galaxies and wielders of fire-mist [Fohat]'. This chiliastic vision supplemented the psychological appeal of belonging to a vast cosmic order.[7]

Besides its racial emphasis, theosophy also stressed the principle of élitism and the value of hierarchy. Blavatsky claimed she received her initiation into the doctrines from two exalted mahatmas or masters called Morya and Koot Hoomi, who dwelt in a remote and secret Himalayan fastness. These adepts were not gods but rather advanced members of our own evolutionary group, who had decided to impart their wisdom to the rest of Aryan mankind through their chosen representative, Madame Blavatsky. Like her masters, she also claimed an exclusive authority on the basis of her occult knowledge or gnosis. Her account of prehistory frequently invoked the sacred authority of élite priesthoods among the root-races of the past. When the Lemurians had fallen into iniquity and sin, only a hierarchy of the elect remained pure in spirit. This remnant became the Lemuro-Atlantean dynasty of priest-kings who took up their abode on the fabulous island of Shamballah in the Gobi Desert. These leaders were linked with Blavatsky's own masters, who were the instructors of the fifth Aryan root-race.[8]

Despite its tortuous argument and the frequent contradictions which arose from the plethora of pseudo-scholarly references throughout the work, *The Secret Doctrine* may be summarized in terms of three basic principles. Firstly, the fact of a God, who is omnipresent, eternal, boundless and immutable. The instrument of this deity is Fohat, an electro-spiritual force which impresses the divine scheme upon the cosmic substance as the 'laws of nature'. Secondly, the rule of periodicity, whereby all creation is subject to an endless cycle of destruction and rebirth. These rounds always terminate at a level spiritually superior to their starting-point. Thirdly, there exists a fundamental unity between all individual souls and the deity, between the microcosm and the macrocosm.[9] But it was hardly this plain theology that guaranteed theosophy its converts. Only the hazy promise of occult initiation shimmering through its countless quotations from ancient beliefs, lost apocryphal writings, and the traditional Gnostic and Hermetic sources of esoteric wisdom can account for the success of her doctrine and the size of her following amongst the educated classes of several countries.

How can one explain the enthusiastic reception of Blavatsky's ideas by significant numbers of Europeans and Americans from the 1880s onwards? Theosophy offered an appealing mixture of ancient religious ideas and new concepts borrowed from the Darwinian theory of evolution and modern science. This syncretic faith thus possessed the power to comfort certain individuals whose traditional outlook had been upset by the discrediting of orthodox religion, by the very rationalizing and de-mystifying progress of science and by the culturally dislocative impact of rapid social and economic change in the late nineteenth century. George L. Mosse has noted that theosophy typified the wave of anti-positivism sweeping Europe at the end of the century and observed that its *outré* notions made a deeper impression in Germany than in other European countries.[10]

Although a foreign hybrid combining romantic Egyptian revivalism, American spiritualism and Hindu beliefs, theosophy enjoyed a considerable vogue in Germany and Austria. Its advent is best understood within a wider neo-romantic protest movement in Wilhelmian Germany known as *Lebensreform* (life reform). This movement represented a middle-class attempt to palliate the ills of modern life, deriving from the growth of the cities and industry. A variety of alternative life-styles—including herbal and natural medicine, vegetarianism, nudism and self-sufficient rural communes—were embraced by small groups of individuals who hoped to restore themselves to a natural existence. The political atmosphere of the movement was apparently liberal and left-wing with its interest in land reform, but there were many overlaps with the *völkisch* movement. Marxian critics have even interpreted it as mere bourgeois escapism from the consequences of capitalism.[11] Theosophy was appropriate to the mood of *Lebensreform* and provided a philosophical rationale for some of its groups.

In July 1884 the first German Theosophical Society was established under the presidency of Wilhelm Hübbe-Schleiden (1846–1916) at Elberfeld, where Blavatsky and her chief collaborator, Henry Steel Olcott, were staying with their theosophical friends, the Gebhards. At this time Hübbe-Schleiden was employed as a senior civil servant at the Colonial Office in Hamburg. He had travelled widely, once managing an estate in West Africa and was a prominent figure in the political lobby for an expanded German overseas empire. Olcott and Hübbe-Schleiden travelled to Munich and Dresden to make contact with scattered theosophists and so lay the basis for a German organization. It has been suggested that this hasty attempt to found a German movement sprang from Blavatsky's desire for a new centre after a scandal involving charges of charlatanism against the theosophists at Madras early in 1884. Blavatsky's methods of producing occult phenomena and messages from her masters had aroused suspicion in her entourage and led eventually to an enquiry and an unfavourable report upon her activities by the London Society for Psychical Research. Unfortunately for Hübbe-Schleiden, his presidency lapsed when the formal German organization dissolved, once the scandal became more widely publicized following the exodus of the theosophists from India in April 1885.[12] Henceforth Blavatsky lived in London and found eager new pupils amongst the upper classes of Victorian England.

In 1886 Hübbe-Schleiden stimulated a more serious awareness of occultism in Germany through the publication of a scholarly monthly periodical, *Die Sphinx*, which was concerned with a discussion of spiritualism, psychical research, and paranormal phenomena from a scientific point of view. Its principal contributors were eminent psychologists, philosophers and historians. Here Max Dessoir expounded hypnotism, while Eduard von Hartmann developed a philosophy of 'individualism', according to which the ego survived death as a discarnate entity, against a background of Kantian thought, Christian theology, and spiritualist speculations. Carl du Prel, the psychical researcher, and his colleague Lazar von Hellenbach, who had held seances with the famous American medium Henry Slade in Vienna, both contributed essays in a similar vein. Another important member of the *Sphinx* circle was Karl Kiesewetter, whose studies in the history of the post-Renaissance esoteric tradition brought knowledge of the scholar magicians, the early modern alchemists and contemporary occultism to a wider audience. While not itself theosophical, Hübbe-Schleiden's periodical was a powerful element in the German occult revival until it ceased publication in 1895.

Besides this scientific current of occultism, there arose in the 1890s a broader German theosophical movement, which derived mainly from the popularizing efforts of Franz Hartmann (1838–1912). Hartmann had been born in Donauwörth and brought up in Kempten, where his father held office as a court doctor. After military service with a Bavarian artillery regiment in 1859, Hartmann began his medical studies at Munich University. While on vacation in France during 1865, he took a post as ship's doctor on a vessel bound for the United States, where he spent the next eighteen years of his life. After completing his training at St Louis he opened an eye clinic and practised there until 1870. He then travelled round Mexico, settled briefly at New Orleans before continuing to Texas in 1873, and in 1878 went to Georgetown in Colorado, where he became coroner in 1882. Besides his medical practice he claimed to have a speculative interest in gold- and silver-mining. By the beginning of the 1870s he had also become interested in American spiritualism, attending the seances of the movement's leading figures such as Mrs Rice Holmes and Kate Wentworth, while immersing himself in the writings of Judge Edmonds and Andrew Jackson Davis. However, following his discovery of *Isis Unveiled*, theosophy replaced spiritualism as his principal diversion. He resolved to visit the theosophists at Madras, travelling there by way of California, Japan and South-East Asia in late 1883. While Blavatsky and Olcott visited Europe in early 1884, Hartmann was appointed acting president of the Society during their absence. He remained at the Society headquarters until the theosophists finally left India in April 1885.[13]

Hartmann's works were firstly devoted to Rosicrucian initiates, Paracelsus, Jakob Boehme and other topics in the Western esoteric tradition, and were published in America and England between 1884 and 1891. However, once he had established himself as a director of a *Lebensreform* sanatorium at Hallein near Salzburg upon his return to Europe in 1885, Hartmann began to disseminate the new wisdom of the East to his own countrymen. In 1889 he founded, together with

Alfredo Pioda and Countess Constance Wachtmeister, the close friend of Blavatsky, a theosophical lay-monastery at Ascona, a place noted for its many anarchist experiments.[14] From 1892 translations of Indian sacred texts and Blavatsky's writings were printed in his periodical, *Lotusblüthen [Lotus Blossoms]* (1892–1900), which was the first German publication to sport the theosophical swastika upon its cover. In the second half of this decade the first peak in German theosophical publishing occurred. Wilhelm Friedrich of Leipzig, the publishers of Hartmann's magazine, issued a twelve-volume book series, *Bibliothek esoterischer Schriften [Library of Esoteric Writings]* (1898–1900), while Hugo Göring, a theosophist in Weimar, edited a thirty-volume book series, *Theosophische Schriften [Theosophical Writings]* (1894–96). Both series consisted of German translations from Blavatsky's successors in England, Annie Besant and Charles Leadbeater, together with original studies by Hartmann and Hübbe-Schleiden. The chief concern of these small books lay with abstruse cosmology, karma, spiritualism and the actuality of the hidden mahatmas. In addition to this output must be mentioned Hartmann's translations of the Bhagavad Gita, the Tao-Te-King and the Tattwa Bodha, together with his own monographs on Buddhism, Christian mysticism and Paracelsus.

Once Hartmann's example had provided the initial impetus, another important periodical sprang up. In 1896 Paul Zillmann founded the *Metaphysische Rundschau [Metaphysical Review]*, a monthly periodical which dealt with many aspects of the esoteric tradition, while also embracing new parapsychological research as a successor to *Die Sphinx*. Zillmann, who lived at Gross-Lichterfelde near Berlin, was an executive committee member of a new German Theosophical Society founded under Hartmann's presidency at Berlin in August 1896, when the American theosophists Katherine Tingley, E. T. Hargrove and C. F. Wright were travelling through Europe to drum up overseas support for their movement.[15] Zillmann's own studies and the articles in his periodical betrayed a marked eclecticism: contributions on yoga, phrenology, astrology, animal magnetism and hypnotism jostled with reprints of the medieval German mystics, a late eighteenth-century rosicrucian-alchemical treatise, and the works of the modern French occultist Gérard Encausse (Papus). Hartmann supplied a fictional story about his discovery of a secret Rosicrucian monastery in the Bavarian Alps, which fed the minds of readers with romantic notions of adepts in the middle of modern Europe.[16] Zillmann was so inspired by the early nineteenth-century mystic Eckhartshausen and his ideas for a secret school of illuminates that he founded an occult lodge in early 1897. This *Wald-Loge* (Forest Lodge) was organized into three quasi-masonic grades of initiation.[17] In Zillmann's entourage there worked the occultist Ferdinand Maack, devoted to the study of newly discovered rays in the context of his own 'dynamosophic' science and an edition of the traditional Rosicrucian texts, the astrologer Albert Kniepf, Indian theosophists and writers on the American movements of Christian Science and New Thought. In his capacity of publisher, Paul Zillmann was an important link between the German occult subculture and the Ariosophists of Vienna, whose works he issued under his own imprint between 1906 and 1908.

The German Theosophical Society had been established in August 1896 as a national branch of the International Theosophical Brotherhood, founded by the American theosophists around Willian Quan Judge and Katherine Tingley. Theosophy remained a sectarian phenomenon in Germany, typified by small and often antagonistic local groups. In late 1900 the editor of the *Neue Metaphysische Rundschau* received annual reports from branch societies in Berlin, Cottbus, Dresden, Essen, Graz, and Leipzig and bemoaned their evident lack of mutual fraternity.[18] However, by 1902, the movement displayed more cohesion with two principal centres at Berlin and Leipzig, supported by a further ten local theosophical societies and about thirty small circles throughout Germany and Austria. Paul Raatz, editor of the periodical *Theosophisches Leben* [*Theosophical Life*, est. April 1898], opened a theosophical centre in the capital, while at Leipzig there existed another centre associated with Arthur Weber, Hermann Rudolf, and Edwin Böhme.[19] Weber had edited his own periodical *Der theosophische Wegweiser* [*The Theosophical Signpost*, est. 1898], while from the newly-founded Theosophical Central Bookshop he issued a book-series, *Geheimwissenschaftliche Vorträge* [*Occult Lectures*] (1902–7), for which Rudolph and Böhme contributed many titles.

While these activities remained largely under the sway of Franz Hartmann and Paul Zillmann, mention must be made of another theosophical tendency in Germany. In 1902 Rudolf Steiner, a young scholar who had studied in Vienna before writing at Weimar a study of Goethe's scientific writings, was made general secretary of the German Theosophical Society at Berlin, founded by London theosophists. Steiner published a periodical, *Luzifer*, at Berlin from 1903 to 1908. However, his mystical Christian interests increasingly estranged him from the theosophists under Annie Besant's strongly Hindu persuasion, so that he finally broke away to found his own Anthroposophical

Society in 1912.[20] It may have been a desire to counter Steiner's influence in the occult subculture which led Hartmann to encourage the publication of several new periodicals. In 1906 a Theosophical Publishing House was established at Leipzig by his young protégé Hugo Vollrath.[21] Under this imprint a wave of occult magazines appeared, including *Der Wanderer* (1906–8), edited by Arthur Weber; *Prana* (1909–19), edited initially by the astrologer Karl Brandler-Pracht and later by Johannes Balzli, secretary of the Leipzig Theosophical Society; and *Theosophie* (est. 1910), edited by Hugo Vollrath. Astrological periodicals and a related book-series, the *Astrologische Rundschau* [*Astrological Review*] and the *Astrologische Bibliothek* [*Astrological Library*], were also issued here from 1910. Hartmann's earlier periodical was revived in 1908 under the title *Neue Lotusblüten* at the Jaeger press, which simultaneously started the *Osiris-Bücher*, a long book-series which introduced many new occultists to the German public.

Meanwhile, other publishers had been entering the field. Karl Rohm, who had visited the English theosophists in London in the late 1890s, started a firm at Lorch in Württemberg after the turn of the century. His publications included reprints of Boehme, Hamann, Jung-Stilling, and Alfred Martin Oppel (A.M.O.), translations of Sir Edward Bulwer-Lytton's romances and the works of contemporary occultists.[22] Johannes Baum's New Thought publishing house was founded in 1912 and moved to Pfullingen in 1919. Although initially concerned with translations of American material, this firm was to play a vital role in German esoteric publishing during the 1920s.[23]

In competition with the theosophists at Leipzig was the firm of Max Altmann, which had commenced occult publishing in 1905. In July 1907 Altmann began to issue the popular *Zentralblatt für Okkultismus*, edited by D. Georgiewitz-Weitzer, who wrote his own works on modern Rosicrucians, alchemy and occult medicine under the pseudonym G. W. Surya. The Leipzig bookseller Heinrich Tränker issued an occult book-series between 1910 and 1912, which included the works of Karl Helmuth and Karl Heise. From 1913 Antonius von der Linden began an ambitious book-series, *Geheime Wissenschaften* [*Secret Sciences*] (1913–20), which consisted of reprints of esoteric texts from the Renaissance scholar Agrippa von Nettesheim, the Rosicrucians and eighteenth-century alchemists, together with commentaries and original texts by modern occultists. From this brief survey it can be deduced that German occult publishing activity reached its second peak between the years 1906 and 1912.[24]

If the German occult subculture was well developed before the First

World War, Vienna could also look back on a ripe tradition of occult interest. The story of this tradition is closely linked with Friedrich Eckstein (1861–1939). The personal secretary of the composer Anton Bruckner, this brilliant polymath cultivated a wide circle of acquaintance amongst the leading thinkers, writers and musicians of Vienna. His penchant for occultism first became evident as a member of a *Lebensreform* group who had practised vegetarianism and discussed the doctrines of Pythagoras and the Neo-Platonists in Vienna at the end of the 1870s. His esoteric interests later extended to German and Spanish mysticism, the legends surrounding the Templars, and the Freemasons, Wagnerian mythology, and oriental religions. In 1880 he befriended the Viennese mathematician Oskar Simony, who was impressed by the metaphysical theories of Professor Friedrich Zöllner of Leipzig. Zöllner had hypothesized that spiritualistic phenomena confirmed the existence of a fourth dimension. Eckstein and Simony were also associated with the Austrian psychical researcher, Lazar von Hellenbach, who performed scientific experiments with mediums in a state of trance and contributed to *Die Sphinx*. Following his cordial meeting with Blavatsky in 1886, Eckstein gathered a group of theosophists in Vienna. During the late 1880s both Franz Hartmann and the young Rudolf Steiner were *habitués* of this circle. Eckstein was also acquainted with the mystical group around the illiterate Christian pietist, Alois Mailänder (1844–1905), who was lionized at Kempten and later at Darmstadt by many theosophists, including Hartmann and Hübbe-Schleiden. Eckstein corresponded with Gustav Meyrink, founder of the Blue Star theosophical lodge at Prague in 1891, who later achieved renown as an occult novelist before the First World War. In 1887 a Vienna Theosophical Society was founded with Eckstein as president and Count Karl zu Leiningen-Billigheim as secretary.

New groups devoted to occultism arose in Vienna after the turn of the century. There existed an Association for Occultism, which maintained a lending-library where its members could consult the works of Zöllner, Hellenbach and du Prel. The Association was close to Philipp Maschlufsky, who began to edit an esoteric periodical, *Die Gnosis*, from 1903. The paper was subsequently acquired by Berlin theosophists who amalgamated it with Rudolf Steiner's *Luzifer*.[26] In December 1907 the Sphinx Reading Club, a similar occult study-group, was founded by Franz Herndl, who wrote two occult novels and was an important member of the List Society.[27] Astrology and other occult sciences were also represented in the Austrian capital. Upon his return from the United States to his native city, Karl

Brandler-Pracht had founded the First Viennese Astrological Society in 1907.[28] According to Josef Greiner's account of Hitler's youth in Vienna, meetings and lectures concerned with astrology, hypnotism and other forms of divination were commonplace in the capital before the outbreak of the war.[29] Given this occult subculture in Vienna, one can better appreciate the local background of the movements around Guido von List and Lanz von Liebenfels, whose racist writings after 1906 owed so much to the modern occult revival in Central Europe.

Although modern occultism was represented by many varied forms, its function appears relatively uniform. Behind the mantic systems of astrology, phrenology and palmistry, no less the doctrines of theosophy, the quasi-sciences of 'dynamosophy', animal magnetism and hypnotism, and a textual antiquarianism concerning the esoteric literature of traditional cabbalists, Rosicrucians, and alchemists, there lay a strong desire to reconcile the findings of modern natural science with a religious view that could restore man to a position of centrality and dignity in the universe. Occult science tended to stress man's intimate and meaningful relationship with the cosmos in terms of 'revealed' correspondences between the microcosm and macrocosm, and strove to counter materialist science, with its emphasis upon tangible and measurable phenomena and its neglect of invisible qualities respecting the spirit and the emotions. These new 'metaphysical' sciences[30] gave individuals a holistic view of themselves and the world in which they lived. This view conferred both a sense of participation in a total meaningful order and, through divination, a means of planning one's affairs in accordance with this order.

The attraction of this world-view was indicated at the beginning of this chapter. Occultism had flourished coincident with the decline of the Roman Empire and once again at the waning of the Middle Ages. It exercised a renewed appeal to those who found the world out of joint due to rapid social and ideological changes at the end of the nineteenth century. Certain individuals, whose sentiments and education inclined them towards an idealistic and romantic perspective, were drawn to the modern occult revival in order to find that sense of order, which had been shaken by the dissolution of erstwhile conventions and beliefs.

Since Ariosophy originated in Vienna, in response to the problems of German nationality and metropolitanism, one must consider the particular kind of theosophy which the Ariosophists adapted to their *völkisch* ideas. A theosophical group had been active in the city as early as 1887, but its members were initially inclined towards a *Biedermeier* tradition of pious 'inwardness' and self-cultivation under the patronage of Marie Lang. Rudolf Steiner was a member of this group and his account of its interests indicates how little sympathy there existed between the 'factual' Buddhistic theosophy of Franz Hartmann, who was also in attendance, and the more spiritual reflective attitude of the rest of the circle.[31] During the 1890s Viennese theosophy appeared to reflect the predilection of the educated classes for piety, subjectivism, and the cult of feelings, a mood which corresponds to the contemporary vogue of the *feuilleton* and literary impressionism in the arts. Schorske has attempted to relate this cultivation of the self to the social plight of the Viennese bourgeoisie at the end of the century. He suggests that this class had begun by supporting the temple of art as a surrogate form of assimilation into the aristocracy, but ended by finding in it an escape, a refuge from the collapse of liberalism and the emergence of vulgar mass-movements.[32] It appears plausible to locate the rise of Viennese theosophy within this cultural context.

When theosophy had become more widely publicized through the German publishing houses at the turn of the century, its ideas reached a larger audience. By this time theosophy represented a detailed body of teachings, as set down in the newly-available translation of Blavatsky's major work *Die Geheimlehre* [*The Secret Doctrine*] (1897–1901) and the numerous abridgements and commentaries by Franz Hartmann, Hermann Rudolph, Edwin Böhme and others. Whereas the earlier Austrian theosophical movement had been defined by the mystical Christianity and personal gnosticism of cultivated individuals, its later manifestation in Vienna corresponded to a disenchantment with Catholicism coupled with the popularization of mythology, folklore and comparative religion. The impetus came largely from Germany, and both List and Lanz drew their knowledge of theosophy from German sources. List was indebted to the Berlin theosophist Max Ferdinand von Sebaldt and counted Franz Hartmann, Hugo Göring, and Paul Zillmann among his supporters. Zillmann was the first to publish both List and Lanz on esoteric subjects. Theosophy in Vienna after 1900 appears to be a quasi-intellectual sectarian religious doctrine of German importation, current among persons wavering in their religious orthodoxy but who were inclined to a religious perspective.

The attraction of theosophy for List, Lanz, and their supporters consisted in its eclecticism with respect to exotic religion, mythology, and esoteric lore, which provided a universal and non-Christian perspective upon the cosmos and the origins of mankind, against which the sources of Teutonic belief, customs and identity, which were germane to *völkisch* speculation, could be located. Given the antipathy towards Catholicism among *völkisch* nationalists and Pan-Germans in Austria at the turn of the century, theosophy commended itself as a scheme of religious beliefs which ignored Christianity in favour of a *mélange* of mythical traditions and pseudo-scientific hypotheses consonant with contemporary anthropology, etymology, and the history of ancient cultures. Furthermore, the very structure of theosophical thought lent itself to *völkisch* adoption. The implicit élitism of the hidden mahatmas with superhuman wisdom was in tune with the longing for a hierarchical social order based on the racial mystique of the *Volk*. The notion of an occult gnosis in theosophy, notably its obscuration due to the superimposition of alien (Christian) beliefs, and its revival by the chosen few, also accorded with the attempt to ascribe a long pedigree to *völkisch* nationalism, especially in view of its really recent origins. In the context of the growth of German nationalism in Austria since 1866, we can see how theosophy, otherwise only tenuously related to *völkisch* thought by notions of race and racial development, could lend both a religious mystique and a universal rationale to the political attitudes of a small minority.

PART 2

The Ariosophists of Vienna

3

Guido von List

GUIDO (VON) LIST was the first popular writer to combine *völkisch* ideology with occultism and theosophy. He also represented an exceptional figure among the *völkisch* publicists in Germany before 1914. First of all, he was a native of Vienna, the capital of Habsburg Austria, which by the turn of the century had stood outside the mainstream of German national development, as exemplified by the Bismarckian Reich, for more than three decades. List, moreover, belonged to an older generation than most of his pre-war fellow ideologues and thus became a cult figure on the eastern edge of the German world. He was regarded by his readers and followers as a bearded old patriarch and a mystical nationalist guru whose clairvoyant gaze had lifted the glorious Aryan and Germanic past of Austria into full view from beneath the debris of foreign influences and Christian culture. In his books and lectures List invited true Germans to behold the clearly discernible remains of a wonderful theocratic Ario-German state, wisely governed by priest-kings and gnostic initiates, in the archaeology, folklore, and landscape of his homeland. He applied himself to cabbalistic and astrological studies and also claimed to be the last of the Armanist magicians, who had formerly wielded authority in the old Aryan world.

Guido Karl Anton List was born in Vienna on 5 October 1848, the eldest son of a prosperous middle-class merchant. Both his mother and his father were descended from trading families that had been settled in the capital for at least two generations. Maria List, the mother of Guido, was the daughter of a builder's merchant, Franz Anton Killian, who had served as the commander of the First Vienna Civil Defence during the anti-royalist 1848 revolution. His father, Karl Anton List, was a leather goods dealer who sold saddlery and other finished articles, while his grandfather, Karl List, had been a publican and vintner by trade. The great-grandfather had also kept an inn.[1]

Guido List was brought up in the second *Bezirk* of the city which lies on the immediate eastern side of the old Danube canal in the centre. Several accounts suggest that List was a happy child in a secure home. In 1851 Anton von Anreiter painted a water-colour portrait of him.[2] Such a commission would indicate that the family was both affluent and identified with the customs of the Vienna bourgeoisie. Young List enjoyed a good relationship with his parents. The Lists delighted in taking their children on country excursions around the capital, and it was these outings which initially established List's love of nature and rural landscape. List also displayed an artistic bent inasmuch as he tried to render these sentiments in both pictures and words, efforts which were encouraged by his father's instruction in drawing and painting. List's surviving sketches date from 1863 (*aet.* 15) and depict castles, prehistoric monuments, and the natural scenery of Lower Austria and Moravia.[3]

Like most Austrians, the List family was Roman Catholic, and List had been duly christened at St Peter's Church in Vienna. However, in 1862, an incident occurred that revealed his lack of interest in orthodox religion. When his father and friends planned to visit the catacombs beneath St Stephen's Cathedral, List was determined to accompany the adults. The dark and narrow vaults made a strong impression on him. He later claimed that he had knelt before a ruined altar in the crypt and sworn to build a temple to Wotan once he had grown up. Evidently he regarded the labyrinth under the cathedral as a pre-Christian shrine dedicated to a pagan deity. List was later to claim that his conversion dated from this revelation.[4]

List wanted to become an artist and a scholar, by which he understood a romantic historian who could read the past from folklore and the landscape. This ambition brought him into conflict with his father, who wanted him to work in the family leather business as the eldest son and heir. List conformed with these paternal expectations and resigned himself to a commercial training, but his submission to the demands of work was by no means total. Henceforth he divided his time between the claims of commerce and a private world of art, imagination and nature-worship. During working hours he would assist his father, but he dedicated all his leisure time to rambling or riding through the countryside in all weathers, while sketching scenes and writing down his experiences.[5] These rural excursions were given direction and focus through List's interest in alpinism and rowing. He was proficient at both sports, becoming a leading member of the Viennese rowing club *Donauhort* and the secretary of the *Österreichischer Alpenverein* (Austrian Alpine Association) in 1871. It is significant that his first published piece appeared in the annual of the Alpine Association. Sport had evidently assumed the role of an active communion with the elemental realms of rivers and mountains.[6]

List's love of nature was inspired by a desire for solitude and escape from the workaday world. He was happiest if he could undertake his excursions alone. Although not averse to the company of friends, he often experienced others as a hindrance to the enjoyment of his inmost being.[7] Surviving descriptions of excursions undertaken in company indicate his withdrawal from the group and a tendency to strike off on a private adventure. His ritualization of such adventures served to make his private world even more exclusive and earned him the reputation of a lone wolf and a mystic. Such rituals are illustrated by his midsummer solstice camps. After a long hike across the Marchfeld, List and his friends had once gone to an inn. When a thunderstorm compelled the group to stay there overnight, List left to celebrate the solstice by sleeping out alone on the Geiselberg hill-fort.[8] Again, on 24 June 1875 he persuaded four friends to take the afternoon off work and to row with him on the Danube. Downstream they came upon the ruins of the Roman town of Carnuntum, where the group camped and caroused into the night. For his friends this was a most congenial evening; for List, lost in reverie, it was the 1500th anniversary of the tribal German victory over the Romans, which he celebrated with a fire and the burial of eight wine bottles in the shape of a swastika beneath the arch of the Pagan Gate.[9]

In later years List frankly explained his attraction to nature as a reaction to the modern world of streets, shops, and factories. He often expressed his dislike of metropolitan Vienna: whenever he left the city for the country he felt he had escaped 'the foggy shroud of the metropolis' and 'fearful scenes of the wild pursuit of profit'. The modern economy had, according to List, led humans astray under the motto of self-seeking individualism.[10] 'One must flee those places where life throbs and seek out lonely spots untouched by human hand in order to lift the magic veil of nature.'[11] His flight into the benign and tranquil realm of nature was an escape from modernity, which he may have associated with paternal pressure towards a career in commerce.

While his father continued to manage the leather business, List could freely indulge his taste for solitude, sports, and long excursions.

But after Karl Anton died in 1877, List was forced to make his own living. Being quite unsuited for commerce, he soon retired from the business and married his first wife, Helene Förster-Peters, on 26 September 1878. He recalled the next decade as a period of hardship,[12] as the couple eked out a very modest existence on scant private means and the small income from List's journalism.[13]

With his business career at an end, List was now able to pursue his interests in literature and history on a full-time basis. From 1877 to 1887 he published numerous articles about the Austrian countryside and the customs of its inhabitants in the newspapers *Heimat, Deutsche Zeitung* and *Neue Welt*, all known for their nationalist sentiment. His studies of landscape were coloured by a pagan interpretation of local place-names, customs and popular legends. A typical early idyll about a group of medieval castles near Melk was published in the *Neue Deutsche Alpenzeitung* in 1877.[14] Because the Austrian Alpine Association had assumed a trans-national status in 1874, thereby ignoring the German-Austrian borders of the 1867 and 1871 settlements, List was in contact with both Austrian and German members of the Association with nationalist and Pan-German attitudes. List now celebrated the fact that the landscape was *native*. The Alps and Danube were revered for their national identity; streams, fields and hills were personified as spirits culled from Teutonic myth and folklore. These early articles were distinguished from the juvenilia by their markedly *völkisch* and nationalist stamp.

During these years List was working at his first full-length novel, *Carnuntum*, inspired by that memorable summer solstice party of 1875. In 1881 he published a short account of his vivid experiences on that occasion. Enthralled by the *genius loci* List had gazed into the distant past of Carnuntum. The streets and splendid buildings of the ruined town rose around him, the ethereal figures of its former inhabitants passed before his mind's eye, and then he witnessed that fateful battle between Germans and Romans, which had led to the fall of the garrison in 375. In his opinion this attack of the Quadi and Marcomanni tribes started the Germanic migrations which eventually led to the sack of Rome in 410 and the collapse of the Empire. To List, the very word Carnuntum evoked the hazy aura of olden Germanic valour, a signal motto recalling the event that put the ancient Germans back on the stage of world history.[15] *Carnuntum*, published in two volumes in 1888, described a romance enacted against this fanciful background.

This specious history was doubly attractive to German nationalists in Austria. In the first place List placed *Austrian*-settled tribes in the van of the assault on Rome. Secondly, his account suggested that these tribal settlers of pre-Roman Austria and the post-Roman barbarian kingdoms of the Dark Ages constituted a continuous native occupation of the homeland. Their high civilization, to use List's terms, had been interrupted only twice in its entire history: once by the Roman colonization of Pannonia lasting from *c.*100 until 375, and secondly with the advent of Christianity, or 'the other Rome'.[16] This account reflected List's loathing of the contemporary Catholic establishment in Austria. The present political order and main confession were shown to be illegitimate, deriving from the imposition of a foreign yoke and the suppression of Germanic culture many centuries before.

This mythology caught the attention of German nationalists in search of legitimations for their own disenchantment with the multinational Austrian state. The earliest recognition of his novel proved most valuable to List. In 1888 there had also appeared an historical work entitled *Der altdeutsche Volksstamm der Quaden* [*The ancient German Quadi tribe*] by Heinrich Kirchmayr. The publisher was the *Verein 'Deutsches Haus'* at Brno, whose president was the industrialist Friedrich Wannieck, chairman of the Prague Iron Company and the First Brno Engineering Company, both major producers of capital goods in the Habsburg empire. The *Verein 'Deutsches Haus'* was a nationalist association for German inhabitants of Brno, who felt encircled by the overwhelmingly Czech population of South Moravia. Wannieck was impressed by the parallels between List's clairvoyant account of the Quadi and the academic study of Kirchmayr. Between Wannieck and List there developed a regular correspondence that laid the basis of a lasting friendship. The *Verein 'Deutsches Haus'* later published three of List's works in its own book-series of nationalist studies of history and literature, while Wannieck's munificence eventually led to the foundation of the List Society twenty years later.[17]

Besides its appeal to this *völkisch* circle at Brno, *Carnuntum* helped to establish List as a familiar figure in the Austrian Pan-German movement associated with the names of Ritter Georg von Schönerer and Karl Wolf. Schönerer had first secured election to the Austrian *Reichsrat* in 1873 and became the outspoken protagonist of anti-Semitism and nationalism amongst the German nationals of the Habsburg empire. He made his first anti-Semitic speech before the assembly in 1878 and demanded the economic and political union of German-speaking Austria with the German Reich in his election address. From 1883 onwards he published a virulently nationalist newspaper *Unverfälschte Deutsche Worte*, which stressed the German identity of Austrian Germans and recommended a separation of German provinces from the remainder of the multi-national Habsburg empire. During this decade Schönerer achieved a modest following in many provincial groups, cultural societies, and sports clubs with similar sentiments. All these numerous associations were concerned with raising nationalist consciousness among the Austrian Germans in a variety of ways: anniversary celebrations for German royalty and culture heroes like the Prussian Kaiser, Bismarck, Moltke, and Wagner; midsummer and yuletide solstice festivals in accordance with ancient custom; and study-groups for the appreciation of German history and literature. List now made his own mark in this milieu during the 1890s.

In 1890 Karl Wolf, a Pan-German parliamentary deputy, had begun publishing the weekly *Ostdeutsche Rundschau* [*East German Review*], the political tenor of which was only slightly less nationalistic than Schönerer's paper. List became a regular contributor. In 1891 the paper published extracts of his recent book, *Deutsch-Mythologische Landschaftsbilder* [*German-Mythological Landscape Pictures*] (1891), which comprised an anthology of his folkloristic journalism from the previous decade. The titles of his articles over the next years witness his tireless interest in the ancient national past of Austria: 1893 saw the publication of 'Götterdämmerung' and 'Allerseelen und der vorchristliche Totenkult des deutschen Volkes' in Wolf's paper;[18] in 1894 came a long serialized article 'Die deutsche Mythologie im Rahmen des Kalenderjahres', and, with a typically *völkisch* touch of peasant romanticism, 'Der Kohlenbrenner, ein nieder-österreichische Volkstype';[19] the celebration of national crafts was more general in his 'Die Blütezeit des deutschen Handwerkers im Mittelalter' of 1895.[20] Studies of magical folklore occurred in the articles 'Der deutsche Zauberglaube im Bauwesen' and 'Mephistopheles'.[21] By the middle of the decade List's nationalist sentiment included anti-Semitism, witness his deprecatory essay 'Die Juden als Staat und Nation'.[22] He also wrote in Aurelius Polzer's *Bote aus dem Waldviertel* [*The Waldviertel Herald*] (est. 1878) and in *Kyffhäuser* (est. 1887), which had hoisted the Pan-German flag at Horn and Salzburg. His topics were heraldry and folk customs concerning baptism, marriage, and burial. In his opinion these traditional institutions all reflected archaic Teutonic practices.[23] List's nationalization of local history and archaeology was followed by Franz Kiessling, author of several books on topography, ancient monuments and customs in Lower Austria. The two men were acquainted and doubtless influenced each other.

Journalism by no means exhausted List's support of the Pan-German cause, for he was also active in the movement as a lecturer and a playwright. On 24 February 1893 he delivered a lecture to the nationalist *Verein 'Deutsche Geschichte'* about the ancient holy priesthood of the Wotan cult. List claimed this extinct faith had been the national religion of the Teutons. Moreover, it was a theme dear to List, since it had formed the subject of an earlier lecture read to members of Wannieck's *Verein 'Deutsches Haus'* in 1892 at Brno. In due course this imaginary priesthood would become the central idea of his political mythology.[24] He was also associated with the *Bund der Germanen*, the *Verein* refounded in January 1894 by Karl Wolf and Karl Iro, the editor of Schönerer's newspaper. On 3 December 1894 this league threw a Germanic evening festival, where diversions included a choir, music and the *première* of List's mythological play *Der Wala Erweckung* [*The Wala's Awakening*], followed by a speech on the German mission. The festival was exclusive to nationalists and the ticket of admission read 'not valid for Jews'.[25] As a member of the strongly nationalistic *Deutscher Turnverein* (German Gymnastic League, est. 1885), List commemorated the 1895 yuletide festival of its Leopoldstadt branch with a rousing oration entitled 'Deutsche Treue', which was subsequently published in *Der Hammer* (est. 1894), the monthly periodical of the German Nationalist Workers' League, and appearing as a supplement to the *Ostdeutsche Rundschau*.

List continued to publish his own literary works throughout the 1890s. In 1893 he had founded, together with Fanny Wschiansky, a belletristic society for the purpose of fostering neo-romantic and nationalist literature in Vienna. This *Literarische Donaugesellschaft* (Danubian Literary Society) was modelled on the fifteenth-century *litteraria sodalita Danubiana* of the Viennese humanist Conrad Celte (1459–1508), about whom List wrote a short biography in 1893. The success of his first novel *Carnuntum* was repeated with two more historical romances set in tribal Germany. *Jung Diethers Heimkehr* [*Young Diether's Homecoming*] (1894) related the story of a young Teuton, who was converted to Christianity by force in the fifth century. The novel closes with the joyful return of the apostate to his original religion of sun-worship. Hardly less melodramatic was the saga *Pipara* (1895), a two-volume novel which recounted the sensational career of Pipara, a Quadi maiden of Eburodunum (Brno), who rose from Roman captivity to the rank of empress. Representatives of the Pan-German movement were glowing in their praise of List's fiction. *Pipara* received enthusiastic reviews in both Schönerer's and Wolf's papers. On 9 April 1895 the editorial board of the *Ostdeutsche Rundschau* convened a Guido List evening in the author's honour. There were poetry-readings and lectures by Ottokar Stauf von der March, editor of the *Tiroler Wochenschrift*, and by Karl Ptak, another editor on Wolf's paper. List also composed lyrical pieces in a mythological and nationalist idiom. After his *Walküren-Weihe* [*The Valkyries' Initiation*] (1895) had been published by Wannieck's association at Brno, the Wieden Singers' Club in South Vienna gave a spring recital on 6 June 1896, when his poem *Ostara's Einzug* was sung. The same choral society organized a List festival to commemorate the silver anniversary of his literary endeavour on 7 April 1897. By this date List had become a celebrity amongst the Pan-German groups of Austria.[26]

List's search for the ancient religion of his country led him towards the pagan deism evidenced by his catechism *Der Unbesiegbare* [*The Invincible*] (1898). On 6 January 1898 he had been visited by the Old Catholic bishop of Bohemia, Nittel von Warnsdorf, who warmly congratulated him on his inauguration of 'a new epoch in the history of religion'.[27] On the later occasion of List's second marriage, in August 1899, to Anna Wittek of Stecky in Bohemia, the wedding was celebrated in the evangelical Protestant church.[28] His wife's Lutheranism reflects the spiritual waverings of many Austrian Pan-Germans, who wished to express their disgust with the multi-national empire by a rejection of its common Catholic faith. Aurelius Polzer had converted formally to Protestantism in 1885; Schönerer followed suit in 1900. This tendency was particularly strong after 1898 in the border areas of German settlement, where Austrian Pan-Germans were encouraged by Schönerer's *Los von Rom* campaign to distinguish themselves from their Czech and Slovene neighbours by a Prussian set of sacred values. It has been estimated that there were ten thousand converts in Austria by 1900, and that over half of these were resident in Bohemia.[29] However, List's *völkisch* bias towards paganism precluded any formal involvement with an alternative Christian confession.

Anna Wittek was the actress who had played the Wala at the evening festival in 1894; she also had given dramatic recitations of List's poetry. Her portrait shows a pretty, young woman dressed in a fashion redolent of *fin-de-siècle* mystery and natural appeal.[30] In her List had found both an inspired and inspiring interpreter for his presentation of the sentimental national past.[31] Following their marriage List dedicated himself exclusively to drama. His plays, *König Vannius* [*King Vannius*] (1899), *Sommer-Sonnwend-Feuerzauber* [*Summer Solstice Fire*

Magic] (1901), and *Das Goldstück* [*The Gold Coin*] (1903), were concerned with royal tragedy, solstice festivals, and a love story in times of yore. An interesting product of this use of the stage as a vehicle for his ideas was the programmatic pamphlet *Der Wiederaufbau von Carnuntum* [*The Reconstruction of Carnuntum*]-(1900). Here List called for a reconstruction of the Roman amphitheatre as an open-air stage for the production of scenarios including dragon-slaying, regattas, bardic contests and *Thinge* (annual Germanic assemblies), which would all carry the symbolism of Wotanism to an ever wider public of Pan-Germans in Austria. List called the projected New Carnuntum a 'German-Austrian Bayreuth' and it was indeed evident that the example of Richard Wagner had served him as a model.[32]

By the turn of the century List had achieved modest success as a writer in the idiom of contemporary neo-romantic and nationalistic genres. His writings focused attention on the heroic past and religious mythology of his native country. The year 1902 witnessed a fundamental change in the character of his ideas: occult notions now entered his fantasy of the ancient Germanic faith. After undergoing an eye operation to relieve a cataract in 1902, List was blind for eleven months. Throughout a long and anxious period of enforced rest, he took solace in pondering the origins of the runes and language.[33] In April 1903 List sent a manuscript about the Aryan proto-language to the Imperial Academy of Sciences in Vienna. This document set out the idea of a monumental pseudo-science concerned with Germanic linguistics and symbology: it was his first attempt to interpret, by means of occult insight, the letters and sounds of the runes and alphabet on the one hand, and the emblems and glyphs of ancient inscriptions on the other. Although the Academy returned his manuscript with no comment, this slight piece grew over the ensuing decade to become the masterpiece of his occult-nationalist researches.[34] In September 1903 the Viennese occult periodical *Die Gnosis* published an article by List, which indicated the new theosophical cast of his thought. Here the author outlined the process of the universe's creation and illustrated its phases with the triskelion and swastika glyphs. A fuller discussion of the theosophical influence on List's writings is reserved for a later chapter.

Between 1903 and 1907 List made occasional use of the aristocratic title 'von' in his name: he finally entered the title in the Vienna address-book of 1907. This entry came to the notice of the nobility archive, which urged an official enquiry. On 2 October 1907 List asserted before the magistrates that his family was descended from

Lower Austrian and Styrian aristocracy. He claimed that his great-grandfather had abandoned the title upon entering a burgher trade (inn keeper), but that he, Guido von List, had resumed the title after leaving commerce for a literary career in 1878. In support of his title List produced a signet ring, which his great-grandfather had allegedly worn. This bore a coat-of-arms displaying two rampant foxes (*List* means cunning in German) upon a quartered field, which was the blazon of the twelfth-century knight, Burckhardt von List, according to an old chronicle.[35]

Although it is possible that List did possess some tenuous claim to nobility, the sociological implications of its assertion in either 1878 or 1907 are more important. Why did List want the title must be our first question. According to his own testimony, List assumed the title once he had abandoned a commercial career. As an author, List felt himself to be a member of a cultivated élite, according to an idealist tradition which had struck deep chords amongst the German middle classes of the nineteenth century. Seen in this light, List's assumption of a noble title represents a socio-cultural confirmation of his desired identity.[36] On the other hand, if his use of the title dates from 1907, as the documents suggest, his self-ennoblement can be regarded as an integral part of his religious fantasy. According to his lectures on the Wotanist priesthood, List believed that this ancient religious élite had formed the first aristocracy of tribal Germany. From 1905 to 1907 he had extended this line through his heraldic studies. These discussions treated heraldry as a system of esoteric family emblems which had been handed down from the old hierarchy to the modern nobility.[37] By claiming an aristocratic title and an armorial device, List was reassuring himself that he was a descendant of the hierarchy as well as its historian. His friend, Lanz von Liebenfels, had also assumed a noble title by 1903 and may have influenced List.[38] The aristocratic trappings of genealogy and heraldry served, through their esoteric interpretation, to reassure men of their identity and worth.

Despite the rebuff of the Imperial Academy, List's fortunes changed. In December 1904 Rudolf Berger raised the matter in parliament and demanded an explanation of List's treatment from the Minister for Culture and Education. This interpellation was signed by fifteen Viennese dignitaries.[39] No redress from the Academy was forthcoming, but the uproar led the supporters of List to moot the founding of a List Society (*Guido-von-List-Gesellschaft*), which would finance and publish a formal series of List's 'researches' into the ancient nationalist past. Both this incident and proposition demonstrate the significant appeal of List's ideas to Pan-Germans and occultists alike.

Around 1905 Friedrich Wannieck, his son Friedrich Oskar Wannieck, Lanz von Liebenfels and some fifty other individuals signed the first announcement concerning support for a List Society. A study of its signatories reveals the widespread and significant support for List amongst public figures in Austria and Germany. Here are the names of Karl Lueger, the anti-Semitic mayor of Vienna; Ludwig von Bernuth, chairman of a *völkisch* health organization; Ferdinand Khull, committee member of the German Language Club; Adolf Harpf, editor of the *Marburger Zeitung*; Hermann Pfister-Schwaighusen, lecturer in linguistics at Darmstadt University and an enthusiastic supporter of Austrian Pan-Germanism; Wilhelm von Pickl-Scharfenstein (Baron von Witkenberg), compiler of several anti-Semitic directories; Amand Freiherr von Schweiger-Lerchenfeld, editor of the popular magazine *Stein der Weisen* and a distinguished army officer; Aurelius Polzer, editor of nationalist newspapers at Horn and Graz; Ernst Wachler, the *völkisch* author and founder of an open-air Germanic theatre in the Harz mountains; Wilhelm Rohmeder, a Pan-German educationist at Munich; Arthur Schulz, editor of a Berlin periodical for *völkisch* educational reform; Friedrich Wiegershaus, chairman of the Elberfeld branch of the powerful *Deutschnationaler Handlungsgehilfen-Verband* [DHV] (German Nationalist Commercial Employees' Association) and Franz Winterstein, committee member of the anti-Semitic German Social Party (DSP) at Kassel. These representatives of Pan-Germanism in Austria and Germany were joined by several occultists: Hugo Göring, editor of theosophical literature at Weimar; Harald Arjuna Grävell van Jostenoode, a theosophical author at Heidelberg; Max Seiling, an esoteric pamphleteer and popular philosopher in Munich; and Paul Zillmann, editor of the *Metaphysische Rundschau* and master of an occult lodge at Berlin. All these men endorsed the foundation of the List Society.[40]

After an official founding ceremony on 2 March 1908, the List Society continued to attract this distinctive mixture of nationalist and occultist supporters. From 1908 to 1912 new members included the deputy Beranek, a co-founder of the *Bund der Germanen* in 1894; Rudolf Berger, committee member of the German Nationalist Workers' League in Vienna; Hermann Brass, chairman of the defensive League of Germans in North Moravia (est. 1886); Dankwart Gerlach, an ardent supporter of the nationalist and romantic Youth Movement; Conrad Glasenapp, the nationalist biographer of Wagner; Colonel Karl Hellwig, a *völkisch* organizer at Kassel; Bernhard Koerner, the heraldic expert and popularizer of middle-class genealogy; Josef Ludwig Reimer, a Pan-German author in Vienna; Philipp Stauff, a virulently anti-Semitic journalist in Berlin; and Karl Herzog, chairman of the Mannheim branch of the DHV. In addition to this roll of nationalists one finds the leading German theosophist Franz Hartmann, the theosophical editor Arthur Weber, the occult novelist Karl Hilm, the theosophist General Blasius von Schemua, the collective membership of the Vienna Theosophical Society, and Karl Heise, a leading figure in the vegetarian and mystical Mazdaznan cult at Zurich. The register implies that List's ideas were acceptable to many intelligent persons drawn from the upper and middle classes of Austria and Germany. Attracted by his unique amalgam of nationalist mythology and esotericism, these men were prepared to contribute ten crowns as an annual society subscription. The main part of the Society's assets derived from the Wannieck family, which put up more than three thousand crowns at its inauguration.[41]

Encouraged by this generous provision, List wrote a series of 'Ario-Germanic research reports' (*Guido-List-Bücherei*) which were based upon his occult interpretations of ancient national culture. Between 1908 and 1911, six reports were issued as booklets under the auspices of the List Society. These publications included a key to the meaning and magical power of the runes (*GLB* 1), a study of the political authority and organization of the Wotanist priesthood (the *Armanenschaft*) (*GLB* 2 and 2a), esoteric interpretations of folklore and place-names (*GLB* 3 and *GLB* 4), and a glossary of secret Aryan messages in hieroglyphs and heraldic devices (*GLB* 5). In 1914 List published his masterpiece of occult linguistics and symbology (*GLB* 6). These seven booklets represent the systematic exposition of his fantasy concerning the religious, political and social institutions of the national past. This fantasy of the past (and a desired present) records a *Weltanschauung* shared by List and his close supporters. It will be the task of later chapters to analyse this *Weltanschauung*.

List's reputation amongst members of the *völkisch* and nationalist subcultures grew in the wake of his first three 'reports' of 1908. The institutions of the Ario-Germans were frequently discussed in the *völkisch* press and other newspapers. From 1909 onwards List's name became well known among *völkisch* groups of Austria and Germany: the *Neues Wiener Tagblatt* and the *Grazer Wochenblatt* praised his discoveries in the ancient national past; *Der Tag*, a Berlin daily paper, credited him with the illumination of a priceless heritage; a French periodical regarded him as 'a teacher of mystical imperialism'.[42] In

February 1911 alone three academic lectures were delivered about him in Vienna and Berlin.[43] Following this acclaim List was fêted by minor authors, who drew upon his 'researches' for their inspiration. In 1907 Jerome Bal, a Hungarian schoolmaster at Levoča, published an occult manual of Magyar heraldry, which he dedicated to List;[44] his example was followed by B. Hanftmann in his study of regional domestic architecture and by Ernst von Wolzogen in his survey of contemporary literature.[45] In June 1909 Wolzogen staged his *völkisch* drama, *Die Maibraut* [*The May Bride*], at Wiesbaden. He had dedicated the play to List in words of deep admiration and was delighted to introduce the old author in person to the audience. A reporter described List as 'a martial, bearded manifestation of Armanism'.[46] In 1912, Karl Heise wrote about seven special and holy runes, indicating that his work was based on the discoveries of 'his dearest teacher Guido von List', while Karl Engelhardt dedicated a mythological idyll to his 'teacher of the Divine'.[47] The German theosophists also acknowledged List's nationalist popularization of their doctrines. Franz Hartmann compared List's work on hieroglyphs to Blavatsky's *Isis Unveiled*, while Johannes Balzli, editor of *Prana*, wrote a biography of List as 'the rediscoverer of ancient Aryan wisdom'.[48]

List's ideas were passed on by means of three principal channels. His ideology, rooted in the conflict of German and Slav national interests within the Habsburg empire, possessed an evident appeal to *völkisch* groups in Germany, which also sought a chauvinist mystique for the defence of Germandom against liberal, socialist, and 'Jewish' political forces in the late Wilhelmian era. The most important carriers of Listian ideas across the border were those members of the List Society in the German Reich who were involved in the founding of the Reichshammerbund and the Germanenorden. Philipp Stauff, Karl Hellwig, Georg Hauerstein, Bernhard Koerner, and Eberhard von Brockhusen were active in both these pre-war anti-Semitic *völkisch* leagues. In subsequent chapters this ideological succession is traced through the Germanenorden and its Munich offshoot, the Thule Society, to the infant Nazi Party after the war. This channel of influence certainly carries most weight in any assessment of List's historical importance.

The second channel concerns several shadowy *völkisch* figures in Germany, whose publicistic activity ensured a wider audience for Listian ideas among the German public both during and after the war. In November 1911 List received a letter from a pseudonymous individual calling himself Tarnhari, who claimed that he was the descendant or reincarnation of a chieftain of the ancient Wölsungen tribe in prehistoric Germany. Tarnhari assured List that his ancestral-clairvoyant memories confirmed List's own reconstruction of the Ario-Germanic traditions and hierarchic institutions. Tarnhari subsequently published two patriotic brochures at Diessen near Munich during the war, later establishing a *völkisch* publishing house at Leipzig. During the early post-war period he was associated with Dietrich Eckart, Hitler's mentor in the early days of the Nazi Party. That Tarnhari popularized List's ideas during the war can be seen from the writings of Ellegaard Ellerbek, a *völkisch*-mystical author, who paid extravagant tribute to both Tarnhari and List. His example was followed by others in the 1920s who wrote about the religion of Armanism and guaranteed this word a certain currency in nationalist usage.[49]

The third channel of Listian influence in Germany concerns those individuals, who specifically built upon his ideas of an occult Aryan-German heritage and elaborated upon the wisdom of the runes, mantic sciences, the Edda, and Teutonic astrology. Rudolf John Gorsleben, Werner von Bülow, Friedrich Bernhard Marby, Herbert Reichstein and Frodi Ingolfson Wehrmann created a complex corpus of armanist-ariosophical lore, which, while associated with the writings of Jörg Lanz von Liebenfels during the 1920s, owed a more significant and acknowledged debt to Guido von List. This later ariosophical movement flourished in Germany during the late 1920s and 1930s. Although these individuals worked in esoteric circles and sought no political involvement, a small coterie of these Edda and runological occultists enjoyed the confidence of Heinrich Himmler during the mid-1930s and contributed to the symbolism and ritual of the SS.[50]

List himself remained a mystical thinker with little organizational ability. However, he did found a tiny inner ring of initiates within the List Society called the HAO, which stood for *Hoher Armanen-Orden* (High Armanen-Order). The HAO was formally founded at the midsummer solstice of 1911, when the most dedicated List Society members in Berlin, Hamburg, and Munich travelled to meet their Austrian colleagues in Vienna. List took this elect on several 'pilgrimages' to certain places in 'the land of Ostara, where the spirit of Hari-Wotan still reigned'. On 23 June 1911 the group visited the cathedral catacombs, where the young List had first sensed this pagan god, and then proceeded to other allegedly Wotanist sanctuaries on the Kahlenberg, on the Leopoldsberg and at Klosterneuburg. Over the next three days, the enthusiasts made their way to Brühl near

Mödling, Burg Kreuzenstein, and finally to Carnuntum. This last expedition marked the climax of these 'pilgrimages to sanctuaries undertaken by our Armanist congregation'. The commemorative photographs of this climax indicate that the congregation numbered only ten persons.[51] The HAO was supposed to be a post for the architects of 'a new Spiritual Germany', but its minute sectarian and pietist nature is all too evident. In April 1915 List convened at Vienna an HAO meeting, which now numbered more Austrian public figures who had gathered to hear List's rousing Easter address.[52]

The HAO was a dead end in terms of historically significant groups, since List chose to work on occult and racial problems throughout the war in the calm of his study. His final 'research report' entitled 'Armanismus und Kabbala' was intended to amplify his earlier speculations on the occult 'correspondences' between various objects and qualities in the physical world, including animals, plants, minerals, colours, sounds, musical notes and numbers, within an esoteric scheme of interpretation. The 'report' was never completed in a publishable form. During 1916 and 1917 List wrote several articles on the approaching national millennium, which was supposed to be realized once the Allies had been defeated; Johannes Balzli published two of these predictions in his *Prana* in 1917.

During the war years List's ideas continued to attract individuals, who sought sacred explanations for the hardships and trials of the war. List received many letters from men at the front who expressed their gratitude for his cheering discoveries; stories of runes and ancient Aryan symbols found on stones far from hearth and home gave them hope in a final victory for the Ario-Germans. List's books were passed around by men in the trenches and field hospitals.[53] At the beginning of 1917 List had a vision which assured him of a final victory for the Central Powers over the Allies, but these hopes were betrayed. The year 1918 brought the Allied blockade of Europe, where food and fuel supplies ran low in the cities. In the early autumn the Habsburg empire began to dissolve and the Austrians were compelled to sue for peace on 3 October 1918. List regarded the catastrophe in a millenarian context: this collapse was necessary as a period of woes before the salvation of the Ario-Germans.

In late 1918 the seventy-year-old guru was in poor health owing to food shortages in Vienna. The following spring List and his wife set off to spend a period of recuperation at the manor-house of Eberhard von Brockhusen, a List Society patron who lived at Langen in Brandenburg. On arrival at the Anhalter Station at Berlin, List was too exhausted to continue the journey. After a doctor had diagnosed a lung inflammation, List's condition deteriorated rapidly. On the morning of 17 May 1919 the Armanist magician and prophet of national revival died in a Berlin guest-house. Following his cremation at Leipzig, the ashes were laid in an urn at Vienna Central Cemetery. Philipp Stauff wrote an obituary which appeared in the *Münchener Beobachter*, a *völkisch* newspaper edited by Rudolf von Sebottendorff that became the official Nazi organ in the course of the next year and remained the leading Party newspaper until 1945. Although List never lived to see the Nazi party, he was honoured by its nascent spirit.[54]

4

Wotanism and Germanic Theosophy

LIST claimed that the ancient Teutons had practised a gnostic religion emphasizing the initiation of man into natural mysteries. He called this religion Wotanism after the principal god in the Germanic pantheon. His basic sources for the ancient religion were the Edda and the runes. The Old Norse poetry of Iceland painted the colourful mythology of its pagan inhabitants, whom List regarded as Wotanist refugees from Christian persecution in early medieval Germany. The Edda thus recorded the myths and beliefs of the ancient Germans. In the Edda, Wotan was worshipped as the god of war and the lord of dead heroes in Valhalla. He was also identified as a magician and a necromancer in the poems. The 'Havamal' and 'Voluspa' described how Wotan performed ritual acts of self-torture in order to win the magical gnosis of natural mysteries. According to late nineteenth-century scholars these acts reflected a form of shamanism. As a result of pain the performer of these rituals gained certain magical and psychical powers.[1] In the 'Havamal' Wotan was wounded by a spear and hung upon a windswept tree without food or drink for nine nights. At the climax of his suffering an understanding of the runes suddenly came to him. He sank down from the tree and then related the eighteen runic spells, which were typically concerned with the secret of immortality, the ability to heal oneself, mastery over one's enemies in battle, the control of the elements and success in love. In the 'Voluspa' Wotan pledged one of his eyes to the well of Mimir in return for mantic knowledge of future events. It is very likely that this myth reminded List of his own occult insights during his period of blindness in 1902.

The runes are best known as an ancient northern script formed by sharp separate lines for writing or cutting upon wood, metal or stone; but they were also used for their magical properties in divination, the casting of lots, invocations and the preparation of amulets and charms. Thus each individual rune possessed its own name and symbolism over and above its phonetic and literary value. List must be acknowledged as the pioneer of *völkisch* rune occultism, for he was the first writer to link the written runes of a particular eighteen-letter series, or futhark, with the runic spells related by Wotan in the 'Havamal'. List attributed a specific individual rune to each of Wotan's verses, adding occult meanings and a summary motto of the spell. These occult meanings and mottoes were supposed to represent the doctrine and maxims of the rediscovered religion of Wotanism. Typical mottoes were: 'Know yourself, then you know everything!'; 'Embrace the universe in yourself, and you can master the universe!'; 'Do not fear Death, he cannot kill you!'; 'Your life rests in God's hand, trust him in yourself!'; 'Marriage is the root of the Aryan race!'; and 'Man is one with God!'[2] The emphasis of these maxims upon the inner power of the human spirit and its identity with God reveals the gnostic nature of Wotanism.

But Wotanism also stressed the mystical union of man with the universe as well as his magical powers. The doctrine described the universe in terms of a ceaseless process of transformation through 'birth', 'being', 'death' and 'rebirth'. The rotation of the planets, the seasonal cycle, the growth and decay of all living organisms confirmed the truth of this simple cyclical cosmology. Behind this process of change List saw the 'primal laws of nature', according to which all change occurred. He claimed that these laws represented an immanent God in Nature. List conceived of all things as an emanation of a spiritual force. Man was an integral part of this unified cosmos and thus obliged to follow a single ethical precept: to live in accordance with Nature. At her bosom all tensions were dissolved in a mystical union between man and the cosmos. A close identity with one's folk and race was reckoned a logical consequence of this closeness to Nature.

The twin doctrines of the magical self and a mystical union in List's gnostic religion of Wotanism typify the contradictory spirit of nineteenth-century Romanticism, itself a literary and spiritual response to the wider cultural and social changes in modern Europe. Writing of the motives of Romanticism, George L. Mosse has observed:

> Bewildered and challenged, men attempted to re-emphasise their own personality. But, since the rate of industrial transformation, as well as its effects, seemed to evade the grasp of reason ... many turned away from rational solutions to their problems and instead delved into their own

emotional depths. This longing for self-identification . . . was accompanied by a contradictory urge to belong to something greater than oneself . . . since existing social conditions were bewildering and oppressive, romantics sought to find the larger, all-encompassing unity outside the prevalent social and economic condition of man.[3]

List also formed his new religion from archaic materials and in opposition to the modern world. His doctrine emphasized the power of the individual spirit and a sanctuary within the cosmos of Nature. As the alleged gnosis of the ancient Germans, this religion was to be revived as the faith and moral cement of a new pan-German realm.

List also adopted the notions of modern theosophy for his reconstruction of the ancient gnosis. His debt to theosophy may be understood in terms of two distinct sources. The first source concerns the writings of Max Ferdinand Sebaldt von Werth (1859–1916). Sebaldt had begun his literary career as the editor of a periodical, *Das angewandte Christentum* [*Applied Christianity*] (1891), in collaboration with Moritz von Egidy, a prominent *Lebensreformer* in Germany. He was also a prolific writer on travel and foreign countries. However, in 1897 he began to publish thick volumes on the subject of sexology. His *'Wanidis'* (1897) and *D.I.S. 'Sexualreligion'* (1897) described the sexual-religion of the Aryans, a sacred practice of eugenics designed to maintain the purity of the race. Both works were published by Wilhelm Friedrich of Leipzig, a publisher known for his many theosophical editions, and were illustrated with the magical curved-armed swastika by the theosophical artist Fidus. Sebaldt subsequently published *Genesis* (1898–1903) in five-volumes, which treated of eroticism, Bacchanalia, libido, and mania within a racist and sexological context.

This Berlin author clearly anticipated Ariosophy by combining racial doctrines with occult notions derived from his own bizarre interpretations of Teutonic mythology. The contents of *'Wanidis'* indicate his penchant for expounding the metaphysical symbolism of the Germanic pantheon. According to Sebaldt, ancient Aryan cosmology was defined by the creative act of the god Mundelföri, who whisked the universe out of a primal fiery chaos. There subsequently arose a polar dualism typified by the opposite principles of matter and spirit, and the male and female sexes. He insisted that eugenics was essential to Aryan superiority, because only a bond of 'pure opposites' could release the primal energy underlying their polarity and thereby generate excellent progeny.[4] Similar notions later appeared in the writings of List over the ensuing years.

The first indication that List knew the work of Sebaldt occurs in his unsigned article 'Germanischer Lichtdienst', published in 1899 in *Der Scherer* [*The Mole-Catcher*], a satirical Tyrolean monthly magazine loosely associated with the Austrian Pan-German movement.[5] Discussing the religious significance of pagan solstice fires, List suggested that this ritual symbolized the original birth of the sun. He also claimed that the swastika was a holy Aryan symbol, since it derived from the *Feuerquirl* (fire whisk) with which Mundelföri had initially twirled the cosmos into being. In September 1903 the Viennese occult periodical *Die Gnosis* published an article by List that indicated his continuing debt to Sebaldt. He discussed the 'old-Aryan sexual religion' and a mystical cosmogony, the phases of which he illustrated with such hieroglyphs as ᛌ ᛌ ⊕ ᛰ ⊕ . He also wrote for the first time about the immortality of the soul, reincarnation and its karmic determination. He distinguished between exoteric (Wotanist) and esoteric (Armanist) forms of religious doctrine and hinted at the total authority of initiates over the ordinary people in ancient Germany. The Teutonic gods, Wotan, Donar and Loki, were interpreted as symbols for esoteric cosmological ideas, the Sebaldtian stamp of which would have been quite evident to contemporaries.[6] This article marked the first stage in List's articulation of a Germanic occult religion, the principal concern of which was racial purity.

In the course of the next few years List's writings became more overtly theosophical. His notes and references indicated such works as Madame Blavatsky's *Die Geheimlehre* (1897–1901), which had been published in German translation by Wilhelm Friedrich in instalments at the turn of the century, and the German edition of William Scott-Elliot's *The Lost Lemuria* (1905), with its descriptions of fabulous sunken continents and lost civilizations. List no longer termed the ancient natives 'Germans' or a 'people', but 'Ario-Germans' and a 'race', as if to stress their identity with the fifth root-race in Blavatsky's ethnological scheme. The Wotanist priesthood, which List had first discussed in the early 1890s, was now transformed into an exalted gnostic élite of initiates (the *Armanenschaft*), which corresponded to the hierophants in *The Secret Doctrine*. *Die Rita der Ario-Germanen* [*The Rite of the Ario-Germans*] (1908) regurgitated substantial parts of the theosophical cosmogony in its putative account of ancient Ario-Germanic belief. The unmanifest and manifest deities, the creation of the universe by divine respiration, a primal fire as the energy source of a force redolent of Fohat, and the gradual evolution of the cosmos according to this agent's obedience to the 'laws of nature' received detailed treatment.

Chapter headings were supplemented with the cryptic theosophy and
Chapter headings were supplemented with the cryptic theosophical sigils  .[7] By now a synthesis of theosophy and Germanic mythology formed the basis of List's *Weltanschauung*. His first three 'research reports' even made occasional use of the word 'theosophy' in their exposition of imaginary ancient Teutonic beliefs.[8]

List displayed considerable knowledge of theosophical detail. Life was graded according to its 'dimensionality', which was supposed to increase as it continued its progress through the rounds. He also mentioned the airships and cyclopean structures of the Atlanteans.[9] *Die Religion der Ario-Germanen* (1910) presented a long discussion of the Hindu cosmic cycles, which had inspired Blavatsky's hypothesis of rounds. List was evidently fascinated by a numerical correspondence between an arithmetical riddle in the 'Grimnismal' of the Edda and the number of years in the kaliyuga, the shortest and most decadent of the Hindu cycles. He acknowledged Blavatsky's *Die Geheimlehre* as the source of his speculations.[10] Astrological analyses also appeared in his work in 1910, the year which witnessed the publication of the first popular German astrological periodicals by the Theosophical Publishing House.[11]

Die Bilderschrift der Ario-Germanen [*The Picture-Writing of the Ario-Germans*] (1910) described the theosophical cosmogony in further detail: List's account of the divine manifestation alluded to the three Logoi and the ensuing rounds of fire, air, water and earth. List depicted these stages with the Blavatskyan-Hindu sigils ○⊙⦶⊖⊕ and identified the first four rounds as the mythological Teutonic realms of Muspilheim, Asgard, Wanenheim and Midgard, which were tenanted respectively by fire-dragons, air-gods, water-giants and mankind. He also evidenced his debt to Blavatsky in his adoption of seven root-races for each round. List claimed that the Ario-Germans represented the fifth and current race in the present round, while ascribing the names of mythical Teutonic giants to the four preceding races. The diluvial Atlanteans were equated with the kinsfolk of the giant Bergelmir, who was supposed to have survived a flood in Norse mythology, while the third race was reckoned to be the kinsmen of the giant Thrudgelmir. In common with Blavatsky, List suggested that this third race (her Lemurians) had been the first to propagate themselves through sexual reproduction. The two earlier races, namely the kinsmen of Ymir and Orgelmir, were androgynous and clearly corresponded to Blavatsky's Astral and Hypoborean races.[12]

This Germanization of theosophy was extended by three tables in the appendix. The first illustrated the evolutionary stages of a round through one complete cycle from unity to multiplicity and back to unity. Corresponding to the theosophical notions of unmanifest and manifest deities, the three Logoi, the five elemental realms (now including ether) and the appearance of mankind, List invoked mythological German equivalents. He called the divine being Allvater, who manifested himself in the three Logoi as Wotan, Wili, and We. A series of anti-clockwise triskelions and swastikas and inverted triangles symbolized stages of cosmic evolution in the downsweep of the cycle (i.e. the evolution from unity to multiplicity), while their clockwise and upright counterparts connoted the return path to the godhead. The skewed super-imposition of these 'falling' and 'rising' sigils created complex sigils like the hexagram and the Maltese Cross ⚜ . List asserted that these latter sigils were utterly sacred, because they embraced the two antithetical forces of all creation: as the representative symbols of the zenith of multiplicity at the outermost limit of the cycle, they denoted the Ario-Germanic god-man, the highest form of life ever to evolve in the universe. Two further tables recorded a cabbalistic scheme of 'correspondences' between plants, trees, birds and deities of the Classical and Germanic pantheons.[13] Franz Hartmann commended this work, comparing its scope with that of Blavatsky's *Isis Unveiled*, and praised List for his discovery of the congruence between Germanic and Hindu doctrines.[14]

In 1914 List published the sixth and last of his 'research reports', *Die Ursprache der Ario-Germanen* [*The Proto-Language of the Ario-Germans*], which introduced yet more theosophical notions into his account of the ancient national past. To the root-races of the Lemurians and Atlanteans he assigned homelands on sunken continents in accordance with the speculations of William Scott-Elliot, whose map he reproduced. List also claimed that the prehistoric megaliths and the huge rocking-stones of Lower Austria indicated the survival of an Atlantean 'island' within the modern European continent. A chart at the end of this work sought to reconcile the geological periods of the Earth, as established by contemporary palaeogeography, with the stages of a theosophical round lasting 4,320,000,000 years, or a *kalpa* in Hindu chronology.[15]

Why did theosophy become such an important part of List's gnosis? One solution is provided by its contemporary vogue and the fact that many supporters of the List Society were interested in the occult. Friedrich Wannieck was both an ardent spiritualist and a firm believer in the theosophical mahatmas, Morya and Koot Hoomi;[16] General Blasius von Schemua (1856–1920) had been associated with the mystical school of Alois Mailänder at Darmstadt since 1890, whose followers included Franz Hartmann and Wilhelm Hübbe-Schleiden. Schemua was a prominent theosophist and also a friend of Demeter Georgiewitz-Weitzer (1873–1949), who edited the *Zentralblatt für Okkultismus* and wrote several occult works under the pseudonym G. W. Surya;[17] Max Seiling had written a study of Mailänder and other books about spiritualism and occultism; Friedrich Schwickert (1857–1930) was interested in the work of Sir Edward Bulwer-Lytton and wrote a study about the elixir of life. He became one of the leading astrologers in Weimar Germany;[18] Karl Heise was a Swiss member of the Mazdaznan cult and, together with his brother Heinrich, ran a commune called 'Aryana' near Zurich;[19] Wladimir von Egloffstein dabbled in chronological speculations about cycles and wrote an esoteric history of the Church. Finally, there was Jörg Lanz-Liebenfels, whose own brand of racist occultism owed much to theosophy. List borrowed several ideas from the younger man: the occult significance of the Templars, the manichaean struggle between the master-races (the Ario-Germans) and the slave races (non-Aryans) and a theory about the original homeland of the Aryans, a vanished polar continent called Arktogäa.[20]

What theosophy offered to these individuals, whose intellect, education and social circumstances made it at all appealing, was an integrated view of the world, in which the present was understood in terms of a remote past. This imaginary past legitimated a variety of social, political, and cultural ideals such as racism, magic, and hierophantic élitism, which were all negations of the modern world. Although this legitimation was not traditional, inasmuch as it was mythological, it was a legitimation that included the apparently scientific findings of the present, a sense of meaning in society and history, and supernatural references. This perspective was likely to appeal to people for whom a variety of contemporary developments were disturbing. At best, these occult beliefs might bolster and justify resistance to processes of social change. At worst, they provided a fantasy world, in respect of which the present could be lamented and the possessors of the true gnosis could comfort themselves in their assumed superior wisdom.

5

The Armanenschaft

LIST'S political mythology of a Wotanist priesthood invoked the political authority of initiates, both in the prehistoric social order and in the modern world. This idea was first formulated in his lectures and articles of the 1890s, but it had emerged as a principal element of his fantasy by 1908. The word *'Armanenschaft'*, which List applied to his ancient hierarchy, can be traced to his spurious adaptation of a Teutonic myth related by Tacitus in his *Germania*.[1] According to the Roman author, the ancient Germans had preserved an account of their origins in traditional songs. These songs celebrated an earth-born god Tuisco and his son Mannus as the founders of their race. To Mannus they assigned three sons, after whom the three constituent tribes of ancient Germany took their names: the coastal tribes were called 'Ingaevones'; those of the interior, 'Hermiones'; and the remainder, 'Istaevones'. Contrary to Tacitus and other classical historians who had attempted to identify these tribes with known appellations, List claimed that these names denoted social estates within the Ario-Germanic nation.[2] He claimed that the 'Ingaevones', the 'Hermiones' and the 'Istaevones' represented the agricultural, the intellectual and the military estates. It was the intellectual estate, a body of priest-kings, that formed the basis of List's political fantasy. He germanized the word 'Hermiones' to 'Armanen', meaning the heirs of the sun-king, while their priesthood was called the *'Armanenschaft'*.[3]

The priest-kings were allegedly responsible for all government and education in ancient society, offices which were legitimized by their profound wisdom. This wisdom was defined by the gnosis of Germanic theosophy. The possession of this gnosis was regarded as the absolute and sacred legitimation of the initiates' political authority, while society was stratified according to each class's degree of initiation into the gnosis. List emphasized that this gnosis was not equally accessible to all members of society. He alluded to a two-tier system of exoteric and esoteric instruction in the gnosis. Exoteric doctrine (Wotanism) assumed the popular form of myths and parabolic tales intended for the lower social classes, while esoteric doctrine (Armanism) was concerned with the mysteries of the gnosis and was restricted to trainees for high office. Since the *Armanenschaft* was the body responsible for education, such a segregation would have been simply administered.[4]

List's description of the *Armanenschaft* structure borrowed concepts from Freemasonry and Rosicrucianism. The élite priesthood was divided into three grades, corresponding to the grades of Entered Apprentice, Fellow Craft and Master Mason in lodge hierarchy. Each grade represented a certain degree of initiation into the gnosis. With a clear image of masonic ritual in mind, List claimed that each grade of the ancient priesthood had its own particular signs, grips and passwords. A novice spent seven years learning the Edda and elementary theosophy, before proceeding to the grade of brother. At this stage in his training he travelled to other Armanist centres, in order to gain working experience as a priest, governor and educator. After seven years in this grade, a suitably qualified brother might proceed to the grade of master as a full initiate. He was then privy to the ultimate secrets of the gnosis, which could not be communicated by language: List characterized these secrets by such occult formulae as 'the lost master-word', 'the unutterable name of God' and 'the philosopher's stone', culled from masonic, cabbalistic and alchemical lore of the eighteenth century, or the ' ⥍ Arehisosur ⥍ ', his own Gothic motto formed by the five vowels.[5] Freemasonry thus provided List with a model for an hierarchical priesthood whose power derived from initiation.

Besides defining the authority of a master over his subordinate brothers, this gnostic gradation underpinned the collective authority of the *Armanenschaft* over the profane majority. The *Armanenschaft* was alleged to have enjoyed 'superior privileges' and possessed an 'exalted and holy status' among the people.[6] They predominated in all affairs of government, while the king and nobility were drawn from a superior college of masters. Since the gnosis of the priesthood combined science, religion and law, its members exercised total authority as teachers, priests and judges.[7] The Armanist centres or 'high places' *(Halgadome)* were the seat of government, the school and the lawcourt.[8] All authority was invested with the absolute legitimacy of sacredness.[9]

In his account of the history of the *Armanenschaft*, List continued to draw on the occult materials of Rosicrucianism, alchemy, the military religious orders and Freemasonry. He claimed that the *Armanenschaft*, following its suppression in ancient Germany, had survived up until the present, inasmuch as its holy gnosis had been fostered by secret societies of Rosicrucians and Freemasons, chivalrous orders and the scholar magicians of the Renaissance who had championed the pursuit of hermetic and cabbalistic sciences. The link between these diverse groups lies in the modern occult revival's debt to the tangled mythology of theosophists and secret societies in the eighteenth century. In order to appreciate List's adoption of these groups as social agents of Armanism during its dark age, these mythologies require explanation.

The story of these mystifications can be properly understood only in relation to the growth of irrationalism in the mid-eighteenth century. This trend was partly a reaction to the practical reforming attitude of enlightened absolute princes in Germany, which appeared to interfere with traditional legal privilege, ecclesiastical immunities or popular prejudice. Enlightened reform represented a threat to many people because its changes destroyed long accepted status and cultural values. Such people found a handy ideological weapon against such innovating tendencies in irrationalism. There were also older sources of the new irrationalism: traditional religious affiliation, pietism and the enduring fascination of a mystical key to the riddles of nature, which found expression in the traditional occult sciences. The new irrationalism was thus a product of the revaluation of the emotive and intuitive faculties, coupled with a fearful distrust of analytical reason, materialism and empiricism. This spiritual mood, widespread in Germany, generated many sects and societies concerned with the occult and mysterious during the second half of the eighteenth century. These groups were responsible for a revival of interest in the arcane materials of alchemy, Rosicrucianism and Freemasonry.[10]

The origins of Rosicrucianism lie at the beginning of the seventeenth century when two anonymous Rosicrucian manifestoes and the related *Chymische Hochzeit* of Johann Valentin Andreae (1586–1654) were printed at Kassel. These manifestoes announced the existence of a secret brotherhood, which desired a 'universal and general reformation of the whole wide world'. The brotherhood was putatively founded by Christian Rosenkreutz, a German mystic who was supposed to have lived from 1378 to 1484. This reformation was to be achieved through the union of Protestantism with magic, alchemy, and cabbalism in concert with contemporary advances in medical and scientific knowledge. Frances Yates has argued that the manifestoes express hopes that focused on Frederick II, the Elector of the Palatine, as a 'politico-religious leader destined to solve the problems of the age', while their contents represented a kind of hermetic revival among Protestant intellectuals at a time when the original hermetic impulses of the fifteenth century Renaissance had waned.[11] The attraction of such a project at a time of violent ideological and religious antagonism before the Thirty Years War is obvious. From these seventeenth-century origins of mystical pietism, utopian hope and hermetic-cabbalistic ideas, the Rosicrucian myth continued to fascinate many intellectuals who felt drawn to its quest for secret knowledge and the promise of moral renewal. Klaus Epstein has noted that the myth attracted conservatives particularly, since it emphasized the value of traditional wisdom for future development.[12]

While the Rosicrucians of the early seventeenth century were only partly concerned with alchemy, the later revivals of the myth laid great stress on their claims to possess the secrets of transmutation and the knowledge of the 'philosopher's stone' or elixir of life. In 1710 a work was published in Breslau with the arcane title *Die warhaffte und vollkommene Bereitung des Philosophischen Steins der Brüderschaft aus dem Orden des Gülden- und Rosen-Creutzes*. Its author was 'Sincerus Renatus', in reality Sigmund Richter, a pastor in Silesia, who had studied the writings of Paracelsus and Jakob Boehme. In the light of other documentary finds around Central Europe, Christopher McIntosh has suggested that a widespread alchemical movement existed under the appellation *Gold- und Rosenkreuz* during the second half of the eighteenth century. In either 1747 or 1757 a quasi-masonic Rosicrucian order of this name was founded at Berlin, with a hierarchy of nine grades based on the cabbalistic Tree of Life. This organization acquired some political significance, since it counted King Frederick William II and his prime minister, Johann Christoph von Wöllner, among its brothers in the late 1780s. The ideology of the order blended mysticism with conservative and anti-Enlightenment attitudes.[13]

List was familiar with Rosicrucian materials, inasmuch as he used the ten-grade cabbalistic hierarchy peculiar to some Rosicrucian orders. He may have gleaned this idea from Franz Hartmann, who was probably familiar with the Rosicrucian structure of the Order of the Golden Dawn in England as a result of his contact with Theodor Reuss, who had founded in 1902 irregular masonic and Rosicrucian lodges in Germany with the authority of William Westcott, a founder member of the Golden Dawn.[14] In any event, literature about the

Rosicrucians was abundant at the beginning of the century in Germany. Both Franz Hartmann and Rudolf Steiner had written about them, while a reprint of a late eighteenth-century alchemical-rosicrucian text was published in Zillmann's periodical during 1905.[15] When List made the further claim that the Rosicrucians of the seventeenth and eighteenth centuries had been agents of the Armanist gnosis, he was thus recruiting a mysterious and durable body of adepts for his secret tradition. Besides the response this would enjoy from theosophists, one must consider the ambition of the original Rosicrucians. In a Listian context, the 'universal and general reformation' connoted a national revival through the rediscovery of traditional Ario-Germanic wisdom.

Before examining the putative Templarist survival of Armanism, the involvement of the Knights Templars with occultism must be mentioned. This complex story introduces two distinct Templar mythologies: the medieval Templar legends and their confusion with Freemasonry in the eighteenth century. Founded in 1118, the original Knights Templars were a crusading military religious order which was forced to leave the Holy Land in 1291. The order subsequently became the victim of a slanderous campaign mounted by the King of France, who coveted their wealth and influence within his realm. He accused the Templars of satanic practices, certain perversions and blasphemies, including the worship of a huge idol fashioned in the shape of a human head. Because of these alleged calumnies the order was ruthlessly suppressed and its leaders burnt in 1314. Despite the probable falsehood of the charges against them, the historical record surrounded the memory of the Templars with a mysterious and heretical aura.[16] This medieval suppression had a certain influence upon the masonic adoption of the Templars.

At the beginning of the eighteenth century the institutions of modern Freemasonry arose. It should be emphasized that this new organization of meeting-houses was institutionally linked with the old working lodges of operative masons and master-builders, which dated from the fourteenth and fifteenth centuries. The Freemasons had begun joining the operative lodges at the end of the seventeenth century to form an organization in which the professional and upper classes could discuss contemporary affairs and business in an enlightened and congenial atmosphere. The new institution inherited the ritual of the older, in that craft traditions became the allegories and symbols of a deistic and fraternal doctrine. After its official foundation in England in 1717, Freemasonry soon migrated to a Continental setting. It was in Germany, where the growth of deviant masonic rites was greatest owing to the profusion of mystical and theosophical sects, that Freemasonry became confused with a Templar heritage.

Although the idea of chivalric Freemasonry first occurred around 1737 in France, the first Templar rite was introduced in Germany in 1755 by Baron Gotthelf von Hund (1722–76). Calling his order the Rite of Strict Observance, Hund claimed to possess secret Templar documents dating from the time of their suppression, which allegedly proved that his order represented the legal Templar succession. Hund speculated that the Templars had been privy to the secrets of the Temple of Solomon in Jerusalem, which was held to be the origin of the Craft. It has been suggested that this chivalric mystification of Freemasonry arose with the express purpose of conferring aristocratic origins upon a middle-class institution with a humble craft background.[17]

Masonic and occultist interest in the Templars during the late eighteenth century influenced scholarship regarding the beliefs and practices of the historical Templars. Attention was focused on their alleged blasphemies, especially the worship of the idolatrous head, in an attempt to relate Templar heresy to exotic religions. One particular account of the head in the trial documents called it 'Baphomet', which was interpreted as a reference to a Muslim deity. This name was also associated with the gnostic cult of the Ophites, which had flourished in the first few centuries AD. Josef von Hammer-Purgstall suggested that the idol derived from surviving conventicles of the cult, with which the Templars had supposedly come into contact during their domicile in the eastern Mediterranean area.[18]

These mythologies entered late nineteenth-century occultism through the influential writings of the French occultist Eliphas Lévi (1810–75), whose writings on magic were studied by Blavatsky.[19] The Templars were once again credited with the possession of arcane knowledge. Occult Templarism flourished among quasi-masonic orders and at least two specifically Templar orders were founded on the Continent around 1900. The Ordo Templi Orientis (OTO) originated in the irregular masonic activities of Theodor Reuss, Franz Hartmann and Karl Kellner between 1895 and 1906; the racist Ordo Novi Templi (ONT) was founded by Lanz von Liebenfels around 1907.[20]

List most probably derived his occult conception of the Templars from a masonic source, but his notion was also coloured by the poetic grail-mythology of *Parsival* which inspired Lanz.[21] He exploited these myths in order to claim that the medieval Templars had been another secret agent of the Armanist gnosis during the benighted Christian epoch. List concluded that the 'Baphomet' idol was not a head but a gnostic sigil. According to List, this sigil was the Maltese Cross, formed by the skewed superimposition of the clockwise and anti-clockwise swastikas. He claimed that the Templars had been put to death for their worship of this most sacred Ario-Germanic symbol, and that the later masonic orders of Templarist inspiration had also fostered the gnosis. List claimed that the Templars and Rosicrucians 'represented the higher grades of the secret priesthood, the spiritual and aristocratic tendency, while the Freemasons signified lower grades . . . the democratic tendency'.[22] But besides the élitist connotations of chivalry, the Templars were important in another respect. Because they had been persecuted for their beliefs, List could more plausibly contend that there had been a conspiracy against any revival of ancient Germanic religion and its priesthood.

In his short essay 'Das Mittelalter im Armanentum', List described a further group of Armanist secret agents. These were the Renaissance humanists, whose interests had focused on the rediscovery of the Hermetic texts. Specifically mentioned by List were Pico della Mirandola (1463–94) and Giordano Bruno (1548–1600) in Italy, and Johann Reuchlin (1455–1522), Johann Trithemius (1462–1516) and Agrippa von Nettesheim (1486–1535) in Germany. List claimed that their revival of neo-Platonist and hermetic-cabbalistic ideas marked an efflorescence of the ancient national gnosis following the weakening of the Catholic stranglehold in medieval Europe.[23] List had already copied 'Aryan' magic sigils from the cryptographic works of Trithemius and lauded Agrippa as an 'old Armanist'.[24] However, it was his exploitation of Reuchlin that lent most plausibility to his fantasy of modern Armanist tradition.

Reuchlin has been acclaimed as the father of German humanism for his pioneering work on Greek and Hebrew texts. Educated at several universities, Reuchlin initially qualified as a lawyer and entered service at the court of Württemberg in 1482. He was ennobled for his services by Emperor Maximilian in 1494. During a visit to Italy Reuchlin had met Pico della Mirandola, who encouraged him to study Hebrew. Reuchlin subsequently developed those ideas which established him as the German representative of Renaissance cabbalism. He was convinced that the philosophy of Plato had its origins in the Jewish mystical books of the Cabbala. These theories were advanced in his treatises *De verbo mirifico* (1494) and *De arte cabbalistica* (1517). Besides his interest in Jewish mysticism, Reuchlin also wrote original studies of the Hebrew language, which paved the way for biblical scholarship based on the oldest sources, while confirming his reputation as a humanist who respected the contributions of other religious traditions besides Christianity.

Around 1510 Johann Pfefferkorn demanded that the Jews of Germany should have their holy books confiscated by the Church in a campaign to force them to convert to Christianity. His demands enjoyed the support of an anti-Semitic ecclesiastical party at Cologne. Reuchlin scorned this kind of religious intolerance and lampooned the arguments of the anti-Semites, only to be accused of heresy by the Dominicans of Cologne. The controversy dragged bitterly on until 1520, when Reuchlin was cleared of these charges. It was Reuchlin's defence of the Jewish texts which led List to believe that he was an initiate of the Armanist gnosis. List claimed that the original priest-kings had entrusted their gnosis verbally to the rabbis of Cologne during the eighth century, in order to safeguard its survival during a wave of Christian persecution. The rabbis had then set these secrets down in cabbalistic books which were erroneously thought to represent a Jewish mystical tradition. The Cologne controversy thus made Reuchlin look as if he was trying to save these very books from the anti-Armanist Church.[25] In this way List cast Reuchlin in the role of a great Armanist reformer struggling against a Catholic conspiracy to suppress the gnosis. List's veneration of Reuchlin even extended to the belief that he himself was the reincarnation of the sixteenth-century humanist.[26]

The Templars, Renaissance humanists, cabbalists and Rosicrucians were thus enlisted in the ranks of an imaginary heritage stretching back from the modern Armanists like List and his followers to the persecuted priest-kings, whose political authority had lapsed at the time of Christianization in early medieval Germany. This secret tradition bridged the gap formed by the Christian epoch between the ancient dispensation and its future revival. By claiming that the *Armanenschaft* had never been destroyed, but had survived in secret conventicles, List could suggest that his own cult was the surviving remnant of the hierophantic political tradition, which had to be revived in order that a glorious pan-German realm could be established in Europe.

List's blueprint for a new pan-German empire was detailed and unambiguous. It called for the ruthless subjection of non-Aryans to Aryan masters in a highly structured hierarchical state. The qualification of candidates for education or positions in public service, the professions and commerce rested solely on their racial purity. The heroic Ario-Germanic race was to be relieved of all wage-labour and demeaning tasks, in order to rule as an exalted élite over the slave castes of non-Aryan peoples.[27] List codified a set of political principles for the new order: strict racial and marital laws were to be observed; a patriarchal society was to be fostered in which only the male head of the house had full majority and only Ario-Germans enjoyed the privileges of freedom and citizenship; each family was to keep a genealogical record attesting its racial purity; a new feudalism was to develop through the creation of large estates which could not be broken up but inherited only by the first-born male in a family.[28] These ideas, published as early as 1911, bear an uncanny resemblance to the Nuremberg racial laws of the 1930s and the Nazi vision of the future.

But List went further still, anticipating the mystical élitism of the SS in Nazi Germany. The hierarchical structure of Ario-Germanic society was based on the cabbalistic Tree of Life.[29] This occult system of ten grades of successively higher initiation into gnostic mysteries served as the basis of the new order. In List's scheme, the two lowest grades denoted the individual and his family, which were in turn subordinate to five specified levels of Armanist authority. Above these there existed three supreme grades, whose absolute authority corresponded to the analogous location of the three highest *sefiroth* on the Tree 'beyond the veil of the abyss'. According to List, the eighth grade comprised the higher nobility, while the ninth was occupied only by the king and his immediate circle. The tenth grade symbolized God. List emphasized the mystical equivalence of the ascending and descending grades and interpreted the traditional cabbalistic motto 'As above, so below' to mean that the Aryan is a god-man.[30] This application of the Tree to a political hierarchy thus located the seat of authority in a sacred zone. While ancient Germanic society was claimed to have been a theocratic state, so the new order was to comprise a special élite, whose power was holy, absolute and mysterious. List's ideal state was a male order with an occult chapter.[31] The similarities with Himmler's plans for an SS order-state are striking.

Documentary evidence proves that List and the members of his HAO relished their sense of membership of a secret élite. List styled himself the Grand Master of the order and was addressed thus by his followers,[32] while other titles were conferred on members in accordance with the hierarchical grades of the ancient priesthood. Bernhard

Koerner was known as the *Arz-Femo-Aithari*, and List also used the dignity of *Arz-Wiho-Aithari*.[33] Both these titles denoted councillors in the ninth grade of the cabbalistic hierarchy. Subordinate only to God and king, these councillors formed the supreme chapter of the priesthood. Initiate status was also ritually celebrated by means of esoteric glyphs upon funerary monuments: Heinrich Winter was buried at Hamburg beneath a rough-hewn stone bearing the swastika in 1911; an entire tumulus with a glyph-ornamented column was designed for Friedrich Oskar Wannieck in 1914; Georg Hauerstein sen. set a swastika-inscribed headstone upon the grave of his first wife at Isernhagen near Hanover in the same year.[34]

The HAO addressed itself to the male sex, the upper and middle classes, and all German patriots in the historically German-settled lands of Central and Eastern Europe. List urged the contemporary aristocracy in particular to resist the pro-Slav interests and democratic tendencies of the contemporary Austrian state and to regard themselves as the heirs of the old priest-kings. List was also a staunch supporter of the Habsburg monarchy and imperial dynasty, which he wished to transform into the figure-head of a new Armanist empire.[35] All these exhortations demonstrate his concern to awaken German nationalist consciousness among the nobility and other groups whose traditional status was threatened by the growth of non-German political influence in Austria.

The myth of an occult élite is not new in European ideology. It has been a perennial theme of post-Enlightenment occultism, which attempts to restore the certainties and security of religious orthodoxy within a sectarian context. Baron von Hund had invoked 'unknown superiors' for his Rite of Strict Observance, Westcott provided for a third order of 'Secret Chiefs' in the Golden Dawn, and Blavatsky spoke of the secret masters of the 'Great White Lodge': all these occult authorities fall within the same tradition.[36] The hidden élite confers an unaccountable authority upon the visible representatives of the cult. The imaginary priest-kings of the past similarly endorsed List's claims to secret knowledge and special authority. At the same time, the putative existence of a modern *Armanenschaft* suggested to believers that the golden age might be soon restored, and that Germany and Austria would be united in a theocratic pan-German realm, wherein non-German interests would play no part. Within thirty-five years this vision was instituted as the foreign policy of the Third Reich.

6

The Secret Heritage

LIST, echoing contemporary Pan-German sentiment, was particularly concerned to associate the Austrian Germans with their compatriots in the Reich. It was important to him that the *Armanenschaft* and its politico-religious rule should have flourished in the Danubian region, as well as in Germany proper, since the earliest times. List accordingly challenged the conventional historical belief that the barbarian migrations had scattered the Celtic tribes of the region, and that it was Charlemagne who had first settled converted Germans on the eastern marches (*Ostmark*) of his large ninth-century empire. He claimed, on the contrary, that the region had witnessed a high development of Ario-Germanic culture several millennia before its Roman colonization (*c*.100–375) and that the Wotanist religion had been continually practised until the imposition of Christianity, principally through Charlemagne, whom he decried as the 'slaughterer of the Saxons' on account of his campaign of conversion on pain of death among the pagans of North Germany.

List believed he had discovered the remnants of this universal armanist-wotanist dispensation all round his native country. Despite the ravages of many centuries, compounded by Christian obliteration, he claimed to discern the vague outlines and scanty relics of a vast forgotten culture both throughout and beyond the German-settled areas of Austria. He found these relics in material archaeological monuments (tumuli, megaliths, hill-forts and castles on earlier pagan sites); in the local names of woods, rivers, hills and fields, many of which dated from pre-Carolingian times and allegedly recalled the names of gods and goddesses in the Germanic pantheon; and in the many legends, folk-tales and customs through which the common country folk were supposed, albeit unconsciously, to inherit and pass on the pale and distorted reflection of ancient Ario-Germanic religious parables and doctrines. By means of his discoveries in these three areas of local historical and folkloristic research, List sought to convince his readers that the western or 'Austrian' half of the Habsburg empire could look back upon a German pagan and national past of immemorial antiquity.

List's vision of the prehistoric past owed little to empirical methods of historical research. His surmises depended rather upon the clairvoyant illumination that certain places induced in his mind. After walking up the Hermannskogel to the north of Vienna, and again while sleeping out overnight on the Geiselberg hill-fort, List fell into a trance and witnessed the heroic and religious events that had allegedly passed in these places centuries before.[1] Armed with this faculty, List was able to divine countless sites of former Armanist association in the Lower Austrian countryside, along the River Danube, high upon the Alps and in Vianiomina (Vienna), the holy Teutonic city of old. The tumuli at Gross Mugl and Deutsch-Altenburg, likewise the hill-forts of Götschenberg, Leisserberg and Obergänserndorf, were all recruited for his list of sanctuaries dedicated to the old faith.[2] The town of Ybbs was, according to List, founded upon a shrine to the Teutonic goddess Isa; the dreary ruins of Aggstein recalled the evil spirit Ägir, while the village of St Nikola lay upon the site of a sanctuary named after Nikuz, the lord of the water-sprites.[3] South of the Danube near Melk, List discerned a huge Armanist temple stretching over many square miles: he regarded the Osterburg, Burg Hohenegg and the woodland church at Mauer as stations in a religious complex which focused on a sacrificial stone, now serving as a plinth for a saint's statue beside the Zeno brook.[4] This exploitation of pre-historic monuments, human settlements and medieval castles for his stock of Armanist *Halgadome* (high places) represented a personal mythology, by means of which List imposed a set of modern German nationalist meanings upon cultural objects. Through this occult interpretation, List sought to nationalize the ancient past in accordance with contemporary Pan-German ideology.

List pursued similar speculations in the case of place-names, which allegedly celebrated the old Germanic religion. He claimed that the god Wotan had been immortalized in such village-names as Wutter-wald, Wulzendorf, Wultendorf and Wilfersdorf, while his wife Frigga (also known as Holla or Freya) was remembered in such place-names as Hollenburg, Hollabrunn, Hollarn, Frauendorf and Frauenburg. Because many of the old pagan shrines had probably not been destroyed, but merely newly consecrated and re-dedicated to Christian saints, in conformity with early missionary policy, List was convinced that place-names containing the words Michael, Rupprecht, Peter and Maria denoted the old deities Wotan, Hruoperaht, Donar and Frigga.[5] Armed with this interpretative key to place-names, List was able to trace an extended network of shrines and sanctuaries dedicated to the gods of the Wotanist religion across the map of modern Austria.

More fruitful and far richer as a source of evidence for the former armanist-wotanist culture of Austria were the numerous popular legends and folk-tales in which List had taken an interest since his childhood. He suggested that the stock figures and motifs in fairy-tales and nursery rhymes such as the ogre, the sleeping emperor, the wild huntsman, and the ratcatcher reflected the parables and teachings of the formerly universal Wotanist religion.[6] When List heard specific folk-tales describing vanished castles, the offspring of supernatural and mortal unions, fratricides, lost lovers, or half-human creatures, he would trace their elements back to the fables of Teutonic mythology and their cosmic significance as symbols for the winter-gods, sun-gods, spring-goddesses and the goddess of Death in the old Ario-Germanic nature-religion.[7] The same interpretations could be applied to popular customs. In a work specifically devoted to the rites of the Ario-Germans, List traced a wide range of legal antiquities and common law practices relating to local jurisdictions and their officers, fines, ordeals, penalties and ceremonial back to ancient Armanist procedures.[8]

Having indicated the former existence of a universal German pagan culture by means of these relics, List sought to increase the plausibility and significance of his golden-age myth by explaining the downfall of the ideal Armanist world in terms of a real and historical institution. Owning to his strong sympathies with the *Los von Rom* movement, Georg von Schönerer's anti-Catholic campaign begun in 1898, List achieved this end with a conspiracy-theory that identified Christianity as the negative and destructive principle in the history of the Ario-Germanic race. If it could be shown that Christian missionaries had been intent upon the destruction of Armanist culture, its actual non-existence in the present could be related to empirical events, while reproaching the neglect of German national interests in modern Austria. List's account of Christianization in the historic German lands reiterated the debilitation of Teutonic vigour and morale and the destruction of German national consciousness. He claimed that the Church's gospel of love and charity had encouraged a deviation from the strict eugenics of 'the old Aryan sexual morality', while its new ecclesiastical foundations had blurred the *Gaue* (traditional ethnic provinces), in order to confuse the Germans in respect of political loyalties and obedience. Lastly, the withdrawal of all educational and religious facilities from the vanquished Germans had reduced them to the level of a helot people.

These moral and political enormities could have been achieved only through the annihilation of the national leadership. According to List, Christian missionary activities began with the humiliation of the *Armanenschaft* and ended with its outright persecution. The sanctuaries were closed down as centres of worship, education and government, thus removing the institutional basis of Armanist authority. Expropriated and impoverished, the priest-kings were compelled to wander through a land which neither recognized their status nor valued their holy gnosis anymore. Many of them fled to Scandinavia or Iceland, while those remaining in Central Europe assumed the status of a pariah caste, subsisting as tinkers, gypsies and strolling players.[9] Christianity completed its suppression of the *Armanenschaft* by its absolute vilification. According to the new faith, the old faith had been the instrument of Satan. Abandoned 'high places' were shunned as the 'castles of Antichrist'; the priest-kings were mythicized into warlocks; the runes acquired the stigma of sorcery; the ancient celebrations were conceived of as a sabbath by the medieval mind, while those who persisted in the old confession were burnt as heretics or witches.

That the Church had demonized the (imaginary) national priest-hood was the ultimate charge in List's own polemic against Christianity. But it was he who had demonized the Church as the sole source of evil in a pan-German scheme of belief. Religious conversion by missionaries or by force (in the case of Charlemagne and the Saxons) represented the most vicious assault upon national integrity ever witnessed, for 'when the Germans had been completely barbarized . . . the Vicar of God ensconced himself upon the bastion of his subjects' artificially induced stupidity and ruled over a shamefully demoralized people which was almost ignorant of its nationality'.[10] Only a conspiracy of such magnitude, entailing a colossal process of national dissolution, could satisfactorily account for the decay of Armanist culture and the downfall of the traditional world.

From medieval times onward the subjugated Germans had learnt of their past only through mendacious foreign accounts. These 'vicious reports from Roman, Greek and Frankish pens' assured the Germans that they had existed in a woefully primitive state before the advent of Christianity. The combined weight of Western historical scholarship relegated them to the status of a cultural latecomer in Europe. Confronted by the fact of Germany's retarded national unification, List invoked his specious occult history to prove the opposite. Because the alleged Christian conspiracy had tried to obliterate all traces of the Armanist past, it followed that its relics would be obscure and inaccessible to the majority of people in the modern world. At this point occultism made its logical appearance in his thought. In order to ensure some dialogue between his myths and the present, List ascribed occult meanings to many familiar cultural materials. These materials possessed an accepted ordinary meaning, but once List had revalued them with an occult meaning, they endorsed his own fantasy of the Armanist past. We have already seen that List's stock of occult Armanist relics included prehistoric monuments, place-names, popular folk-tales and customs. But these artefacts and traditions simply posited an unconscious survival of former Armanist culture in a diluted, distorted and misunderstood form. List claimed that there also existed a consciously cultivated secret Armanist heritage, which had been started with the explicit expectation of an Armanist restoration at the end of the Christian epoch.

List's account of the secret Armanist heritage returns us to the time when the German tribes were subject to enforced conversion to Christianity. The priest-kings had soon realized the inevitable outcome of this process and consequently set about the creation of secret societies, which would be responsible for fostering the holy gnosis during the Christian era. Within conventicles known as *Kalander*, the national priesthood translated all records of their wisdom into a secret language called the *Kala* or *hochheilige heimliche Acht*, which was comprehensible only to initiates.[11] This language enabled the fugitive priest-kings to communicate metaphysical and religious material surreptitiously and to leave a record of their gnosis to posterity. List coined the verb *verkalen* to denote the translation of esoteric Armanist wisdom into an occult code of words, symbols, or gestures. This occult language, in the context of its re-translation, permitted List to interpret a very broad range of cultural material in confirmation of the hidden Armanist gnosis.

Since Freemasonry and lodge hierarchy were the models for the priesthood, List extended this idea as a way of proving that the ancient wisdom had survived. He imagined the secret *Kalander* as the social precursors of the medieval corporations of guilds, akin to masonic lodges in their hierarchy of apprentice, journeyman, and master. The medieval guilds typically possessed a craft secret, which protected its members from outside competition. List, however, suggested that these commercial craft secrets were a cover for the occult gnosis, the esoteric meaning of which was probably not even apparent to the members of the guilds, since the memory of the priest-kings had faded in the medieval mind. The three particular corporations of guildsmen, whom List cited as the conscious or unconscious carriers of tradition, comprised the skalds and minstrels, the heralds and masons, and lastly the officers of the secret medieval *vehmgericht*. Their respective 'kalic' forms of the gnosis were medieval songs, heraldic devices and architectural decoration, and legal antiquities.

List's claim that a college of heralds had existed as a guild organization in the early medieval period was essential to his belief that such a corporation had safeguarded the ancient gnosis. The source of this fallacy is easily explained. Because heraldry signified a method of personal identification by means of hereditary marks borne on a shield, some historians have been tempted to date heraldry from the time when warriors first decorated their shields for battle. Formal heraldry dates from the second quarter of the twelfth century, when armorial bearings on shields began to be repeated in subsequent generations of the original bearer's family. The utility of this practice in largely illiterate societies was considerable; because of the growth and complexity of the practice, kings founded colleges of heralds to administer the design and award of arms at the beginning of the fifteenth century. List's interest in heraldry arose for three specific reasons. Firstly, he could claim that it was a practice deriving from pre-Christian times. Secondly, the colourful blazon could be interpreted as a graphical and occult form of the secret gnosis. Lastly, the genealogical nature and widespread use of heraldry connoted the survival of the esoteric tradition throughout the Christian epoch in all parts of Europe.

List first advanced the theory that heraldic devices were based on the magical runes in 1891. He rejected the thesis of the historian Erich Gritzner, that the science dated back to the time of the Crusades, by demonstrating the correspondence between the heraldic divisions of the shield and the runic forms.[12] After his adoption of theosophical ideas in 1903, List adduced other supposedly Armanist sigils, including triskelions, swastikas, and sun-wheels, for the secret heraldic heritage. He expounded his theories in a series of articles in the *Leipziger Illustrierte Zeitung* between 1905 and 1907. In his treatise *Das Geheimnis der Runen* [*The Secret of the Runes*] (1908) he showed how the runic forms could be discerned in the heraldic divisions; their occultation arose from the fact that the non-initiate was distracted by the brightly tinctured fields of the shield, so that the dividing lines themselves were not apparent. The fa-rune ᚠ corresponded to the blazon per pale sinister side bend sinister; the thurr-rune ᚦ to a series of blazons incorporating the pile charge, and the gibor-rune (or swastika) ᛤ to a variety of blazons based on kinked pale, fess and bend. Besides these runes, List also detected the swastika in several heraldic crosses.[13]

This was just a beginning. Assisted by Bernhard Koerner (1875–1952), a List Society member and an officer of the Royal Prussian College of Arms since 1903, List supplemented these modest claims with a heraldic manual, which demonstrated the presence of the remaining runes and numerous glyphs of Armanist provenance in at least five hundred coats-of-arms, many of which were still borne by the modern aristocracy of Germany and Austria. In this compendium of pictorial Armanist relics List developed an occult key to interpret the furs, tinctures, divisions and charges of almost any coat-of-arms. The three furs, pean, ermine and vair, identified the bearer of the arms as a member of the three ancient social estates, the farmers, the priest-kings and the warriors. Each colour and metal similarly corresponded to a specific concept in Armanist doctrine. Gules yielded the 'kalic' word *ruoth*, which denoted Ario-Germanic law; vert referred to hope and resurrection; argent symbolized knowledge, wisdom and God.[14] From this system of correspondences List was able to decipher any heraldic device as a cryptic motto conveying the old gnosis. Some of his solutions were simple: the argent and azure gyrony charge in the Brockhausen arms was interpreted to mean 'Heed the law and safeguard wisdom',[15] but the esoteric meanings became more complex and less consistent when List introduced the magical sigils taken from the works of Johann Trithemius. List identified a heraldic device corresponding to the sign of the earth-spirit in Rembrandt's etching 'The Magician' (*c*.1632). This quartered escutcheon charge per saltire or and azure with twin orles in alternate gules, argent and sable meant 'I long for the illuminating Armanist salvation, wisdom and law, because the heavenly commandment issues from the darkness and God blesses from the light'.[16] List completed this arbitrary system of interpretation with occult meanings for the heraldic animals. He claimed that the dragon, eagle, worm, and lion symbolized the four elements, fire, air, water and earth, while the serpent stood for the fifth (theosophical) element of ether. Since the griffin was a synthetic creature, combining parts of the other animals, List concluded that it denoted the whole cosmos.[17]

List's materials were practically unlimited owing to Koerner's tireless interest in heraldic occultism. The arms of states, towns and noble families were all interpreted as the secret cultural relics of the ancient order. Burgundy, Moravia, Silesia, and Carniola had enshrined the old gnosis in their state arms, while the civic arms of Cologne, Basle, and Mainz also possessed an esoteric meaning. The nobilities of Mecklenburg, Brandenburg, Styria, and Carinthia were likewise shown to be the traditional representatives of the old hierarchy on account of their coats-of-arms.[18] List multiplied such examples to posit the existence of a widespread Armanist counterculture throughout Central Europe and beyond.

As the genealogical principle was the essence of heraldry it followed logically that this secret heritage led to the contemporary aristocracy. The German aristocracy, whose political authority had been eroded since the French Revolution, might derive comfort from List's exhortation that it was composed largely of 'descendants of old hierocratic families'.[19] The secret gnosis in their arms was an esoteric legitimation of their hereditary authority against the populist and democratic tendencies of the modern age. Friedrich Freiherr von Gaisberg (1857–1932), a List Society member and a Württemberg nobleman, was drawn to List's occult legitimation of aristocratic authority. At the turn of the century he had founded the St Michael Association for the study of the peerage and the 'preservation of their hereditary interests as an estate'. List dedicated one of his 'research reports' to Gaisberg and interpreted his coat-of-arms to mean 'Salvation! Laws are the principal gnosis of Armanism; the creative power of God shines out of the darkness'.[20] Such laws naturally guaranteed the authority of the aristocracy and held out the hope of its restitution.

This heraldic and genealogical occultism did not appeal only to aristocrats. The contemporary existence of several groups devoted to the study of middle-class pedigrees indicates that List's occult heraldry had a wider bourgeois audience. Bernhard Koerner had established a Roland Association at Berlin, having assumed the editorship of a twenty-volume handbook of middle-class genealogy from 1899. The Roland Association in Dresden under the chairmanship of Hermann Unbescheid had pursued *völkish* research into heraldic matters since January 1902. Another group called the Central Agency for German Family History was established by Hans Breymann at Leipzig in February 1904.[21] For the individuals who joined such groups, heraldry and genealogy connoted a search for identity in the form of time-honoured tradition, a precious heritage and an imaginarily secure image of the feudal past. Heraldry conjured a colourful tableau of knights, feudal privileges and castles, an image which formed a pleasant antithesis to the socio-cultural tendencies of the present. This quest connoted a hunger for obsolescent social structure and political authority, which were undermined by the institutions of the modern world. One might recall that both List and Lanz were self-ennobling bourgeois. Given this middle-class fascination for seigneurial trappings, List's heraldic occultism possessed considerable appeal.

List's architectural occultism was similar to that of heraldry with regard to both its forms and appeal. In 1889 he had suggested that the corbels on the west arch of St Stephen's Cathedral made allegorical references to ancient doctrine. The mystifications of medieval masons allowed all stone sculpture to be treated as a secret 'kalic' code, the meaning of which had always remained a craft concern. This notion dated from a time when List was acquainted with Friedrich von Schmidt (d. 1891), the master-builder of the cathedral, from whom he gleaned a knowledge of operative masonic lore.[22] Once List adopted the theosophical sigils, he was able to extend this architectural occultism in a geometrical sense. According to List, the holy Armanist triskelion, swastika and other sigils could be detected in the design of late Gothic curvilinear tracery and rose windows dating from the fifteenth century.[23] The technical nature of this kind of occultism was most plausible, a fact borne out by its perennial appearance amongst occultists.[24] But the idea appealed for two further reasons. In the first place, contemporaries were familiar with the notion of masonic secrets, so that it seemed probable that medieval craftsman had worked their mysteries into the fabric of their creations for subsequent generations to decipher. Secondly, given the contemporary Gothic Revival in Germany, List's suggestion that Gothic architecture contained ancient secrets would have found a readymade response.[25] He also emphasized the traditional atmosphere of the Armanist world with Gothic artwork and the occasional use of a bold *Fraktur* typeface in his publications.

The vehmgericht constituted the last of List's guilds and was supposed to have translated the holy Armanist gnosis into a 'kalic' form so that it might survive the Christian epoch. Since the vehmgericht really was a secret institution, founded to administer law in the Holy Roman Empire between the early thirteenth and sixteenth centuries, it seemed a most effective agent for List's occult heritage. Vehmic law most probably originated in pre-Carolingian times, but it was not until the late twelfth century that it assumed historical significance. At this time the imperial jurisdiction was being usurped by the new territorial princes, who were striving to assume the political authority of the old feudal estates. To counter this modern tendency the Archbishop of Cologne placed himself at the head of a long-standing system of local courts, which were to pass capital sentences in the name of the Emperor. An old parochial institution thus assumed a new historical role. From their origin in Westphalia these vehmgerichts soon spread throughout the Empire wherever conservative men sought to hinder the power of the princes. However, with the stabilization of political conditions, such a system of justice became superfluous. The vehmgericht was consequently restricted to Westphalia at the beginning of the sixteenth century and finally abolished in 1811.

The organization of the vehmgericht was based on the jurisdiction of countless local courts. Sessions were held either publicly or in secret, attended only by the members of the particular court and the judge, to whom they owed allegiance, wherever they travelled in the Empire. New members were sworn to secrecy concerning all matters relating to the vehmgericht and took an oath that they would bring any case within the competence of the court to its notice. They were then initiated into the passwords and secret signs of the organization before being presented with the symbols of their office: a rope and a dagger inscribed with the letters S.S.G.G., which stood for the obscure vehmic motto 'String, Stone, Grass, Green'. Henceforth, the novices would fight to maintain old feudal privileges against their usurpers and bring the offenders to trial.

This was the historical reality of the vehmgericht, but it later became the subject of a romantic mythology. Owing to its secret means and traditional ends—the protection of historic rights against the centralizing tendencies of princely rule—the vehmgericht came to symbolize a heroic and radical institution to the authors and historians of the Romantic period. The now largely forgotten Gothic novels published in Germany between 1780 and 1820 were primarily responsible for the creation of an enduring popular image of the vehmgericht as a secret but powerful body exercising true justice against local despots and their lackeys in distant days of medieval strife. These Gothic tales dwelt upon the mystique of the secret courts. In the middle of the night an officer of the vehmgericht would fasten the summons to the door of the accused, or simply transfix it with his vehmic dagger upon the town-gates. In obedience to this summons the accused would then make his way to the appointed place. On a remote moonlit heath or at a lonely crossroad the vehmgericht gathered to judge the accused. If the man were innocent, he would be acquitted; if guilty, he would be hanged on the spot. Failure to appear in accordance with the summons would be taken as satisfactory proof of guilt. The fugitive would then be executed by vehmic assassins, who waylaid him outside low taverns, on woodland paths or wheresoever he tried to flee.[26]

List was quite familiar with this sensational image of the vehmgericht. In 1891 he described a vehmgericht session which was supposed to have occurred at the castle of Rauhenstein against this pseudo-medieval background; the summons, the dagger, secret passages, dungeons, torture-chambers and midnight gloom all served to make his secret Armanist guild both vivid and plausible to a popular audience.[27] Besides its familiarity, the vehmgericht possessed several other attributes, which made it a fitting historical vehicle for List's occult tradition. In the first place, even academic historians admitted that the vehmgerichts had originally derived from local courts which dated back to pre-Christian times. List could therefore claim that the vehmgericht was a secret Armanist guild. Since administration and justice had been important functions of the priest-kings, it could be argued that the vehmgerichts represented a clandestine survival of Ario-Germanic law. List adduced many occult notions to prove this. The obscure letters on the vehmic dagger were reckoned to be a transliteration of a double sig-rune followed by two swastikas ᛋᛋ卐卐 , while the 'kalic' word *ruoth* (meaning law) suggested that any cultural feature which was either red *(rot)* or in the shape of a wheel *(Rad)* concealed the existence of a former vehmgericht. According to these irrational speculations, List believed that all the common red wayside crucifixes and wheelcrosses in Catholic regions of Central Europe marked the erstwhile locations of secret Armanist courts; he found these in abundance throughout Lower Austria, Bohemia, and even in the suburbs of Vienna.[28]

Secondly, the avowed purpose of the vehmgericht was appropriate to List's secret tradition. He also attributed other ideological motives to the courts than had been the historical case. In 1905 List published a short account of a vehmgericht which was supposed to have held its sessions at Rothenkreuz near Stecky in the fifteenth century. This was the period of the Hussite wars and a time of lawlessness throughout Central Europe. From List's account it is clear that he regarded these religious wars as a Czech campaign of attrition against the German minorities of Bohemia. His vehmgericht acted accordingly as the defender of German rights against Czech tyranny. This projection of modern nationalist sentiment into the past was obviously addressed to contemporary German minorities. Published in the annual of a *völkisch* association in North Moravia, this tale would doubtless be seen as a vindication of its readers' anti-Czech attitudes.[29]

The vehmgericht was an ideal agent for List's hidden heritage. Its secret means connoted a mysterious élitism, but also implied a popular institution offering comfort to those who groaned beneath an upstart tyrant's heel. Its relics could now be rediscovered and its function revived. The vehmgericht could rise again to restore order in a world where modern tendencies appeared to some individuals as a threat to their culture. List and his followers found satisfaction in this fantasy of a militant, omnipresent, yet hidden force that appeared to promise the restoration of a new pan-German empire. This fantasy was grimly fulfilled in the aftermath of the lost war when extreme right-wing nationalists, calling themselves vehmic assassins, murdered several politicians of the new German Republic.

List had marshalled all sorts of occult evidence for the existence of a prehistoric national culture in the heart of the hereditary Habsburg lands. The archaeological monuments, the place-names, and the legends, folk-tales and customs of the Danubian region were interpreted in such a way as to prove that this part of Central Europe had participated in a universal and superior German civilization of great antiquity. List's invocation of a secret, consciously created Armanist heritage in the form of heraldry, architectural decoration, and legal antiquities also progressed from the celebration of past Germanic glory to an analysis of the historic measures taken by the old priest-kings to ensure its eventual restoration. The occult meanings which he ascribed to these materials indicated the political testament and expectations of the last representatives of a lost unitary Ario-Germanic nation. The time for that restoration was now come. List's secret heritage augured the imminent transformation of Austria and Germany into a new pan-German empire.

7

The German Millennium

FRITZ SAXL, the German historian of Renaissance ideas, was an early observer of the renewed interest in fortune-telling at the beginning of the twentieth century. He dated its origins to around 1910, while noting that a number of periodicals devoted to astrology sprang up over the next decade in Germany, accompanied by textbooks, prophecies and reprints of astrological classics. In due course palmistry, numerology, cabbalism and tarot supplemented astrology to form the principal scientific bases of a popular divinatory movement which grew prodigiously in the 1920s. Saxl reflected that, although these sciences may be erroneous from a logical point of view, the imaginative or religious background of such a popular movement is of the greatest importance. A theoretical concern with the measurement of data for a system of correspondences between natural phenomena and human affairs retains a neutral scientific status, but its predictive tenor can be regarded legitimately as a function of human hopes and needs. Indeed, such foretelling of future events may become vitally important to individuals and groups that are subject to anxiety or deprivation. Saxl similarly regarded prophecy as a symptom of widespread social unease at a time when the traditional expectations of certain groups appeared to be frustrated. He considered its modern manifestation to be one of the omens of the First World War.[1]

List's prophecies were addressed collectively to the German nation and appeared to fulfil a similar function to individual fortune-telling. He foretold that an age of universal prosperity was approaching to alleviate the tribulations of German nationalists in Central Europe. This optimistic forward-looking attitude did not contradict his paeans to the past. The prophecy of a happy national future complemented his nostalgia for a lost golden age inasmuch as it denoted the restoration of his imaginary traditional world. Past and future represented the twin poles of a counter-ideal in time generated by a profound disenchantment with the present; the secret Armanist heritage throughout the allegedly benighted Christian epoch formed a bridge between these two ideal ages; such Armanist survivals were both the relics of the old dispensation and the heralds of the new order. This chapter examines the nature of List's prophecy and assesses its social significance and appeal, showing how his cyclical conception of time initially sponsored the idea of fluctuatory fortune, and how these sentiments were later modified by the idea of ultimate salvation and a linear conception of history.

List's cyclical vision of time was derived from his three sources of theological inspiration: the holy world of Nature, Norse mythology and modern theosophy. It has already been shown how the elementary content of Armanist doctrine focused upon the 'laws of nature', which ostensibly determined the periodicity of all planetary and organic cycles in the cosmos. List frequently invoked these cosmic rhythms in his early pieces on national landscape:[2] that their sustaining laws assumed the status of a divine principle in his later writings testifies to his belief in cyclical time. Secondly, one must consider the import of Norse myths in this respect. List's references to the *Fimbulwinter* and the *Götterdämmerung* suggest that he was familiar with those pagan legends, according to which there came a mighty winter after which the whole earth was consumed by fire and flood before rising anew, 'fertile, green and fair as never before, cleansed of all its sufferings and evil'.[3] According to these myths, the cycle of destruction and creation was repeated indefinitely. Lastly, List's adoption of theosophy with its cosmic rounds, and the individual's successive reincarnation in each round, served to confirm his conviction in the recurrence of all things.

Such cyclical notions of time may coexist with ideas of salvation and redemption, but these cannot enjoy any unique or final status. The termination of any given cycle heralds spiritual evolution and cosmic renovation, but the implacable logic of the cycle will still prevail: the organism will decline and perish recurrently into eternity. List rejected this oriental fatalism regarding time and destiny in favour of Judaeo-Christian notions of salvation. Although he had adopted theosophical materials for his cosmology, he was loath to accept its limited soteriology. His hopes for a restoration of the traditional world and a national revival led him to the materials of Western apocalyptic. Its explicit assumptions of linear time and a unique, final redemption jar continually with the cyclical implications of theosophy throughout his writings. In the light of List's vilification of Christianity, this adoption is ironic. In due course List's vision of a pan-German empire was almost wholly based on Western apocalyptic.

Both Jewish and Christian apocalypses distinguish themselves from other forms of prophecy by asserting an absolute and qualitative difference between the present age and the future. This dualistic and linear time scheme is represented by the juxtaposition of a pessimistic view of the present with a fantastic and joyful image of the future. The present age is devalued by a depressing account of the hardships and misfortunes that have befallen the people. The apocalyptic writer often indicates that the world is subject to an increasing physical and moral degeneration: *mundus iam senescit*. These complaints can extend to the charge that the world is under the dominion of Satan or other evil powers. At a point in the narrative coincident with the time of the apocalypse's composition, this historical survey gives way to prophecy proper. It is predicted that the former ills will be exacerbated by yet worse adversities. There will be signs of an ultimate catastrophe, such as violent climatic changes, drought, earthquakes and fire. Finally the evil spirit of this first age may appear as a dragon or other beast to torment mankind. The end of this age approaches as these so-called 'messianic woes' become increasingly intolerable. A divine warrior-leader will suddenly intervene to liberate his chosen people from their affliction. This messiah will bind or destroy the evil tyrant before establishing his own divine and incorruptible kingdom on earth. These acts initiate a new second age, when the joyful elect of the redeemed will know no suffering nor want; this new world will not be subject to the ordinary laws of nature and physical limitation; happiness and good fortune will reign eternally.[4]

The essential features of Western apocalyptic prophecy can be discerned in these broad outlines. A first, woeful, even evil age proceeds to its climax, when a new age dawns wherein the former sufferers will be redeemed and exalted. Such prophecy possesses enormous appeal for those beset by severe adversity. Norman Cohn has shown how certain disoriented social groups in medieval Europe took these apocalypses quite literally.[5] Whenever particular hardships occurred, apocalyptic groups would discern the traditional signs of those final 'messianic woes'. Tyrants were regularly identified with the monstrous beast of the last days, an incarnation of the Antichrist. The sufferers took comfort in expectation of a messianic redeemer, who would fulfil the prophecy by establishing the felicitous millennium in which they would participate as an elect. These hopes might lead the sufferers to conceive of themselves as a messianic vanguard and they engaged in rebellious activities against the Establishment in order to secure themselves a worthy place in the new world. The degree of such militancy would stand in a relationship to the supposed proximity of salvation.[6]

The survival of these ancient religious fantasies in the landscape of Western revolutionary imagination suggests that these myths satisfy a deep-seated demand for comfort and hope at times of oppression and strife. But poverty, pestilence, and war were all commonplace in medieval Europe and did not in themselves generate apocalyptic beliefs: a millenarian tradition had also to be present. Once a personal *Lebenswelt* has been upset by disaster it is easy to see apocalyptic as a fundamental and religious system of explanation. The putative source of the disaster is identified as an absolute evil power, the destruction of which is anticipated with hopes of the millenium. Absolute categories of good and evil, order and sin, restore cognitive harmony in the minds of the deprived and disoriented. Eschatological ideas have thus remained a perennial fantasy within the Judaeo-Christian orbit of religious influence.

List echoed traditional apocalyptic by expressing extreme pessimism about many aspects of modern Austrian society. His concern was greatest with regard to the nationality question. The status of German language and culture in Austria had been increasingly challenged by the Slavs of the empire over the preceding decades. The process had been furthered by the Taafe government or 'Iron Ring', which had derived its support from a broad base of clerical, conservative, and slavophile interests from 1879 until 1893. A triumph of Slav interests appeared to have been achieved in 1897 when Count Badeni introduced his language decrees, whereby all civil servants in Bohemia would have to speak both Czech and German, a qualification which would have clearly discriminated against the Germans. List fulminated against the clerical and socialist parties that favoured Slav interests and, drawing on the contemporary slogans of the Schönererite Pan-German and *Los von Rom* movements, he denounced the national outrage of Czech priests being appointed to German parishes in the ethnic borderlands and decried the preponderance of Slav civil servants in the bureaucracy.[7]

His critique of contemporary Austria also embraced wider social and economic issues. He bemoaned the current economic tendencies towards *laissez-faire* capitalism and large-scale enterprise, because they undermined the existence of artisans, craftsmen and small middle-class entrepreneurs. He complained that commerce had lost its former ethical code and regarded the decline of the guilds as the collapse of the 'bastions of the burgher-world'.[8] List's own concept of economic order was based nostalgically on those pre-capitalist modes of finance and production which were hard-pressed by modernization. He viewed the growth of modern banking and other financial institutions as the machinations of an immoral minority who speculated with paper tokens at the expense of honest men engaged in the production of tangible and proper goods. He condemned all finance as usury and indulged in period anti-Semitic sentiments culled from the newspapers of Georg von Schönerer and Aurelius Polzer. He finally recounted the story of the Vienna stock exchange crash of 1873 as the inevitable outcome of modern business practice.

List's critique of the new economics actually typified the attitude of many Austrian contemporaries. Since only a fraction of industrialization could be ascribed to autochthonous entrepreneurs, with the State and foreign investors playing the major role, domestic investment generally came from the banks and credit institutions. For this reason capitalism was regarded as the preserve of a small, closed group. This attitude was reinforced after the 1873 crash, when the wider public had no further desire to speculate in equities. Pulzer has commented that, when the growth of capitalism was a process with which the majority of the population could not identify itself, feelings of pessimistic anger and pseudo-revolutionary conservatism were bound to assert themselves.[9] List's innovation consisted in channelling these sentiments into an expression of apocalyptic protest.

List was no less pessimistic concerning modern political and cultural tendencies. A staunch defender of the monarchical principle and the Habsburg dynasty, he denounced all popular and democratic institutions of representation. Parliamentarianism was pure nonsense since it was based on the premiss that a majority of votes, however well or ill informed, should determine policy.[10] Contemporary cultural movements were condemned likewise: feminism testified to the worthlessness of the age; modern painting (the Seccessionists) represented the rape of German art; theatre was dominated by foreign and Jewish patrons. These period clichés reflected the apocalyptic notion that the world was subject to a process of physical and moral degeneration.

Following the idiom of other contemporary *völkisch* writers, List regarded the rural peasantry as the physical guarantors of a healthy nation. As a result of urban migration in the late nineteenth century, this peasantry was decreasing. List visited abandoned and depopulated farmsteads in Lower Austria, forming a dismal opinion of their wider implications. The decline of the peasant estate was, in his view, symptomatic of national decrepitude. Moreover, while the rural population dwindled, the increasing urban population gave further cause for dismay. The population of Vienna had tripled between 1870 and 1890 and urban services had clearly failed to keep pace. One-third of the city residents lived in dwellings of two rooms or less, and the city possessed one of the highest tuberculosis rates in Europe.[11] List observed that the majority of rural immigrants fell victim to these overcrowded conditions; wretched accommodation and poor food completed the debilitation of the nation's youth. This physical decay of the nation was accompanied by moral degeneration. Like a medieval moralist enumerating the deadly sins, List compared modern urban culture to the perversions of the late Roman and Byzantine civilizations.[12]

It is evident that List's description of contemporary Austria amounted to a fundamental devaluation of the present. The entire industrial-urban complex together with its emergent social and political institutions was utterly condemned. List followed the apocalyptic model even further by claiming that this situation was due to the dominion of evil powers. The dissolution of traditional social practices and institutions posited, in List's view, a simpler and more conscious agent of change than the play of market forces, social circumstances, and structural changes of the economy. List sought a more concrete personification of these widespread socio-economic transformations in the monolithic conspiracy of the Great International Party. This imaginary body represented an anthropomorphic conception of social forces, whereby all historical change was explained by reference to agents with volition. Its origins could be detected in the Christian conspiracy against the old Ario-Germanic hierarchy. In the present the wiles of the Great International Party could be discerned in the financial institutions, the political parties and their neglect of German national interests, and in the advocates of emancipation, reform and international co-operation. The obvious paradox of a monolithic agency working behind the manifest pluralism of modern secular society should not obscure List's debt to apocalyptic logic: the identification of a single nefarious power lent a religious and revolutionary appeal to his critique of Austrian society. The Great International Party was the satanic incarnation of the present age, intangible yet monstrous and malevolent.[13]

In the face of this oppression List began to search for the signs of national salvation in accordance with the traditional apocalyptic model. He devised several theories to prove that these signs were already evident by borrowing chronological notions from Hindu cosmology and Western astrology. By 1910 he had developed an interest in cosmic cycles following their theosophical popularization as rounds. These speculations concerning the regular creation and destruction of all organisms within the cosmos enabled List to invoke apocalyptic hopes by positing the end of a cycle close in time to his own day: the start of another cycle corresponded to the advent of a new age. List indulged in abstruse calculations based on Blavatsky's figures concerning the cycles, in order to conclude that a significant cycle had terminated in 1897.[14] A further quarry of apocalyptic calculation was found in the materials of the contemporary German astrological revival amongst theosophists. Blavatsky had already referred to the solar or sidereal year, which was the time taken by the planets to take up their original alignment in the next house of the zodiac. She defined this period as $c.25{,}868$ terrestrial years. List quoted this very figure and thus derived the sidereal season, which lasted $c.6{,}467$ terrestrial years. Since seasonal changes played a central role in his pantheistic mythology, his application of the sidereal concept to apocalyptic was logical. In a series of articles published during the war, List claimed that the 'cosmic-fluid influences of the sidereal seasons' exercised a powerful force upon human affairs.[15] An 'armanisto-cabbalistic' calculation convinced him that the winter solstice of 1899 had simultaneously been the winter solstice of the current sidereal year. The tribulations of the modern age and the suffering unleashed by the First World War were regarded as manifestations of those cosmic equinoctial gales before the onset of the sidereal spring. This season represented an absolutely and qualitatively distinct period in the history of mankind. Within this astrological framework of specu-lation, the 'messianic woes' appeared as the cosmically determined heralds of redemption.[16]

Another sign, which gave List cause for messianic optimism, was his receipt of a letter in November 1911 from an individual calling himself Tarnhari. This man, whose name literally meant 'the hidden lord', claimed to be descended from the ancient tribe of the Wölsungen. This mysterious emissary from the distant past assured List that his rediscoveries concerning the Ario-Germanic past tallied with his own ancestral-clairvoyant memories. Tarnhari also confirmed the existence of the *Armanenschaft*: he claimed that he had been earlier reincarnated as a leading priest-king of the old élite.[17] Although

Tarnhari primarily vindicated the past pole of his fantasy, List regarded the appearance of this reincarnated chieftain as a good omen of imminent national redemption on the future pole.[18] A further indication of the messianic hopes attaching to Tarnhari may be deduced from a letter from Friedrich Wannieck to List, written in the early months of the war. The old patron suggested that Tarnhari should reveal himself openly, now that Germany stood in an hour of need.[19]

These various signs indicated the imminent destruction of the satanic antagonist. List demanded the annihilation of the Great International Party in order that the Ario-Germans could enter the promised land of happiness and prosperity.[20] In 1911 he voiced a prophecy of millenarian combat, which strangely anticipated the naval and military hostilities of the First World War:

> *Ja, noch einmal sollen die Funken aus den ario-germanisch-deutschen-österreich-ichischen Schlachtschiffen stieben, noch einmal sollen Donars Schlachtenblitze aus den Kolossalkanonen unserer Dreadnoughts zischelnd züngeln, noch einmal sollen unsere Völkerheere . . . nach Süden und Westen . . . wettern, um [den Feind] zu schlagen . . . damit Ordnung geschaffen werde.*[21]

> [Yes, the Ario-German-Austrian battleships shall once more send sparks flying, Donar's lightning shall once more shoot sizzling from the giant guns of our dreadnoughts, our national armies shall once more storm southwards and westwards to smash the enemy and create order.]

These battles are consistent with the apocalyptic model. An enormous revolt, redolent of the twilight of the gods or the barbarian migrations, will smash the infernal enemy to create a righteous and pan-German order.

This prognostication of a German war of aggression against the non-German world was rooted in List's desire for apocalyptic vengeance. He recognized that an international war could satisfy his demand for a more visible, tangible, and anti-German enemy than the imaginary Great International Party. This translation of millenarian struggle into a war of nations also spared List the hopeless and undesirable revolt against the domestic establishment, the traditional features of which he was anxious to conserve. This conjunction of chiliastic bellicosity and a disinclination towards authentic social revolution is corroborated by the predilection for national wars on the part of many conservative revolutionaries and fascists in Europe.[22]

The outbreak of the First World War was greeted with jubilation in all belligerent countries. Some historians have suggested that this popular response evidenced a widespread desire for novelty after several seemingly stagnant decades. Others have noted a burgeoning imperialism coupled with the wish for distraction from pressing social reforms. In Germany there flourished the 'Ideas of 1914', an intellectual formulation of the general feeling of relief that national unity had overcome social division in the face of a foreign enemy. The pre-war cultural pessimists identified the former national ills with the insidious influence of the western democracies, which were now to be vanquished by the sword. It is against this euphoric reaction that List's apocalyptic attitude to the war must be understood.[23]

In April 1915 List convened a meeting of the HAO in Vienna. He delivered an Easter oration in which he welcomed the war as the onset of a millenarian struggle that would usher in the new age. He warned that this age of transition would initially witness a sharpening of adversity, 'frightful outrages and maddening torments'. But these trials would eventually separate the good from the bad for all time, since all true Germans 'were preparing a new age, in which nothing pertaining to the old age could survive unless it was Armanist in nature'.[24] The war played an important role in List's millenarian fantasy. International hostilities represented the 'messianic woes' with their increasingly intolerable misfortunes and also acted as a divine court of judgement which would divide the people into the eschato-logical camps of the saved and the damned. He closed his oration with an expression of temporal dualism perfectly consistent with traditional Western apocalyptic.

The attitudes of his cult followers towards the war corresponded closely to his own. Tarnhari spoke of the war as a 'holy august emergency', while Ellegaard Ellerbek dated his letters according to the day of 'the holiest war'. List adopted a similar chronology by completing his apocalyptic piece entitled 'Es wird einmal...!' with the date 'Vienna, on the thousandth day of the Holiest War, 22 April 1917', and celebrating the day by having a studio-photograph taken of himself working in his study. Numerous other pieces of correspondence from List's circle repeat this view of the war as a sacred crusade against the demonic hosts; its harsh trials, whether encountered in the trenches or the hungry cities, were to be borne joyfully on account of their apocalyptic significance.[25]

This positive attitude towards suffering prompts its comparison with a phenomenon that Michael Barkun has defined as the 'disaster utopia'. Barkun observes the ambiguity of disaster which, while obviously subjecting people to deprivation, can also produce unusual feelings of well-being. He notes that disasters often induce a temporary sense of common purpose and that 'invidious social distinctions disappear in a suddenly opened and democratized atmosphere'.[26] This evaluation accords well with the euphoria implicit in the 'Ideas of 1914', and also illuminates List's enthusiasm for the actual hardships of war. Because a belief in the millennium often assumes the occurrence of disasters that precede the epiphany, the sense of fellowship in the midst of actual disasters can appear to confirm the millenarian expectations. For List, suffering augured salvation.[27]

How did List actually envisage this collective salvation? For his descriptions of the millennium he tended to make use of mythological materials drawn from medieval German apocalyptic, Norse legends, and modern theosophy in order to convey its fantastic nature. He related the medieval tale of Emperor Frederick Barbarossa who lay sleeping inside the Kyffhäuser mountain. Once he awakened, Barbarossa would unleash a wave of Teutonic fury across the world prior to the establishment of German hegemony. This tale owed its inspiration to a complex of medieval millenarian hopes which had originally crystallized around the Hohenstauffen emperors in the thirteenth century. Owing to a variety of historical and cultural circumstances, these hopes later lit upon the Habsburg emperors Frederick IV and Maximilian I in the fifteenth century. One millenarian tract of the period entitled *Gamaleon* had told of a future German emperor who was to overthrow the French monarchy and the Papacy. The Church of Rome would be expropriated and all its clergy exterminated. Once their oppressors had been vanquished, the Germans would be exalted over all other peoples. In place of the Pope a new German patriarch at Mainz would preside over a new Church subordinate to the emperor, a new Frederick, whose dominion would embrace the entire earth.[28]

List's own vision of the Armanist millennium owed much to this mixture of crude early nationalism with the tradition of popular eschatology. As in those early modern manifestoes one finds the same belief in a primitive German world in which the divine will was once realized and which had been the source of all good until it was undermined by a conspiracy of inferior, non-Germanic peoples, the Church, the capitalists, the Jews, the liberals, or whatever. This ideal world would be restored by a new aristocracy under a God-sent saviour who would fulfil the religious and political expectations of the oppressed. List drew upon the traditions of this obscure historical chiliasm by claiming that the reigns of Frederick IV and Maximilian I betokened a renaissance of the Armanist spirit, the thrust of which had been sadly aborted by the conspiratorial Lutheran Reformation.[29] It is further significant that List was attracted to the ideas of Giordano Bruno, the sixteenth-century philosopher and heretic. Bruno had proclaimed that Judaism and Christianity had corrupted the ancient and true religion, by which he meant the mysticism and the magic of the Egyptian *Hermetica*, which had enjoyed considerable popularity amongst the Neoplatonists of the Renaissance. Bruno also wanted a new dispensation based on the rediscovered ancient gnosis. This conjunction of millenarian hopes and cabbalistic thought also appeared in List's vision of the new Germany. With great approval he quoted Bruno: 'O Jove, let the Germans realise their own strength . . . and they will not be men, but gods'.[30]

A particular Norse legend offered another vision of the millenium which is important for this analysis. As early as 1891, List had discovered a verse of the 'Voluspa' which invoked an awesome and benevolent messianic figure:

> *Denn es kommt ein Reicher zum Ringe der Rater,*
> *Ein Starke von Oben beendet den Streit,*
> *Mit schlichtenden Schlüssen entscheidet er alles,*
> *Bleiben soll ewig, was er gebeut [gebot].*[31]

> [A wealthy man joins the circle of counsellors,
> A Strong One from Above ends the faction,
> He settles everything with fair decisions,
> Whatever he ordains shall endure for ever.]

This *Starke von Oben* (Strong One from Above) became a stock phrase in all List's subsequent references to the millennium. An ostensibly superhuman individual would end all human factions and confusion with the establishment of an eternal order. This divine dictator possessed particular appeal for those who lamented the uncertain nature of industrial society. List eagerly anticipated the advent of this leader, whose monolithic world of certainties would fulfil the socio-political conditions of his national millennium.

Lastly, theosophy offered an occult vision of the millennium. Towards the end of the war, List suggested that the Austrian and German victims of the slaughter on the battle-fronts would be reincarnated as a collective messianic body. He applied the principle of karma to claim that the hundred thousands of war-dead would be reborn with innate millenarian fervour: these young men would then form the élite messianic corps in a later post-war national revolution. From his calculations based on 'cosmic and astrological laws', List deduced that the years 1914, 1923 and 1932 had an intimate relation with the coming Armanist millennium. He favoured the year 1932 as the time when a divine force would possess the collective unconsciousness of the German people. This generation of resurrected revolutionaries would become sensitive to the divine force and constitute a fanatic league which would usher in the new age. Order, national revenge, and fervour would then transform modern pluralist society into a monolithic, eternal, and incorruptible state.[32] This totalitarian vision was List's blueprint for the future Greater Germanic Reich. In his anticipation of Nazi Germany, his calculation was only one year out.

8

Jörg Lanz von Liebenfels
and Theozoology

REFERENCE has already been made to List's younger contemporary,
Jörg Lanz von Liebenfels, who was among the old guru's earliest
patrons, having made his first acquaintance, together with the
Wanniecks, at Gars am Kamp in 1893. Lanz also celebrated a lost
proto-Aryan world, but his theories did not possess the *völkisch* aura of
List's Armanism with its eulogy of ancient Teutons and their customs.
His thought is based instead on radical theology, an idiosyncratic view
of history and abstruse scientific speculation. Lanz causes one to
glimpse a strange prehistoric world of god-like Aryan supermen, a
medieval Europe dominated by patrician religious and military
orders, and a visionary New Age peopled with racist knights, mystics,
and sages. At the heart of his 'ario-christian' doctrine lies a dualistic
heresy which describes the battling forces of Good and Evil, typified
by the Aryan ace-men and their saviour Frauja, a Gothic name for
Jesus, who calls for the sacrificial extermination of the sub-men, the
'apelings' and all other racial inferiors. Lanz drew his terminology
from a variety of contemporary disciplines in the humanities and the
natural sciences, including anthropology, physics, and zoology, but
the functional similarity of his mythology with the relatively simple
völkisch notions of List with respect to their common political concerns
and purpose should not be overlooked. Lanz has already been the
subject of two analytical studies and he has now assumed his place as
one of Hitler's pre-war mentors at Vienna in standard biographies of
the Führer.[1]

The man who styled himself Jörg Lanz von Liebenfels and
furthermore claimed to have been born on 1 May 1872 at Messina, the
son of Baron Johann Lancz de Liebenfels and his wife Katharina, *née*
Skala, was actually born on 19 July 1874 in Vienna-Penzing, the son of
Johann Lanz, a schoolmaster, and his wife Katharina, *née* Hoffenreich.

He was christened simply Adolf Josef. Contrary to his adult fantasy of aristocratic and Sicilian origins, he was brought up by middle-class parents who were decended on the paternal side from a long line of Viennese burghers dating from the early eighteenth century.[2] During his childhood he acquired a romantic interest in the medieval past and its religious orders, which he revered as the spiritual élite of a remote age. By his own and often unreliable account, he developed an enthusiasm for the military order of the Templar Knights and steeped himself in fanciful lore concerning their castles and legends.[3] These sentiments may have motivated his decision to enter the Cistercian novitiate at Heiligenkreuz Abbey near Vienna. Despite opposition from his family, he was inducted into the order as Brother Georg on 31 July 1893 (aet. 19).

Heiligenkreuz Abbey was a formative influence in Lanz's life. The plain white stone and austere flags of the magnificent Romanesque church nave, the vaulted cloister garth, the richly illuminated stained glass and the graves of the twelfth-century Babenberg dukes were deeply imbued with an atmosphere of medieval and chivalrous romance. Lanz was an enthusiastic novice and made good progress, taking the solemn vows on 12 September 1897 and assuming teaching duties in the seminary from 19 September 1898.[4] While monastic life fulfilled his sentimental desire for identification with the old holy élites, these years at Heiligenkreuz also gave him an exceptional opportunity to extend his education under the learned tutelage of his novice-master, Nivard Schlögl, who professed the Old Testament and oriental languages. Lanz's later writings bear the stamp of a thorough grounding in Bible knowledge, the exegesis of rare apocryphal and gnostic texts, and the religious traditions and languages of the Near East. He was also an assiduous student of the Abbey's history and published his studies in several learned journals.[5]

The very first of his published works is important since it reveals the earliest indication of his incipient heresy and sectarian *Weltanschauung*. The relevant piece was a commentary upon a tombstone relief excavated from the cloister flagstones in May 1894. This relief portrayed a nobleman, mistakenly identified as Berthold von Treun (d. 1254), treading upon an unidentifiable beast. Lanz interpreted this scene as an allegorical depiction of the eternal struggle between the forces of good and evil, represented here by the nobleman and the strange animal.[6] Lanz was particularly intrigued by this bestial representation of the evil principle. His reflections upon the literal implications of this allegory convinced him that the root of all evil in the world actually had a sub-human animal nature. He began to study zoology in order to find a solution to this problem. Taking the Scriptures, apocrypha, modern archaeological discoveries, and anthropology as his further sources, Lanz assimilated current racist ideas into a dualistic religion. He finally identified the blue-eyed, blond-haired Aryan race, as defined by such contemporary Social Darwinist writers as Carl Penka, Ludwig Woltmann, and Ludwig Wilser, as the good principle, and the various dark races of negroes, mongols and 'mediterraneanoids' as the evil principle. Lanz's distinctive contribution to racist ideology was this translation of scientific ideas and prejudice into a gnostic doctrine, which typified the blond and dark races as cosmic entities working respectively for order and chaos in the universe.

It is difficult to know how far these ideas had developed during Lanz's novitiate. His teacher Schlögl disdained the Jews of the Old Testament as an arrogant and exclusive religious group, while his Bible translations were placed on the Index of forbidden books by the Church because of his anti-Semitic prejudice. Lanz may well have begun thinking along racist lines under Schlögl's influence. However, it is likely that these burgeoning unorthodox notions would have also caused considerable friction between himself and his superiors. After a period of tension and unhappiness arising from his desire for physical and intellectual freedom, Lanz renounced his holy vows and left Heiligenkreuz on 27 April 1899 (aet. 24).[7] His departure was viewed in a different light by the Abbey authorities. The register refers to his 'surrender to the lies of the world and carnal love'.[8] Lanz, however, defiantly justified his apostasy with the assertion that the Cistercian order had betrayed its original (i.e. racist) doctrines and that he could engage in its reform better from outside. His three anti-clerical books, published shortly after leaving the Abbey, testify to this attitude.[9] Other evidence suggests that he joined Schönerer's Pan-German movement and converted to Protestantism.[10] He is also supposed to have married upon leaving the order. Such an action would have compelled the renunciation of his vows and might explain the otherwise enigmatic reference to 'carnal love'.[11]

Henceforth Lanz was free to develop his own religious ideas. The years from 1900 to 1905 witness an extraordinary dynamism in Lanz's intellectual development and enterprise. He enrolled as a member of at least two learned societies where he had an opportunity to meet eminent historians and scientists. He took out three patents on inventions including a technical apparatus and a motor.[12] He also commenced writing for such *völkisch* and Social Darwinist periodicals as Theodor Fritsch's *Hammer* (est. January 1902) and Ludwig Woltmann's *Politisch-Anthropologische Revue* (est. April 1902). One of Lanz's articles contained more than a hundred references to scholarly texts and articles, thereby confirming the depth of his recent studies in anthropology, palaeontology and mythology. This piece records Lanz's first publication along scientific lines. Since Lanz was using a doctoral title by 1902, he may have written a dissertation on a topic in this prehistoric field.[13]

In 1903 Lanz published a long article in a periodical for biblical research. Entitled 'Anthropozoon biblicum', this learned investigation of the past extended his earlier theological and scientific hypotheses. He began by analysing the mystery cults described by the ancient authors Herodotus, Euhemarus, Plutarch, Strabo, and Pliny. He concluded that the antique civilizations had strictly maintained a secret associated with the sexual domain, since its mention always occurred within the context of orgiastic rituals. He was also convinced that the principal locale of such cults had lain in the Near East.[14] Turning from these conclusions, Lanz pursued his enquiries in the light of recent archaeological discoveries in Assyria. Two particular reliefs with cuneiform inscriptions provided the key to the riddle of these cults: the relief of Ashurnasirpal II (883–859 BC) and the black obelisk of Shalmaneser III (858–824 BC). Both these artefacts had been discovered and excavated at Nimrud in 1848 by the British orientalist Sir Austen Henry Layard.[15]

Both reliefs depicted Assyrians leading strange beasts of several species in the manner of pets. The accompanying cuneiform inscription on the former related that the King of Musri (a territory lying to the east of the Gulf of Aquaba) had sent these small beasts (*pagatu*) as tribute to Ashurnasirpal II. Similar animals were also reportedly received from the kings of the Patineans and the Egyptians. The text continued that Ashurnasirpal had bred these animals in his zoological garden at Calah. The inscription on the latter alluded to two other species of beasts (*baziati* and *udumi*), which had also arrived as tribute from Musri.[16] A welter of philological fallacies and circumstantial evidence taken from current anthropology and ethnology enabled Lanz to set up a series of hypotheses regarding the subject of the reliefs.[17]

He suggested that the *pagatu* and *baziati* were really the pygmies of recent scientific research and discovery; most importantly, he claimed that the Aryan race had committed bestiality with this lower species, which derived from an earlier and quite distinct branch of animal evolution.[18] The writings of the ancients, the findings of modern archaeology and anthropology, and substantial sections of the Old Testament were supposed to corroborate this terrible practice of miscegenation. The remaining sections of the article were devoted to a meticulous exegesis of the Books of Moses, Job, Enoch, and the Prophets in support of this hypothesis. The article thus completed the initial phase in the development of Lanz's neo-gnostic religion. He had identified the source of all evil in the world and discovered the authentic meaning of the Scriptures. According to his theology the Fall simply denoted the racial compromise of the Aryans due to wicked interbreeding with lower animal species. The consequence of these persistent sins, later institutionalized as satanic cults, was the creation of several mixed races, which threatened the proper and sacred authority of the Aryans throughout the world, especially in Germany where this race was most numerous. With this definition of sin, the sexo-racist gnosis offered an explanation for the wretched human condition that Lanz subjectively perceived in modern Central Europe.

Within a year Lanz published his fundamental statement of doctrine. Its very title, *Theozoologie oder die Kunde von den Sodoms-Äfflingen und dem Götter-Elektron* [*Theo-Zoology or the Lore of the Sodom-Apelings and the Electron of the Gods*] (1905), distils the gnostic essence of Lanz's thought. It was a strange amalgam of religious beliefs drawn from traditional Judaeo-Christian sources, yet modified in the light of new life-sciences: hence theo-zoology. The book repeated the basic hypotheses of the earlier article within an expanded scheme of biblical interpretation spanning both Testaments. The first section sought to understand the origin and nature of the pygmies. Four chapters entitled Gaia (earth), Pege (water), Pyr (fire) and Aither (air) described the satanic realm by relating the story of the first pygmy, called Adam, who spawned a race of beast-men (*Anthropozoa*).[19] Lanz employed a cryptic scheme of translation, whereby the words 'earth', 'stone', 'wood', 'bread', 'gold', 'water', 'fire' and 'air' all connoted 'beast-man', while the verbs 'to name', 'to see', 'to know' and 'to cover' meant 'to copulate with' and so on, in order to create a monomaniacal view of the ancient world.[20] According to Lanz, the chief pursuit of antiquity appeared to have been the rearing of love-pygmies (*Buhlzwerge*) for deviant sexual pleasure.[21] The prime purpose of the Old Testament had been to warn the chosen people (the Aryans!) against the consequences of this bestial idolatory.

Lanz's discussion of the divine principle involved the adoption of more modern scientific materials. It has already been shown how swiftly Lanz appropriated the findings of contemporary archaeology and anthropology for his doctrine: he was no less sensitive to the recent discoveries in the fields of electronics and radiology. The earliest of such discoveries to inspire Lanz concerned the thermionic emission of electrons from hot bodies as observed by Blondlot and called N-rays in 1887. Within a few years Wilhelm Röntgen had discovered X-rays, for which he was awarded the Nobel prize in 1901. In addition to these forms of electromagnetic radiation came the discovery of radioactivity by the Curies in 1898. They subsequently succeeded in isolating the source elements polonium and radium in 1902 and duly received the Nobel prize. These exciting discoveries of radiation captured popular imagination, an influence that was given further force by the application of radio communication between 1898 and 1904, following the work of Marconi and Hertz.

Lanz appreciated the popular appeal of these futuristic forms of energy and exploited such notions for his descriptions of the gods.[22] He began by asserting that the gods were but earlier and superior forms of life (*Theozoa*), quite distinct from Adam's spawn of *Anthropozoa*. Following the hint of Wilhelm Bölsche (1861–1939), a popular zoological writer who may have owed his inspiration on this point to theosophy, Lanz claimed that these early beings had possessed extraordinary sensory organs for the reception and transmission of electrical signals. These organs bestowed the powers of telepathy and omniscience upon their owners but had atrophied into the supposedly superfluous pituitary and pineal glands in modern man owing to the miscegenation of the god-men with the beast-men. However, Lanz claimed that a universal programme of segregation could restore these powers to the Aryans as the closest descendants of the god-men.[23]

The next four chapters, entitled Pater, Pneuma, Hyios, and Ekklesia, followed the account of the New Testament; attention was focused on the coming of Christ and his revival of the sexo-racist gnosis in order to redeem his chosen people, namely the Aryan race. Christ's miracles, his magical powers and the transfiguration all served to confirm his electronic nature. Lanz substantiated this hypothesis with quotations from the apocryphal Acts of John, the Oxyrhynchus Sayings and the Gnostic apocrypha known as the *Pistis Sophia*, which was the subject of contemporary German scholarship.[24] Lanz finally interpreted the Passion as the attempted rape and perversion of Christ by pygmies urged on by the disciples of the satanic bestial cults devoted to interbreeding.[25]

These frequently obscene and always radical interpretations of the Scriptures logically embraced the familiar Judaeo-Christian notions of linear history and an apocalypse. In place of the formerly distinct divine and demonic species, there had developed several mixed races of which the Aryans were the least corrupt. However, throughout all recorded history the inferior races had sought to tyrannize the Aryans by dragging them down the evolutionary ladder by means of their promiscuity. The history of religion described the struggle between the bestial and endogamous cults. At the end of this neo-manichaean temporal scheme stood the promise of final redemption and the Second Coming. Lanz's concept of the millennium was clearly generated by an overwhelming sense of cultural pessimism. He regarded the modern world as the domain of utter evil:

Die Zeit is gekommen! Verkommen und verelendet ist die alte Sodomsbrut in Vorderasien und um's ganze Mittelmeer herum . . . Unsere Leiber sind vergrindet trotz aller Seifen, verudumt, verpagutet und verbaziatet. Nie war das Leben der Menschen trotz aller technischen Errungenschaften so armselig wie heute. Teuflische Menschenbestien drücken von oben, schlachten gewissenlos Millionen Menschen in mörderischen Kriegen, die zur Bereicherung ihres persönlichen Geldbeutels geführt werden. Wilde Menschenbestien rütteln von unten her an den festen Säulen der Kultur . . . Was wollt ihr da noch eine Hölle im Jenseits! Ist die, in der wir leben, und die in uns brennt, nicht schauerlich genug?[26]

[The time has come! The old brood of Sodom is degenerate and wretched in the Middle East and all round the Mediterranean . . . Our bodies are scurfy despite all soaps, they are udumized, pagatized and baziatized [verbs of corruption formed from the Assyrian names for the pygmies]. The life of man has never been so miserable as today in spite of all technical achievements. Demonic beast-men oppress us from above, slaughtering without conscience millions of people in murderous wars waged for their own personal gain. Wild beast-men shake the pillars of culture from below . . . Why do you seek a hell in the next world! Is not the hell in which we live and which burns inside us [i.e. the stigma of corrupt blood] sufficiently dreadful?]

These 'messianic woes' corresponded to Lanz's subjective perception of widespread socio-cultural disorder in Europe. These woes heralded the approach of the millennium in the form of a sexo-racist religious revival among the Aryans. The time had indeed come. The ascendancy of the inferior races both in Europe and in its colonial orbit had to be reversed. At this point Lanz betrayed the illiberal, pan-German and monarchical sentiments underlying his entire theozoological doctrine. The lower classes of society were confused with the inferior races' progeny and charged with the frustration of German greatness and world dominion; they would have to be exterminated in accordance with the logic of traditional Western apocalyptic. Lanz fulminated against the false Christian tradition of compassion for the weak and inferior and demanded that the nation deal ruthlessly with the underprivileged. Socialism, democracy and feminism were the most important targets for this merciless mission on account of their emancipatory force.[27] Women in particular were regarded as a special problem, since they were supposedly more prone to bestial lust than men. Only their strict subjection to Aryan husbands could guarantee the success of racial purification and the deification of the Aryan race. The process would be accelerated by the humane extermination of the inferior races through an enforced programme of sterilization and castration.[28]

The similarity between Lanz's proposals and the later practices of Himmler's SS *Lebensborn* maternity organization, and the Nazi plans for the disposal of the Jews and the treatment of the enslaved Slav populations in the East, indicate the survival of these mental reflexes over a generation. Lanz's advocacy of brood-mothers in eugenic convents (*Zuchtklöster*), served by pure-blooded Aryan stud-males (*Ehehelfer*), was revived in the Third Reich with Himmler's anticipation of polygamy for his SS, the preferential care of unmarried mothers in SS maternity homes, and his musings on the education and marriage of Chosen Women (*Hohe Frauen*). Lanz's specific recommendations for the disposal of the racial inferiors were various and included: deportation to Madagascar; enslavement; incineration as a sacrifice to God; and use as beasts of burden. Both the psychopathology of the Nazi holocaust and the subjugation of non-Aryans in the East were presaged by Lanz's grim speculations.[29]

The millennium revealed itself as a fabulous German landscape, at once futuristic and aristocratic. Lanz claimed that traces of the holy electronic power still prevailed in the old princely dynasties of Germany. Provided that their pedigree had remained thoroughly noble, these families were the closest living descendants of the former god-men. Lanz emphasized that these princes had always cultivated genius, innovation and art at their castles and courts, thus providing the sole historical instrument of progress. In contrast there stood the spiritual deadweight of the inferior castes, which constantly sought to jeopardize this progress with their sentimental and vulgar demands for a share in power, regardless of their racial and gnostic incapacity. In the sphere of foreign affairs Lanz urged every right-thinking Aryan-German to recognize this truth abroad and take legitimate possession of their global birthright. Germany could no longer allow 'the apish louts to fleece the world', since the entire planet was her natural colony with a farm for every bold soldier and, in accordance with the hierarchical principle of racial purity, a country estate for every officer.[30]

An apocalyptic battle would be released upon the corrupt and resistant world, in order to attain this racist millennium. Lanz's words anticipated List's own prophecy of the First World War: '*Unter dem Jubel der befreiten Gottmenschen würden wir den ganzen Erdball erobern . . . es soll geschürt werden, bis die Funken aus den Schloten deutscher Schlachtschiffe stieben, und die Feuerstrahlen aus deutschen Geschützen zucken . . . und Ordnung gemacht unter der zänkischen Udumubande [wird]*'[31] ['Amid the jubilation of the liberated god-men we would conquer the whole planet . . . the fire should be raked until sparks fly from the barrels of German battleships and flashes start from German cannon . . . and order created among the quarrelsome Udumu-band']. This envisaged order was a pan-German racist and hierarchical paradise, which included gnostic hierophants, a new caste of warriors and a world revolution to establish eternal German hegemony:

> *Aber es soll nicht mehr lange dauern, da wird im Lande des Elektrons und des heiligen Graals ein neues Priestergeschlecht entstehen . . . Grosse Fürsten, starke Krieger, gottbegeisterte Priester, Sänger mit beredter Zunge, Weltweise mit hellen Augen werden aus Deutschlands urheiliger Göttererde erstehen, den Sodomsäfflingen wieder die Ketten anlegen, die Kirche des heiligen Geistes . . . aufrichten und die Erde zu einer 'Insel der Glückseligen' machen.*[32]

[But it will not last much longer, for a new priesthood will arise in the land of the electron and the holy grail . . . Great princes, doughty warriors, inspired priests, eloquent bards and visionary sages will arise from the ancient holy soil of Germany and enchain the apes of Sodom, establish the Church of the Holy Spirit and transform the earth into the 'Isles of the Blessed'.]

This apocalypse fused several German intellectual traditions into a millenarian vision of the new fatherland. The bards and sages of early Romanticism marched with the princes and soldiers of pre-industrial conservatism into a religious paradise, defined by such neo-gnostic symbols as the Holy Grail, the electron and the Church of the Holy Spirit. Its attainment was conditional upon the total subjugation of the inferiors. *Theozoologie* thus represented an extraordinary compilation of theological and scientific ideas in support of the restoration of aristocratic authority in a pan-German realm.

In spring 1905 Lanz co-operated with several distinguished theologians in the production of a scholarly edition of early Jewish texts. This publication was undertaken by an editorial panel representing the viewpoints of Judaism, Catholicism and Protestantism: Moritz Altschüler, the rabbinical scholar who was a member of the List Society and edited the *Vierteljahrsschrift für Bibelkunde*; Wilhelm A. Neumann, a professor of theology and a canon of Heiligenkreuz Abbey; and August Wünsche, a professor of oriental studies. The publisher's announcement of the forthcoming series entitled *Monumenta Judaica* reveals the ambitious nature of their endeavour. The first part, 'Bibliotheca Targuminica', proposed to edit the earliest Aramaic sources for the Pentateuch; subsequent sections were planned for editions of its Samarian, Syriac, Gothic and Arabic recensions. The second part, 'Bibliotheca Talmudica', was intended to study the influence of Babylonian and Assyrian ideas upon the Jewish religious tradition.[33] Lanz's selection as the Catholic editor instead of Neumann, and his use of the titles 'Dr. phil. et theol., prof. et presb. ord. Cist.', suggests a certain standing among theologians and a reconciliation with the establishment at Heiligenkreuz.[34] He was invited to contribute because of his knowledge of the Septuagint and Vulgate texts and the Gothic Bible of Wulfila. The series did not fully materialize and only five volumes had appeared under the title *Orbis antiquitatum* by 1908. Lanz was responsible for an edition of the Book of Genesis from both the Septuagint and Vulgate texts.

Journalism soon lured Lanz away from further theological scholarship while his increasing association with *völkisch* and anti-Semitic parties after 1905 precluded this kind of collaboration in Judaic research. His contributions to Fritsch's *Hammer* (a pioneer anti-Semitic periodical) and the establishment of his own organ *Ostara* in late 1905 were perhaps as much a cause of the termination of the *Monumenta Judaica* as the over-ambitiousness of the project. The *Ostara* (named after the pagan goddess of spring) was commenced as a periodical addressed to political and economic problems in the Habsburg empire from an illiberal and Pan-German point of view. Each issue was written exclusively by a single author. These included 'sc', Adolf Harpf, Ludwig von Bernuth, Adolf Wahrmund, and Harald Grävell van Jostenoode besides Lanz during the issue of the first twenty-five numbers until July 1908. Some of these contributors are familiar as supporters of the List Society (est. March 1908). The periodical manifesto informed its readers that the *Ostara* was the first and only 'racial-economic' magazine, which intended to apply anthropological findings practically, in order to combat scientifically the revolt of the inferiors and to protect the noble European race. The publication of 'theozoological' ideas amongst a broad readership required that the magazine discuss racism in relation to all aspects of social life, including science, politics, technology, art and literature.[35] From July 1908 until the end of the First World War, Lanz managed to write no less than seventy-one issues himself. Their stock themes were racial somatology, anti-feminism, anti-parliamentarianism and the spiritual differences between the blond and dark races in the fields of sexual behaviour, art, philosophy, commerce, politics, and warfare, and caste law derived from the Hindu codes of Manu.[36] The First World War was eventually documented as an eschatological phase of the manichaean struggle between the blonds and the darks.[37]

The years between 1908 and 1918 witnessed Lanz's increasing debt to contemporary *völkisch* publicists, with whom he corresponded. The *Ostara* was faithful to its announced intentions by tracing the harmful socio-economic and cultural consequences of the inferior races' emancipation in all spheres of public life. These analyses were accompanied by empirical data gathered from contemporary journalism. Their subjects may be traced in the titles of the series. Among numbers 26 to 89 seven were narrowly concerned with a classification of racial types (in 1909), eighteen were devoted to the subjects of sex, women and prostitution (chiefly between 1909 and 1913), twenty-nine to spiritual and physical comparisons between the blonds and darks and nine to religious and occult subjects, which usually formed the philosophical basis of racial manichaeism. Here one can trace Lanz's debt to the theosophical and occult subcultures.

The principal theosophist of Lanz's acquaintance, with the exception of Guido List, was Harald Grävell van Jostenoode (1856–1932), who lived in Heidelberg. By 1908 this proto-Ariosophist had written several *völkisch* texts imbued with a mixture of Christian and Buddhist piety, including the strongly theosophical *Aryavarta* (1905) and he had also contributed to a variety of nationalist and theosophical periodicals. He subsequently edited Franz Hartmann's *Neue Lotusblüten* in 1913 after the latter's death. In July 1906 Grävell wrote an *Ostara* number, in which he demanded the return of the Habsburg crown jewels to the German Reich. This claim symbolized a potent millenarian hope of contemporary Austrian Pan-Germans. A century earlier, on 6 August

1806, the Holy Roman Empire had been formally dissolved, with the last emperors having resided in Vienna, where the imperial regalia had remained. The Second Reich, established by Bismarck in 1871 and excluding Austria, represented the focus of rising national fortunes to the Pan-Germans of the multi-national Habsburg empire in the east. The return of the regalia to a new imperial capital at Nuremberg would, to these individuals, have represented the restoration of a neo-Carolingian Greater Germanic Empire under Hohenzollern rule, which would reabsorb the historic German territories of Austria, Bohemia and Moravia. Twelve statutes, based on racist, nationalist, anti-capitalist and anti-feminist sentiments, together with a blueprint for a national Church inspired by mystical and theosophical piety, completed Grävell's guidelines for a pan-German empire which was ultimately to include Belgium, Holland, and Scandinavia.[38]

The next indication of a theosophical bias in the *Ostara* was Grävell's second contribution in July 1908. Here he outlined a thoroughly theosophical conception of race and a programme for the restoration of Aryan authority in the world. His quoted occult sources were texts by Annie Besant, Blavatsky's successor as leader of the international Theosophical Society at London, and Rudolf Steiner, the Secretary General of its German branch in Berlin.[39] Grävell's theosophical contribution was followed by Lanz's *Bibeldokumente* series (1907–8) at the occult publishing house of Paul Zillmann. Here the new theosophical direction of Lanz's thought, previously indicated only by Grävell's contributions to his magazine, is quite explicit.

The second number of this series, *Die Theosophie und die assyrischen 'Menschentiere' [Theosophy and the Assyrian 'Man-Beasts']*, showed how Lanz was now exploiting the materials of modern theosophy, as he had already done in the cases of archaeology and anthropology, in order to substantiate his own neo-gnostic religion. He began by giving a selective exegesis of Blavatsky's major text *Die Geheimlehre* (1897–1901), comparing her occult anthropogeny favourably with the findings of contemporary palaeontology. He evidently shared her belief in the sunken continents of Lemuria and Atlantis and reproduced a palaeogeographical map of the world for comparison with the map of Lemuria, drawn by the English theosophist, William Scott-Elliot.[40] He compared her discussions of the lapsed third eye in man with those of Bölsche and Klaatsch, while recognizing his *pagatu, udumi* and *baziati* of Assyrian lore in her account of prehistoric monsters. Finally, and most important, Lanz found a striking theosophical confirmation of his bestial conception of the Fall. The eighth stanza of Dzyan, verses 30–2, had related how the early Lemurians first developed into two distinct sexes and how they brought about a Fall from divine grace by interbreeding with attractive but inferior species and producing monsters: '*Sie nahmen Weiber, die schön anzusehen waren, Weiber von den Gemütlosen, den Schwachköpfigen. Sie brachten Ungetüme hervor, bösartige Dämonen*'[41]['They took she-animals unto themselves, she-animals which were beautiful but the daughters of those with no soul nor intelligence. Monsters they bred, evil demons']. Lanz concluded his favourable evaluation of the Secret Doctrine with a comparison of Blavatsky's scheme of five root-races and the anthropogenic theory of the palaeontologist Stratz, published in *Naturgeschichte der Menschen* (1904). According to Lanz, the fourth root-race of Atlanteans had divided into pure and bestial sub-species, corresponding to the early anthropoids and the anthropomorphic apes. The fateful mistake of the former's descendants, the fifth root-race of Aryans or *homo sapiens*, had been persistent interbreeding with the latter's descendants.[42]

Lanz's adoption of theosophy for this sexo-racist gnosis falls within the context of a wider familiarity with the quasi-scientific ideas of the contemporary Monist League in Germany.[43] The earliest indication of this familiarity is provided by an *Ostara* number of 1910. Here Lanz discussed such philosophies as the Monism of Ernst Haeckel and Wilhelm Ostwald, and the neo-vitalism of Bergson's plagiarists in Germany. Although Haeckel considered himself a materialist, his romantic *Naturphilosophie* and 'pan-psychism' (a belief in the world soul and its manifestation as energy in all matter) were far from reflecting ordinary mechanistic materialism. Lanz, who contributed to *Das freie Wort*, a Monist periodical, subscribed to similar ideas, and also imputed such a 'pan-psychic' tradition to the writings of medieval and early modern mystics, Albertus Magnus, Comenius, Boehme and Angelus Silesius. He claimed that this 'idealistic monism' was consistent with the progressive outlook of the heroic Aryan race, while materialism connoted an earthbound, pessimistic attitude characteristic of the lower dark races.[44] These esoteric claims should not obscure Lanz's debt to the contemporary Monist movement.

This 'idealism', which may be traced to early nineteenth-century Romanticism and later philosophies of will and vitalism, together with the materials of Monism and modern occultism, formed the intellectual basis of Lanz's previously theological sexo-racist gnosis. Lanz was convinced that this doctrine of energy had lain at the heart of an imaginary tradition of 'ario-christian' mysticism, originally practised by the Aryan god-men and perpetuated by the monastic traditions of the West. The earliest biblical writings and the foundations of St Benedict of Nursia, St Bernard of Clairvaux and St Bruno had been followed by an apostolic succession of 'ario-christian' mystics, including Meister Eckhart, Paracelsus, Johann Georg Hamann, Jung-Stilling, and Carl du Prel.[45] This register of historical agents of the secret gnosis demonstrates well how Lanz recruited the several Western traditions of monastic reform, medieval mysticism, Renaissance hermeticism, eighteenth-century theosophy and modern occultism for a cryptic tradition of theozoological gnosis. The need to posit a mythological tradition for his illiberal and racist views shows how similar his ideas are to those of List despite the difference of their theological and cultural preferences. Like List, Lanz was also claiming an élite status for the guardians and priests of this secret tradition.

Lanz extended his ideological debt to occultism when he began to apply the materials of the contemporary German astrological revival to his fantasies of an apocalyptic victory for the Central Powers during the First World War. Since this revival had a specifically theosophical background in Germany, most of the new astrological texts by Karl Brandler-Pracht, Otto Pöllner, Ernst Tiede, and Albert Kniepf appeared under the imprint of the Theosophical Publishing House at Leipzig after 1910.[46] In January 1915 Lanz reviewed the astrological literature of Pöllner and Tiede. Pöllner's first work, *Mundan-Astrologie* [*Mundane Astrology*] (1914), laid the basis of political astrology by casting the horoscopes of states, peoples and cities, in order to determine their future destiny, while his second work, *Schicksal und Sterne* [*Destiny and the Stars*] (1914), traced the careers of European royalty according to the dictates of their natal horoscopes. Tiede gave an analysis of all belligerent state-leaders' horoscopes, before declaring that there was a two to one chance of victory for the Central Powers.[47] In the spring Lanz published further reviews of astrological and prophetic literature by Arthur Grobe-Wutischky, Brandler-Pracht and Albert Kniepf, who had applied the predictions of the early modern French seer Michael Nostradamus (1503–66) to the present European conflict.[48]

By August 1915 Lanz had sufficiently assimilated the new astrological and prophetic ideas to apply them to his own millenarian interpretation of the war. Following the theories of Pöllner and a Dutch astrologer writing under the pseudonym C. Libra, Lanz assigned to all major countries a planet and a zodiacal sign, the astrological properties of which corresponded to the culture and spirit of their racial stock according to the precepts of the 'ario-christian' gnosis.[49] This 'racial-metaphysical' astrology was then applied to the international hostilities. Having reviewed the events of 1914 and 1915 in the light of this neo-gnostic apocalyptic, Lanz turned to prophecy proper. The present war supposedly signalled that messianic 'fullness of time'. Increasing racial confusion, enormous military and cultural upheavals concluded by a new Mongol invasion of Europe during the period 1960 to 1988 traced the course of the incipient 'messianic woes' to the climax of demonic dominion on earth. This hard trial heralded the millennium, when a new Church of the Holy Spirit would arise to create a supra-national Aryan state, the government of which would fall to an eternal priesthood privy to the secrets of the ancient sexo-racist gnosis. The geographical origin of this coming racist millennium was the city of Vienna, which would assume a dominant role in the new politico-religious world order.[50]

In the late 1920s Lanz invoked an astrological scheme of apocalyptic prophecy, by which he could interpret the course of Western political and religious development. He took the Platonic year lasting 26,280 terrestrial years as a basic chronological unit, and then derived the 'cosmic month' of 2,190 years, which was divided into *three* 'cosmic weeks', each of which lasted approximately 730 years and defined a particular cultural epoch. One 'cosmic week' was supposed to have commenced in AD 480 at the birth of St Benedict of Nursia, widely regarded as the founder of medieval Western monasticism. In the period 480–1210 society was ruled by 'spiritual-chivalrous master-orders' (Benedictines, Cistercians, Templars and Teutonic Knights), because Mars was in Pisces. By contrast, the rule of the vulgar masses characterized the period 1210–1920, because the moon was in Pisces: the Turks and Jews weakened the European polity and the spread of towns, capitalism and the ideologies of democracy and nationalism encouraged the ascendancy of the proletariat and racial inferiors. Turning to prophecy proper, Lanz foretold that the next period 1920–2640 would witness the revival of hierarchies, because Jupiter would be in Pisces: '*Nicht mehr Parlamente . . . sondern weise Priesterfürsten, geniale, ariosophisch-mystisch geschulte Patrizier und Führer ritterlich-geistlicher Geheimorden werden die Geschicke der Völker leiten*' ['No longer will parliaments determine the fate of the people. In their place will rule wise priest-kings, genial patricians with an understanding of ario-sophical mysticism and leaders of chivalrous and spiritual secret orders']. Lanz hailed Spain, Italy, and Hungary as the 'Jupiter countries', precursors of the approaching global reformation, because of their right-wing dictatorships during the 1920s.[51]

The principal features of Lanz's ideology prior to 1918 were thus the notion of an occult gnosis, its historical lapse or suppression as an established religion owing to satanic design, and its imminent resurrection in order to secure the cosmos for a new Aryan élite, with which Lanz clearly identified himself. The nature of this élite forms the subject of the next chapter. But Lanz's revolutionary vision also possesses a specifically Austrian quality. His invocation 'Austria erit in orbe ultima', the motto of the Habsburg emperors in the fifteenth and sixteenth centuries, recalls a baroque vision of Catholic world-rule which was peculiar to Southern Europe. In view of Lanz's profound attachment as a young man to ecclesiastical ritual, ceremonial, and culture, it seems likely that this vision of a new world-order was inspired, like the old Habsburg sense of mission and 'desire for planetary conquest, an empire on which the sun never sets', by the grandeur and universality of Catholicism in Austria.[52]

9

The Order of the New Templars

LANZ'S desire to found a chivalrous order evolved directly from his racist-élitist gnosis. Although his theology was formally complete by 1905, he had not yet identified its historical agents beyond the Israelites and the early Christians. In the course of the *Ostara* series this rudimentary definition was extended to include eminent medieval saints, monastic founders, and mystics; these individual agents of the gnosis were supplemented by the reformed monastic orders and the associated military orders of the Crusades. This choice reflects personal preferences. His adoption of chivalrous agents for the gnostic tradition was fostered by a complex of factors involving his own psychological disposition and the neo-romantic climate of Austrian and German culture at the turn of the century. Even as a boy Lanz had felt drawn to the Middle Ages and its pageant of knights, noblemen, and monks. His decision to enter the Cistercian novitiate owed much to these sentiments, and it is likely that his adult desire to identify with the aristocracy derived from similar fantasies. As a scion of the German nobility, Lanz could feel assured of a tangible link with a venerable tradition that transcended the present.

Adolf Josef Lanz was born of middle-class parents, whose male forebears can be traced back to the early eighteenth century, so it seems improbable that his claims to aristocratic lineage were legitimate.[1] Some scant evidence can nevertheless be found to vindicate these claims. The name 'Liebenfels', which Lanz had hyphenated to his own by 1903,[2] indicated his descent from an old Swiss-Swabian family originating in the fifteenth century. Lanz also used the blazon of this family, an eagle wing argent upon a gules field. The founder of this line, Hans Lanz, had been a barber-surgeon at Meersburg before rapidly ascending the social scale. After joining an aristocratic fraternity at Constance in 1454, he married a noblewoman in 1463, thereby acquiring a title to her estates including Schloss Liebenfels near Mammern. Between 1471 and 1475 Hans Lanz acted as town magistrate at Constance. He was subsequently ennobled by Emperor Frederick III, with whom he stood in high favour for his representation of Austrian interests in Switzerland. Having been granted the title Lanz von Liebenfels, he bore the eagle wing argent upon a gules field blazon of the Liebenfels family, which had died out at the end of the fourteenth century. The descendants of Hans Lanz von Liebenfels (d. 1502) held high offices in Church and State: women in three successive generations became princess-abbesses at Säckingen during the eighteenth century. The family cannot be traced later than c. 1790.[3]

In 1878 one C. von Lantz, a Russian army colonel serving in Austria, also thought that he was related to the Lanz von Liebenfels, but his connection with the Viennese family is unproven.[4] In 1899 a handbook of bourgeois heraldry described Lanz's family as the Viennese line of the noble Lanz von Liebenfels, a family of 'Bavarian origin, some of whose descendants had settled in Silesia and other foreign countries'. The decorated Russian officer was also mentioned but not identified as a close relative.[5] Although there is no further evidence of an emigration to Eastern Europe, it remains conceivable that Lanz's ancestor, Matthias Lanz (b. 1720), was a derogated descendant of such emigrants. Besides this slight evidence for a genealogical link, several rumours spread amongst Lanz's friends regarding his marital title to the name: one story records his marriage to a Liebenfels upon leaving the abbey in 1899, another relates that he was on intimate terms with a family called von Liebenfels-Frascati.[6] Whether it was an oral tradition of noble origins amongst his own family or a liaison with a noble family which led Lanz to assume an aristocratic title will probably never be known with certainty, despite extensive ancestral research by his followers.[7] The real importance of this obscure genealogical issue concerns Lanz's later foundation of a chivalrous order. While noble status satisfied his desire for membership of an enduring traditional élite, his own order could fulfil a similar function.

Besides these fantasies of nobility, one must consider his romantic reverence for holy orders, which was compounded by a subsequent interest in the Knights Templars. Lanz's first interest in the Templars stemmed from a reading of the medieval lays concerning Parsifal and the knights of the Grail. These epics were enjoying a contemporary vogue owing to their operatic treatment by Richard Wagner and the subsequent popularization of their mythology by such neo-romantic authors as Erwin Kolbenheyer and Friedrich Lienhard between 1900 and 1914. In their novels mystical pilgrimages and chivalrous heroism combined to create an emotional climate in which the figure of the grail-knight denoted the spiritual man's search for eternal values in a modern trivialized world based on materialistic assumptions.[8] Given Lanz's contacts with contemporary *Lebensreform* groups, this symbolism would have been quite familiar to him. By 1907 he had concluded that the 'Templeisen' knights of Grail association were really the historical Templars, whose valiant conduct in the Holy Land had guaranteed their transformation into an archetype of religious chivalry in the thirteenth century.[9]

The Templar knights were closely associated with the Cistercian order. St Bernard of Clairvaux, the Cistercian founder, had composed the Templar rule in 1128 and later addressed a laudation to the knights for their martial championship of the Christian cause. Lanz's own regard for the Templars was probably reinforced by the fact that he had been a Cistercian himself. According to his fantasy, these knights had actually championed the racist gnosis during the Middle Ages. Their ambition had been the creation of 'a Greater Germanic order-state, which would encompass the entire Mediterranean area and extend its sphere of influence deep into the Middle East'.[10] In 1913 he published a short study, in which the grail was interpreted as an electrical symbol pertaining to the 'panpsychic' powers of the pure-blooded Aryan race. The quest of the 'Templeisen' for the Grail was a metaphor for the strict eugenic practices of the Templar knights designed to breed god-men.[11] The Templars had become the key historical agent of Lanz's sexo-racist gnosis before 1914.

Ideas of piety and chivalry, sentiments which were widespread in theosophical and neo-romantic subcultures, thus fused with modern notions of racial salvation, élitism, and pan-Germanism in this 'ario-heroic' image of the Templars. Their trial and suppression in 1312 acquired an occult meaning within this sectarian *Weltanschauung*. The brutal suppression of this noble order accordingly signified the triumph of the racial inferiors who had long sought to remove the chief advocates of the eugenic cult. The ascendancy of these inferiors in Europe, coupled with the burgeoning racial chaos of the following centuries, had corrupted 'ario-christian' civilization and thus created the disorder of the modern world. Nor did Lanz restrict himself to nostalgic visions of a glorious past. Once he had unearthed the true occult meaning of the Scriptures, supposedly suppressed by the post-thirteenth-century Establishment, it remained to revive the racist gnosis in the present. Lanz decided to refound the lapsed military order as his own Ordo Novi Templi (ONT) for a new crusade.

With the aid of his Viennese friends Lanz purchased Burg Werfenstein as the headquarters of his order in 1907. This castle was a romantic medieval ruin perched upon a sheer rock cliff above the River Danube at the village of Struden near Grein in Upper Austria.[12] In the December 1907 issue of *Ostara*, Lanz published a programme of the ONT, describing the order as an Aryan mutual-aid association founded to foster racial consciousness through genealogical and heraldic research, beauty-contests, and the foundation of racist utopias in the underdeveloped parts of the world. He also wrote that he was founding a museum of Aryan anthropology, for which he had secured a suitable site (i.e. Burg Werfenstein).[13] Lanz celebrated Christmas Day 1907 by hoisting a swastika flag upon the tower of Burg Werfenstein.[14] Franz Herndl, who inhabited a hermitage upon Wörth Island opposite the castle, remembers that two flags were flown: the first displayed the Liebenfels blazon, while the second showed a red swastika surrounded by four blue fleurs-de-lis upon a golden field.[15] The image of a feudal lord was heightened by Lanz's increasing use of heraldic seals: one showed his blazon and carried the inscription 'Jörg Lanz de Liebenfels, Dom. de Werfenstein eges.', while another related to the ONT.[16] He also celebrated the ancient origins of his castle in a study which suggested that Werfenstein was a site associated with the Nibelungs of the fifth century.[17] By these devices, Lanz gave ritual expression both to his own nobility and his fulfilment of a traditional mission.

The earliest activities of the ONT appear to have been festivals held at Burg Werfenstein during 1908. Once in the spring several hundred guests arrived by steamer from Vienna to the sound of small cannon fire from the beflagged castle. After luncheon at local inns, the large party listened to a concert in the castle courtyard; festivities lasted late into the night with bonfires and choir-singing. This event was widely reported in the national press, thus helping to publicize the ideas of the *Ostara* to a broader audience.[18] Alongside these profane celebrations of Pan-German inspiration Lanz was creating a liturgy and ceremonial for his order, which remained largely secret to non-initiates. At this time Lanz began to devise a rule for the ONT in the form of the kind of disciplinary code observed by traditional religious orders. Although it was not printed until after the First World War, it is probable that a similar manuscript document circulated among members of the order much earlier. Historical evidence concerning this rule provides a picture of the development of sectarian activities between 1908 and 1918.

The nine articles of the rule comprised a statement of the order's purpose and basis; an account of brothers' rights and duties; a brief description of the order's rituals and several articles concerning ceremonial, including hierarchy, vestments and heraldry. Lastly, the rule added articles pertaining to order property and the procedure for disputes and resignation.[19] The first article described the ONT as a racial-religious association, which could be joined only by persons of predominantly pure blood, namely those who were more or less blond-haired, blue-eyed and possessed of an 'ario-heroic' figure according to Lanz's analysis of racial somatology in the *Ostara* issues of 1908 and 1909.[20] This aristocratic association existed to harmonize science, art and ethics into a gnostic religion that was to foster the maintenance of the threatened Aryan race in all countries of the world. Its first commandment exhorted each to love his neighbour, by which Lanz understood the racial kinsman. The duties of brothers embraced professional, social, scientific and religious fields of activity. Members of the order were required to display preference towards other brothers and racial equals in matters concerning professional appointments, welfare, and business. They were also charged with the recruitment of suitable novices and expected to contract eugenically proper marriages. Brothers of means were encouraged to found new ONT houses on sites distinguished by natural beauty and historical association, especially of a monastic or Templar character: such houses were to form 'ario-christian' centres and racial utopias in Europe and overseas.[21]

While the scientific activities of the brothers involved research into genealogy and anthropology, their religious practices introduce the esoteric aspect of the order. These practices stressed the traditional status of both order and doctrine by using a quasi-orthodox liturgy of psalms, prayers and readings accompanied by organ music. During the 1920s Lanz composed several copious ritual books, which reflected his Catholic and Cistercian inspiration. The basic text was the *Hebdomadarium*, which contained the three offices for each day of the week, namely matins, prime and compline. Each office had a space for a reading relating to 'ario-christian' doctrine from the *Festivarium NT*. This book of festival readings comprised three volumes: the *Legendarium* provided readings describing the historical and cultural traditions of the racial religion for matins on each day of the year. The materials for its 1,400 pages were drawn from orthodox

Christianity, modern science and the acts of the New Templars; the other volumes, the *Evangelarium* and the *Visionarium*,performed a similar function in the prime and compline offices. These ritual books were supplemented by a hymnal (*Cantuarium*), a book of psalms and an *Imaginarium NT* of devotional pictures, all of which fused the orthodox forms and beliefs of Catholicism with the sexo-racist gnosis. According to Lanz, these rituals were designed to beautify and ennoble the lives of brothers by relating them to the waxing and waning of nature through a full religious calendar.[22] As such, these practices reflect the central function of the sect: the restoration of socio-cultural order through rituals using a traditional yet also racist form of liturgy in an aesthetically pleasing and communal setting.

Besides this liturgy Lanz made provision for a hierarchy of orders. According to the rule brothers were divided into seven orders corresponding to their service and degree of racial purity. The lowest order consisted of Servers (SNT), who were either less than 50 per cent racially pure, as defined by Lanz's racial somatology, or persons under twenty-four years who had not yet undergone a racial test. The next order was formed by Familiars (FNT), persons who had made themselves of especial service to the ONT but did not wish for a formal reception. The following order of Novices (NNT) included all members aged over twenty-four years and being more than 50 per cent racially pure, who had not yet been tested for advancement to the superior orders. These orders comprised the Masters (MONT) and the Canons (CONT) who possessed respectively 50–75 and 75–100 per cent degrees of racial purity. The two highest orders of the hierarchy were those of Presbyter (pONT) and Prior (PONT). Any Master or Canon was eligible for promotion to the order of Presbyter once he had founded a new house or site for the ONT. His rights included the saying of office and celebration of mass, but excluded the reception and investiture of brothers. A Presbyter whose chapter exceeded five Masters or Canons was eligible for installation as a Prior, who enjoyed all rights of holy office. On all occasions the brothers observed this order of precedence, while ranking according to the date of their reception within each order.[23]

Lanz embellished his hierarchy with a description of the vestments, heraldic device and title proper to the order of each brother. The basic robe worn by all brothers was a white cowled habit decorated with a red chivalric cross, the form of which varied according to the bearer's order. Presbyters wore additionally a red biretta and stole, while a Prior also carried a golden staff. This ritualism extended to the blazons placed above the seats in the chapter-house. Each brother's family coat-of-arms was mounted upon a baroque surround, the exact design of which corresponded to his order. The surround also displayed an angel and a faun, which represented the dualistic gnosis of the ONT. Lastly, brothers chose an order-name which they used in the formula 'Fra + Name + order + house', e.g. Fra Detlef CONT ad Werfenstein. The style of address for brothers was 'honorabilis' and 'reverendus' for Presbyters and Priors.[24] It will be obvious that this fusion of orthodox monastic and racist symbolism in the hierarchy ceremonial worked to emphasize the central importance of the gnosis in the minds of brothers.

The ONT liturgy and ceremonial acquired this form in 1921, but may have been practised earlier. The extent to which this meticulous rule was observed up until the end of the First World War can be inferred from scattered references in the *Ostara* numbers. In 1911 Lanz first described Burg Werfenstein as the priory of the order.[25] Regular receptions had apparently taken place as early as 1908,[26] and the use of order-names and orders began to develop before the war. By 1912 Lanz was calling himself Prior of the Order,[27] while other brothers were mentioned in the *Ostara* numbers between 1913 and 1918. A devotional poem, entitled 'Templeisenlehre', was published by Fra Erwin NNT von Werfenstein in 1913, while Detlef Schmude, an early enthusiast in Germany, signed his contributions as Fra Detlef CONT zu Werfenstein in 1915. Other brothers called Rainald, Curt and Theoderich, were styled CONT, MONT and SNT, respectively. By 1915, the erstwhile Novice Erwin had advanced to the order of Canon.[28]

Besides this minor ceremonial, several other activities indicate the development of sectarian consciousness during the war. These activities include the composition of devotional songs and verse, and the decoration of the priory with votive paintings. In 1915 and 1916 Lanz issued a New Templar breviary in two parts which contained 'ario-christian' psalms and canticles written by himself and his closest followers. These pieces were based on traditional Christian texts, but their meaning was changed in a racist and gnostic sense, thus anticipating the later ritual books. The strident supplication to Christ-Frauja (a Gothic name for Jesus) for racial salvation and the sacrifice and extermination of the inferior races reflected the familiar dualist doctrine.[29] Votive paintings for the Blue Templar Room at Burg Werfenstein included that of Hugo de Payns, founder and first Grand Master of the Templars and that of Saint Bernard embracing the suffering Christ.[30] All these details confirm the evolution of order ritual at an early date before or during the war.

New Templar religiosity also sustained brothers in the field. Fra Detlef wrote a series of devotional poems about St Bernard, the Templars and fortitude, while serving in the German army on the eastern front in Poland during 1915. These poems celebrated the saint's protection of his servants and their blessing as priests of the racist gnosis. Fra Curt also composed a martial poem after the battles of the Nidda.[31] Other poems described the River Danube and Burg Werfenstein as sacred sites of the holy gnosis. Such verse celebrated the shining image of the castle-priory against the dark valley of racial chaos; above the sunlit battlements of the 'castle of the Grail' fluttered the swastika flag, while white-cowled brothers performed the holy office in the grove below.[32]

Ritual activity in the order clearly occurred before and during the war, but it is difficult to know how many individuals were involved in the esoteric side of the ONT. In addition to the already-mentioned full brothers of the order, Lanz created several Familiars, including August Strindberg, Guido von List, General Blasius von Schemua, Gustav Simons, the inventor of a reform diet bread in Vienna, and Wilhelm Diefenbach, the pioneer of reform-culture and teacher of the theosophical artist Hugo Höppener (Fidus).[33] Lanz also claimed that Lord Kitchener and Karl Kraus, the Austrian satirist, were *Ostara* readers. The popularity of the *Ostara* proves that the ONT was familiar to a great number of Austrians, particularly in Vienna. Survivors of the period recall that the *Ostara* was widely distributed from city tobacco-kiosks and was widely read in the right-wing students' fencing associations, while Lanz claimed an enormous edition of 100,000 copies in 1907.[34] One may conclude that the chauvinist and racist ideas of Lanz were broadly endorsed by *Ostara* readers, even if only a small minority were admitted to the esoteric practices of the New Templars.

After the first *Ostara* series was terminated in early 1917, only a few second editions of earlier numbers were issued. By the time of the armistice in November 1918, the extensive dissolution of the Habsburg empire was painfully apparent. Mutinies, food riots, and secessionist revolts in the provinces of Carniola, Bohemia, and Moravia announced the collapse of imperial rule after nearly four hundred years. During the turmoil of autumn 1918, which appeared to confirm his darkest predictions concerning the triumph of the inferior races, Lanz left Vienna for Hungary. His first post-war publication, *Weltende und Weltwende* (1923), described the subsequent events and conditions in apocalyptic terms. The food shortages, the currency crises and soaring cost of living, and the ubiquitous presence of Allied missions, intended to control the enforcement of territorial changes and economic reparations, confirmed his belief that a monstrous conspiracy was responsible for the destruction of historic political entities, the removal of traditional élites, and the economic demoralization of the upper and middle classes. Henceforth, a rabid anti-Semitism and a belief in a 'Jewish-Bolshevik-Freemasonic' alliance characterize his 'ario-christian' ideology.

The events of 1918–23, which transformed the political map of Central and Eastern Europe, were cataclysmic, particularly for those who identified themselves with the pre-war order. The revolution and civil war in Germany and Russia, the triumph of popular over aristocratic forms of government, and the rise of parvenus represented a colossal manifestation of disorder in the minds of many individuals. People who had perceived a threat to their cultural norms before 1914 were now confronted with experiences appearing to verify their worst fears. Only against this chaotic political and economic background can the new relevance of New Templar doctrine in the post-war period be appreciated: for those who were subject to this sense of disorientation, the ONT could offer the promise of a crusade for absolute values against a dispensation of chaos and darkness. The post-war history of the ONT introduces the sectarian revival of Lanz's sexo-racist gnosis in each of the three defeated Central European nations.

The principal actor in the post-war German revival of the order was Detlef Schmude. His enthusiasm for the order had led him to found its second priory at Hollenberg near Kornelimünster on 9 February 1914.[35] After service in the German army Schmude returned in 1918 to Grossottersleben in the Harz where he wrote a novel based on his experiences in the ONT. *Vom Schwingen und Klingen und göttlichen Dingen* [*Vibrations, Resonances and Divine Things*] (1919) focused on the life-enhancing value of occult mental vibrations between persons involved in devotional activities based on *Lebensreform*. The novel described a young man's woodland chapel consecrated to mystical Christian worship and its circle of guardians. Besides its explicit indication of ONT ceremonial, including the order habits and baroque heraldry with the angel-faun symbolism, the book reveals a close affinity to the literature of the 'quest' in points of theme and style.[36] But Schmude was also active in a practical capacity. In March 1919 he was engaged as an army captain in the organization of a volunteer work-camp corps at Magdeburg. This corps was intended to generate a will to work amongst the unemployed in the chaotic post-war economy by means of co-operative housing and agrarian schemes.[37]

Schmude began to generate support for the order in Germany soon after the war. In June 1921 he organized the printing of the ONT rule at Magdeburg, in which he, a certain Johann Walthari Wölfl and Lanz signed as the Priors of Hollenberg, Werfenstein and Marienkamp.[38] In 1922 he started to publish a second *Ostara* series, in which the first nineteen numbers, originally written by various Pan-German authors in 1905–7, were to be replaced by new issues, which included a second serial edition of *Theozoologie*. His first number, *Die Ostara und das Reich der Blonden*, reiterated the 'ario-christian' canon with abundant quotations from Lanz: 'racial history is the key to the understanding of politics', and 'all ugliness and evil stems from interbreeding'. Schmude distinguished five racial types and examined the causes of cultural collapse, while claiming that 'all oriental and ancient States had declined with the appearance of mob-rule and the dictatorship of the proletariat, as soon as the inferior races had won the upper hand over the blond "ario-heroic" ruling caste'.[39] These words reveal the significance of Lanz's old racial theories to individuals distressed by the effects of defeat, economic collapse, and revolution upon their traditional values.

At this time Schmude met Friedrich Franz von Hochberg (1875–1954), a Silesian count and a cousin of the ruling Prince of Pless. He had pursued a military career in the Prussian Army but had retired at the end of the war to commence practice as an architect near Zittau in Saxony from 1920. At the village Wanscha he ran his 'Rosenbauhütte' (Rose-Lodge), which specialized in designs for country-house architecture. Hochberg greatly bemoaned the contemporary state of affairs in Germany. He may have been obliged to resign his commission in the army due to Allied directives on military reductions, and his family estate at Rohnstock was threatened by Polish incursions until the German Freecorps victory of 1921. Hochberg joined the ONT in a troubled state of mind. He was designated Presbyter at Hollenberg by May 1923; the following December he admitted that the ONT was his sole comfort in '*diesem üblen Zwergen-und Tschandalenlande*'[40]['in this evil land of pygmies and *Tschandale'*].

In spring 1924 Schmude travelled to Persia, hoping to found an ONT colony at Tabriz. Hochberg assumed the duties of Prior at Hollenberg during his eighteen-month absence. The subsequent activities of this priory testify to his enthusiasm and organizational energy. In that year three chapters were held by the German brothers of the order: a Whitsun chapter on 7/8 June at Burg H., where the thirteen brothers present included Friedbert Asboga, a writer on astrological magic and medicine, and Konrad Weitbrecht, a Swabian forester who led an ONT group in his region; a September chapter on 20/21 September in South Germany for the Swabian circle; finally, an Advent chapter on 29/30 November at Hanover, where Hochberg and Weitbrecht were joined by about ten other brothers. The numbers in attendance were evidently small and one cannot be sure of their social background. While several of the Swabians had rural occupations, it is recorded that Prince Hans Heinrich XV of Pless made several donations to the order. Brothers' descriptions of their experiences at the chapters emphasize mystical atmosphere, the romance of Gothic and chivalrous trappings and the beauty of nature. The general tone of feeling was a pleasure in the temporary suspension of mundane and unpleasant aspects of life and a sense of peace and order.[41]

The priory of Hollenberg consisted of brothers in widely separated parts of Germany and possessed no fixed seat. Efforts were made to find a suitable building, in order to give the priory this symbol of unity. In March 1924 Weitbrecht received a million Austrian crowns, collected by the brothers of the priories of Werfenstein and Marien-kamp, for a seat in South Germany. Hochberg meanwhile made five hundred gold marks available for the purchase of the small ancient earthwork of Wickeloh near Gross-Oesingen in Lower Saxony on 26 March 1925.[42] Although construction commenced here that summer, the priory of Hollenberg was wound up after Schmude had deemed its survival unlikely due to adverse economic circumstances in Germany upon his return in January 1926. Its brothers thus transferred to the obedience of Werfenstein, while Schmude dissolved the priory with effect from 15 April 1926.[43] But the ONT did not lapse in Germany. Hochberg later bought the small fort at Dietfurt near Sigmaringen, where the priory of Staufen was formally consecrated on 31 December 1927. The Swabian circle and other German brothers performed the order rituals in the grotto chapel beneath the fort under the priorate of Hochberg until the end of the 1930s.[44]

Another circle planning the foundation of a new ONT house in North Germany developed among the brothers of the former Hollenberg chapter who had transferred exceptionally to the obedience of Marienkamp. This circle was led by Georg Hauerstein jun., the son of

Georg Hauerstein, a friend of List and an ONT brother associated with Schmude before the war. Having joined the Hollenberg chapter in 1922, the younger Hauerstein (Fra Eberhard) pioneered the Wickeloh project near his own racist utopia on the Lüneburg Heath. He sold his land in 1926 and bought a house at Prerow on the Baltic Sea coast, which he ran as a pension called 'Haus Ostara'.[45] He then acquired a religious interest in an ancient earthwork called the Hertesburg near Prerow, and established a fund for its purchase in August 1926, to which the Hungarian brothers and the Berlin palmist, Ernst Issberner-Haldane, contributed.[46] A wooden church was built on this site the next year and was consecrated as the Hertesburg presbytery on 8 November 1927. This foundation was related to medieval Templar lore and also to the mythical sunken city of Rethra-Vineta, supposedly the cradle of the 'ario-heroic' race in the pseudo-traditional history of the ONT.[47] Here Hauerstein generated a new centre of sectarian activity and issued two book-series in the early 1930s until the site was compulsorily acquired by Hermann Göring's Reich Forestry Commission as part of the Darss National Park in October 1935. Hauerstein then established a new presbytery of Petena at the Püttenhof near Waging in Bavaria.[48] Besides these ritual ONT activities in Germany, the doctrine of Lanz was cultivated by a secular group around the occult-racist publisher Herbert Reichstein from October 1925.

The last years of the war had brought Lanz a contact and friend whose wealth and patronage was to prove the salvation of the order in Austria after the war. Johann Walthari Wölfl was an industrialist who lived in Vienna-Hietzing and who had become an *Ostara* reader by early 1918. He was sufficiently inspired by the ONT to offer Lanz substantial funds on the condition that he became Prior of Werfenstein. Wölfl assumed this dignity following Lanz's departure for Hungary. Under his priorate the Austrian section of the order flourished. The membership of some 50-60 brothers made frequent endowments of money, books, and ceremonial objects for the ornamentation of the priory. A small antique organ was procured from Schloss Steyeregg and the office was regularly performed on Sundays and other holy festivals. Although no chapter took place in 1923 owing to the unfavourable political climate in the new socialist Republic, a solemn Whitsun chapter was held at Werfenstein on 7/8 June 1924, attended by Wölfl, Lanz's two brothers Herwik and Friedolin, and twelve other brothers. The celebrations began at midnight in the castle grove with the consecration of water and fire, followed by the reception and investiture of new brothers. The next morning matins and the prime were said in the grove followed by meditation, a conference in the Blue Templar Room, and a tour of the castle with an opportunity to admire the panoramic view of the River Danube below. In the afternoon compline was said followed by songs ending at four o'clock. The lasting impression of the chapter is recorded in a brother's letter: 'an inner sense of community, an intimate and clear tranquillity and harmony . . . '.[49] This Whitsun chapter was repeated in 1925 and 1926.

Wölfl was responsible in the 1920s for several order-publications which, together with Lanz's recently composed office books, extended the liturgical basis of the ONT. In April 1923 he began to issue the *Tabularium*, a monthly diary intended for restricted circulation among brothers. Each of the three archpriories supplied its own notes relating to receptions, investitures, endowments, and significant events. A directory of worship for the whole period was also included. Reprints of extracts from brothers' letters relating to their religious enthusiasm for the gnosis formed a final section. In the summer of 1925 Wölfl started two further series, the *Librarium* and the *Examinatorium*. The former comprised short studies relating to the alleged medieval antecedents of the order, the castle-priory Werfenstein, and *Lebensreform*; the latter offered a question-and-answer synopsis of all order matters so that new brothers were quickly and comprehensively apprised of its history, traditions, and ceremonial. The neo-Cistercian and pseudo-traditional tendency of these texts is plainly evident.[50]

Wölfl devoted himself to exoteric publications in the late 1920s and carried Lanz's doctrine afresh to a wider Austrian audience. In May 1926 he had received an authorization from Lanz to publish a third *Ostara* series, which duly commenced in February 1927 with an introductory issue by himself.[51] Between 1927 and 1931 most of a hundred projected numbers were published with illustrated covers in a more luxurious format than those before the war. Wölfl also introduced ONT ideas to a new right-wing public in Vienna through an association called the Lumenclub, which was founded on 11 November 1932. This group was formed to combat 'the ugly, sickly and rotten aspects of contemporary culture' by the generation of 'an ethical and spiritually sublime way of life'. Although this manifesto echoed pre-war theosophical and *Lebensreform* sentiments, the Lumen-club was closely linked with the *Ostara-Rundschau (Panarische Revue)*, which Wölfl had begun to publish in April 1931. This review was based on the concept of pan-Aryan co-operation between right-wing radical groups of the world. Its directory of useful addresses indicated the offices of Italian and French fascist organs, the Nazi *Völkischer Beobachter*, and patriotic and racist associations in Great Britain and the United States.[52] That the Lumenclub was an ONT front is confirmed by the membership of its committee in 1936: Wölfl, Walter Krenn (Fra Parsifal), and Theodor Czepl (Fra Theoderich, later Dietrich). The Lumenclub issued its own broadsheet and convened lectures and acted as a growth centre for the illegal Nazi party in Austria in the years preceding the downfall of the Republic and the *Anschluss* with Germany in March 1938. However, despite their modest contribution to the rise of Austrian fascism, the Lumenclub and the ONT were suppressed by the Gestapo in March 1942, according to a party edict of December 1938 applying to many sectarian groups.[53]

The movements of Lanz during the 1920s provide a record of ONT activity in Hungary. At the end of 1918 Lanz had left Austria, the new socialist administration of which confirmed his suspicions regarding the triumph of racial inferiors in the heart of Christian Europe, and gone to live in Budapest. Here he became involved in counter-revolutionary activities against the numerous short-lived administrations and the Romanian invasion in 1918–19. He joined the *Ébredö Magyarok* (Awakening Hungarians), a secret patriotic association founded in 1917 among soldiers discharged from the war. During the autumn of 1918, when the old Hungary was in dissolution and Karolyi's government seemed unable or unwilling to defend her national interests, this and several other right-wing associations organized themselves in defence of Hungary's territorial integrity without and her social stability within. The *Ébredö Magyarok* regarded themselves as the chief executants of the internal White Terror directed against members of Karolyi's and Kun's revolutions, the Communists, and the Jews, though many smaller bodies shared the work with them. During the Communist revolution, Lanz was nearly executed by a firing-squad of insurgents on Easter Sunday 1919; it was the second time he had found himself under sentence of death for his part in the counter-revolution. Although the history of the secret associations is confused and obscure, Lanz's involvement must have brought him into contact with prominent Hungarian right-wing radicals and thus exercised a polarizing influence upon his political ideas. It is significant that his new anti-Semitic and anti-Bolshevist notions date from this year.[54]

Following the victory of the Hungarian counter-revolution under the auspices of a coalition including the conservative Christian National Union in early 1920, Lanz served in a Christian National press agency attached to the Hungarian Foreign Office, where he was engaged in writing reactionary articles for the daily newspapers *Pester Post* and *Pester Zeitung*. Hungary was a far more favourable domicile than Austria for a person of Lanz's political views in these troubled years. Lanz remained in Budapest, posing as an 'expatriate German baron' in conservative circles. His subsequent literary endeavour was divided between reactionary journalism, the composition of the ONT office books, and occult studies. Since the latter included astrology and cabbalism, it is evident that Lanz was an early participant in the burgeoning post-war occult subculture in Central Europe.

The affairs of the ONT in Hungary initially focused on Lanz's acquaintances in the capital where he had established his priory of Marienkamp in 1921. The brothers of this chapter were mostly overseas. One Fra Bertram was a post-war emigrant to Argentina; a New Yorker identified as a German nobleman (K. v. L.) was known as Fra Chlodio, while the Austrian chemical engineer Albrecht von Gröling (b.1881), known as Fra Amalarich, worked in London, Texas, and California. He was the son of Albrecht Friedrich von Gröling (b.1851), a formerly prominent Viennese Pan-German associated with Georg von Schönerer before the war. Together with Fra Amalarich MONT and Fra Archibald MONT, Lanz published a cabbalistic study, while an active correspondence existed between him, his expatriate brothers, and brothers at the two other archpriories. This limited activity expanded after Lanz had purchased the ruined thirteenth-century church of Szent Balázs near the village of Szentantalfa on the northern shore of Lake Balaton on 6 January 1926 as a seat for the priory of Marienkamp. Local Hungarian friends Ladislaus and Wilhelm were appointed the priory's keepers and restoration began in the following April. A description of the church amid a riot of vernal blossom testifies to Lanz's sense of religious *renovatio* at their first visit:

Am 3. April 1926, fuhren Hon. Fra. Ladislaus, Fra. Wilhelm M.O.N.T. und Rev. Fra. Georg P.O.N.T. nach St. Blas . . . Ergreifend schöne Osterlandschaft: braunviolettes Waldgebirge, die weite smaragdgrüne Seefläche, ultramarinblaue, unendliche Ebenen, ganz unwirklich über dem See schwebend, blausilberner Himmel, aus weissen und zart rosafarbigen blühenden Mandel-, Kirschen- und Pfirsischbäumen dunkelgrauviolett aufsteigend das alte Gemäuer des Propstei- priorats.[55]

[On 3 April 1926 Hon. Fra. Ladislaus, Fra. Wilhelm MONT and Rev. Fra. Georg PONT travelled to Szent Balázs . . . The Easter landscape was breathtakingly beautiful. The brown-violet hues of the wooded hills, the expansive emerald green surface of Lake Balaton, countless ultramarine strata hanging magically above the water and the silvery blue sky. Among the white and pale pink blossom of the almond, cherry and peach trees stood the ancient grey-violet masonry of the priory.]

In due course Lanz established a dubious body of tradition to support his claim that the church had been a medieval Templar house. He was aided in this enterprise by the Hungarian scholar and royalist, B. Raynald, who joined the ONT.[56]

Here in Hungary, a country which had largely succeeded in restoring pre-war social and political conditions, Lanz saw a future for the ONT. Assisted by peasants and craftsmen from the nearby villages of Balatoncsicso and Szentjakabfa, Lanz restored the church for the purposes of divine office and summer residence by mid-1927. The accounts of his surviving Hungarian workers characterize the Marien-kamp-Szent Balázs priory as a utopian country commune consisting of Lanz, his noble Hungarian lady friend, her exotic cats, and foreign visitors. Lanz also maintained a lively dialogue with Hungarian royalists and Germanophiles like Tordai von Szügy and Paul Horn, a Member of Parliament at Budapest with astrological interests, so that rumours of German espionage at the colony circulated widely. Lanz himself cut an eccentric patrician figure in the neighbourhood. He conducted theological debates with the local Catholic priests and even encouraged the villagers to have their infants baptized at the priory.[57] The church was decorated in the liturgical manner of the ONT: gnostic murals of St Blasius, St George and the 'electrotheonic grail-dove' were complemented by the familiar blazonry on flag and door.[58] Two accounts of chapters survive from the summer of 1928. The first describes an ecstatic reunion of brothers and Prior after the late arrival of Master Ortwin and friends from Budapest, while the second records the investiture of Georg Hauerstein jun. and Friedrich Schwickert, the astrologer and one-time List Society member, as Presbyters. This particular celebration was distinguished by the transfiguration of the order-flag into a visual record of theozoological evolution.[59] Both the theme of the murals and the pietistic descriptions of the chapters evidence the sense of holy crusade amongst the brothers who gathered at this remote rural site. Their mission recalled the Christian bastion which Hungary once presented to invading Mongol hordes and Turks in medieval times. Lanz's modern racist ideology and his New Templars thus fell within an old established Magyar tradition of defence. Hungarian brothers later founded a tiny ONT presbytery below the Vaskapu hill at Pilisszentkereszt in northern Hungary in September 1937.[60]

The affairs of the ONT in Central Europe petered out following the establishment of authoritarian regimes and the outbreak of war. Lanz left Hungary for Switzerland in 1933 and began to issue a new series of his writings from Lucerne. Initially impressed by Hitler, he seems to have had less sympathy with the National Socialists once the Third Reich was established. In Germany his works were printed at Barth near the Darss peninsular and distributed from the nearby Hertesburg under Hauerstein's auspices until 1935. After this year a Vienna publisher was involved until late 1937, when no more of his writings appeared until after 1945 in Switzerland. Paul Horn remained responsible for the order in Hungary right through the war but the German and Austrian sections of the ONT were officially suspended in the early 1940s. The zenith of ONT activity occurred between 1925 and 1935. By the end of its career the ONT had colonized seven sites, of which no more than five were ever simultaneously active; the total roll of brothers received into the order probably never exceeded three hundred. The evolution of the order, both as a conception and an institution, reflects the growth of Lanz's own interests and cultural discoveries within the enduring paradigm of his racist prejudice and his attachment to monastic and chivalrous forms.

The significance of the ONT lies in what it expressed rather than in anything it achieved. It was a symptom of diffusely expressed feelings of discontent and the amalgam of its concerns, interests, and styles clearly touched subterranean anxiety in Austrian and German society. Its élitist and millenarian responses to this anxiety complemented a genocidal impulse. The ultimate aim of the ONT was world salvation through eugenic selection and the extermination of racial inferiors.

PART 3

Ariosophy in Germany

10

The Germanenorden

BECAUSE List preferred the role of mystagogue and master within a group of disciples,[1] the task of transmitting his ideas fell to his followers who joined racist organizations in Wilhelmian Germany. Such men included Colonel Karl August Hellwig, Georg Hauerstein sen., Bernhard Koerner, Philipp Stauff, and Eberhard von Brockhusen, who were all deeply imbued with List's ideas. They carried List's occult-nationalist ideas to historically significant right-wing organizations in the German Reich. Hellwig and Hauerstein were among the founders of the Reichshammerbund at Leipzig in May 1912, while Koerner, Stauff, and Brockhusen occupied key posts in the Germanenorden, its clandestine sister organization. The story of Ariosophy in Germany will finally introduce Rudolf von Sebottendorff, an admirer of both List and Lanz von Liebenfels, who established between 1917 and 1919 two racist sects at Munich whence the National Socialist German Workers' (Nazi) Party originated.

Both the Reichshammerbund and the Germanenorden were virulently anti-Semitic groups, the origins of which lie in the organizing ability of Theodor Fritsch, a major figure of pre-war German anti-Semitism, and in the politics of Germany between 1900 and 1914. Fritsch was born of Saxon peasant parents on 28 October 1852 at Wiesenau near Leipzig, where he trained as a milling engineer.[2] He soon developed those publishing and organizational skills which marked both his professional and political activities. From October 1880 he edited the *Kleine Mühlen-Journal* [*Small Mills Journal*], starting a second milling periodical in 1882 and seeking to organize the millers into a German Millers' League.

Fritsch was concerned that small tradesmen and craftsmen were threatened by the growth of larger firms, factories, and mass production. He sought to mitigate these threats through the new guild. His championship of small-business interests was complemented by anti-Semitic attitudes. Fritsch attributed the new economic order to the growing influence of Jewish business and finance in Germany. He had published in 1881 a collection of pan-German and anti-Semitic sayings as *Leuchtkugeln [Fire-Balls]*. In 1887 he wrote his *Antisemiten-Katechismus* and a long pamphlet series entitled *Brennende Fragen [Burning Questions]*. His first anti-Semitic organization was the *Leipziger Reformverein* (est. 1884), for which he issued a periodical, *Antisemitische Correspondenz*, from 1885. In June 1889 at Bochum, an anti-Semitic conference, attended by many representatives from France, Hungary, Germany and Austria, including Georg von Schönerer, led to the establishment of two German anti-Semitic parliamentary parties, the *Deutsch-Soziale Partei* under the leadership of Max Liebermann von Sonnenberg, and the *Antisemitische Volkspartei*, led by the peasant-rousing demagogue Otto Böckel.[3]

Fritsch did not offer himself as a candidate for these parties because he was convinced that anti-Semitism could not succeed as a political force in parliament. His conviction in the ineffectiveness of parliamentary anti-Semitism proved to be correct. When more than one party existed after the Bochum conference, their competition led to a reduction in the number of successful anti-Semitic candidates at the Reichstag elections. But coalitions led to other problems. After the two parties merged in 1894 as the *Deutsch-Soziale Reformpartei*, the desire for parliamentary co-operation and convergence caused such moderation in the manifesto as to lead to a marked reduction of emphasis on anti-Semitism in favour of an appeal to more conservative and middle-class economic interests. By 1903 the anti-Semites in parliament had been all but absorbed by the Conservative government and were increasingly dependent on agreements with such extra-parliamentary bodies as the Agrarian League and the German Nationalist Commercial Employees' Association. The *Deutsch-Soziale Reformpartei* secured only six seats in the elections of 1907 and a mere three in 1912.

Fritsch denounced the Jews as racial aliens. In his *Zur Bekämpfung zweitausendjähriger Irrthümer [Contesting the Falsehoods of Two Thousand Years]* (1886), he stressed 'Aryandom' and its relation to Germanic traditions within a pagan context. Fritsch wanted a reorganization of the intellectual, economic, social, and political life of the nation in which Jews had no place. This development in Fritsch's thought found its reflection in the publication of more 'scientific' studies of race towards the end of the 1890s. While Arthur de Gobineau (1816–82) had written a cameo of racial evolution and decline, concluding that the Aryans were destined to extinction beneath the ocean of black and yellow races, Vacher de Lapouge (1854–1936) and Houston Stewart Chamberlain (1855–1927) wrote under the influence of the new zoological and biological sciences and introduced the Jews as the race most detrimental to Aryan racial supremacy. Unlike Gobineau, with his reliance upon linguistics as the standard of racial distinction, these later racist writers were interested in skull measurements and other physical characteristics such as hair and eye colouring.

Fritsch wanted to establish a broad and powerful anti-Semitic movement outside parliament, where it would be most effective. In October 1901 he sent a circular to some three hundred individuals who had earlier been active party anti-Semites. The response was disappointing, but in January 1902 he founded the *Hammer*, initially a monthly, later a fortnightly periodical, which was to act as a crystallization point of the new movement. In 1905 the *Hammer* readers, then numbering more than three thousand persons, began organizing themselves into local *Hammer-Gemeinden* (Hammer-Groups). The members of these groups came largely from the declining *Jugendbundbewegung* (Youth League Movement) and the German Nationalist Commercial Employees' Association (DHV).[4] In 1908 these groups used the name *Deutsche Erneuerungs-Gemeinde* (German Renewal Groups): their membership was interested in anti-capitalist forms of land reform designed to invigorate the peasantry, the garden city movement, and *Lebensreform*.[5] This spontaneous local organization was actively encouraged by Fritsch. In 1904 his collaborator, Paul Förster, had published an appeal for a *völkisch* general staff to spearhead a nationalist-racist revival of Germany and so unite the many groups and leagues which sought to establish more German colonies overseas, to build a mightier navy to compete with England, and generally to enhance the international prestige of the German Reich under Hohenzollern rule, while 'cleansing' the nation of allegedly insidious social agents at home, principally identified as the Socialists, the Jews, and any other opponents of belligerent German imperialism.[6]

In March 1912 Fritsch recalled the weakness of the earlier anti-Semitic political parties and demanded a new anti-Semitic organization 'above the parties'.[7] The year 1912 was crucial for those individuals who were worried at the state of the nation. The second Moroccan crisis of July 1911, when the government sent a gunboat to Agadir to put pressure on the French to guarantee the German iron interests in West Morocco and to cede parts of the French Congo to Germany, had demonstrated that German colonialism was still hampered by the French and the British. This imperial disappointment was compounded by a domestic shock at the Reichstag elections of January 1912, when the Social Democratic Party won 110 seats, a large gain on its former 43 seats. The foremost losers of the elections were the Conservatives and anti-Semites, who retained only 68 of the 109 seats they had held in the parliament of 1907. These alarming events stirred Heinrich Class, the anti-Semitic chairman of the *Alldeutscher Verband* (Pan-German League) to publish a political manifesto, *Wenn ich der Kaiser wär!* [*If I were Kaiser!*] (1912), in which he appealed for a dictatorship and the suspension of parliament and denounced the Jews in a violent diatribe. Fritsch reviewed the book in the *Hammer* and recommended his readers to act immediately.[8] At a meeting at his Leipzig home on 24/25 May 1912 Fritsch and some twenty prominent Pan-Germans and anti-Semites formally founded two groups to indoctrinate German society.[9] Karl August Hellwig, a retired colonel living at Kassel and a List Society member since March 1908, headed the Reichshammerbund, a confederation of all existing Hammer groups; Hermann Pohl, a sealer of weights and measures at Magdeburg, became the chief officer of the Germanenorden, a secret twin organization.

The influence of List's ideas was evident in the first of these organizations. Hellwig had already drafted a constitution for the Reichshammerbund in February 1912. The executive body was formed by the *Bundeswart*, an office occupied by Hellwig, the *Ehrenbundeswart*, an honorary office held by Theodor Fritsch, and an *Armanen-Rat* of the twelve members. This latter appellation indicates Hellwig's Listian inspiration. Prospective members of the Reichshammerbund were obliged to guarantee their Aryan blood and that of their spouses, while leaflets formed the principal weapon in the struggle against the Jews. A set of guidelines followed in April 1912, which urged collaboration with Catholics and a broad spread of propaganda amongst workers, farmers, teachers, civil servants and officers of the armed forces, with particular efforts amongst the students at universities.[10] The correspondence of Julius Rüttinger, head of the Reichshammerbund branch in Nuremberg, reflects the slow progress of the organization and a persistent trend towards internal disputes and petty concerns. At the end of 1912, the Nuremberg group reported a total membership of twenty-three persons, of which only ten attended meetings on average, and a balance of 5.58 marks from a total annual income of 94.64 marks.[11] By June 1913 only nineteen branches of the Reichshammerbund existed throughout Germany, of which the liveliest appears to have been in Hamburg. Despite thousands of leaflets and determined canvassing, the league could claim no more than a few hundred members.

The history of the Germanenorden is both more complex and involved with List's ideas. The notion of an anti-Semitic group organized like a secret quasi-masonic lodge appears to have arisen amongst *völkisch* activists around 1910. Some anti-Semites were convinced that the powerful influence of Jews in German public life could be understood only as the result of a widespread Jewish secret conspiracy; it was supposed that such a conspiracy could best be combatted by a similar anti-Semitic organization.[12] In spring 1910 Philipp Stauff, a prominent *völkisch* journalist, mentioned in his correspondence the idea of an anti-Semitic lodge with the names of members kept secret to prevent enemy penetration.[13] The following year Johannes Hering, who belonged to the local Hammer group in Munich as well as the *Alldeutscher Verband*, and who was friendly with both List and Lanz von Liebenfels wrote to Stauff about Freemasonry. Hering stated that he had been a Freemason since 1894, but that this 'ancient Germanic institution' had been polluted by Jewish and parvenu ideas: he concluded that a revived Aryan lodge would be a boon to anti-Semites.[14]

In late 1911 Hermann Pohl sent a circular on this subject to some fifty potential anti-Semitic collaborators. Pohl stated that the Hammer group in Magdeburg had already formed a lodge upon appropriate racial principles with a ritual based on Germanic pagan tradition. He enthused about the use of lodge ceremony for anti-Semitic organizations: the solemnity, the mysterious effects, and the hierarchical discipline produced a unanimity that was rare among small *völkisch* groups. Pohl urged his correspondents to join his movement and form lodges of their own, adding that this project had the full support of Theodor Fritsch.[15] The origins of this Magdeburg lodge are documented in an inaccurate polemic against Pohl in late 1918. According to this source the Hammer group was established in Magdeburg in autumn 1910, and a certain Heinnatz wished to found an inner core of members in the form of a lodge. The membership consulted Fritsch, who replied that this idea had already been mooted by other Hammer groups. The Wotan lodge was accordingly instituted on 5 April 1911, with Hermann Pohl elected Master. On 15 April a Grand Lodge was founded with Theodor Fritsch as Grand Master, but the work of formulating rules and rituals was undertaken by the Wotan lodge. On 12 March 1912 the organization adopted the name

Germanenorden upon the suggestion of Fritsch.[16]

The year 1912 witnessed the rapid establishment of Germanenorden lodges throughout Northern and Eastern Germany. In January Pohl wrote a manifesto for the 'loyal lodges', which indicated his desire for a fervent rather than numerous following, which would usher in an 'Aryan-Germanic religious revival' stressing obedience and devotion to the cause of a pan-German 'Armanist Empire' (*Armanenreich*). He called for the rebirth of a racially pure German nation in which the 'parasitic and revolutionary mob-races (Jews, anarchist cross-breeds and gipsies)' would be deported.[17] Pohl issued the first Germanenorden newsletter that July in which he recorded that lodges had been ceremonially founded at Breslau, Dresden, and Königsberg in the spring, while lodges at Berlin and Hamburg had been already working prior to this time. Brothers in Bromberg, Nuremberg, Thuringia, and Düsseldorf were recruiting with a view to constituting themselves as lodges in the near future. The total roll of brothers at this time numbered 140 and by December 1912 the Germanenorden numbered 316 brothers distributed as follows: Breslau 99, Dresden 100, Königsberg 42, Hamburg 27, Berlin 30 and Hanover 18.[18] In the following January a lodge was established at Duisburg with 30 brothers. Pohl now dropped the title 'Secretary' and styled himself 'Chancellor' of the Order.[19] Lodges were established in Nuremberg and Munich in the course of 1913 but the success of these southern provinces of the Order was limited in comparison with those in Northern and Eastern Germany.[20] A Reichshammerbund group was founded at Munich in spring 1914 by Wilhelm Rohmeder, chairman of the *Deutscher Schulverein* and a member of the List Society since 1908. There was much duplication of membership between the two organizations.[21]

This history of the early Germanenorden must be supplemented by an account of its aims, rules, and rituals. According to a circular of the Franconian province, the principal aim of the Germanenorden was the monitoring of the Jews and their activities by the creation of a centre to which all anti-Semitic material would flow for distribution. Subsidiary aims included the mutual aid of brothers in respect of business introductions, contracts, and finance. Lastly, all brothers were committed to the circulation of *völkisch* journals, especially the *Hammer*, their 'sharpest weapon against Jewry and other enemies of the people'.[22] The articles of the Germanenorden betray an overt ariosophical influence. All nationals, male or female, of flawless Germanic descent were eligible for admission to the Order. Application forms requested details about the colour of the applicant's hair, eyes, and skin.[23] The ideal coloration was blond to dark blond hair, blue to light brown eyes, and pale skin. Further details regarding the personal particulars of the applicant's parents and grandparents, and in the case of married applicants, those of the spouse were also required.[24]

A guide to recruitment ruled that physically handicapped and 'unpleasant looking' persons were barred from admission and referred the prospective candidate to those *Ostara* numbers devoted to racial somatology published between 1908 and 1913.[25] A Germanenorden newsletter related that the articles of the Order had been formulated after discussions with Karl August Hellwig of the *Armanenschaft*. The ritual was also ascribed to *Armanenschaft* ceremony, but the suggestion that brothers of the higher grades in the Germanenorden be called *Armanen* was vetoed by the *Armanenschaft*. These statements imply that Hellwig was in touch with a contemporary body called the *Armanenschaft*, which can be identified either as the *Armanen-Rat* of the Reichshammerbund or the HAO, the chief German representative of which was Philipp Stauff at Berlin.[26]

The emblems of the Germanenorden indicate a further source of ariosophical inspiration. From the middle of 1916 the official Order newsletter, the *Allgemeine Ordens-Nachrichten*, began to display on its front cover a curved-armed swastika superimposed upon a cross ⋇ .[27] In due course advertisements for *völkisch* jewellery, rings, pendants and tie-pins, incorporating various runes and the swastika, appeared in this publication. The supplying firm, Haus Ecklöh of Lüdenscheid in Westphalia, worked from designs submitted by members of the List Society during the war.[28] Although the swastika was current among several contemporary *völkisch* associations in Germany, it was through the Germanenorden and the Thule Society, its successor organization in post-war Munich, that this device came to be adopted by the National Socialists.[29]

The ceremony and ritual of the Germanenorden demonstrate its strange synthesis of racist, masonic, and Wagnerian inspiration. A summons to an initiation ceremony of the Berlin province on 11 January 1914 informed brothers that this was a frock-coat and white-tie affair and that any new candidates would have to submit to racial tests by the Berlin phrenologist, Robert Burger-Villingen, who had devised the 'plastometer', his own instrument for determining the relative Aryan purity of a subject by means of cranial measurements.[30] A surviving ritual document of *c.*1912 describes the initiation of novices into the lowest grade of the Order. While the novices waited in an adjoining room, the brothers assembled in the ceremonial room of the lodge. The Master took his place at the front of the room beneath the baldachin flanked on either side by two Knights wearing white robes and helmets adorned with horns and leaning on their swords. In front of these sat the Treasurer and Secretary wearing white masonic sashes, while the Herald took up his position in the centre of the room. At the back of the room in the grove of the Grail stood the Bard in a white gown, before him the Master of Ceremonies in a blue gown, while the other lodge brothers stood in a semicircle around him as far as the tables of the Treasurer and Secretary. Behind the grove of the Grail was a music room where a harmonium and piano were accompanied by a small choir of 'forest elves'.

The ceremony began with soft harmonium music, while the brothers sang the Pilgrims' Chorus from Wagner's *Tannhäuser*. The ritual commenced in candlelight with brothers making the sign of the swastika ⊓ and the Master reciprocating. Then the blindfolded novices, clad in pilgrimage mantles, were ushered by the Master of Ceremonies into the room. Here the Master told them of the Order's Ario-Germanic and aristocratic *Weltanschauung*, before the Bard lit the sacred flame in the grove and the novices were divested of their mantles and blindfolds. At this point the Master seized Wotan's spear and held it before him, while the two Knights crossed their swords upon it. A series of calls and responses, accompanied by music from *Lohengrin*, completed the oath of the novices. Their consecration followed with cries from the 'forest elves' as the new brothers were led into the grove of the Grail around the Bard's sacred flame.[31] With the ritual personifying lodge officers as archetypal figures in Germanic mythology, this ceremonial must have exercised a potent influence on the candidates.

The war threw the Germanenorden into confusion when many brothers joined up. Julius Rüttinger, the Master of the Franconian province, went early to the front. Hermann Pohl wrote to him in November 1914 that finance had become a serious problem with nearly half the brethren of the nation serving in the armed forces: 'the war came upon us too soon, the Germanenorden was not yet properly organized and crystallized, and if the war lasts much longer, the Order will go to pieces. A great number of brothers have already been killed in action.'[32] Despite Pohl's concern for the survival of the Order, several prominent brothers were unimpressed by his leadership. In July 1914 the Master of the Leipzig lodge had politely proposed that Pohl retire, while in 1915 members of the Berlin lodge attempted a separatist schism.[33] In late 1915 Töpfer, Rüttinger's successor at Nuremberg, wrote that brothers were now weary of the ritual, ceremony and banquets, which Pohl regarded as the main purpose of the Order.[34]

Matters came to a head at a Thuringian province meeting held at Gotha on 8 October 1916, attended both by Thuringian brethren and those of neighbouring provinces.[35] The Berlin brothers urged the Gotha assembly to relieve Pohl of his office as Chancellor. Incensed by this thankless response to his unstinting efforts on behalf of the Order since 1911, Pohl immediately declared himself Chancellor of a schismatic Germanenorden Walvater of the Holy Grail, which succeeded in carrying with it the already established lodges in the provinces of Silesia (Breslau), Hamburg, Berlin, and the Osterland (Gera). Pohl's supporters at Berlin were G. W. Freese and Bräunlich, who founded new Berlin lodges in the city and at Gross-Lichterfelde.[36] The original Order was subsequently headed by Generalmajor Erwin von Heimerdinger (b.1856) as Chancellor, Dr Gensch as Treasurer, and Bernhard Koerner as Grand Keeper of Pedigrees (*Grosssippenwahrer*), an office in line with his genealogical and heraldic interests. Strict secrecy was still demanded in all Order correspondence and these officers at Berlin stated that they would henceforth be known only anonymously by the runes ᛡ, ᚦ and ᚷ. Philipp Stauff and Eberhard von Brockhusen were also mentioned as principal officers in the loyalist Berlin province.[37]

This new focus of loyalist Order activities in Berlin may have been due to the efforts of Philipp Stauff. Born on 26 March 1876 at Moosbach, Stauff had gained experience as a journalist before publishing his own nationalist newspaper *Wegweiser und Wegwarte* at Enzisweiler on Lake Constance from 1907. By 1910 he had moved to Kulmbach in Franconia, where he assumed the editorship of another newspaper in the same vein. Stauff was intent on founding an association of *völkisch* authors, an ambition realized in late 1910 after he had canvassed some hundred prominent nationalist, racist and anti-Semitic writers, including Adolf Bartels, Ludwig Wilser, Johannes Hering and Lanz von Liebenfels. In early 1912 Stauff moved to Berlin where he continued his *völkisch* publishing. He published a directory of contemporary pan-German and anti-Semitic groups as *Das deutsche Wehrbuch* [*The German Defence Book*] (1912) and, on behalf of Heinrich Kraeger, who with Alfred Brunner founded the *Deutsch-Sozialistische Partei* in 1918, he issued the *Semi-Gotha* and *Semi-Alliancen*, genealogical handbooks which purported to identify Jews amongst the German aristocracy. This project was not intended to discredit the nobility but to assist the 'cleansing' process inherent in so much anti-Semitic psychology. These handbooks appeared in serial form between 1912 and 1914 and involved Stauff in a legal suit.[38] A similar handbook, the *Semi-Kürschner*, modelled on Kürschner's German Literary Calendar, listed Jews active in public life as authors, actors, bankers, officers, doctors and lawyers, and involved Stauff in a stormy correspondence of denials and protests throughout 1914.[39]

Stauff had become a List Society member at Kulmbach in 1910, swiftly graduating to the intimate circle around the Master. He was among the pilgrims who travelled to Vienna in June 1911 to participate in the HAO celebrations and rambles to sites of Armanist association. In 1912 Stauff became a committee member of the Society and a generous patron. His esoteric treatise *Runenhäuser [Rune Houses]* (1912) extended the Listian thesis of 'armanist' relics with the claim that the ancient runic wisdom had been enshrined in the geometric configuration of beams in half-timbered houses throughout Germany. In early 1913 Stauff was involved in a series of spiritualist seances which claimed to have communicated with long dead priest-kings of the old religion.[40] Documentary evidence exists to suggest that Stauff was also close to the Ordo Novi Templi before the war.[41]

Confusion reigned in Order affairs after the schism of 1916. Pohl had retained the stamps and stationery of the old Order so that he could issue circulars and newsletters in the name of the loyalist Order, a practice that led many aspirant candidates of the loyalist lodges to his group. Members of the two Orders became convinced that the Order had been dissolved, so great was the confusion. Bernhard Koerner, who had been serving as a cavalry captain in France since 1915, wrote to List in January 1917 that the Germanenorden had now become extinct. Despite the dispatch of authoritative circulars, the lodge officers were quite out of touch with Order affairs by this stage.[42]

After the armistice in November 1918 former brothers of the loyalist Germanenorden set about its revival. The Grand Master, Eberhard von Brockhusen (1869–1939), was a Brandenburg landowner and a generous List Society patron. He was rather preoccupied with the revolt of Polish labourers on his estates, and complained that Order administration was chaotic owing to the lack of a constitution; in early 1919 he asked Erwin von Heimerdinger to relieve him of his office.[43] Although Stauff informed Brockhusen that his resignation had been accepted at the beginning of March, the affair seemed to drag on as Brockhusen was still pleading for a constitutional reform in

the summer, and accusing Stauff of slander. Brockhusen's correspondence reveals a deep dismay at post-war conditions and a hatred
of the Poles.[44] In the late summer Heimerdinger abdicated the
Chancellorship in favour of the Grand Duke Johann Albrecht of
Mecklenburg, who was very enthusiastic about the Order and the
Free Corps expedition to the Baltic countries in 1919. The Order soon
lost this prominent patron when he died of a heart attack on 6
February 1920.[45] Brockhusen remained in office and finally got his
constitution accepted in 1921, which provided for an extraordinarily
complex organization of grades, rings, and provincial 'citadels'
(*Burgen*) supposed to generate secrecy for a nationwide system of local
groups having many links with militant *völkisch* associations, including
the *Deutschvölkischer Schutz- und Trutzbund*.[46]

Despite the petty and futile debates of its senior officers in Berlin,
the Germanenorden provinces initiated clandestine activities involving
the assassination of public figures associated with the new German
Republic, the loathsome symbol of defeat and disgrace to radical
nationalists. The Germanenorden was used as a cover-organization
for the recruitment of political assassins in 1921. The murderers of
Matthias Erzberger, the former Reich Finance Minister and the hated
signatory of the armistice, were Heinrich Schulz and Heinrich
Tillessen, who had been strongly influenced by *völkisch* propaganda
after demobilization at the end of the war. They had settled in June
1920 in Regensburg, where they met Lorenz Mesch, the local leader of
the Germanenorden. In May 1921 Schulz and Tillessen went to
Munich where they received their orders to kill Erzberger from a
person who claimed to have the authority of the Germanenorden. The
attempted assassination of Maximilian Harden, the republican author,
was also traced to the Order. The impressive secrecy and ideology of
the Order thus inspired *völkisch* fanatics to murder the Jewish and
republican enemies of the German nation in a modern 'Vehm'.[47]

After 1921 the loyalist Germanenorden became a single group
among the numerous right-wing and anti-Semitic organizations
claiming the support of disgruntled and revanchist Germans in the
Weimar Republic. For the story of Germanenorden influence on
Nazism one must return to Hermann Pohl and his Germanenorden
Walvater, which first attracted the interest of Rudolf von Sebottendorff
in late 1916. Sebottendorff joined the schismatic order and revived its
Bavarian province in Munich at Christmas 1917, thus laying the basis
of an important *völkisch* organization which witnessed the birth of the
National Socialist Party. Without this man it is likely that both the

Germanenorden and Ariosophy would have been condemned to oblivion.

11

Rudolf von Sebottendorff
and the Thule Society

SEBOTTENDORFF first became involved in German *völkisch* activities at a late stage of the war, but his early life is still important. Compared to most *völkisch* agitators in imperial Germany, Sebottendorff seems a cosmopolitan adventurer. His penchant for shady deals and espionage led him into subterfuges which also earned him the reputation of a trickster. The son of a working-class Prussian family, Sebottendorff made an early break with his background by going to sea and working in the Middle East. A study of his early movements enables one to understand better those experiences which fashioned his attitudes and otherwise equipped him to play his not insignificant part in the counter-revolutionary operations at Munich in 1918 and 1919.*

The man who called himself Baron Rudolf von Sebottendorff was, in common with the Ariosophists he admired, no more than a self-styled aristocrat. He was born on 9 November 1875 at Hoyerswerda, a Saxon market town lying on the Lausitz Heath north-east of Dresden, the son of Ernst Rudolf Glauer, a locomotive driver, and his wife Christiane Henriette, *née* Müller. He was christened Adam Alfred Rudolf Glauer.[1] According to his semi-fictional autobiography, the Glauer family was descended on the male side from a French soldier,

---

*Before examining his life before this period, a note on sources is in order. Besides official documents relating to birth, marriage and residence, all accounts of his life date from 1918 onwards. In addition to a brief biographical sketch in Ernst Tiede's *Astrologisches Lexikon* (1922), there exist two semi-autobiographical novels, *Erwin Haller* (1918-1919) and *Der Talisman des Rosenkreuzers* [*The Rosicrucian's Talisman*] (1925). Although these works contain much imaginary material, their mention of specific dates and events, certain of which are both very local and confirmed by independent sources, justifies their treatment with caution as historical aids. For this documentation of Sebottendorff's early life I am indebted to Ellic Howe's unpublished typescript 'Rudolph Freiherr von Sebottendorff' (1968), a copy of which is deposited in the Institut für Zeitgeschichte, Munich.

Lieutenant Torre (1789–1821), who had been stranded after the Battle of Katzbach (1813) at the village of Alzenau (Olszanica), about 18 kilometres north-east of Löwenberg (Lwówek Slaski) in Prussian Silesia. This Frenchman was the alleged great-grandfather of Rudolf Glauer. Torre married a local farmer's daughter who gave birth to a son in 1818, who himself married in 1845 and was killed in the street fighting at Berlin during the 1848 revolution. As natives of Silesia the family were strongly pro-Prussian in their political affiliations: the name Torre was probably changed to Glauer for this reason. Ernst Rudolf Glauer was born about 1846 and served in both the Austro-Prussian campaign of 1866 and the Franco-Prussian War. Following his discharge from the army in 1871 he took up his appointment as a railwayman at Hoyerswerda. He died in June 1893, leaving his orphaned son sufficient funds to complete his secondary schooling and commence study in engineering.[2]

While the biographical details in Tiede state that young Glauer attended the Ilmenau Technical School, the autobiography indicates an earlier period of practical training with the engineering firm of J. E. Christoph at Niesky.[3] We next encounter Glauer staying with old friends at the inn in Koblenz near Hoyerswerda over the Christmas break of his second semester at the Berlin-Charlottenburg Polytechnic. He mentioned that he had not seen these friends for two years. If one takes 1893 (the year of his father's death) as an initial date in the account, this brings one to Christmas 1896, a few weeks after his twenty-first birthday. There is also a reference to the necessity of a visit to Hoyerswerda in connection with his recent coming of age.[4] Glauer remained in Berlin until the end of the summer semester, reporting then for his year's military service in the navy on 1 October 1897. Rejected on grounds of a tendency to hernia, Glauer tutored privately in Hanover until March 1898. However, he had to abandon his post after accompanying his pupils' mother on an illicit journey which took them to Nice, Monte Carlo, Genoa, and Lucerne.[5]

Having failed to complete his studies, Glauer could not hope to secure a qualified post in Germany. Like many young contemporaries, Glauer felt confined in his homeland and decided to go to sea. After signing on as a stoker for six months, Glauer sailed in the H.H. Meier (5140 tons) on 2 April 1898 from Bremerhaven to New York, returning to Bremerhaven on 3 May.[6] He subsequently found work on the S.S. Ems (4912 tons) in September 1899. While this steamer was docked in Naples on its way to New York, Glauer was informed of a vacancy for an electrician on board the S.S. Prinz Regent Luitpold (6288 tons).

Since this vessel was on its maiden voyage to Sydney, Glauer decided to seize this chance to visit Australia. He was taken off the Ems and, after a few days' waiting, sailed from Naples in the Prinz Regent Luitpold on 15 February 1900.[7] During the voyage Glauer was persuaded by another seaman to desert ship and try their luck prospecting for gold in Western Australia. After docking at Freemantle on 13 March, Glauer and his friend travelled via Southern Cross and Coolgardie to their concession in the North Coolgardie Goldfield on the eastern edge of the Great Victoria Desert. The venture was doomed by the death of the friend in June. Glauer returned to Freemantle to embark for Egypt, where he had an introduction given him by a Parsee at Coolgardie.[8] Thus ended Glauer's time at sea, a period marked by foreign adventure, youthful ambition, and technical experience in large modern steamships.

Arriving at Alexandria in July 1900, Glauer travelled directly to Cairo to meet Hussein Pasha, an influential Turkish landowner who was in the service of the Khedive Abbas Hilmi. According to Tiede, Glauer worked in the service of the Khedive as a technician from 1897 to 1900; according to *Der Talisman des Rosenkreuzers*, Glauer spent less than a month in Cairo before travelling on to Constantinople, as Hussein Pasha spent the summers in Turkey at his house on the Asian shore of the Bosporus.[9] In the absence of further evidence, it seems likely that Glauer spent sufficient time in Egypt to gain some impression of its people and culture. Although still paying substantial tribute to the Ottoman Sultan, Egypt had become a prosperous country by the late 1890s under the successful Anglo-Egyptian condominium, established in 1882 to safeguard the stability of the country and the power of the Khedive against the revolts of factions which had earlier misgoverned the economy for their own benefit. Sir Evelyn Baring, who served as British consul-general, wrote in 1901 that 'the foundations on which the well-being and material prosperity of a civilized community should rest have been laid . . . the institution of slavery is virtually defunct. The corvée (labour done in lieu of taxes by vassals) has been practically abolished.' But this progress had not been without cost. Here Glauer gained his first impressions of a developing country and saw the problems arising from westernization and religious or nationalist reaction.

At the end of July 1900 Glauer sailed the thousand mile voyage from Alexandria to Constantinople via Piraeus and Izmir. On his arrival at the Golden Horn he was taken by caïque up the Bosporus to the country home of Hussein Pasha at Çubuklu near Beykoz.

Although still intending to return home to resume his studies, Glauer was so enchanted by the country, its customs, and his gracious host that he decided to stay on. After learning Turkish from the imam of the Beykoz mosque, and familiarizing himself with the manners of the people through frequent visits to Stamboul, Glauer agreed to work from October 1900 for a year as surveyor on the Anatolian estates of Hussein near Bandirma and at Yenikiöy near Bursa. Here there was a large area on the slopes of Mount Olympus, which Hussein was settling with Turkish returnees from the former Ottoman provinces of Bulgaria. Glauer made plans to build modest houses to replace the primitive huts already there. A small brick-making plant and a saw-mill were organized. There were also plans to plant mulberry trees for silkworm breeding and hazel trees for the European chocolate industry. A contract with the firm of Nestlé was struck and a road was laid from the village to Bursa.[10]

Besides gaining further technical and managerial experience in Turkey, Glauer began a serious study of occultism. An interest in exotic religion had already been kindled when he saw the Mevlevi sect of whirling dervishes and visited the Cheops Pyramid at El-Gîza in July 1900. His companion Ibrahim had told him of the cosmological and numerological significance of the pyramids and aroused Glauer's curiosity about the occult gnosis of ancient theocracies.[11] Hussein Pasha, his wealthy and learned host, practised a form of Sufism and discussed these matters with Glauer. At Bursa he made the acquaintance of the Termudi family, who were Greek Jews from Salonica. Old Termudi had retired from business to devote himself to a study of the Cabbala and collecting alchemical and Rosicrucian texts, while his eldest son Abraham managed their bank at Bursa and a younger brother ran a branch establishment at Salonica. Apart from the banking business the Termudi family also traded in silkworm cocoons and raw silk. The Termudis were Freemasons in a lodge that may have been affiliated to the French Rite of Memphis, which had spread in the Levant and the Middle East. Glauer was initiated into the lodge by old Termudi and subsequently inherited his occult library.[12] In one of these books Glauer discovered a note from Hussein Pasha, describing the secret mystical exercises of traditional Islamic alchemists, still practised by the Baktâshî sect of dervishes.[13] When Glauer returned to Turkey in 1908, he continued to study Islamic mysticism, which in his opinion shared a common Aryan source with the Germanic runes.

The account in *Der Talisman des Rosenkreuzers* implies that Glauer remained at the Yenikiöy estate until 1908, moving then to Constantinople, but official documents suggest otherwise. He is recorded as resident in Munich from September 1902 until April 1903, when he left for Probstzella, a small village in Thuringia. He stated that he was a fitter by trade.[14] A further record also places him in Germany after 1901. At Dresden on 25 March 1905 Glauer married Klara Voss, a Saxon farmer's daughter from Bischofswerda. But the marriage broke down and the couple obtained a divorce in Berlin on 5 May 1907.[15] Years later a newspaper reported that Glauer had appeared in court at Berlin, charged with forgery and other deceptions.[16] Glauer may have been obliquely referring to this incident, when he described how he had pondered upon a dilemma in the Freiburg minster during 1908— perhaps this clash with the authorities and the decision to leave Germany.[17]

By the end of 1908 Glauer was in Constantinople. The story of *Erwin Haller* (1918–19) describes a train journey in September from Breslau to Constanta, whence he sailed by Romanian vessel to the capital. This account implies that Haller/Glauer had been attracted by the economic prospects arising from the Young Turk revolution of July 1908, which had established a constitutional monarchy and the rule of parliament. At Constantinople he made several Swiss and German contacts involved in the import trade and German-financed projects including the Baghdad railway, but he could not find employment himself. He finally chanced upon a temporary teaching job at a colony of Kievan Jews on the slopes of the Alem Dağ, about 30 kilometres from Scutari (Üsküdar). He returned to Constantinople at Easter 1909 and witnessed the reactionary counter-revolution of Sultan Abdul-Hamid II, who had been deposed the preceding summer. After several days of bloody fighting the Young Turks re-established their authority and exiled the Sultan. Here it is worth mentioning that the masonic lodge, which Glauer had joined at Bursa in 1901, may have been a local cadre of the pre-revolutionary Secret Society of Union and Progress, founded on the model of Freemasonry by Salonican Turks to generate liberal consciousness during the repressive reign of the Sultan.[18]

Given Glauer's alleged interest in the westernization of Turkey, it is hard to account for his obscurantist and reactionary political attitudes during the collapse of the old order and the revolution in Germany. Glauer is supposed to have given lectures on esoteric subjects at his apartment in the Pera (Beyoğlu) district of Constantinople, subsequently founding a mystical lodge in December 1910. At this time he was writing a study of the Baktāshī dervishes, an antinomian mystical order widely spread and influential in Turkey and connected by legend with the origin of the Janissaries, the medieval instrument of pan-Ottoman dominion in the Balkans. A link between the Baktāshī order and European Freemasonry has also been alleged.[19] Glauer's political views were primarily inspired by a religious orientation: the anti-materialism of pan-Ottoman mysticism, alchemy, and Rosicrucianism, combined with a post-war hatred of Bolshevism, which he identified as the acme of materialism, led him to embrace anti-democratic ideas. His politics find an historical parallel in the support of King Frederick William II for the *Gold- und Rosenkreuzer Orden*, which opposed the rational and modernizing forces of the Enlightenment with its mystical irrationalism in Prussia during the 1780s.[20]

This complex of politico-religious attitudes may also account for Glauer's fantasy of aristocratic origins. His adoption of the name and title 'von Sebottendorff von der Rose' deserves detailed examination, as does the genealogy of the family, for any light it can throw on the cloudy issue. According to one explanation, Glauer claimed that he was naturalized as a Turkish citizen in 1911 and subsequently adopted by an expatriate Baron Heinrich von Sebottendorff under Turkish law. Since this act was not recognized in Germany, the new Rudolf von Sebottendorff had the adoption repeated by Siegmund von Sebottendorff von der Rose (1843–1915) at Wiesbaden in 1914 and later for good measure by his widow Maria at Baden-Baden.[21] In another declaration, Glauer claimed that he had been naturalized and adopted by an American of this name at Constantinople in 1908.[22] Although the adoption would have been valid only with the express permission of the Kaiser, Glauer's claimed relationship with the Sebottendorffs was endorsed by the family. Rudolf Freiherr von Sebottendorff and his second wife, Freifrau Anna, were described as mourning cousins in the funerary notice of Siegmund.[23]

The Sebottendorff family were originally lords of several villages on the Baltic coast during the early Middle Ages. An ancestor served as a diplomat to Emperor Otto II (d. 983), from whom he received the dignity of imperial knight and a coat-of-arms showing a root of cinnamon. By the end of the twelfth century the Balt family had migrated south to Silesia, an area of predominant Slav settlement then being colonized by German knights and peasants. From the thirteenth to the sixteenth century the family flourished in at least four lines and achieved eminent office in the service of the Empire. By the eighteenth century two lines were still extant. Carl Moritz von Sebottendorff

(1698–1760), the head of the von der Rose line, moved south to Austria. Almost all his male descendants served in the Habsburg army, residing variously in Vienna, Linz, and Brno; the remaining Lortzendorff line occupied posts in the Prussian army, since Silesia had passed from Austrian to Prussian administration under Frederick the Great in 1742.[24]

Glauer appears to have based his claim of adoption on both lines of the family. The only members of the family bearing the name Heinrich or living in America at the appropriate time came from the Prussian line. A certain Heinrich von Sebottendorff (b. 1825) was living in 1887 at Görlitz, a town not far from Hoyerswerda. A common Silesian background might account for a relative of this Heinrich befriending Glauer in Constantinople. But when this adoption was reckoned invalid, Glauer approached the aged Austrian representative of the family, Siegmund von Sebottendorff von der Rose. Both lines sported the cinnamon blazon, which Glauer subsequently bore as his own. Besides the family's Silesian association and the Austrian line's involvement with Freemasonry during the late eighteenth century, it is difficult to know why Glauer should have latched on to this name, if the connection was entirely imaginary. In due course hostile rumours surrounded the issue with further confusion: one may only be certain that Glauer wished to use the name and pose as a baron. Since he came to be known by this name, this account will henceforth refer to him as Rudolf von Sebottendorff.

Sebottendorff's second period in Turkey lasted four years. After fighting and receiving wounds in the Turkish forces during the Second Balkan War (October–December 1912), he returned to Germany, establishing himself at Berlin in early 1913.[25] His activities and movements during the first half of the Great War are rather obscure. He claimed that he was at Breslau in 1913, where he financed the Göbel tank. Since this machine was a failure, his enterprise cannot have been rewarded.[26] Besides frequent visits to Siegmund von Sebottendorff at Wiesbaden, several accounts link him with Dresden at this time. When Siegmund died in October 1915 Sebottendorff was living at Kleinzschachwitz, a fashionable suburb lying on the banks of the River Elbe. Here he built a large villa in spacious grounds (now Meusslitzer Strasse 41) for 50,000 gold marks. Sebottendorff then became the subject of unfavourable rumours and he suddenly left.[27] He later claimed that he had been the victim of a slanderous campaign concerning the fortune of his second wife. On 15 July 1915 at Vienna, Sebottendorff had married a divorcee, Berta Anna Iffland. As the daughter of the late Friedrich Wilhelm Müller, a wealthy Berlin merchant, she possessed significant funds in trust. Sebottendorff stated that Max Alsberg, the Berlin lawyer responsible for her estate, became hostile when relieved of his lucrative appointment following the marriage. Alsberg allegedly incited Heindl, a senior Dresden police officer, to defame Sebottendorff as a fortune-hunter.[28] Sebottendorff also had trouble with the Berlin authorities on account of his Turkish nationality, which prevented his conscription into the German army.[29]

After a succession of moves to Frankfurt and Berlin, Sebottendorff and his wife settled in 1916 at Bad Aibling, an elegant Bavarian spa. From here Sebottendorff consulted Georg Gaubatz, his Munich lawyer, in order to secure the police files relating to his contested Turkish nationality. Gaubatz happened to show him a newspaper advertisement for the Germanenorden which summoned fair-haired and blue-eyed German men and women of pure Aryan descent to join the Order. Three cryptic runes stood beneath this message. Sebottendorff was intrigued and acquired membership. In September 1916 Sebottendorff decided to visit a chief of the mysterious Germanenorden at Berlin.[30] This individual turned out to be Hermann Pohl. Pohl and Sebottendorff talked about the runes, the esoteric meaning of which seems to have interested the latter in the Order. Pohl explained that he had come to a study of the runes through Guido von List, and that he was convinced that racial miscegenation, especially with Jews, was responsible for obscuring the Aryans' knowledge of the magical powers of the runes. He believed that this gnosis could be revived once the race had been purified of foreign contamination.

When Sebottendorff enquired about the future of the Order, the other man said this would be clear once a meeting could be held to settle the confusion in Order affairs. Shortly before Christmas Sebottendorff received news that the Order had been reconstituted with Pohl as Chancellor. This information confirms that Sebottendorff had made contact with Pohl just before the schism.[31] At his meeting with Pohl, Sebottendorff had asked for a list of possible Order candidates in Bavaria. Upon his return to Bad Aibling he received about a hundred addresses and was entrusted with the task of working up the moribund Bavarian province of the Order. Throughout 1917 Sebottendorff was very active on Pohl's behalf. His correspondence with the people whose addresses he had received grew in volume. He began to visit them, and these visits led to regular group meetings and lectures. There was also a lively correspondence with Pohl, who had meanwhile rented a floor for a lodge in a house near the Potsdamer Bahnhof of Berlin. A dedication ceremony, to which Sebottendorff was invited, was held on 21 December 1917. Sebottendorff's offer to publish a monthly Order periodical was warmly received by the brothers: the first number of *Runen* appeared in January 1918. He also agreed to assume the financial burden of the *Allgemeine Ordens-Nachrichten* newsletter, which was for members only. At this meeting Sebottendorff was formally elected Master of the Bavarian province.[32]

During 1918 Sebottendorff met an art student, the wounded veteran Walter Nauhaus, who became his right-hand man in the recruitment campaign. Nauhaus was a kindred spirit in two important respects: he shared an expatriate background and an interest in the occult. The son of a German missionary, he was born on 29 September 1892 at Botsabelo in Transvaal.[33] During the Boer War the English garrisoned nearby Middelburg, where the family lived from July 1901 to June 1902. Following the death of his father the family returned to Germany in late 1906. The family settled in Berlin, where Nauhaus began to study wood-carving in 1908. His leisure time was spent visiting relatives in Pomerania and Silesia, or rambling through the Prussian and Thuringian countryside with a *völkisch* youth group, an indication of his romantic attachment to the new fatherland. At the outbreak of war he joined a Pomeranian regiment, which saw early action on the Western Front, and Nauhaus was badly wounded near Chalons on 10 November 1914. He was not discharged from hospital until autumn 1915. Unfit for further military service, he devoted himself at Berlin to *völkisch* studies and joined the Germanen-orden in 1916, becoming a keeper of pedigrees. His reading ranged from Guido von List's 'researches' to astrology, chiromancy, and the writings of Peryt Shou. In a letter to List he admitted to an interest in the Cabbala, and in Hindu and Egyptian religious beliefs. Like Sebottendorff, Nauhaus was fascinated by the mystical ideologies of ancient theocracies and secret cults.[34] In April 1917 Nauhaus followed his art teacher Professor Wackerle to Munich, where he soon opened his own studio.

Sebottendorff and Nauhaus organized their activities so that Nauhaus would concentrate on the recruitment of younger members. Progress was initially slow, but the pace quickened as the year progressed. Sebottendorff claimed that the Order province numbered 200 members in spring 1918; the following autumn there were 1,500 members in all Bavaria with 250 in the capital.[35] Sebottendorff had held the meetings at his Munich apartment on the Zweigstrasse until July 1918 when five large club rooms with accommodation for 300 guests were leased from the fashionable Hotel Vierjahreszeiten. Sebottendorff, Gaubatz, and Hering made arrangements for a formal dedication ceremony, which was attended by Hermann Pohl, G. W. Freese and other Germanenorden Walvater brethren from Berlin and Leipzig on 18 August 1918. A week later a large investiture of novices took place, followed by a lecture from Pohl on the 'sun-castles' of Bad Aibling, which possessed esoteric national significance; Hering spoke also on German mythology.[36] Hering's diary records frequent meetings after this date: the lodge was convoked at least once a week for investitures, lectures, and excursions during the autumn. Lodge ceremony involved the use of a piano, harmonium, and female choir. Since these ritual Germanenorden activities were supplemented by overt right-wing meetings the term Thule Society had been adopted as a cover-name for the Order to spare it the unwelcome attentions of socialist and pro-Republican elements. The rooms were decorated with the Thule emblem showing a long dagger superimposed on a shining swastika sun-wheel.

On Saturday evening, 9 November 1918, there was a 'musical rehearsal' in the Thule rooms. During the previous forty-eight hours there had been a bloodless revolution in Bavaria. The Wittelsbach royal family had made a hasty and ignominious flight, the wartime government had resigned, and the Soviet Workers' and Soldiers' Councils had assumed authority. The Bavarian revolution preceded that in Berlin by two days and was headed by a bohemian Jewish journalist. Kurt Eisner had been prominent as a pacifist and the leader of the Independent ('minority') Social Democrats in Munich. He had played an important part in the anti-war strikes of January 1918 for which he was gaoled until October. Against the background of domestic collapse in the defeated country he proclaimed a Socialist Republic, assuming the premiership and ministry of foreign affairs in a cabinet consisting of both 'majority' and 'minority' socialists. The members of the Thule Society, in common with others on the political right-wing in Munich, were dumbfounded by these unexpected and traumatic events. Germany was defeated, the Kaiser and ruling princes were abdicating, while republics were proclaimed by Jewish socialists. The *völkisch* fatherland for which they had fought so long and hard had vanished overnight.

It was in response to this disaster that Sebottendorff delivered an impassioned oration to the Thule that evening. The alleged text betrays a striking mixture of monarchical, anti-Semitic and ariosophical sentiment:

> *Wir erlebten gestern den Zusammenbruch alles dessen, was uns vertraut, was uns lieb und wert war. An Stelle unserer blutsverwandten Fürsten herrscht unser Todfeind: Juda. Was sich aus dem Chaos entwickeln wird, wissen wir noch nicht. Wir können as ahnen. Eine Zeit wird kommen des Kampfes, der bittersten Not, eine Zeit der Gefahr! ... So lange ich hier den eisernen Hammer halte, bin ich gewillt die Thule in diesen Kampf einzusetzen! . . . Unser Orden ist ein Germanenorden, Germanisch ist die Treue. Unser Gott ist Walvater, seine Rune ist die Aarrune. Und die Dreiheit: Wodan, Wili, We ist die Einheit der Dreiheit . . . Die Aarrune bedeutet Arier, Urfeuer, Sonne, Adler. Und der Adler ist das Symbol der Arier. Um die Fähigkeit der Selbstverbrennung des Adlers zu bezeichnen, wurde er rot ausgeführt . . . von heut ab ist der rote Adler unser Symbol, er soll uns mahnen, dass wir durch den Tod gehen müssen, um leben zu können.* [37]

[Yesterday we experienced the collapse of everything which was familiar, dear and valuable to us. In the place of our princes of Germanic blood rules our deadly enemy: Judah. What will come of this chaos, we do not know yet. But we can guess. A time will come of struggle, the most bitter need, a time of danger . . . As long as I hold the iron hammer [a reference to his Master's hammer], I am determined to pledge the Thule to this struggle. Our Order is a Germanic Order, loyalty is also Germanic. Our god is Walvater, his rune is the Ar-rune. And the trinity: Wotan, Wili, We is the unity of the trinity. The Ar-rune signifies Aryan, primal fire, the sun and the eagle. And the eagle is the symbol of the Aryans. In order to depict the eagle's capacity for self-immolation by fire, it is coloured red. From today on our symbol is the red eagle, which warns us that we must die in order to live.]

Sebottendorff's references to the Ar-rune (λ) and the mystical resurrection of the eagle, which should become the militant symbol of the Aryans, are evidence of an unmistakable Listian influence. In 1908 List had claimed that the Ar-rune denoted the sun, the primal fire, the Aryans and the eagle, while also alluding to the death and resurrection of the eagle as a specifically Germanic symbol of rebirth. [38] He also described the trinity of Wotan, Wili, and We in his Germanic-theosophical cosmogony of 1910. [39] The name Thule may also be traced to ariosophical inspiration. The term derived from the name given to the northernmost land discovered by Pytheas in about 300 BC. Sebottendorff identified his 'Ultima Thule' as Iceland; as the supposed outpost of Germanic refugees in List's works, this country held an eminent position in the Armanist doctrine. [40] Exhorting Thule members to fight 'until the swastika rises victoriously out of the icy darkness', Sebottendorff closed his speech with a racist-theosophical poem written by Philipp Stauff. On the basis of this fustian rodomontade and its ariosophical mumbo-jumbo, one might be tempted to dismiss both Sebottendorff and the Thule Society. However, Sebottendorff subsequently emerges as an important organizer of the nationalist reaction to the Eisner government and the succeeding Communist Republics at Munich in journalistic, military and political fields. Ariosophy had found a leader in the counter-revolution.

Several months after the Nazi seizure of power in 1933, Sebottendorff published a book with the sensational title *Bevor Hitler kam: Urkundliches aus der Frühzeit der nationalsozialistischen Bewegung* [*Before Hitler Came: The early years of the Nazi movement*]. It related details of its author's activities in Bavaria during the war and revolution in support of a prefatory thesis:

> Thule members were the people to whom Hitler first turned, and who first allied themselves with Hitler. The armanent of the coming Führer consisted—besides the Thule Society itself—of the *Deutscher Arbeiterverein*, founded in the Thule by Brother Karl Harrer at Munich, and the *Deutsch-Sozialistische Partei*, headed there by Hans Georg Grassinger, whose organ was the *Münchener Beobachter*, later the *Völkischer Beobachter*. From these three sources Hitler created the *Nationalsozialistische Arbeiterpartei*.[41]

Reginald Phelps has examined these claims in detail upon the basis of archival sources and independent accounts, concluding that Sebottendorff's claims have some substance.[42]

Sebottendorff's statement that he provided the journalistic basis of the Nazi party is quite correct. The *Beobachter* was a minor weekly which had been published in the eastern suburbs of Munich since 1868. It presented mostly local stories with a middle-class, somewhat anti-clerical and anti-Semitic bias, and was owned from 1900 onwards by Franz Eher. When Eher died in June 1918, the paper ceased publication until Sebottendorff purchased it for 5,000 marks. He renamed it *Münchener Beobachter und Sportblatt* and included sporting features to win a youthful readership for his trenchant anti-Semitic editorial.[43] From July 1918 until May 1919 the newspaper office was at the Thule premises. After the Soviet revolution at Munich in 1919 Sebottendorff moved the office to the premises occupied by H. G. Grassinger's local branch of the *Deutsch-Sozialistische Partei* (DSP), another anti-Semitic nationalist group founded in 1918. Henceforth Grassinger was the newspaper's production manager and the paper was his party's official organ in Munich.

The financial history of the paper after Sebottendorff left Munich in

July 1919 indicates its gradual acquisition by the National Socialist Party. The DSP editors became divided amongst themselves in the summer, and Sebottendorff summoned his sister Dora Kunze and the paper's nominal proprietor, his mistress Käthe Bierbaumer, for a conference at Constance to clarify the position and dismiss unsuitable personnel. The paper was then converted into a limited liability company. The issued capital of the new company, Franz Eher Verlag Nachf., was 120,000 marks held by two shareholders: Bierbaumer's holding represented 110,000 marks, while Kunze's was 10,000 marks. However, by 20 March 1920 the shareholders were as follows:

Gottfried Feder	10,000 marks
Franz Xaver Eder	10,000
Franz von Freilitzsch	20,000
Wilhelm Gutberlet	10,000
Theodor Heuss	10,000
Karl Alfred Braun	3,500
Dora Kunze	10,000
Käthe Bierbaumer	46,500

Gottfried Feder was one of Hitler's earliest followers; Freilitzsch and Heuss were members of the Thule. It will be clear that Sebottendorff, through his women, had lost a controlling interest by early 1920. By 17 December 1920 all the shares were in the hands of Anton Drexler as nominee for the National Socialist Party. They were transferred to Adolf Hitler in November 1921.[44]

Sebottendorff's second contribution to the nationalist reaction concerns military operations. The Thule stockpiled weapons for Lehmann's Pan-Germans during November 1918 in the event of an armed counter-revolution against Eisner's government. Two schemes for intervention were hatched. Early in December Sebottendorff planned to kidnap Eisner at a rally in Bad Aibling, but this failed. An attempt to expand counter-revolutionary activity through the establishment of a vigilante civilian guard (*Bürgerwehr*), organized by Rudolf Buttmann and Heinz Kurz of the Thule, was also unsuccessful once the Left in the city became suspicious.[45] More effective was Sebottendorff's foundation of the *Kampfbund Thule* during the period of the Communist Republic in Munich, when the legal government had taken refuge at Bamberg. Battle training was held clandestinely at Eching, several kilometres north of Munich; Communist organizations were penetrated, and Sebottendorff was authorized by the cabinet at Bamberg to recruit Bavarians for a Free Corps attack upon the embattled capital. There was a busy traffic in forged railway passes, which enabled Thule members and sympathizers to leave Munich and travel to a marshalling-point at Treuchtlingen. These men contributed to the forces of the Bund Oberland in the successful White onslaught against the Communist-held city from 30 April to 3 May 1919.

Eisner had been assassinated on 21 February by Count Arco auf Valley, a young Jew resentful at his exclusion from the Thule who wished to prove his nationalist commitment. Disorder was henceforth endemic. A shaky coalition government was established by 'majority' Social Democrats under Johannes Hoffmann, but the cabinet was compelled to flee to Bamberg as the situation deteriorated in early April. On 6 April a group of anarchist intellectuals proclaimed the Bavarian Soviet Republic, inspired by the example of Béla Kun in Hungary, who had sent a wave of red inspiration up the Danube to defeated Austria and Germany. After this quixotic administration had fallen within a week, a more serious Communist band seized power on 13 April. Leadership was vested in the Russian emigrés Leviné-Nissen, Axelrod, and Levien, who had been blooded in the 1905 Russian revolution. Their reign of terror was mitigated only by its inefficiency: violent decree followed decree; drunken soldiers of the 'Red Army' ran through the streets plundering and looting; schools, banks, and newspaper offices were shut.

After trying unsuccessfully to build a counter-revolutionary army at Bamberg, Hoffman was forced on 15 April to invite the aid of the Von Epp and other Free Corps, whose anti-Republican sympathies had previously led to their being banned in Bavaria. As the ring of White troops tightened around Munich, the Communists raided nationalist strongpoints within the city. They broke into the Thule premises on 26 April and arrested the secretary Countess Heila von Westarp and in the course of the day six more members were taken. The Red commandant Egelhofer proclaimed the next day that 'a band of criminals . . . of the so-called upper classes . . . arch reactionaries, agents and touts for the Whites', had been captured. The hostages were taken to the cellar of the Luitpold Gymnasium, which had served as a Red Army post since mid-April. The seven Thule members and three other men were shot on 30 April as a reprisal for reports of the killing of Red prisoners by Whites at Starnberg. Four of the seven Thulists were titled aristocrats including Prince Gustav von Thurn und Taxis, who was related to several European royal families. Munich and the world looked on aghast.[46]

The shooting of the hostages enraged the hitherto quiescent Munich citizenry. Rumours spread, compounding the deed with accounts of frightful atrocities. The White troops accelerated their advance and began to enter the city on 1 May, finding a citizen uprising organized by the Thule in progress. The fighting was heavy and tempers ran high on account of the murdered hostages. In return hundreds were shot, including many who had not even remotely favoured the Communist Republic. When the storm was over, the Hoffmann government was returned to power. A parliamentary government of 'majority' Socialists and parties to their right was formed, but it was evident that actual authority had slipped from the Social Democrats owing to their reliance on anti-Republican elements. Everywhere in Germany the old social and political forces had regained strength between January and May 1919, but nowhere were the successes of the counter-revolution so great as in Bavaria. Because of its propaganda and counter-revolutionary action, and also because of the martyrdom of its hostages, the Thule Society and the Germanen-orden had a major share in the creation of a raw and rancorous atmosphere at Munich in which extremist movements like National Socialism could thrive.

Besides his journalism and military ventures, Sebottendorff generated a centre of political discussion and assembly for many groups in the nationalist reaction. When the revolution had initially broken out in November 1918, many *völkisch* groups lost their premises, as landlords felt obliged to give no opposition to the new Republican government. Sebottendorff claimed that the Thule rooms in the Hotel Vierjahres-zeiten became a haven for such groups; hospitality was extended to the National Liberal Party of Hans Dahn, the Pan-Germans, and the *Deutscher Schulverein* of Wilhelm Rohmeder, while Thule guests included Gottfried Feder, Alfred Rosenberg, Dietrich Eckart, and Rudolf Hess, all to achieve prominence in the Nazi Party.[47] A study of the membership list reveals that the Thule supporters were drawn principally from lawyers, judges, university professors, aristocratic members of the Wittelsbach royal entourage, industrialists, doctors, scientists, and rich businessmen like the proprietor of the elegant Hotel Vierjahreszeiten.[48]

The pan-German and anti-Semitic ideology of the Thule Society was supplemented by Sebottendorff's penchant for Ariosophy in his public eulogies of Fritsch, List, Lanz von Liebenfels and Stauff. This intellectual tendency is evidenced by the Thule study-rings formed to investigate Germanic law under Hering, Nordic culture under

Nauhaus, and heraldry and genealogy under Anton Daumenlang, which are all familiar fields of gnostic racism. However, in autumn 1918 Sebottendorff had attempted to extend the appeal of the Thule's nationalist ideology for the working classes by entrusting Karl Harrer (1890–1926), a sports reporter on a Munich evening paper, with the formation of a workers' ring.[49] Although Sebottendorff called this ring the *Deutscher Arbeiterverein*, it is clearly identical to the *Politische Arbeiter-Zirkel*, founded in October 1918. Its members included Harrer as chairman, Anton Drexler, the most active member, and Michael Lotter as secretary. This tiny group, with only three to seven members in regular attendance, met weekly through the winter. Harrer lectured on such subjects as the causes of military defeat, the Jewish enemy, and anti-English sentiment.[50] In December Drexler urged the discussion circle to found a political party and the *Deutsche Arbeiterpartei* (German Workers' Party) (DAP) was formally founded in the Fürstenfelder Hof tavern on 5 January 1919, its supporters coming chiefly from the ranks of Drexler's colleagues at the locomotive works. Drexler's constitution for the party was accepted by twenty-four men and he was elected chairman.[51]

The precise relationship of the new party with the workers' ring of Thulean inspiration remains indeterminate. Franz Dannehl, a Thule member and a DAP speaker, claims to have discussed the founding of the party with Harrer at the Hotel Vierjahreszeiten, but Drexler's pamphlet *Mein politisches Erwachen* (1919) mentions neither Dannehl nor Harrer nor the foundation of the party. Although the minutes of the ring indicate no discussions of racist *Weltanschauung* beyond a rudimentary form of anti-Semitism, it is probable that Harrer's *völkisch* ideas infiltrated the ring and influenced Drexler and the DAP, which was transformed a year later, at the end of February 1920, into the National Socialist German Workers' Party (NSDAP). However, the DAP line was predominantly one of extreme political and social nationalism, and not based on the Aryan-racist-occult pattern of the Germanenorden.

Adolf Hitler first encountered the DAP at a meeting on 12 September 1919. Originally sent as an army spy to monitor the group, Hitler joined the tiny party and lectured to large audiences in taverns from November. He was interested in a mass political party and impatient with the small conspiratory nature of the group. In December he drafted regulations for the committee, giving it full authority and preventing any 'side government' by a 'circle or lodge'. This was aimed at Harrer, who bowed out of office in January 1920.[52]

1. Guido von List in 1910

2.   3.

List Society Patrons
2. Friedrich Wannieck
3. Friedrich Oskar Wannieck
4. Blasius von Schemua
5. Philipp Stauff
6. Bernhard Koerner

4.

5.

6.

7.

8.

9.

Runes and Occult Heraldry

7. List, *Das Geheimnis der Runen* (1908)
8. List, *Die Bilderschrift der Ario-Germanen* (1910)
9. Tarnhari, name-runes and occult coat-of-arms, *c*.1915

10.

Armanist Ritual
10. HAO pilgrimage to Carnuntum, June 1911

11. Funerary tumulus for F. O. Wannieck in Munich, 1914

11.

12. Jörg Lanz von Liebenfels PONT

14.

13.

New Templar Doctrine
13. Flagstone showing knight and beast, excavated at Heiligenkreuz Abbey in 1894
14. *Ostara* illustration, 1922

16.

15.

17.

18.

ONT Priories
15. Burg Werfenstein
16. Werfenstein ex-libris
17. Templar Room at Burg
    Werfenstein
18. Marienkamp-Szt. Balázs
19. Staufen

19.

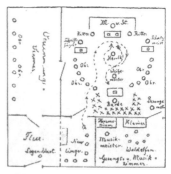

20.

21.

22.

The Germanenorden
20. Theodor Fritsch
21. Lodge ceremony for novices, *c*.1912
22. Founding meeting of Order at Leipzig, 24/25 May 1912

23.

24. Rudolf von Sebottendorff
24. Thule Society emblem, 1919

25.

26.

25. Herbert Reichstein
26. Frodi Ingolfson Wehrmann
27. Gregor Schwartz-Bostunitsch

27

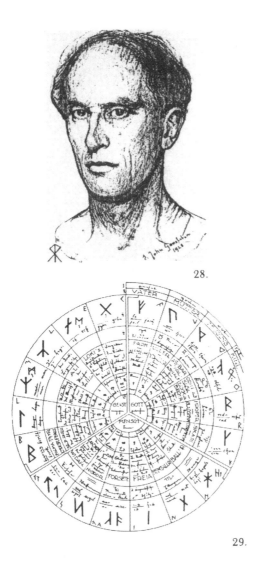

28.

29.

28. Rudolf John Gorsleben
29. Werner von Bülow's 'world-rune-clock'

30. Karl Maria Wiligut in July 1945

31.

32.

31. Wiligut family seal, 1933
32. SS *Totenkopfring* design, 1941

33. SS-Oberführer Weisthor (K. M. Wiligut) in 1936

The contemptuous attack of Hitler on *'völkisch* wandering scholars' in *Mein Kampf* presumably echoes his quarrel with Harrer and the conspiratory *lodge* approach of groups like the Thule Society and the Germanenorden, just as it proclaims that open mass political *party* activity is essential to success.

Although the DAP and the Thule Society diverged in their views on ideology and action, there was a direct line of symbological succession between the two groups in the form of the swastika. Friedrich Krohn, a Thulean and a member of the Germanenorden since 1913, had earned the reputation of a DAP expert as a result of his collection of some 2,500 books on *völkisch* subjects for the use of party members. In May 1919 Krohn wrote a memorandum with the title 'Ist das Hakenkreuz als Symbol nationalsozialistischer Partei geeignet?' ['Is the swastika suitable as the symbol of the National Socialist Party?'], in which he proposed the left-handed swastika (i.e. clockwise in common with those of the theosophists and the Germanenorden) as the symbol of the DAP. He evidently preferred the sign in this direction on account of its Buddhistical interpretation as a talisman of fortune and health, whereas its right-handed (i.e. anti-clockwise) counterpart betokened decline and death. (However, since most Listian swastikas and the device of the Thule Society had been right-handed, it is clear that there was no standard usage regarding the direction of the swastika in the *völkisch* tradition). Hitler actually favoured a right-handed, straight-armed swastika and prevailed upon Krohn in DAP committee discussions to revise his design. Krohn was responsible for the colour scheme of a black swastika in a white circle on a red background. At the foundation meeting of the local Starnberg group of the NSDAP on 20 May 1920, this swastika, originally proposed by Krohn and modified by Hitler, made its first public appearance as the flag of the new movement.[53] It is therefore possible to trace the origin of the Nazi symbol back through the emblems of the Germanenorden and ultimately to Guido von List.

Sebottendorff's subsequent career might be the blueprint for a *'völkisch* wandering scholar'. Following the angry reaction of Thule members who held him negligently responsible for the loss of the membership lists to the hostages' killers, Sebottendorff attended no further Thule meetings after 22 June 1919. His political adventure was now over and he had to find a new career. Since 1913 he had been a keen student of astrology and this became his principal activity when he succeeded Ernst Tiede as editor of the periodical *Astrologische Rundschau* in October 1920. Tiede had inspired Lanz von Liebenfels with his prophetic literature at the outbreak of war. He had subsequently published a markedly occult-racist text, *Ur-Arische Gotteserkenntnis* [*Ancient Aryan God-Knowledge*] (1917), which described the mysteries and sun-religions of the ancient Aryan theocracies, and he corresponded with Guido von List about theosophy and 'armanist' wisdom in the Old Testament.[54] Sebottendorff followed in these footsteps. Between 1921 and 1923 he wrote no less than seven astrological text-books which enjoyed a high prestige among contemporary German astrologers for their empirical precision and clarity. He also edited the periodical at Bad Sachsa in the Harz mountains until 1923. He was always fond of small fashionable spa towns, where he could pose as a baron.

In spring 1923 Sebottendorff left for the lakeside resorts of Switzerland. At Lugano he completed his occult treatise on the Baktāshī dervishes and their relationship to the alchemists and Rosicrucians. After staying in Switzerland throughout 1924 he returned to Turkey. From 1926 until 1928 he acted as the honorary Mexican consul in Istanbul, subsequently travelling in the United States and Central America between 1929 and 1931. At some stage he acquired the knighthood of the Imperial Constantine Order, a royalist and chivalrous league, whose anti-Bolshevik ideology and noble trappings must have been dear to his heart.[55] He returned to Munich in 1933 to revive the Thule Society in the Third Reich, but soon fell into disfavour with the Nazi authorities on account of his claims to have been the precursor of early National Socialism. He was briefly interned at the beginning of 1934.[56] Again Sebottendorff made his way to Turkey via Switzerland, and eventually found employment under Herbert Rittlinger in the German Intelligence Service at Istanbul during the war. His former chief recalled him as a penurious and amiable old gentleman, whose information was regrettably useless. When the Germans left Istanbul in September 1944, Sebottendorff received funds to keep him modestly for a year. After the war Rittlinger received reliable information that the old baron had thrown himself into the Bosporus on 9 May 1945. As his last known contact, Rittlinger has the final word: 'the old and lonely baron was at the end of his tether; no money, cut off and without the slightest hope of ending his days with even the most slender resources. The day the armistice was signed, with the implication of total defeat, would have depressed him even further.'[57] Thus ended the life of the adventurer who had introduced Ariosophy to the Nazi Party.

12

The Holy Runes
and the Edda Society

IN 1918 the old Wilhelmian world in Germany was swept irrevocably away. The war had been finally lost after four years' now seemingly futile sacrifice of lives, loved ones, youthful hopes and ambitions, and economic resources. The shock of military defeat was compounded by its unexpectedness following recent successes on the Western Front and the collapse of Russia. The sudden armistice encouraged a 'stab in the back' legend, whereby a conspiracy of socialists and Jews at home was supposed to have betrayed the armies in the field. The harsh conditions of the Versailles peace settlement imposed further burdens on the weary and confused country: former Reich territories were ceded, war reparations of money and industrial output were demanded, and the occupation by foreign troops completed the humiliation of the nation. The Kaiser and other ruling princes had abdicated, while in their place unfamiliar politicians set about the establishment of a parliamentary democracy, typically perceived as the creature of the victors and hostile interests. Between 1918 and 1923 Germany was convulsed by local uprisings and civil war, several attempted putschs, frontier skirmishes with Poland, and disastrous domestic inflation. The chaos of the new Republic made a miserable contrast with the imperial glitter and pompous splendour of the gilded pre-war era. Germany suffered a political and cultural trauma as it painfully sought adjustment to its new circumstances.

These wretched conditions naturally favoured the emergence of myths and ideologies concerned with the restoration of the supposed halcyon past or at least the removal of those influences deemed responsible for Germany's terrible downfall. Although a tiny minority of monarchists intrigued for the return of the exiled Kaiser, most new right-wing movements represented a revolutionary break with the Second Reich. Apocalyptic nationalist poetry aimed at the Allies flourished and *völkisch* groups sprang up to fulminate against the Jews, the communists, and the Freemasons. Nationalist revolutionaries embraced a romantic freebooter spirit and joined the Free Corps, private armies which fought in the Baltic states, against Poland, and also against communist rebels in Germany. Other neo-conservatives preached the necessity of a new feudal order, a corporate state, or a Third Reich. The pre-war youth movement expanded with the proliferation of leagues devoted to the celebration of their own exclusive male community, athletic adventure and romantic nationalism.[1]

Fresh support for the occult-nationalist ideas of Guido von List formed on the visionary fringes of the post-war *völkisch* movement. In many cases this was a matter of old supporters reaching new audiences. Ellegaard Ellerbek, List's ardent war-time admirer, embarked on a vigorous anti-Republican campaign which utilized an astonishing variety of gnostic, theosophical, and anti-Semitic notions to vilify the Allies, denounce materialism, and to elevate the Germans to the status of god-men. His *Versailler Visionen* (1919) described the subtle aura suspended over each of the European nations as a function of their spiritual character and concluded with an 'occult-armanistic' exhortation to his countrymen: 'Do you know that you are gods?' The next year he published a novel entitled *Sönne Sonnings Söhne auf Sonnensee* (1920), which mixed a farrago of solar symbolism with an account of a *völkisch* utopia and contained four letters from Guido von List in an appendix. Ellerbek lectured widely in Germany, claiming that the Germans were blood descendants of the ancient pagan gods, and wrote anti-Semitic articles in a mystical vein for Dietrich Eckart's paper *Auf gut deutsch [In Plain German]*. His imagination was both apocalyptic and catastrophic during the revolutionary period. Once he declared that a frieze in the house of Walther Rathenau, Foreign Minister of the new Republic, depicted the execution of all living kings and attracted considerable public notice when the Jewish politician was assassinated shortly afterwards. Ellerbek was even remembered in the prison diary of Alfred Rosenberg, as he awaited execution at Nuremberg in 1946.

The List Society continued at new headquarters in Berlin under the enthusiastic leadership of Philipp Stauff, the chief German disciple of the old master. From his home at Moltkestrasse 46a in Berlin-Lichterfelde Stauff published new editions of List's Ario-Germanic researches between 1920 and 1922. Following his suicide on 17 July 1923 his widow Berta Stauff took over the administration of the publishing house and the Society continued to serve as a meeting-point between pre-war members, the Germanenorden, and new-comers throughout the 1920s. Tarnhari frequented the Stauff home, as did Günther Kirchhoff, an occultist with a penchant for genealogy and Germanic prehistory. Eberhard von Brockhusen, Grand Master of the Germanenorden, acted as President of the Society until his death in March 1939. The political influence of the List Society was limited, as its principal function was a social forum for the Stauff circle and their *völkisch* contacts at Berlin. The more activist contribution of the Germanenorden and the Thule Society to counter-revolution at Munich immediately after the war will be obvious.

Whereas these individuals and groups essentially cultivated the traditional Armanism of List, a new post-war Aryan occultist move-ment was started by Rudolf John Gorsleben (1883–1930). On the basis of the runes, occultism, and the Edda, Gorsleben created an original racist mystery-religion which illuminated the priceless magical heritage of the Aryans and justified their spiritual and political world-supremacy. Born on 16 March 1883 at Metz, Gorsleben was brought up in Alsace-Lorraine, a French province which had been annexed by the German Reich in 1871 after its victory in the Franco-Prussian war. The inhabitants of this area spoke a German dialect and wavered in their political allegiance between Berlin and Paris, thus encouraging the local growth of Pan-Germanism during the 1890s. Gorsleben encountered nationalism at an early age in this borderland; as a staunch German patriot he was proud to trace his ancestry back to a fourteenth-century noble family in Thuringia. Little is known of his youth except that he arrived in Munich sometime before the First World War. His first ambitions concerned a career in the theatre, for he published a play called *Der Rastaquär* (1913), which had a short run in the city. He then turned to journalism and edited a pamphlet magazine devoted to nationalist and Pan-German ideas, *Allgemeine Flugblätter Deutscher Nation*. At the outbreak of war Gorsleben volunteered for service with a Bavarian regiment, which fought for two years on the Western Front. He then transferred to a German unit attached to the Turkish army in Arabia, fighting against the Bedouin tribes and their British supporters in Palestine. Gorsleben held the rank of lieutenant and won twelve military distinctions. He also kept a wartime diary, from which an extract about his Arabian campaign was later published. Even these early writings reflect a strong interest in mythology and the importance of race in historical development.[2]

At the end of the war Gorsleben returned to Munich. The revolutionary period politicized him further and he became associated with the Thule Society. In April 1919 he was arrested together with Dietrich Eckart by communist insurgents during the Soviet revolution in the city. Only Eckart's quick-witted answers under interrogation prevented their summary execution in common with the other Thule hostages.[3] On 18 December 1920 Gorsleben delivered a lecture entitled 'The Aryan Man' to the Thule. In his diary of society meetings Johannes Hering commented on the occult tendencies in Gorsleben's thought and their later efflorescence in his mature doctrine of Aryan mysticism.[4] Over the next two years Gorsleben was highly active in local revolutionary right-wing politics. In July 1921 he became Gauleiter of the South Bavarian section of the radical anti-Semitic *Deutschvölkischer Schutz- und Trutzbund*, which was then competing with the early Nazi party for support in Southern Germany. By December 1921 Gorsleben had decided to break with the league's central office at Hamburg and he formed a new alliance with Julius Streicher—who later edited *Der Stürmer* under Nazi auspices—finding considerable support at Regensburg and Nuremberg. Gorsleben also worked closely with Lorenz Mesch, the Germanenorden chief in Regensburg, whose protégés Schulz and Tillessen carried out the Erzberger assassination.[5] However, after a stormy period of internal party strife, Gorsleben retired from *völkisch* politics to devote his time fully to literary and ideological interests. He embarked upon a major translation of the Edda, which he regarded as a distillation of old Aryan religion.

In 1920 Gorsleben had acquired a floundering Munich weekly newspaper called *Die Republik*, which he renamed *Deutsche Freiheit* [*German Freedom*] and edited in a *völkisch* spirit. His contributors included Friedrich Wichtl, the Austrian theorist of masonic world-conspiracy, and Hans F. K. Günther, the racist anthropologist. Between 1920 and 1925 the paper adhered to a conventional nationalist line, save for its occasional references to the occult powers of the Aryan race. From late 1926 onwards this supranational mystical racism prevailed in the magazine as Gorsleben began to expound his own brand of Aryan occultism. His doctrine corresponded to modern occultism and theosophy in several respects: it regarded astrology, cabbalism and magic as its metaphysical bases; its ultimate objective was the creation of a racially pure humanity and the spiritual advancement of the Aryans; the precondition of such advancement was the re-activation of occult powers inherent in each Aryan individual, enabling him to master the natural world; any mechanistic or materialistic conception of reality was rejected out of hand; lastly, it propagated the advent of a new age, in which the Aryan would regain his former splendour and authority in the world. The later works of Gorsleben presented such doctrine as the rediscovered wisdom of the ancient Aryans. His periodical henceforth carried the sub-title 'Monatsschrift für arische Gottes- und Welterkenntnis' and was renamed *Arische Freiheit [Aryan Freedom]* in 1927.

Gorsleben's actual racism was based on Social Darwinism and later eulogies of the Aryan type. He derived the word 'race' from *rata*, an old Norse term meaning 'root', in order to conclude that God and race were identical. He claimed that the Aryans were 'the sons of the sun, the sons of the gods, the supreme manifestation of life' and described their world-view as heroic, inasmuch as the Aryans sacrificed individual benefit for the good of the world. Indeed, their vocation was the settlement and conquest of the whole world. Gorsleben inveighed against the vulgar, corrupt, and wretched modern world as the sad result of racial mixing and comforted the (relatively) pure Germans with such words as 'Know that your body is the temple of God. God dwells within you.' He maintained that racial mixing was always detrimental for the racially superior partner, since his purity was debased in the progeny, and he repeated the common *völkisch* conviction that woman could be 'impregnated' by intercourse, even when no conception occurred, so that her subsequent offspring bore the characteristics of her first lover. Given these overwhelming pressures towards the increasing bastardization of the German descendants of the Aryan race, only the strict practice of segregation and eugenics could guarantee the reversal of racial contamination in the world.[6]

But Gorsleben emphasized the spiritual reawakening and occult education of the Aryans even more than this imperative to proper breeding practices. The esoteric importance of the runes was central to his account of the magical Aryan world-view and these ideas distinguished him sharply from other *völkisch* writers. Prehistorians generally accepted that the runes had possessed a symbolism over and above their phonetic value and use in writing, so that they were accordingly used for divination, the casting of lots, magical invocations, and the preparation of amulets and charms. Gorsleben sought to reconstruct this spiritual science of the runes and their magical uses. In the first place he regarded the runes as conductors of a subtle energy that animated the entire universe, and therefore as devices which could be used to influence the material world and the course of events. The runes were a link between the macrocosm and the microcosm of Aryan man, a representation of God in the world. 'The runes had arisen from the original relationship between the human racial spirit of the god-sons and the world-spirit, and they could lead the true seeker back to his cosmic homeland and offer a mystical union with God.'[7] Gorsleben illustrated these neo-gnostic notions by numerous diagrams showing the individual runes within the most sacred rune, the hagall rune [✳], and the presence of this rune in such symbols and devices as the hexagram, the heraldic lily, the world-ash of Norse mythology, magical squares, and the Cheops pyramid in Egypt.[8] He also developed an occult doctrine of crystals, according to which the spirit of any individual could be seen mediumistically as a specific type of crystal. The crystal types indicated the aptitude and destiny of the subject. Gorsleben declared that the crystals were but solid geometrical projections of the runes, in order to prove their cosmic importance yet again.[9]

Gorsleben elaborated these theories with a wide variety of geo-metrical, numerological, and etymological constructs. The cube was 'unpacked' to produce a Christian cross, the hagall rune was trans-formed into various solar symbols, and the word 'crystal' (*Kristall*) was derived from *Krist-All*, thus indicating an ancient Krist religion of Atlantean and Aryan provenance which had been supposedly bowdlerized as the new gospel of Jesus. As evidence for this prehistoric Krist religion Gorsleben produced many examples of crosses from antique civilizations throughout the world and even traced the monogram of Christ [✕] to a variant form of the hagall rune [✳]. The highly arcane nature of Gorsleben's gnosis is evident from the cover of *Deutsche Freiheit* in December 1926, the second special issue devoted to Armanen-wisdom: the theme 'From Hag-All to Krist-All' is graphically illustrated by the familiar hagall rune, incorporating a hexagram and a hexagon, and the variant hagall rune superimposed on a set of concentric circles. Beneath these two occult symbols are printed the words 'Ask' and 'Embla', the numerical expressions 3 x 3 and 7 + 9, and the cryptic question 'human sacrifice?'. The usual magazine logotype stands in the centre of the page: two curved-arm swastikas within a hexagram formed by two triangles and flanked by the motto 'Like is only understood by like'.

This esoteric representation of ancient Aryan wisdom bears a structural resemblance to the notions of Guido von List, whom Gorsleben often quoted with approval. Gorsleben expanded and buttressed his own exposition of Aryan religion with an impressive array of examples and illustrations drawn from numerous scholarly studies in prehistory, archaeology, ethnology, and art history. His great life-work, *Hoch-Zeit der Menschheit* [*The Zenith of Humanity*] (1930), which described the former glory of the Aryan world, reproduced over a hundred plates from such works, including photographs, line drawings, diagrams, and maps. The lost civilization of Atlantis, the megalithic stone circles of Europe, archaeological finds, ornaments, bas-reliefs, the various rune futharks, astrology, and mathematical theorems were all discussed as evidence for the former high civilization of the Aryans. Their wisdom was similarly held to have survived in a wide variety of cultural forms, including the runic shapes of beams in half-timbered houses, coats-of-arms, countless symbols and words, and even in the picture *Melencolia* by Albrecht Dürer.[10]

Gorsleben regarded old Icelandic literature, especially the Edda, as 'the richest source of Aryan intellectual history'.[11] On 29 November 1925 he founded an Aryan study-group called the Edda Society at his farmhouse in Dinkelsbühl, a romantic medieval town in Franconia. The members of the Society were mostly authors in their own right and contributed to Gorsleben's eclectic reconstruction of the Aryan religion. Werner von Bülow (1870–1947), the Grand Master of the Society, was a retired civil servant from West Prussia who owned the Hotel Karwendel at Mittenwald in Upper Bavaria. He designed a 'world-rune-clock', which showed the correspondence of the eighteen runes with the colours, the zodiacal signs, the gods of the months, numbers, skaldic names, and the Listian trinity of 'birth', 'being', and 'death'.[12] Similar ideas were expressed in his short work *Der Ewigkeitsgehalt der eddischen Runen und Zahlen* (1925). The treasurer of the Society was Friedrich Schaefer at Mühlhausen, whose wife Käthe kept open house for another occult-*völkisch* group which gathered round Karl Maria Wiligut in the early 1930s. Other members of the Edda Society included Martin Brücher and Albert March, who had written an esoteric book on German nationalism involving a quasi-Listian proto-language and the principle of parallax;[13] Karl Nüse, a prominent *völkisch* private scholar; Otto Sigfrid Reuter, the leader of the Germanic Belief Fellowship and author of many books on astrology, prehistoric pagan religion, and the Edda; Carl Reinhold Petter, president of a pan-Aryan league at Danzig; and Mathilde von Kemnitz, a prolific *völkisch* writer who spearheaded the Ludendorff movement after her marriage to the general in September 1926.[14] Gorsleben was Chancellor of the Society and his periodical *Deutsche Freiheit*, later *Arische Freiheit*, was published as the organ of the Society. After Gorsleben's death, due to a long-standing heart complaint, on 23 August 1930 at Bad Homburg, Bülow took over the editorship and the paper was renamed *Hag All All Hag*, later simply *Hagal*, and continued publication up until 1939.

During the 1930s Bülow ran the Edda Society according to its original principles of research into the Edda and other relics of the ancient Aryan religion. However, in 1933 the Society explicitly declared its adherence to the National Socialist world-view in a new memorandum.[15] The magazine *Hag All All Hag* remained principally concerned with the interpretation of Edda verse, mythology and ancient monuments with the runes acting as interpretative devices on the basis of their phonetic and numerical values. Bülow was particularly interested in the myths surrounding Odin, Brunhild, Gudrun, and Heimdall, but other contributors focused more narrowly on the symbolism of specific buildings or regional localities. Political issues were also occasionally addressed. It was claimed that the Nazi revolution in Germany was taking place according to higher cosmic laws and that it was necessary to subordinate personal interests to those of the community; articles also marked the *Anschluss* of Austria and the annexation of Bohemia and Moravia.[16] In 1934 *Hagal* devoted three numbers to the ancestral memory and family traditions of Karl Maria Wiligut, the elderly *völkisch* seer who was recruited into the SS for his clairvoyant knowledge of the ancient Germanic past. In this and subsequent years Bülow emphasized such family traditions as the supreme key to an understanding of the old Aryan beliefs.[17] Günther Kirchhoff, a post-war List Society member and a correspondent of Wiligut, contributed several articles on heraldry, astrology, and local history. Other important writers for the magazine included Ida Schulze, Karl Nüse, Richard Anders, and Josef Heinsch, a leading proponent of the German school of geomancy or sacred geography.

Besides Gorsleben, Bülow, and the Edda Society there were other advocates of rune occultism during the 1920s and 1930s. These individuals cultivated a highly practical engagement with the runes within a less explicitly Aryan racist context. Friedrich Bernhard Marby (1882–1966) founded a mystical school of rune occultism which emphasized the beneficial and healing properties of the runes when used as incantations or gymnastic postures in imitation of their forms. Born on 10 May 1882 at Aurich in North Friesland, Marby had served an apprenticeship to a printer in Hanover, where he remained until 1915. During these years he developed his rune theories, as a result of contact with the literature of Guido von List. After moving in 1917 to Stuttgart, where he worked as an editor on the regional newspaper, Marby became deeply interested in astrology, whose precepts he combined with the rune tradition. In 1924 he started his own paper *Der eigene Weg* and published several short monographs on the runes and their use in meditation and health-building in his *Marby-Runen-Bücherei* book series from 1931 onwards. Between 1928 and 1930 he also pursued his own ancestral research in Sweden and Denmark. Denounced as an anti-Nazi occultist during the Third Reich, Marby was sent to Welzheim concentration camp in 1936. After more than eight years' captivity at Flossenbürg and Dachau, he was finally freed by the invading Allied armies in April 1945. Marby resumed his occult researches after the war, writing new books and editing his magazine *Forschung und Erfahrung* until his death on 3 December 1966.[18]

In the scientific idiom of the early twentieth century Marby regarded man as a sensitive receiver and transmitter of cosmic waves and rays, which animated the entire universe and whose specific nature and effect were dependent on planetary influences, earth magnetism, and the physical form of the landscape. Within this macrocosmic-microcosmic model Marby saw the runes not just as letters or phonetic values but as representations of postures and movements which man could perform in order to improve his reception of these cosmic influences. He therefore devised a system of rune-gymnastics whereby the subject imitated the forms of runes, in order to enjoy the particular influences associated with them. The repetition of the rune sound as a vocal incantation or mantra was also recommended. Both practices indicate a certain debt to yoga, which was familiar to esoteric groups in Germany following its theosophical popularization after the First World War. Marby conceived of the ancient Aryan and Germanic holy places as rune training-grounds, typically sited in craters, on mountains and hills, and in the vicinity of water due to its magnetic and reflective properties. His ideas were imbued with Listian usage: the sanctuaries were described as *Halgadome* and were formerly tended by the Albruna, Thruda, and Wala priestesses; the esoteric interpretation of coats-of-arms also helped to locate places with such associations. After the war Marby devoted himself to astrological practice and studied such matters as the shape of towers and church spires in relation to local planetary influence.[19]

Siegfried Adolf Kummer (b. 1899) similarly emphasized the practical side of rune occultism. In 1927 he founded the rune school Runa at Dresden, which collaborated with the Ariosophical summer school of the Richter brothers at Bärenstein in 1932. Using the traditions of ritual magic, Kummer instructed his pupils to draw a protective magical circle inscribed with the names of the Germanic gods upon the floor and to use a candelabrum, censor, and aspersorium as they performed rune exercises and invocations. Supplementary practices included rune-yodelling and rune-grips, whereby the hand and fingers were used to form a particular rune in the course of meditation. Kummer's writings made frequent reference to List and Gorsleben and were illustrated with pictures of the grail and a 'Nordic' temple.[20] Both Kummer and Marby were censured by Wiligut in his capacity as Himmler's counsellor on magical and religious subjects for bringing the holy Aryan heritage into disrepute and ridicule and this criticism may have led to Marby's harsh treatment in the Third Reich.[21]

Georg Lomer (1877–1957) was yet another occultist in the *völkisch* tradition, but his teachings were involved with astrology rather than rune occultism. Born on 12 September 1877 at Loosten near Wismar, Lomer qualified as a physician before coming into contact with the theosophical movement in Germany after the First World War. While his earliest publications concerned a critique of Christianity, his writings between 1920 and 1925 were devoted to alternative forms of medical diagnosis and treatment based on dream-interpretation, auto-suggestion, and palmistry. It was not until the middle of the decade that his astrological interests became evident. In 1925 he contributed an astrological and graphological supplement, together with the famous astrologer Elsbeth Ebertin, to the old-established theosophical periodical *Zum Licht*. By 1929 he had taken the magazine over, publishing it from Hanover as *Asgard* and sub-titled 'a fighting sheet for the gods of the homeland'. His burgeoning tendency towards a pagan world-view was manifest in *Hakenkreuz und Sowjetstern* (1925), a short treatise pondering the deeper meanings of these symbols and their movements, and in *Die Götter der Heimat* (1927), which fused a new Germanic religion with astrological ideas. In common with the other post-war Aryan occultists, Lomer essentially used occult materials to illuminate the forgotten Aryan heritage. Contributors to *Asgard* included Marby, Ernst Wachler, a pre-war List Society member and a pioneer of open-air *völkisch* theatre, and Gregor Schwartz-Bostunitsch, a mystical anti-communist and conspiracy-theorist.

The wide range and confusing variety of racist occultism during the years of the Republic and the Third Reich might tempt one to dismiss the phenomenon as a crankish outgrowth of a larger occult movement in German society during a troubled period in history. While it is undeniably true that these astrologers, rune magicians, and Edda mystics were occultists, to leave the matter there is to fail to understand the basic ideological and political motive of this special kind of occultism. All these thinkers were united in a profound reaction to the contemporary world. They perceived the German Republic as vulgar, corrupt, and the symbol of defeat. As cultural pessimists they lifted their eyes from the frustrations and disappointments of the present to behold a vision of high Aryan culture in a fabulous prehistoric past. Astrology, the myths of the Edda and the runes, whether mysteriously whispered or cut as strange magical characters, all represented a marvellous link with that golden age. They were also the promissory tokens of a new era, in which magic, mystical vision, and world-power would be restored to all true-born Germans.

13

Herbert Reichstein
and Ariosophy

WHEN Lanz von Liebenfels first coined the term 'Ariosophy' in 1915, his familiarity with contemporary occultism was already considerable.[1] Astrology, as it had developed before and during the First World War, reprints of Nostradamus's prophecies, works on premonitions, telepathy, and psychical research, all combined to provide Lanz with a compendium of modern occultism. After the war, Lanz was absorbed in a study of astrology, which bore fruit in his *Praktisch-empirisches Handbuch der ariosophischen Astrologie*, completed in August 1923. On finding a new publisher in October 1925, Lanz wrote a formal statement of his doctrine. He summarized the basic tenets of Ariosophy as a belief in a quasi-monist 'pan-psychic' energy, identical with God, which animated the entire universe but found its most perfect manifestation in the blond-haired, blue-eyed Aryan. He reiterated the familiar canon that all cultural achievement in the world could be traced to an Aryan origin. Lanz stated the basic concern of Ariosophy as the study of differences between the 'blonds' and the 'darks', while emphasizing the importance of such auxiliary sciences as palmistry, astrology, heraldry, the doctrine of periods, the study of names and a related form of cabbalism. He claimed that heraldic devices and names were the visible and audible hieroglyphs, in which the Aryan ancestors had cryptically recorded the history and karma of their families. Palmistry and astrology provided a similar means of studying the Aryan soul.[2]

This endorsement of occult sciences, especially palmistry and name-cabbalism, is significant for two reasons. In the first place, it indicates his friendly collaboration with a circle of racist character-ologists around the publisher Herbert Reichstein from 1925 until 1929, when he withdrew to devote himself fully to the Ordo Novi Templi; secondly, Lanz profited from this contact inasmuch as he gathered fresh materials for his doctrine from the burgeoning post-war occult movement, which was developing special studies in astrology, graphology, palmistry, yoga, dream-interpretation, and many forms of regimen conducive to health and personal happiness. Significant figures in this milieu were Gustav Meyrink, Franz Spunda, and Peryt Shou, who wrote novels with occult themes, and a larger group of writers, who wrote specialist studies in occult science. The publishing house of Johannes Baum at Pfullingen provided a forum for such studies in the context of its New Thought series: between 1920 and 1925, Baum commenced the issue of at least four book-series, which popularized such topics as homoeopathy, meditation, breathing-exercises, yoga, esoteric Christianity, and oriental religions in pamphlets by Karl Otto Schmidt, Georg Lomer, Willy Adelmann-Huttula, Hans Hänig, Heinrich Jürgens, and others. If one considers the continued publication and influence of several theosophical periodicals and books together with the output of Baum, it is clear that there existed a rich crop of German occult literature in the years immediately following the military defeat and domestic collapse of the country.[3] In this context post-war Ariosophy assumes the status of a particular strand in a varied and colourful ideological subculture, which was principally concerned with the anxieties and uncertainties of individuals in a period of cultural disruption.

The nature of Herbert Reichstein's peculiar contribution to this subculture is best understood through an account of his colleagues. The historical origins of his movement are found in a Berlin group of occultists which formed around 1920. The chief figures in this group were Ernst Issberner-Haldane, a palmist; Frodi Ingolfson Wehrmann, an astrologer; Robert H. Brotz, a graphologist, and Wilhelm Wulff, an astrologer whom Heinrich Himmler consulted in the last weeks of the Second World War.[4] According to Issberner-Haldane, who called this company the 'Swastika-Circle', Wehrmann was an ardent supporter of Guido von List's speculations about the ancient Germanic priest-kings. Born on 6 February 1889 and of Friesian descent, Wehrmann had served as an artillery captain in the war. He was regarded as an expert in ancient Nordic history and runology, and also versed in astrology, numerology, and the study of karma.[5] Another acquaintance recalled his passionate dedication to the cause of his *Volk* and his desire to save the heroic Aryans through the extermination of inferior races. Although he had allegedly first discovered the theories of Lanz after the war, he was credited with an assiduous study of mystical and occult texts after 1920.[6] These reports are corroborated by a later, unsympathetic record of his early occult studies. His first publication, *Die Wirkung der Sonne in den zwölf Tierkreisen* [*The Influence of the Sun in the Twelve Houses of the Zodiac*] (1923), constituted an unacknowledged plagiarism of an English text, which Issberner-Haldane had translated for him.[7] Wehrmann first collaborated with Reichstein in late 1925, and wrote two numbers in his book-series, *Ariosophische Bibliothek*, in 1926.[8]

Issberner-Haldane's life history is more accessible than that of Wehrmann, since he wrote an autobiography. According to this account, Issberner-Haldane was born on 11 June 1886 in Kohlberg on the Baltic Sea. His interest in palmistry was allegedly first aroused in boyhood, when an elder brother bought him a book on the subject. In 1900 he was apprenticed to a businessman in Kohlberg, where he remained until he was eighteen years old. After a short period of military service, he worked in his uncle's tobacco-business at Berlin, later managing a branch in Thuringia. In summer 1910 Issberner-Haldane realized his long-cherished desire to emigrate to Australia, in order to escape the confines of Germany, the culture of which he despised as narrow, philistine, and militaristic. The account of his outward voyage from Bremerhaven via Suez and Colombo is cast in the style of a *Bildungsroman*, whereby the young emigrant meets several interesting individuals, who harbour anti-Semitic and racist ideas. Paragini, a sculptor at Genoa, pronounced upon the importance of racial features for his art, and denied the existence of any creativity among the Jews. Back on board, Dr Jeffersen, a Scottish gentleman, was presented as an astrologer with an interest in the writings of Lanz; Mr Hewalt, another Briton, was also well versed in Lanz's neo-manichaean racism, and displayed a wide knowledge of sexology and several branches of occultism. In Ceylon Issberner-Haldane had an opportunity to consult an Indian fortune-teller and witnessed the feats of an old fakir. The account of these encounters and experiences was supposed to document the gradual dawning of the importance of racism and occultism in Issberner-Haldane's mind, while he continued to develop his studies in palmistry.[9]

After working from autumn 1910 until early 1912 on various farms in the outback of New South Wales and South Australia, Issberner-Haldane travelled to South America. In Rio de Janiero he noticed the brothels were full of girls with Aryan features, clear evidence of a Jewish world-conspiracy to debase the female youth of the superior race. While travelling up the River Amazon to Manaos, Issberner-Haldane composed a dissertation on palmistry, for which he received the title Professor *honoris causa* from an unnamed and probably bogus university. While visiting Peru he wandered upon the Andes, where he experienced a mystical trance bringing initiation into the mysteries and higher meaning of human existence; he also received esoteric instruction from Devaswara Lama, an itinerant Persian sage.[10] Returning to Australia, he worked on farms in Queensland until spring 1914, when he decided to travel to the United States via Germany. He broke his journey at Colombo, in order to visit the holy city of Benares. Here he met a yogi called Ramachiro, who explained the theory of the human aura, before conjuring a series of visions showing scenes in the lives of Issberner-Haldane's former incarnations during antiquity and the medieval period.[11]

After his arrival in Germany at the end of July 1914, Issberner-Haldane intended to visit relatives before travelling on to the United States. With the outbreak of international hostilities, he was interned as an Australian citizen and spent the ensuing four years in prison-camps at Hassenberg, Holzminden, and Ruhleben. Following his release in November 1918, Issberner-Haldane went to live in Berlin, where he opened a palmist practice. Here he met his new colleagues in the post-war German occult subculture. Although still tempted to found a racist utopia in Queensland or California, he remained in Berlin, where he published his first text on palmistry in 1921. In 1926 he began a quarterly periodical *Die Chiromantie*, which was advertised as the official organ of the Association of Palmists in Germany.[12] He first became associated with Reichstein in late 1925, while his periodical was absorbed by that of the latter in late 1929. He joined the ONT in early 1927 after meeting Lanz in either Vienna or Budapest. He subsequently opened a racist commune, the *Svastika-Heim*, near Arkona on the Isle of Rügen which assumed the status of an ONT house.[13]

Herbert Reichstein, the publicist responsible for capturing these and other individuals for his periodical and characterological institute, was born on 25 January 1892 at Haynau in Silesia, but almost nothing is known about his youth or experiences. In October 1925 he was approached by Lanz, who asked him to become his publisher.[14] Reichstein agreed and simultaneously announced himself the director of the *Deutsche Arbeitsgemeinschaft für Menschenkenntnis und Menschenschicksal*, based at Oestrich im Rheingau. He conceived of this association as a mutual aid group and working forum for all occultists concerned with the characterological and divinatory sciences in a racist context, including astrology, graphology, phrenology, 'psycho-physiognomy', and palmistry. The organ of the association was his *Zeitschrift für Menschenkenntnis und Menschenschicksal*, which published articles by occultists together with advertisements for their private consultation.

In an introductory article Reichstein outlined the objectives of his association. Given the chaos caused by the lost war and political upheavals, he claimed that a soundly based science of human character was essential, in order that individuals might prepare themselves better for their fate and learn how to make the best of it. Reichstein denied that he was peddling a form of fortune-telling and emphasized the functions of such a science as a means of determining one's own character and that of others, thus providing information on the likely outcome of individual action in an increasingly complex world, which demanded more and more significant decisions on the part of the individual. The entire project stood squarely upon the basis of a racist *Weltanschauung*, according to which the members of the association regarded themselves as Aryans and pledged themselves to the advancement of racial purity.[15] Reichstein was clearly appealing to a market amongst those whose sense of uncertainty and disorder had led them to seek an occult key to the solution of their problems and the promotion of success in their personal and business affairs. Reichstein's Ariosophy thus grafted the racist canon on to a body of mantic lore, the demand for which was frankly admitted to be the result of post-war tribulations.

In the first issue of the periodical, dated October 1925, Reichstein announced the collaboration of recognized occultists in his project, including Issberner-Haldane, Lanz von Liebenfels, Wilhelm Wulff, and G. W. Surya.[16] In December 1925 he began the issue of a book-series, *Ariosophische Bibliothek*, which proposed to publicize Lanz's theories in a wide field ranging from astrology to heraldry, while bringing this kind of 'practical self-realization' to its readers. A notice in the first number indicated that Frodi Ingolfson Wehrmann, Herbert Gerstner, and Reinhold Ebertin, the astrologer, had joined his association.[17] The second number of his periodical appeared in February 1926 as *Zeitschrift für Menschenkenntnis und Schicksalsforschung*, while the prolix title of his institute was changed to the Ariosophical Society, in order to stress its patronage of Aryan occult sciences for the benefit of Aryans. He had meanwhile moved to Düsseldorf-Unterrath. In the course of 1926 other contributors to the periodical included Robert H. Brotz, Karl Kern, Walter Horst, Theodor Czepl, Detlef Schmude, G. Engelhardt, Freiherr Stromer von Reichenbach, an authority on occult cycles, which he had systematized into his own science of historionomy, Prince Max von Löwenstein, Edmund von Wecus, and Ernst Tiede.[18] By the end of 1927 these contributors had been augmented by Lanz's Hungarian contacts, Paul Horn and Wilhelm Tordai von Szügy.

In 1928, Reichstein acquired two more important contributors, both of whom deserve detailed introduction. Gregor Schwartz-Bostunitsch was a Russian *emigré*, whose direct personal experience of the Revolution had lent his thought a virulently anti-Bolshevik stamp coupled with an unwavering belief in a Jewish world-conspiracy.[19] Born on 1 December 1883 at Kiev, Grigorij Bostunič was of mixed parentage: his father was descended from a patrician family in Riga, while his maternal grandparents were Serbian and Bavarian. Because of this grandmother's family connection, the young Bostunič visited Germany regularly. After qualifying as a lawyer in Kiev in 1908, Bostunič turned to literary pursuits on a full-time basis, interests which he had already cultivated as a student. In 1910 he established his own newspaper, *Der Südkopeken*, which was running to a daily edition of 100,000 copies by 1914. In this year he became Professor for Theatrical and Literary History at the Lisenko Institute and later assumed the directorship of the Railway Theatre at Kiev. The military collapse of Russia and the Revolution signalled the end of this academic and literary career. An ardent opponent of the Reds, Bostunič was active as an anti-Bolshevik agitator and speaker in towns captured by the Whites under Generals Denekin and Wrangel. This political activity also brought him into contact with the idea of a Jewish-Masonic-Bolshevik conspiracy and its alleged world-programme, the Protocols of the Elders of Zion.[20] In 1920 Bostunič was condemned to death *in contumaciam* by the Bolsheviks, but he was able to flee to Bulgaria.

After fleeing his native country, Bostunič began a life characterized by personal rootlessness and a search for new values to sustain him. This search led him to occultism. He referred to a meeting with his first teacher in transcendental matters in the Caucasus during 1917/18, and also to his contacts among Bulgarian theosophists in 1920. James Webb has argued that the Caucasian teacher was most probably G. I. Gurdjieff, while the Bulgarian theosophists were almost certainly associated with the 'Master' Petr Deunov, who had blended Blavatsky's esoteric racism with a vision of Slav messianism.[21] After an abortive attempt to return to Russia in October 1920 Bostunič lived in Belgrade. During the next two years he travelled in Yugoslavia, lecturing on the Jewish-Masonic conspiracy to disgruntled German nationalists in the former Austrian provinces of the new state. His first book, *Freemasonry and the Russian Revolution*, was published in Russian at Novi Sad in 1922, appearing subsequently in extracts in German nationalist and right-wing periodicals between 1923 and 1926. In August 1922 Bostunič emigrated to Germany, where he again lectured on conspiracy-theories. According to his view of the post-war world, all undesirable change and disorder could be traced to the malevolent wiles of a Jewish-Masonic-Bolshevik conspiracy. Nor had his interest in occultism flagged. In 1923 he became an enthusiastic Anthroposophist, but by 1929 he had reviled Rudolf Steiner's movement as another agent of the nefarious conspiracy. Such a specific reversal of opinion did not modify his fundamentally manichaean and occult vision of history. Following his naturalization as a German citizen in 1924, he changed his name to Schwartz-Bostunitsch. He first encountered Herbert Reichstein at Düsseldorf during winter 1926. Reichstein quickly recognized his burning sense of mission and secured his collaboration with the Ariosophical Society. In February 1928 he was quoted as being available to lecture on the relationship between the Russian and German soul and hailed as an expert on secret and supranational powers.[22]

Besides his involvement in the ariosophical movement, Schwartz-Bostunitsch was active in Nazi political circles. After working for Alfred Rosenberg's *Weltdienst* news agency in the 1920s, he then switched his allegiance to the rising SS. Despite his age, deafness and a heart ailment, Schwartz-Bostunitsch was determined to serve the new Germany to the limits of his ability. He travelled widely as a lecturer on Freemasonry, the Jews, and other conspiracies to Nazi organizations in Germany and later in the occupied countries; he also wished to endow a proposed institute for conspiracy studies with his own library of 40,000 volumes on such topics. His letters to Himmler during the 1930s express fanatical dedication to the German racial mission and his SS patron. Owing to his unorthodox ideas he was barred from lecturing in uniform, but was nevertheless appointed an honorary SS 'professor' in 1942. He and his wife, together with the library, were evacuated in early 1944 from Berlin to Schloss Gneisenau at Erdmannsdorf (Riesengebirge) in Silesia for safety's sake. Later that year Schwartz-Bostunitsch was promoted SS-Standartenführer (colonel) upon the personal recommendation of Himmler.[23] His unique political career had taken him from anti-Semitism in pre-revolutionary Russia to a wholehearted identification with Nazi Germany.

The other contributor, whom Reichstein won for the Ariosophical Society in 1928, was Rudolf John Gorsleben. From January 1927 Gorsleben's periodical had appeared under the title *Arische Freiheit*; in January 1928 it was amalgamated with Reichstein's characterological periodical, which was now entitled *Zeitschrift für Geistes- und Wissenschaftsreform*. His peculiar brand of occultism, which discerned Aryan symbols in both the natural and human realms, is witnessed by his articles during this year: 'Arische Schau ist Urschau', 'Der radioaktive Mensch', 'Beitrag zur Christosmythe', 'Hag-All-Rune und Cheopspyramide', 'Runen-Raunen-Rechten-Rat'.[24] In this respect, Gorsleben was closer to the Listian tradition than was Reichstein. The collaboration between the two was short-lived and Gorsleben resumed independent publication of his periodical in 1929. He completed his occult studies with the masterpiece *Hoch-Zeit der Menschheit* (1930) and died, comparatively young, on 23 August 1930.[25] During the late 1920s, he had been affiliated as Fra Rig to the ONT priory of Staufen.[26]

As Reichstein had stated in early 1926, the Ariosophical Society intended to place the findings of characterological and mantic science at the disposal of all deserving Aryans, who were beset by a sense of chaos and uncertainty in the post-war world. In August 1928 a statement was published which emphasized the status of ariosophical characterologists as heirs to the hierophantic tradition of the *Armanenschaft*. At Pforzheim, where Reichstein now had his base, the *Neue Kalandsgesellschaft* (NKG) was proclaimed. The new title of the association was felt by members to have a more Listian tone. The task of this body, according to Wehrmann and Reichstein, was 'the realization of the will of the old Germanic initiates, the priest-kings or *Armanen* in our own age'.[27] There followed a list of collaborators, which included the new names of Franz Friedrich von Hochberg, Professor Morawe, songmaster Schwartz, Konrad Duënsing, and Hermann Wieland, the *völkisch* historian of Atlantis. Lecture tours of the NKG for the forthcoming winter were announced: Wehrmann was available to give courses on karmic astrology and Ariosophy; Gregor Schwartz-Bostunitsch on Freemasonry and Bolshevism; Issberner-Haldane on palmistry and yoga (on which he had published a text-book in June 1928); Robert Brotz on graphology; Herbert Reichstein on Ariosophy, astrology and name-cabbalism. The latter science was based upon the Jewish notion of correspondences between letters and numbers, albeit in a very simple and popular form: the sum of the numerical equivalents of the letters in a person's name allegedly yielded information regarding his nature and destiny.[28] The intellectual leadership of the NKG remained in the hands of Lanz von Liebenfels, who had already contributed 'ariomantic' studies of Guido von List, Ernst Issberner-Haldane, and Benito Mussolini.[29]

During the years from 1929 until 1931 the NKG did succeed in publicizing ariosophical ideas in many German towns through lectures and meetings. The Christmas celebrations of the NKG group at Heidelberg on 29 December 1928 were reported with enthusiasm, while a new NKG branch was inaugurated on 10 January 1929 at Stuttgart, following a well-received lecture by Reichstein.[30] In March 1929 an ambitious programme of lecture tours was announced, with visits to Karlsruhe, Dresden, Erfurt, Magdeburg, Vienna, and Budapest.[31] During the summer Reichstein made the acquaintance of Grete Steinhoff, who allegedly read the character of a person from their names by a 'mediumistic' method in contrast to Reichstein's cabbalistic procedure. Following their meeting Grete Steinhoff became a member of the NKG lecturing staff. In November she and Reichstein planned a joint lecture tour with visits to Cologne, Kassel, Mannheim, Mainz, Nuremberg, Ansbach, Munich, and Vienna.[32] Another group of characterologists at Dresden, the *Zirkel für praktische Menschenkenntnis*, under the leadership of Georg Richter, an occult author with an interest in magnetic healing and telepathy, declared its amalgamation with the NKG in November 1929. This group convened regular meetings through the winter and during 1930; associates included Alfred Richter, a herbalist, and Kurt Hartmann, a bookseller who had undertaken the distribution of Reichstein's periodical in Northern and Eastern Germany.[33]

Towards the end of 1929 internal tensions within the Reichstein group erupted with the resignation of Frodi Ingolfson Wehrmann from the NKG. The signs of this rupture had been ominously increasing since January 1929, when Wehrmann assumed the editorship of the periodical after having moved to Pforzheim from Berlin. References to his unpractical management and his domineering style of leadership in the NKG, which he took over in February, indicate a strain in his relationship with Reichstein, which probably led to his removal from editorial office at the end of August 1929. It is also possible that Wehrmann felt sufficiently encouraged by the popularity of his masterpiece in multi-disciplinary fortune-telling *Dein Schicksal* (1929) to devote himself independently to private practice.[34] A legal action between Reichstein and Wehrmann, accompanied by denunciations from Issberner-Haldane, records the rapid alienation of Wehrmann from his former friends during 1930.[35]

Wehrmann subsequently indulged in a cult of right-wing revolutionary activism by harking back to his wartime service as a 'frontline soldier' and organizing the Pforzheim branch of the National Socialist *Sturmabteilung* (SA). Despite this new identification with the freebooter spirit, prevalent among the Freikorps between 1918 and 1923 and again after the economic crash of 1929, Wehrmann was still preoccupied with occultism. This unusual ideological mixture was demonstrated by his own periodical *Der Wehrmann* (1930–3), which declared its championship of 'Gothic spiritual life', German mysticism, and eugenics in the sense of a 'frontline struggle'. Since Wehrmann's earlier writings had often embraced a violently millenarian doctrine, calling for a destruction of all racial inferiors and the establishment of a Greater Germanic Empire, he may be considered one of the few racist occultists who turned from literary apocalyptic to military activism. Wehrmann remained at Pforzheim, where he lost everything in an air-raid during February 1945. He contracted pneumonia and died in Calw on 19 April 1945.[36]

In April 1931 Reichstein moved his publishing house from Pforzheim to Pressbaum in the Wienerwald. At this time he published a new appeal for the co-ordination of all ariosophically inclined groups or persons in an *Ariosophische Kulturzentrale* (AKZ), which was yet another appellation for his group of racist occultists. He claimed that member groups already existed in Berlin under the direction of Karl Kern; in Munich under Wilhelm von Arbter; in Dresden under Georg Richter; in Leipzig under Ludwig Götz, and in Vienna under himself. From Pressbaum Reichstein enjoyed personal contact with the Austrian ONT in Vienna. In June 1931 an Ariosophical School was opened at the AKZ (now Pfalzauerstrasse 97). This school was advertised as a holiday pension set in the healthy and attractive surroundings of the Wienerwald, with morning instruction in mental and physical training according to ariosophical principles. Reichstein proposed to lecture on name-cabbalism, while visits from Karl Kern, Issberner-Haldane, and Alfred Judt, a specialist in biorhythms, were anticipated in the late summer. Kern had recently distinguished himself with the publication of the *Handbuch der Ariosophie* (1932) and an edited reprint of Johann Praetorius's characterological classic, *Mensch und Charakter* (1703).[37] Following its first successful summer season, the Ariosophical School reopened in May 1932. After the formal celebration of Lanz von Liebenfels's sixtieth birthday with music, lectures, and ariosophical psalms on 8 May 1932, the courses in name-cabbalism, runic occultism, yoga and breathing-exercises, and 'runic gymnastics' began.[38] The latter speciality owed its origin to the writer and publicist Friedrich Bernhard Marby, who had edited his own astrological-ariosophical periodical, *Der eigene Weg*, since 1924. Marby believed that an individual was able to draw down beneficial cosmic forces upon himself by assuming postures in the form of prescribed runes.[39]

Reichstein's periodical reflects the widespread interest among certain sections of German and Austrian society for all manner of health cures, revelations, reassurances, and techniques of self-realization in troubled times. There also existed a marked tendency to embrace several contemporary fringe-sciences and to adopt other forms of current occult beliefs, as if this eclecticism could help to bolster the other ingredients of the doctrine: the 'space energy' (*Raumkraft*) theories of Karl Schappeller, the discoveries of Frenzolf Schmid concerning the healing properties of certain hitherto unidentified rays, and the healing methods of unorthodox doctors were championed by Reichstein.[40] Eccentric cosmological theories also found acceptance: witness the issue devoted to Hanns Hörbiger's World Ice Theory,[41] and Lanz's enthusiastic review of Karl E. Neupert's *Die Umwälzung, die Erde—das All* (1930), which proposed a Hollow Earth Theory, whereby the earth's surface was supposed to be concave, while observable space within this hollow sphere constituted the entire universe.[42] This readiness to profess a belief in abstruse and unconventional doctrines is most plausibly explicable as the consequence of a desire for ideological alliances within the subculture of occult and irrationalist modes of thought.

Following the economic crash in late 1929 Reichstein and his circle began to take an active interest in the fortunes of the Nazi party. Lanz had established a precedent for the admiration of fascist movements, having enthused over the right-wing regimes of Spain, Italy, and Hungary since 1925. In early 1930, Reichstein published cabbalistic horoscopes for the German Republic, Adolf Hitler, and the National Socialist German Workers' Party (NSDAP). While he reckoned that the Republic was subject to 'saturnine influences' and 'black magical forces', his calculations convinced him that the year would bring great success to Hitler and his party.[43] In April 1931 he published an apocalyptic number entitled 'Das Dritte Reich!', which, according to an occult threefold division of body, spirit, and soul, identified the National Socialist Party as the material power-factor, which would realize ariosophical culture and doctrine as its moving spirit- and soul-factors. This abstruse division of roles was allegedly based on

Lanz's *Bibliomystikon*, the 'Attalantic' revelational scriptures supposedly dating from 85,000 BC and discovered by Frenzolf Schmid, and the astrological writings of Georg Lomer. In spring 1932 Reichstein hailed Hitler as 'an instrument of God'.[44] This mood of apocalyptic expectation was given further force by a series of articles by Ernst Lachmann, who sought to predict the future of Germany during the period from 1930 to 1932 on the basis of the 'historionomy' of Stromer von Reichenbach.[45] After the Nazi seizure of power in Germany, Reichstein moved in April 1933 from his Austrian base to Berlin, in order 'to be at the centre of the revival of a nationally awakened Germany'.[46] At the capital he and Karl Kern began the publication of *Arische Rundschau [Aryan Review]*, a weekly newspaper which professed the struggle against Judah, Rome, and Freemasonry in the context of ariosophical racism and occult predictions. Reichstein subsequently issued a book-series, *Das Weistum des Volkes [The Wisdom of the Volk]* (1934–5), which embraced a 'religion of blood kinship'. Reichstein died in relative obscurity at Freiburg in 1944.[47]

The achievement of Reichstein's characterological group and periodical remains the modest popularization of ariosophical ideas among small circles in German cities, an activity which maintained its appeal even during the so-called years of stability from 1924 to 1929, but which peaked between 1929 and 1933 as the sense of domestic strife sharpened with economic recession and political polarization. In this context the ariosophical lecture tours were typical of a widespread and heterogeneous upsurge of revivalists, quacks, and confidence men. Rudolf Olden, a contemporary journalist, has described the antics of sectarians, inventors, and even alchemists, who formed the ranks of these wonder-workers. They found their credulous converts not only among the poor and ignorant, but also among industrialists, generals, and ex-royalty.[48] Sefton Delmer has written that the shock of Germany's defeat, the inflation, the get-rich-quick boom that followed stabilization, the influx of foreign money, and the ensuing economic crash, all combined to produce an atmosphere of unreality, which encouraged the emergence of a caste of 'miracle men'.[49] Reichstein's advertisements for revelational books, horoscopes, and other mantic consultations, special medical preparations, soaps, salves, and toothpastes, no less his warning against competitive 'charlatans', demonstrate his membership of this caste. The statements of the Reichstein circle regarding their indebtedness to Lanz von Liebenfels all expressed gratitude for their salvation from a meaningless life and depression.[50] Ariosophy was a single element in a diffuse subculture geared to the alleviation of stress and disappointment among individuals who felt a profound betrayal of their expectations and cultural values during the final years of the German Republic.

14

Karl Maria Wiligut
The Private Magus of Heinrich Himmler

THE Armanists, Ariosophists, and rune occultists we have encountered so far all conform to a certain sectarian stereotype. Their doctrines cited exalted and superhuman ancestors, whose ancient gnostic rule had brought the Aryans wisdom, power, and prosperity in a prehistoric age until it was supplanted by an alien and hostile culture. These ancestors were supposed to have encoded their salvation-bringing knowledge in cryptic forms (e.g. runes, myths, and traditions), which could be deciphered ultimately only by their spiritual heirs, the modern sectarians. List, Lanz von Liebenfels, Gorsleben, and others attracted disciples with the lure of such doctrines, which were intensively disseminated within the sect, while certain of their ideas and symbols filtered through to wider social groupings. These men thus contributed importantly to the mythological mood of the Nazi era, but they cannot be said to have directly influenced the actions of persons in positions of political power and responsibility.

Karl Maria Wiligut (1866–1946), the so-called Rasputin of Himmler, did achieve such influence. By virtue of his alleged possession of ancestral memory and an inspired representation of archaic Germanic traditions, he became the favoured mentor of Reichsführer-SS Heinrich Himmler on mythological subjects and was given an official assignment for prehistorical research in the SS between 1933 and 1939. During the period of his service he was promoted from SS-Hauptsturmführer (captain) to SS-Brigadeführer (brigadier) upon the personal recommendation of Himmler. Consulted by his patron on a wide range of issues, Wiligut's influence extended to the design of the *Totenkopfring* (death's head ring) worn by members of the SS, the conception of the Wewelsburg as the order-castle of the SS, and the adoption of other ceremonial designed to bestow a traditional aura upon the SS ideology of élitism, racial purity, and territorial conquest. But who was Karl

Maria Wiligut, and how did he come to exercise this extraordinary influence?

The answer to the latter question reflects largely on the character of Himmler himself. Among the top leaders of the Third Reich, Himmler appears the most ambiguous personality, motivated simultaneously by a capacity for rational planning and by unreal fantasies. His zeal for order, punctuality, and administrative detail, and the pedantic impression of an 'intelligent primary school teacher', were seemingly belied by his enthusiasm for the utopian, the romantic and even the occult.[1] It was Himmler's idealistic imagination which led to a visionary conception of the SS and its future role: his black-uniformed troops would provide both the bloodstock of the future Aryan master-race and the ideological élite of an ever-expanding Greater Germanic Reich. Himmler busied himself from 1930 onwards with various projects designed to express the moral purpose and ideological mission of the SS. The marriage regulations of 1931, his plans for an SS officers' college at the Wewelsburg in 1933, and his close collaboration with Richard Walther Darré, the chief Nazi theorist of 'blood and soil', are representative of these projects. In 1935 he established with Darré the Ahnenerbe, an initially independent institute, with a mandate to pursue research into Germanic prehistory and archaeology. The Ahnenerbe was subsequently incorporated into the SS, its academic staff carrying SS rank and wearing SS uniform.[2] It is only within this context of Himmler's quest for Germanic roots to underpin his SS ideology that one can understand his patronage of the 66-year-old *völkisch* occultist Karl Maria Wiligut.

Wiligut was born on 10 December 1866 in Vienna.[3] Both his father and his grandfather had served as officers in the Austrian army and the eldest son followed this family tradition. At the age of fourteen he began attending the imperial cadet school at Vienna-Breitensee and in December 1884 he joined the 99th infantry regiment at Mostar in Herzegovina. He was promoted second lieutenant in November 1888, lieutenant in 1892, and captain in 1903. During this early period of his military career, he served with the 99th, 88th and 47th infantry regiments in various parts of the Habsburg empire. As early as the turn of the century Wiligut had demonstrated some literary ambition with the publication of verse, typically characterized by the celebration of nature, mythological subjects, and regimental history. His treatment of mythology was explicitly nationalistic in *Seyfrieds Runen* (1903), a collection of poems devoted to the legends surrounding the Rabenstein at Znaim on the Austrian-Moravian border. Wiligut's introduction referred to the 'Germanic origin' of place-names and reflected the mood of contemporary folklore studies by Franz Kiessling and Guido List. The book was published by Friedrich Schalk, who had also issued some of List's early work. At this time Wiligut was described in his military files as having good social connections, which may be a reference to his membership in the Schlarraffia, a quasi-masonic lodge which he had joined at Görz in 1889, attaining the grade of Knight and office of Chancellor prior to his resignation in 1909. His lodge-name was Lobesam which also appeared on the title-page of his book. However, there is no evidence that this lodge was allied to the Pan-German movement, nor does Wiligut appear to have been associated with any other nationalist organization in imperial Austria.

In May 1912 Wiligut was promoted to major and was still serving with the 47th infantry regiment at the outbreak of war. In October 1914 he became a staff officer in the 30th infantry regiment, witnessing action against the Russian army in the Carpathians along the north-eastern flank of the empire. Following an exhausting campaign during which he was either in battle or on long night-marches, Wiligut was promoted to lieutenant-colonel and transferred back to Graz to organize reinforcements for the 14th and 49th infantry regiments. He was then posted to the Italian front, where he held a succession of commands between June 1915 and the following spring. In June 1916 he was appointed commanding officer of the Salzburg district reserves and promoted to the rank of colonel in August 1917. In the course of the war he was decorated for bravery and highly commended by his senior officers. Field Marshal Daniel described him as 'a sterling character . . . an extremely skilful, conscientious officer . . . suitable for regimental command', a judgement shared by other high-ranking commanders. In May 1918 Wiligut was recalled from the front in South Tyrol and placed in command of camps for returned soldiers at Zolkiew, north of Lemberg (L'vov) in the Ukraine. After nearly forty years' professional military service he was discharged on 1 January 1919 and he retired to Salzburg.[4]

Wiligut's subsequent importance to *völkisch* groups and the SS rested on his reputation as the last descendant of a long line of Germanic sages, the Uiligotis of the *Asa-Uana-Sippe*, which dated back to a remote prehistoric era. Wiligut claimed to possess ancestral-clairvoyant memory, which enabled him to recall the history and experiences of his tribe over thousands of years. It is difficult to establish when Wiligut first identified with this tradition as pre-war documents are scarce. He claimed that he received instruction on the runes from his grandfather Karl Wiligut (1794–1883), and dated his formal initiation into the family secrets by his father from 1890;[5] a series of nine pagan commandments was supposedly written by him as early as July 1908. The only source for Wiligut's pre-war pagan tradition is Theodor Czepl of the Order of the New Templars who evidently knew of Wiligut around 1908 through an occult circle in Vienna, whose members included Willy Thaler, a cousin of Wiligut, his wife Marie Thaler, the well-known actress, and several ONT brothers.[6] It was on the basis of this former acquaintance that Lanz von Liebenfels gave Czepl the assignment of making renewed contact with Wiligut after the war, since by this time rumours of his 'secret German kingship' were current in the *völkisch* subculture. Czepl accordingly visited Wiligut on three occasions, once spending as long as seven weeks at his Salzburg home in the winter of 1920–1. He recorded his experiences with Wiligut in an extensive memorandum prepared for the ONT.[7]

Wiligut told Czepl that he was the bearer of a secret line of German royalty and showed him tomes on heraldry and his own coat-of-arms and family seal as proof of this claim. He obliquely stated that 'his crown lay in the imperial palace at Goslar and his sword in a stone grave at Steinamanger'. On the basis of his ancestral-clairvoyant memory he described the religious practices, military organization, and constitutional arrangements of the ancient Germans in terms that also closely resembled the earlier revelations of Guido von List. But Wiligut also maintained that the Bible had been originally written in Germany; he evidently identified with an Irminist religion, which was distinct from and the opponent of Wotanism, celebrating a Germanic god Krist, which the Christian religion had later bowdlerized and appropriated as its own saviour. Wiligut also welcomed Lanz's intended publication of a second *Ostara* series for the light this might throw on the real Aryan origins of Christianity. Wiligut presented Czepl at his departure with a poem entitled 'German Faith', which fused mystical pietism with hopes of national redemption. From this meeting with Czepl it may be deduced that Wiligut's doctrine blended the Teutonic archaism of List with the Ario-Christianity of Lanz, albeit in a novel form. It is also likely that his ideas about Krist influenced Gorsleben in the 1920s.

These elements of Wiligut's doctrine may be confidently dated back to around 1920. Their later elaboration is best studied in the copious writings of his Austrian disciple, Ernst Rüdiger (1885–1952), whom he initially met during the war and with whom he collaborated over the next decade. According to Rüdiger, Wiligut attributed to the ancient Germans a history, culture, and religion of far greater antiquity than that generally accepted by academic prehistorians. His chronology began around 228,000 BC, when there were three suns in the sky and the earth was populated with giants, dwarves, and other supposedly mythical beings. History proper began for Wiligut when his ancestors, the Adler-Wiligoten, helped restore peaceful conditions after a long period of strife and thereby inaugurated the 'second Boso culture', which witnessed the foundation of the city Arual-Jöruvallas (Goslar) in 78,000 BC. Subsequent millenia were described in a detailed record of tribal conflicts and mass migrations to fabulous continents of theosophical tradition. Around 12,500 BC the Irminist religion of Krist was proclaimed, becoming the universal faith of the Germans until it was challenged by the schismatic Wotanists. In 9600 BC a climax occurred in the continuous wars between the two religions. Baldur-Chrestos, a holy prophet of Irminism, was crucified by Wotanists at Goslar. However, the prophet escaped to Asia and the battle of faiths persisted over the following centuries. The Wotanists ultimately succeeded in destroying the Irminist sacred centre at Goslar in 1200 BC and the Irminists founded a new temple at the Exsternsteine near Detmold. But this was taken by the Wotanists in 460 before being finally sacked in its corrupt form by Charlemagne during his campaign against the pagan Saxons in the ninth century.[8]

Wiligut ascribed a continuous and important role to his ancestors in this account of the past. The Wiligotis had been *Ueiskuinigs* (wise kings), tracing their descent from the union of the *Asen* (air gods) and *Wanen* (water gods) when the earth was still populated by mythical beings. Later the tribe ruled over a kingdom in the Burgenland, which is why Wiligut attributed a traditional importance to Steinamanger and Vienna comparable to that of Goslar in his recollections from ancestral-clairvoyant memory. At the time of Charlemagne's brutal persecution of the pagans in North Germany, the Wiliguts in that area were supposed to have escaped from Frankish captivity and fled to the Faroe Islands and thence to Central Russia. There the Wiliguts founded the town of Vilna as the capital of an extensive Gothic empire, whose existence had been subsequently obliterated by hostile Christian and Russian interests. Finally, the family migrated in 1242 to Hungary, where they enjoyed respite from the vigilance of the Catholic Church and the enmity of the Wotanists as a result of the chaotic conditions created by the Tartar invasions. Throughout its history, the Wiligut family had remained staunchly loyal to the Irminist faith. Among other notable members of his tribe, Wiligut mentioned Armin the Cherusker and Wittukind, both heroic figures in early Germanic history. It will be evident from this epic account of putative genealogy and family history that Wiligut's prehistorical speculations primarily served as a stage upon which he could project the experiences and importance of his own ancestors.[9]

In the early 1920s Wiligut became convinced that he was the victim of the age-old persecution of his tribe and the Irminist religion. He identified this modern conspiracy against him in the Catholic Church, Jewry, and Freemasonry, and also blamed them for the lost war and the collapse of the Habsburg empire. In order to publicize his ideas among other disgruntled patriots in the new socialist Austrian Republic, he founded an anti-Semitic league at Salzburg and edited a newspaper entitled *Der eiserne Besen* [*The Iron Broom*], in which he fiercely attacked both the Jews and the Freemasons. At this time, Wiligut's marriage came under great strain. In 1907 he had married Malwine Leuts von Treuenringen from Bozen, who bore him two daughters, Gertrud (b.1907) and Lotte (b.1910). A son, twinned with one of the daughters, had died in infancy, thereby foiling the traditional inheritance of secret tribal knowledge by the eldest male heir. Wiligut had come to resent his wife for this loss and became increasingly moody at home during his retirement. His wife, for her part, thought little of his tradition and was also incensed at Wiligut's ill-advised financial guarantee of a commercial venture undertaken by a former officer comrade. Wiligut subsequently claimed that this man was another agent of the conspiracy against him. Matters abruptly climaxed in November 1924 when Wiligut was involuntarily committed to the Salzburg mental asylum, where he was certified insane and remained an inmate until his release in early 1927. The full report on his condition referred to his violence at home, including threats to kill his wife, grandiose projects, eccentric behaviour, and occult interests, before diagnosing a history of schizophrenia involving megalomaniac and paranoid delusions. A Salzburg court ruled him incompetent to administer his own affairs on the basis of this medical evidence.[10]

During his confinement Wiligut continued to correspond with those loyal associates whose belief in his traditions and ancestral memory remained unshaken. These friends were his Austrian disciples, Ernst Rüdiger and Friedrich Teltscher at Innsbruck, and in Germany Friedrich Schiller (ONT) and several members of the Edda Society, including Werner von Bülow, Richard Anders (ONT), and the treasurer's wife, Käthe Schaefer-Gerdau. Thanks to their support and encouragement, Wiligut was able to resume his activities as a Germanic sage following his release from the asylum. In 1932 Wiligut fled his family, the stigma of Salzburg, and the state of Austria. He emigrated to Germany and settled in the Bogenhausen suburb of Munich. Continuing his ancestral researches, he now became a celebrity among the rune occultists of Germany. He was a welcome long-term guest at the home of Käthe Schaefer-Gerdau in Mühlhausen, where a circle known as the 'Free Sons of the North and Baltic Seas' gathered to hear his family traditions and oracular wisdom. In early 1933 the Edda Society printed a long description and interpretation of Wiligut's family seal as an outstanding example of 'Armanist runo-logical heritage'.[11] During the summer of 1934 the Society began publishing pages of rune-rhymes, numerological wisdom, and myth-ological verse by Jarl Widar (Wiligut's new *nom de plume*) in its magazine *Hagal*.[12] The editorial introduction to the July number declared that the magazine had entered a new era and was henceforth committed to the dissemination of a newly-discovered source of wisdom. It also suggested that both List and Gorsleben might have been indebted to similar family traditions.[13]

Wiligut clearly recognized the sympathy between his own mythology and the apocalyptic hopes unleashed in Germany by the Nazi revolution of January 1933. So did others. His old friend Richard Anders, now an SS officer, introduced the old mystic to his chief Heinrich Himmler. The latter was evidently impressed by Wiligut's ancestral-clairvoyant memory and decided to exploit as fully as possible this unique source of information on ancient Germanic religion and traditions. In September 1933 Wiligut joined the SS under the pseudonym Karl Maria Weisthor and was appointed head of a Department for Pre- and Early History within the Race and Settlement Main Office *(Rasse- und Siedlungshauptamt)* of the SS based at Munich. His duties here appear to have consisted in committing examples of his ancestral memory to paper, discussing his family traditions with Himmler, and being generally available to comment on prehistoric subjects. During 1934, his first full year of SS service, Weisthor found favour with his new master. Correspondence over this and ensuing years indicates a most cordial relationship between Himmler and Weisthor, even extending to the exchange of birthday telegrams and gifts. More importantly, Weisthor's correspondence contained many items relating to the Wiligut family tradition, such as rhymed verse on rune-wisdom, mythological poetry, essays on cosmology and the epochs of world prehistory, a copy of his nine pagan commandments from 1908 with a runic transliteration, and an Irminist paternoster in Gothic language. Most of these items were scrupulously initialled by Himmler and kept among his private papers.[14] In April 1934 Weisthor had been promoted SS-Standartenführer (colonel) to reflect his former rank in the imperial Austrian army and in October 1934 he was appointed head of Section VIII (Archives) at the Race and Settlement Main Office. His promotion to SS-Oberführer (lieutenant-brigadier) followed the next month.

In August 1934 Weisthor brought Günther Kirchhoff, a fellow enthusiast for Germanic prehistory with whom he had corresponded since the spring, to the attention of Himmler. Günther Kirchhoff (1892–1975) lived at Gaggenau near Baden-Baden in the Black Forest. A member of the post-war List Society at Berlin and an associate of Tarnhari, Kirchhoff was interested in genealogy and interpreted legends as reflections of actual prehistorical incident. He also speculated on the existence of geodetic energy-lines across whole continents.[15] Greatly impressed by his letters, Weisthor sent the Kirchhoff correspondence to Himmler, with the excited comment that 'there were still thank goodness other "initiates" besides himself who read the times correctly'. He also noted pregnantly that Kirchhoff used a family seal.[16] Within a fortnight Weisthor followed up by sending another Kirchhoff essay entitled 'Rotbart von Kyffhäuser' to Himmler and Reichsminister Walther Darré with the vigorous recommendation that 'its content was of momentous importance both with respect to our own prehistoric past and for its links with the present' and asked the two leaders to study the piece before the Party Day in order that they might discuss it in detail together.[17] The essay described the organization of prehistoric Germany with explicit reference to List's *Armanenschaft*. Kirchhoff claimed that ancient Europe had been ruled by the Great Three, namely the Uiskunig of Goslar, King Arthur of Stonehenge, and Ermanrich of Vineta or Vilna. Subordinate to them was the Great King of Thuringia, Günther the Redbeard, whose tribe migrated to Scotland in 800 BC, where it became known as the Kirkpatrick clan. Kirchhoff deduced his own blood kinship with both the Günther tribe and the Kirkpatricks on the basis of Listian etymology and adopted a coat-of-arms like the town arms of Erfurt in Thuringia to demonstrate this family link. This essay was representative of the fifty or so manuscripts, written on subjects ranging from the Nibelungs to the Rosicrucians, which Kirchhoff submitted to the Reichsführer-SS Personal Staff and the Ahnenerbe between 1936 and 1944.[18]

184

When Kirchhoff started to write about the prehistoric religious significance of the Murg valley near Baden-Baden in the spring of 1936, Weisthor lost no further time in making his personal acquaintance and visited Gaggenau. Accompanied by Kirchhoff, Weisthor undertook an eight-day survey of this Black Forest district in June 1936. His formal report to the SS filled 87 typed pages and included 168 photographs of old half-timbered houses, architectural ornament (including sculpture, coats-of-arms, runes, and other symbols), crosses, inscriptions, and natural and man-made rock formations in the forest. On the basis of this fund of Listian relics Weisthor concluded that the area centring on Schloss Eberstein constituted a gigantic Irminist religious complex depicting the 'eye of God in the triangle' in place-names and topographical features. This religious symbol had first been discussed in one of his *Hagal* articles: the 'revolving eye' (*Draugh*) consisted of an isosceles triangle whose corners symbolized the spirit-point, the energy-point, and the matter-point on a circumscribing circle denoting karma, along which consciousness moved on its path of increasing transcendental awareness. While this notion appears to be quite specific to Weisthor, the references to occult architectural symbolism and the vehmgericht in his report indicate the influence of List or Gorsleben, most probably via Kirchhoff. Weisthor made at least five such land surveys around Germany, discovering a cruciform Irminist complex in the sacred Goslar area.[19]

Confident of Weisthor's patronage, Kirchhoff ultimately exhausted the patience of the Ahnenerbe, which Himmler had ordered to study his essays. One SS academic, appointed to examine a ritual stone at Baden-Baden and other Kirchhoff discoveries in April 1937, reported that Kirchhoff did not understand how to evaluate evidence, that his dating was absurd, and that his library contained many occult works by List, Koerner, and Gorsleben but almost nothing relating to scholarly prehistorical research.[20] When the Ahnenerbe rejected his essay on the Church in early 1938, Kirchhoff angrily accused the institute of participating in a Catholic conspiracy. Having by now had enough of Kirchhoff's endless submissions, the Ahnenerbe took a hard line, describing him as a 'fantasist of the worst kind' and his work as 'rubbish' in their reports.[21] Nevertheless, Himmler still wanted to know why Kirchhoff was being neglected by the Ahnenerbe and took a great interest in his description of a hexagonal religious complex in the countryside around the Raidenstein near Gaggenau. Kirchhoff connected this stone with the family traditions of Tarnhari, whose alleged sixteenth-century ancestor had borne the name Lautrer von

Döfering zum Raidenstein. Himmler insisted that the recalcitrant Ahnenerbe pursue the matter with Kirchhoff but the proposed archaeological dig was postponed indefinitely at the outbreak of the war.[22] The real importance of this dispute is its demonstration of Himmler's essential support for a lay occultist in the face of academic opposition from his staff in the Ahnenerbe. The fact that Weisthor and Kirchhoff continued to win the attention and favour of the Reichsführer-SS over their heads must have rankled badly with the members of the institute. For his part, Kirchhoff continued writing to the Ahnenerbe during the war. His last surviving letter to the Nazi authorities is a thirty-page occult treatise on the cause of German war reversals, addressed to Adolf Hitler via Himmler in late 1944.[23]

The development of the Wewelsburg near Paderborn as the SS order-castle and ceremonial centre must represent Weisthor's most spectacular contribution to the Third Reich. During the Nazi electoral campaign of January 1933 Himmler travelled through Westphalia, making his first acquaintance with 'the land of Hermann and Widukind'. The mythical atmosphere of the Teutoburger Forest, a drive up to the Hermannsdenkmal in fog, and the romantic Grevenburg castle, where the Führer's party stayed overnight, impressed Himmler deeply and made him think of acquiring a castle in this area for SS purposes.[24] After two other castles had been considered in the course of the year, Himmler viewed the Wewelsburg with members of his Personal Staff on 3 November 1933 and made his choice that very evening. After a further visit in April, the castle was officially taken over by the SS in August 1934. The Wewelsburg began its new career as a museum and SS officers' college for ideological education within the Race and Settlement Main Office, but was then placed under the direct control of the Reichsführer-SS Personal Staff in February 1935. This transfer reflected the increasing importance of the castle to Himmler and the germination of his plans for an SS order-castle, comparable to the Marienburg of the medieval Teutonic Knights.

The impetus for this changing conception of the Wewelsburg came almost certainly from Weisthor, who had accompanied Himmler on his visits to the castle.[25] Weisthor predicted that the castle was destined to become a magical German strongpoint in a future conflict between Europe and Asia. This idea was based on an old Westphalian legend, which had found romantic expression in a nineteenth-century poem.[26] This described an old shepherd's vision of a 'Battle at the Birchtree' in which an enormous army from the East would be finally beaten by the West. Weisthor brought this legend to Himmler's notice, claiming that the Wewelsburg was the 'bastion' against which this 'new Hun invasion' would be broken in fulfilment of the old prophecy. Karl Wolff, Chief Adjutant of the Personal Staff, recalled that Himmler was very moved by Weisthor's idea, which squared with his own notion of the SS's future role in the defence of Europe in a coming East-West confrontation which he expected in one to two hundred years' time.[27] While it cannot be definitely proved that Weisthor influenced the choice of the Wewelsburg in late 1933, his interpretation of the legend and other discussions with Himmler contributed importantly to the new conception of the Wewelsburg as an SS order-castle from 1935 onwards.

Weisthor also had an important influence on the development of SS ritual. In the course of his visits to the Wewelsburg, he established a warm friendship with the castle commandant, Manfred von Knobelsdorff. Inspired by their exchanges on religion and traditions, Knobelsdorff enthusiastically sought to revive the Irminist faith through various rituals held at the castle. These included pagan wedding ceremonies for SS officers and their brides, at which Weisthor officiated with an ivory-handled stick bound with blue ribbon and carved with runes, and the annual spring, harvest and solstice festivals for both the SS garrison and the villagers.[28] Knobelsdorff also closed his letters to Weisthor with the expression 'in Irminist loyalty' as a token of his interest in the old religion.[29] Himmler also commissioned Weisthor with the design of the SS *Totenkopfring*, a tangible symbol of membership in an order demanding complete obedience and loyalty. The ring was bestowed by Himmler personally and accompanied by a certificate describing its ornament and meaning. The ornament comprised a death's head, the double sig-rune, a swastika, a hagall rune, and the rune group ᚺᚺᛉ , which indicated the traditions of Weisthor.[30] The ring was moreover ritually linked with the Wewelsburg: in 1938 Himmler declared that the rings of all dead SS men and officers were to be returned for safekeeping in a chest at the castle as a symbolic expression of their enduring community in the order.[31] Here again, symbols and rituals demonstrate Weisthor's contribution to the ceremonial and pseudo-religion of the SS.

Himmler's ultimate plans for the Wewelsburg reflect its cult importance in the SS. In the large domed circular room of the massive enlarged north tower were to hang the coats-of-arms devised for dead SS-Gruppenführer; in the vault or SS-Obergruppenführer hall below unspecified ceremonies were envisaged. In the wings of the castle the study-rooms had already been named and furnished after figures representing a 'nordic mythology' such as Widukind, King Heinrich, Henry the Lion, King Arthur and the Grail. Area plans dating from between 1940 and 1942 provided for the relocation of the village some distance away and the building of an enormous architectural complex consisting of halls, galleries, towers, turrets, and curtain walls arranged in a semi-circular form on the hillside around the original medieval castle. Photographs of models showing the project, due for completion in the 1960s, suggest that Himmler dreamed of creating an SS vatican on an enormous scale at the centre of a millenarian Greater Germanic Reich.[32] It also seems likely that this visionary city would have witnessed the celebration of ancient religion and traditions initially revealed by Weisthor in the 1930s.

By spring 1935 Weisthor had moved from Munich to Berlin, where he continued his work in the Chief Adjutant's office of the Reichsführer-SS Personal Staff. This transfer to the top entourage indicates how highly Himmler valued Weisthor and their discussions together. According to eye witnesses, he was now busier than ever, surrounded by adjutants, orderlies, and the general hustle and bustle of government at the Reich capital. An official car collected Weisthor daily from his private villa in exclusive Grunewald, often before he had finished his breakfast, in order that the elderly officer could meet a demanding schedule of meetings, correspondence, and travel. Frequent social visitors to the villa at Kaspar Theyss Strasse 33 included Heinrich Himmler, Joachim von Leers, Edmund Kiss, Otto Rahn, Richard Anders, and Friedrich Schiller.[33] Besides his involvement with the Wewelsburg and his land surveys in the Black Forest and elsewhere, Weisthor continued to produce examples of his family traditions such as the Halgarita mottoes, Germanic mantras designed to stimulate ancestral memory, a Gotos calendar with verse for 1937, and the design for the SS *Totenkopfring*. An interesting political example of his work is a blueprint for the re-establishment of the Irminist religion in Germany which detailed provisions for restrictions on the priesthood, the nationalization of all ecclesiastical property, and the restoration and conservation of ancient monuments.[34] In September 1936 he was promoted SS-Brigadeführer (brigadier) in the Reichsführer-SS Personal Staff.

Otto Rahn (1904–39), the gifted young author and historian, also worked with Weisthor during his Berlin period. Born on 18 February 1904 at Michelstadt in Odenwald, Rahn had completed his university studies in literature and philology by 1928. Having become deeply interested in the medieval Cathars and grail legends, he researched and travelled widely in Provence, Catalonia, Italy, and Switzerland over the next five years. He ultimately fused the troubadour and *Minnesang* traditions, the Cathar heresy, and the legends of the grail to posit a gnostic religion of Gothic origin which had been brutally suppressed by the medieval Catholic Church, in his romantic history *Kreuzzug gegen den Gral [Crusade against the Grail]* (1933), which won him a European audience. After 1933 Rahn lived at Berlin and devoted himself to further studies in this vein. His quest for a Germanic religious tradition based on heresies and legends interested Himmler, who sought Rahn's collaboration in SS-sponsored research. In May 1935 Rahn joined Weisthor's department as a civilian. He joined the SS formally in March 1936 and was promoted to SS-Unterscharführer (NCO) the following month. The same year he undertook a research tour of Iceland under SS auspices and subsequently published a travel journal of his quest for the Cathar-Gothic tradition across Europe as *Luzifers Hofgesinde [Lucifer's Servants]* (1937). Following four months' military service with the SS-Death's Head Division 'Oberbayern' at Dachau concentration camp in late 1937, he was granted leave to devote himself fully to writing until his unexplained resignation from the SS in February 1939. He died shortly afterwards on 13 March 1939 due to exposure while walking on the mountains near Kufstein.[35]

Otto Rahn belongs to a European genre of romantic travel writers and historians. Among his triumphs of pastoral and atmospheric narrative are his vivid descriptions of the summer countryside in Hesse, the valleys of South Tyrol, the rocky fastness of Montségur and the local village where he spent a snowbound winter, and the desolation and monotony of Iceland. While Rahn's muse and middlebrow scholarship distinguish him from the whimsical Aryan occultists devoted to rune and megalith, there exists a certain identity of interests and motives between them. This common ground concerns the search for a lost Germanic tradition, supposedly obscured or destroyed by the Catholic Church and other hostile interests. In September 1935 Rahn wrote excitedly to Weisthor about the places he was visiting in his hunt for grail traditions in Germany, asking complete confidence in the matter with the exception of Himmler.[36] The attempt to discover such a tradition indicates the passion shared by Rahn, Weisthor and Himmler alike. All three men believed a secret key to ancient pagan culture could be found in the present.

When the SS decided to evaluate the ideological standpoint of

Evola, the Italian idealist philosopher, Weisthor was consulted. Baron Julius Evola (1898–1974) preached a doctrine of élitism and anti-modernity based on an Aryan-Nordic tradition defined by solar mythology and the male aristocratic principle as opposed to the female principle of democracy. These ideas found expression in his books on racism, grail-mysticism, and archaic traditions. Not entirely acceptable to the official fascist party line in Italy, Evola had begun to seek recognition abroad: his German editions comprised *Heidnischer Imperialismus* [*Pagan Imperialism*] (1933) and *Erhebung wider die moderne Welt* [*Revolt against the Modern World*] (1935). In early 1938 the SS started to investigate his ideas and Weisthor was asked to comment on a lecture delivered by Evola at Berlin in December 1937. Three further lectures were given in June 1938 and again Himmler referred the matter to Weisthor, with the additional request that he review Evola's book on pagan imperialism from the perspective of his own traditions. Weisthor replied that Evola worked from a basic Aryan concept but was quite ignorant of prehistoric Germanic institutions and their meaning. He also observed that this defect was representative of the ideological differences between fascist Italy and Nazi Germany and could ultimately prejudice the permanency of their alliance. Wiligut's report was evidently respected. In due course the SS ordered that Evola's activities in the Third Reich should be discouraged.[37]

The exact events leading up to Weisthor's resignation from the SS remain clouded in uncertainty. It is said that the old seer's health was in swift decline despite powerful medication intended to maintain his vitality and mental faculties; also that this very medication caused unfortunate changes in habit and personality, including heavy smoking and alcoholism. Given the jealousy surrounding Weisthor, any incompetence would have been quickly noted. However, Weisthor's psychiatric history still remained a closely guarded secret, for his *curriculum vitae* of May 1937 had been sealed after confidential scrutiny. But in November 1938 Karl Wolff visited Malwine Wiligut at Salzburg, whereupon his earlier certification became known and a source of embarrassment to Himmler. In February 1939 Wolff informed Weisthor's staff that the SS-Brigadeführer had retired on his own application for reasons of age and poor health and that his office would be dissolved. Himmler requested the return of Weisthor's SS *Totenkopfring*, dagger, and sword, which he sentimentally kept under personal lock and key. Weisthor's official retirement from the SS was dated 28 August 1939.[38]

The SS continued to look after Wiligut in retirement, but the final years of his life are a record of oblivion and pitiable wanderings in wartime Germany. Elsa Baltrusch, a member of the Reichsführer-SS Personal Staff, was appointed Wiligut's housekeeper and they were allocated quarters in Aufkirchen. This soon proved too remote for Wiligut after being in the thick of things in Berlin, so they moved to his beloved Goslar in May 1940. Their accommodation at the Werderhof in the town was then unfortunately requisitioned as a medical research establishment in 1943, whereupon the couple moved to a small SS guest-house on the Wörthersee in Carinthia and spent the remainder of the war in Austria. After being evicted and assigned to a refugee camp at St Johann near Velden by the English occupying forces, Wiligut suffered a stroke resulting in partial paralysis and loss of speech. He and his companion were subsequently permitted to return to his old family home at Salzburg, but the unhappy past made this an unsatisfactory arrangement for everyone concerned. Wiligut wanted to go back to his elective homeland Germany, so the pair travelled on to Baltrusch's own family at Arolsen in December 1945. The journey proved too much for the old man and he was hospitalized on arrival. Karl Maria Wiligut died on 3 January 1946, the last of his secret line.[39]

15

Ariosophy and Adolf Hitler

THE reactionary political motives and revolutionary expectations of the various Armanists, Ariosophists, and rune occultists admit of comparison with the ideas of National Socialism. The enthusiasm of the Aryan occultists for Nazism has already been noted: Lanz von Liebenfels wrote in 1932 'Hitler is one of our pupils',[1] and both Werner von Bülow and Herbert Reichstein applauded the advent of the Third Reich in their magazines. But our final question must be to what extent Ariosophy actually influenced Nazism. Some answers to this problem have already been given. The lineage of the early Nazi Party in respect of its sponsors, newspaper, and symbol has been traced to the Thule Society, the Germanenorden, and thus to the ideas of Guido von List. It has also been shown how Himmler officially patronized Karl Maria Wiligut, whose prehistorical speculations were rooted in the ideas of List and his Armanist epigones. In order to complete our enquiry, attention must now be focused on the beliefs of Adolf Hitler and their possible debt to Ariosophy.[2]

Friedrich Heer has described the various towns where the young Hitler lived, commenting on their cultural atmosphere and potential influence upon him. In 1889 Hitler was born at Braunau am Inn, a riverside town on the Austrian-Bavarian border where his father served as an imperial customs officer. Between 1892 and 1895 his father was posted to Passau. The dominant baroque Catholic culture of this old ecclesiastical centre was visibly expressed in the cathedral, churches, monasteries, and chapels of the town, the ubiquitous clergy and the rich liturgical festivals. Heer has suggested that this ambience may have instilled a religious-millenarian awareness in the infant Hitler which later characterized his emotional outlook and world-view. Such an influence would have been subsequently deepened by his attendance at the Benedictine monastery school at Lambach from

1897 to 1899. Here Hitler is said to have been happy, taking an active part in the ceremonial and pageantry of the church which again dominated the face of this town.[3] The frequent depiction of village churches, monasteries and the monumental ecclesiastical architecture of Vienna in Hitler's own paintings between 1906 and 1913 provides further evidence of his attraction to the visual metaphor of the Catholic Church and its thousand-year continuity in his Austrian homeland.[4] This deep involvement in Catholic culture could imply an imaginative disposition towards the dualist-millenarian ideas of Ariosophy.

Hitler's period at Linz from 1900 to 1905 was less fortunate. The sophisticated urban environment put great pressure on a boy more used to school life in small towns and the country and his academic performance deteriorated. But in this town Hitler encountered nationalism and Pan-Germanism. Linz was close to the Czech-settled lands of South Bohemia and the incursion of Czech immigrants, business, and property interests was warily watched by the Austrian Germans of the town. Hitler's history master, Dr Leopold Pötsch, was prominent in several nationalist *Vereine* and also introduced his boys to epic periods of German history with magic lantern shows on the Nibelungs, Charlemagne, Bismarck, and the establishment of the Second Reich. Hitler was always enthusiastic for these history lessons and his belief in 'Germany' as a mother symbol of romantic *Volk* identity and imperial continuity may be traced to his school experiences in Linz. Heer has elicited from survivors several descriptions of Hitler's childhood interest in German racial characteristics and his segregation of classmates into Germans and non-Germans.[5] This early fixation on mother Germany across the border in the context of both manichaean and millenarian ideas would also find an echo in the writings of both List and Lanz von Liebenfels.

At a more rational level, Hitler's independent move to Vienna for formal artistic training was prompted by his interests and ambitions, but his life in the capital was fatally flawed by his failure to secure admission to the Academy of Fine Arts. Following his initial rejection in October 1907 and the death of his mother that Christmas, Hitler returned to Vienna in February 1908 in order to lead the life of a private artist-student with modest means. Together with August Kubizek, his boyhood friend from Linz, he enjoyed the galleries, the city architecture, and Wagner operas until the summer. However, his increasing sense of exclusion from a proper artistic career, his aversion to any other kind of work, and the steady depletion of his funds gradually vitiated this idyll. In November 1908 he vanished from his shared lodging and henceforth lived alone. The slow descent into genteel poverty followed by destitution had begun. Now Hitler experienced the dark side of life in the city. The dingy rented rooms, the crowded soup-kitchens and the filthy flop-houses, the poor streets teeming with foreign immigrants from the provinces, and the Jews with their strange garb and customs, represented a fallen world. Vienna and the multi-racial Habsburg empire appeared to Hitler in his misfortune as the complete antithesis of his fairytale image of mother Germany and her pure national culture. In such a mood Hitler would have been deeply receptive to the manichaean comic-book dualism of blonds and darks, heroes and sub-men, Aryans and *Tschandalen*, described in the *Ostara* of Lanz von Liebenfels.

But what is the evidence for Hitler's acquaintance with the *Ostara* and its determinative influence besides these earlier predisposing factors? In the first place, the chronology is unobjectionable. By the middle of 1908 Lanz had already published 25 *Ostara* numbers and would have published a further 40 numbers before Hitler finally left Vienna in May 1913. In view of the similarity of their ideas relating to the glorification and preservation of the endangered Aryan race, the suppression and ultimate extermination of the non-Aryans, and the establishment of a fabulous Aryan-German millennial empire, the link between the two men looks highly probable. Hitler stated subsequently in *Mein Kampf* that his experiences at Vienna had laid the granite foundation of his outlook and that he had studied racist pamphlets at this time.[6] The likelihood of a local ideological influence again seems substantial. Earlier Hitler biographers tended to confine their surveys of Hitler's supposed sources of inspiration to intellectually respectable writers on racial superiority and anti-Semitism such as Gobineau, Nietzsche, Wagner, and Chamberlain. But there is no evidence that Hitler read their scholarly works. It is altogether more likely that he would have picked up ideas to rationalize his own dualist outlook and fixation on Germany from cheap and accessible pamphlets in contemporary Vienna.

Austrian scholars were the first to suggest that Hitler gleaned the materials for his racist political ideas from the trivial literature of Lanz von Liebenfels. As early as the 1930s August M. Knoll used to ridicule the Nazis before his student audiences at the University of Vienna by observing that the German leader had simply taken his ideas from the locally notorious and scurrilous *Ostara*. This originally polemical speculation was first pursued by Wilfried Daim after the war. Daim was a psychologist with a particular interest in sectarian beliefs and political ideologies. When Knoll mentioned the congruence of Lanz's bizarre ideas with Nazi aims, Daim was very interested as a result of his plan to write a book about Nazism as a perverse religious system. The existence of a sectarian father behind Nazi ideology would lend great weight to his thesis. It was soon discovered that Lanz was still alive and the two scholars arranged to interview him at his home in Vienna-Grinzing. On 11 May 1951 Lanz told Daim that Hitler had visited him at the *Ostara* office in Rodaun during 1909. Lanz recalled that Hitler mentioned his living in the Felberstrasse, where he had been able to obtain the *Ostara* at a nearby tobacco-kiosk. He said that he was interested in the racial theories of Lanz and wished to buy some back numbers in order to complete his collection. Lanz noticed that Hitler looked very poor and gave him the requested back numbers free, as well as two crowns for his return fare to the city centre.

Lanz's statement was confirmed by several pieces of independent evidence. According to police records, Hitler was indeed resident from 18 November 1908 to 20 August 1909 at Felberstrasse 22/[16], a dreary street on the north side of the Westbahnhof, where he had moved after abruptly quitting the room he shared with August Kubizek. Daim also discovered from the Austrian Tobacco Authority that a kiosk had been leased at this time on the ground floor of Felberstrasse 18. Lanz is not likely to have known these details unless told them by Hitler himself. The mention of Hitler's poverty also rings true, for Hitler's funds began to run very low in the course of 1909; the autumn and winter witnessed the most wretched period of his life when he was forced into short-stay warming-houses and doss-houses for heat and shelter at night. Finally, it must be remembered that Lanz would have been unlikely to fabricate an association with Hitler and Nazi ideology in 1951: Vienna was under Allied occupation and political investigations were still in progress. It therefore seems most probable that Hitler did visit Lanz and that he was a regular *Ostara* reader.[7]

In order to corroborate Lanz's testimony further, Daim subsequently interviewed Josef Greiner, whom he regarded as the principal surviving witness of Hitler's life in Vienna after 1908. In his post-war Hitler biography *Das Ende der Hitler-Mythos* (1947), Greiner claimed to have been friendly with Hitler at the men's hostel on the Meldemann-strasse in Vienna-Brigittenau, where Hitler lived from February 1910 until his departure for Munich in May 1913. On 31 December 1955 Greiner supplied Daim with further details about Hitler's life in the hostel. He recalled that Hitler possessed a substantial *Ostara* collection—there must have been at least fifty numbers in a stack about 25 centimetres in thickness. When showed copies of the first *Ostara* series by Daim, Greiner said he remembered the distinctive comet design on the covers of the earliest numbers. He also claimed to remember Hitler engaging in heated discussions with a fellow-boarder called Grill about the racial ideas of Lanz von Liebenfels. In a later conversation with Daim, Greiner stated that Hitler and Grill had once travelled out to Heiligenkreuz Abbey to ask for Lanz's current address.[8]

Despite Daim's conviction that Greiner's memory seemed reliable and his statements authentic, his testimony must be regarded with the utmost caution. In the first place, Greiner's Hitler biography has been found so inaccurate and even simply inventive on points of detail that several scholars have doubted whether Greiner ever knew Hitler at all.[9] The most important doubts concerning his authenticity as a source concern his dating. Greiner stated to Jetzinger that he befriended Hitler at the hostel in 1907 and that their acquaintance ended when he went to study engineering at Berlin in late 1909. Since Hitler did not move into the hostel until early 1910, Greiner cannot have met Hitler, unless he had mistaken the dates. On the other hand, the memoirs of Reinhold Hanisch, another hostel inmate and the salesman of Hitler's paintings, do refer to a man called Greiner at the hostel.[10] This mention would suggest that Greiner did know Hitler at the hostel, but that he forgot the exact date. But Greiner's facility for invention was still apparent in his testimony to Daim: Hitler cannot have possibly wanted to learn Lanz's address from the Heiligenkreuz monks if he already possessed *Ostara* numbers which gave an office address, nor if he had recently visited Lanz in 1909. This visit to the abbey cannot have occurred earlier, because neither man had met Grill, Hitler's companion on the alleged Heiligenkreuz excursion, until they moved into the hostel in 1910. The only valuable evidence in Greiner's testimony relating to the possible influence of Lanz on Hitler is that Hitler possessed an *Ostara* collection and that he often discussed Lanz's theories with Grill during his time at the men's hostel.

On the basis of these testimonies by Lanz and Greiner, the internal evidence of an ideological congruence between Lanz and Hitler may be reviewed. The most important similarity is their manichaean-dualist outlook: the world is divided into the light blue-blond Aryan heroes and the dark non-Aryan demons, working respectively for good and evil, order and chaos, salvation and destruction, in the universe. The Aryan is regarded by both men as the source and instrument of all that is fine, noble, and constructive, while the non-Aryan is allegedly bent upon confusion, subversion, and corruption. Lanz's detailed provisions for Aryan supremacy were also echoed in the Third Reich: decrees banning inter-racial marriages, the extinction of inferior races and the proliferation of pure-blooded Germans by means of polygamy, and the care of unmarried mothers in the SS *Lebensborn* maternity homes were all anticipated in the *Ostara*. Lanz's attitudes to sex and marriage were also shared by Hitler. Both men emphasized the propagative value of marital relations and regarded women ambivalently. Lanz described women as 'grown-up children' yet condemned their capricious tendency to foil the breeding of a master-race by their sexual preference for racial inferiors. Hitler also treated women as pets, and his own sexual relations were characterized by a mixture of reverence, fear, and disgust.

But Hitler would not have accepted other parts of Lanz's ideology. Lanz wanted a pan-Aryan state under Habsburg rule in Vienna, while Hitler despised the Austrian dynasty, averting his gaze from its racial Babylon to the German motherland across the border. Lanz's doctrine was also deeply imbued with Catholic and Cistercian liturgy: prayer, communion, the advent of a racially pure Christ-Frauja messiah, the establishment of priories for the Order of the New Templars, and the elaboration of ceremony would have possessed little appeal for Hitler, who rejected the ritual of Catholicism as an adolescent and later saw himself as the new German messiah. On the other hand, Hitler's enthusiasm for Wagner's chivalrous portrayal of the grail, its guardian knights and their idealism would have made him receptive to Lanz's notion of a crusading order dedicated to the purity of Aryan blood. In a conversation of 1934 Hitler paid tribute to this notion: 'How can we arrest racial decay? Shall we form a select company of the really initiated? An Order, the brotherhood of Templars round the holy grail of pure blood?'[11] This utterance could be traced to a pre-war encounter with Lanz and his Order of the New Templars as well as to the operas of Richard Wagner.

During the Third Reich Lanz is supposed to have been forbidden to publish, and his organizations, the ONT and the Lumenclub, were officially dissolved by order of the Gestapo.[12] These measures were most probably the result of the general Nazi policy of suppressing lodge organizations and esoteric groups, but it is also possible that Hitler wished to avoid any connection being made between his own political ideas and the sectarian doctrine of Lanz. A single Lanz monograph, *Das Buch der Psalmen teutsch* (1926), stands among the surviving 2,000 volumes of Hitler's personal library,[13] but this is neither conclusive evidence that the book was read nor does it essentially relate to Lanz's ideology, being a later liturgical work. It also remains a fact that Hitler never mentioned the name of Lanz in any recorded conversation, speech, or document. If Hitler had been importantly influenced by his contact with the *Ostara*, he cannot be said to have ever acknowledged this debt. However, given his rapid political advance in Germany during the 1920s, and his titanic stature in the 1930s, it is not likely that he would point to the scurrilous pamphlets of an abstruse mystic in Vienna as his original inspiration.

On the basis of the available evidence, then, it seems most probable that Hitler did read and collect the *Ostara* in Vienna. Its contents served to rationalize and consolidate his emerging convictions about the dualist nature of humanity and world-development and buttressed his own sense of mission to save the world. If his acquaintance with the series was limited to the numbers that appeared between late 1908 and the middle of 1909, he must have been interested in Lanz's empirical studies of racial characteristics, the differences between the blonds and the darks and the discussion of women, feminism, and sexuality in these particular issues. If he continued to collect numbers at the men's hostel between 1910 and May 1913, he would have become familiar with the full scope of Lanz's manichaean fantasy of the struggle between the blonds and the darks for racial and political supremacy. Only his continued subscription at Munich would have introduced him to Lanz's concept of the grail as the central mystery of the Aryan race-cult and to materials about the 'ario-christian' Templars. But even if Hitler read no further *Ostara* numbers after leaving Vienna, he would still have absorbed the essential aspects of Lanz's Ariosophy: the longing for an Aryan theocracy in the form of a divinely-ordained dictatorship of blue-blond Germans over all racial inferiors; the belief in an evil conspiracy of such inferiors against the heroic Germans throughout history; and the apocalyptic expectation of a pan-German millennium that would realize Aryan world-supremacy. Such black-and-white dualism was the granite foundation of Hitler's political outlook for life.

The evidence for Hitler's knowledge of Guido von List and his Armanism is less firm and rests upon the testimony of a third party and some literary inferences. When Daim delivered a lecture at Munich in 1959 about Lanz von Liebenfels, he mentioned his associate List in the subculture of Aryan occultism at Vienna. Daim was subsequently approached by a certain Elsa Schmidt-Falk, who claimed that Hitler had regularly visited her and her late husband in Munich. At these meetings Hitler frequently mentioned his reading List and quoted the old master's books with enthusiasm. Hitler also told her that some members of the List Society at Vienna had given him a letter of introduction to the President of the Society at Munich, but this came to nothing as Wannieck was 'either mortally ill or had already died' by the time Hitler finally arrived in Munich.[14] A further Munich source could corroborate Hitler's interest in List. In 1921 Dr Babette Steininger, an early Nazi Party member, presented Hitler with Tagore's essay on nationalism as a birthday present. On the flyleaf she wrote a personal dedication: 'To Adolf Hitler my dear Armanen-brother'.[15] Her use of the esoteric term suggests a shared interest in the work of List. A final indication that Hitler might have been familiar with List's themes is provided by Kubizek's description of Hitler's draft for a play he wrote at their shared lodging in 1908. The drama was based on the conflict between Christian missionaries and the Germanic priests of a pagan shrine in the Bavarian mountains.[16] Hitler might have easily taken this idea from List's *Die Armanenschaft der Ario-Germanen*, published earlier in the same year.

Elsa Schmidt-Falk was in charge of a genealogical research group within the Nazi Party at Munich during the 1920s. She claims that she often met Hitler, whom she also knew from his Vienna period. According to her, Hitler was particularly inspired by List's *Deutsch-Mythologische Landschaftsbilder*, of which he possessed the first edition. He also had a high opinion of *Der Unbesiegbare* (1898) and discussed most of the Ario-Germanic researches with her. Her other claims included the following statements: Hitler was inspired by List to undertake subterranean explorations at St Stephen's Cathedral in Vienna; Hitler was so intrigued by List's burial of the wine bottles at Carnuntum in 1875 that he wanted to exhume this 'first swastika' once he had annexed Austria; Hitler's delight over List's regional folklore led him to suggest that she write a 'Bayrisch-Mythologische Land-schaftsbilder' about the environs of Munich; other Nazi leaders, including Ludendorff, Hess, and Eckart, were supposed to have read List.[17]

The full range of Schmidt-Falk's claims make her testimony rather dubious. There is no evidence for Hitler ever having a particular interest in either archaeology or folklore. If Hitler had read only the first edition of *Deutsch-Mythologische Landschaftsbilder*, he would not have been familiar with the Carnuntum swastika story, which appeared in the second edition of 1913. The source of her knowledge concerning the reading of Eckart, Hess, and Ludendorff is unspecified, nor is it clear when she first heard Hitler speak about the annexation of Austria. Both statements would indicate her involvement with the Nazi movement from at least 1923 through to the Third Reich. Hitler's interest in genealogy, besides his own, with especial reference to the ancestry of other Nazi leaders, which she allegedly undertook to research for him, is also unproven. But even if Schmidt-Falk's testimony were dismissed altogether, there remains Steininger's dedication of 1921, which implies a knowledge of List on the part of Hitler.

The political aspects of List's thought would have appealed to the young Hitler. List fulminated against the political emergence and nationalism of the Czechs, a sentiment in accord with Hitler's feelings at Linz. List also condemned the fantastic monolithic conspiracy of the Great International Party against the Germans and its manifestations as democracy, parliamentarianism, feminism, and 'Jewish' influences in the arts, press, and business. List's sharp division of the world into Aryans and non-Aryans also paralleled the dualistic doctrine of Lanz von Liebenfels. In his blueprint for the restoration of an Armanist state, List prescribed a rigid hierarchy of offices, levels of authority and traditional administrative districts (*Gaue*), which were subsequently emulated by *völkisch* leagues, the early Nazi Party, and the Third Reich. While the Aryans enjoyed many privileges and all political rights, the non-Aryans were to be trampled on as servants and slaves. List also preached the advent of a pan-German millennium, a new Ario-Germanic state with world-hegemony. Hitler could have identified with all this and also with List's romantic evocation of the ancient Armanist world with its heroic leaders and their institutions.

It is less likely that Hitler would have appreciated the antiquarian tendency of List's work. Hitler was certainly interested in Germanic legends and mythology,[18] but he never wished to pursue their survival in folklore, customs, or place-names. He was interested in neither heraldry nor genealogy. Hitler's interest in mythology was related primarily to the ideals and deeds of heroes and their musical interpretation in the operas of Richard Wagner. Before 1913 Hitler's utopia was mother Germany across the border rather than a prehistoric golden age indicated by the occult interpretation of myths and traditions in Austria. Hitler's love of Germany would also have precluded any sympathy with List's celebration of the Habsburg dynasty as an Armanist survival and Vianio nina-Vienna as the holy Aryan city of old. Once Hitler had moved to Germany, he is unlikely to have either maintained or subsequently developed an interest in an Austrian *völkisch* antiquary. As in the case of Lanz, Hitler would have been attracted to the basic manichaean dualism of List's racism, but his occult traditions would have held less appeal.

Hitler left Vienna at the end of May 1913 and travelled westwards to the land of his dreams. On arrival in Munich his heart leapt at the sights and sounds of a truly German city. He took lodgings with a tailor's family at Schleissheimerstrasse 34 and registered with the police as a 'painter and artist'. He spent the following months exploring the Bavarian capital and its environs and eking out a modest living as a relatively successful painter of postcard views. Many of his Munich paintings survive but there is little further evidence of his activities at Munich before his call-up in August 1914.[19] No documents have been found to link him with the Germanenorden, the Reichs-hammerbund, or other *völkisch* groups in the city prior to the First World War. Hitler did once refer to his reading Philipp Stauff after volunteering for the German army in 1914.[20] Stauff impressed him concerning the dominance of Jewry in the German press, but there was no indication that Hitler knew anything about his sectarian and esoteric interests.

Hitler's disinterest in *völkisch* ideas relating to ancient Germanic institutions and traditions is reflected in the development of the early Nazi Party under his leadership. While the Thule Society and the Germanenorden were devoted to the Aryan-racist-occult cultural complex, their successor organizations stressed the lost war, the betrayal of Germany by politicians, and bitter anti-Semitism in their discussions and propaganda. Rudolf von Sebottendorff, the founder-leader of the Thule Society and an admirer of List, Lanz, and Stauff, encouraged the establishment of the Political Workers' Circle (PAZ) with respect to mundane grievances in order to catch 'the man in the street'. The German Workers' Party (DAP) also had little concern for *völkisch*-cultural materials. There is no evidence that Hitler ever attended the Thule Society. Sebottendorff quitted the Thule after the hostage fiasco in June 1919, while Hitler first encountered the DAP in September 1919. Johannes Hering's diary of Society meetings mentioned the presence of other Nazi leaders between 1920 and 1923, but not Hitler himself.[21] Once Hitler was in firm control of the DAP, the party's chief attribute was anti-Semitic oratory at public meetings and street activism, while any *völkisch*-cultural interests were relegated to the preserve of back room enthusiasts.

In *Mein Kampf* Hitler denounced the '*völkisch* wandering scholars' and cultists as ineffectual fighters in the battle for Germany's salvation and poured scorn on their antiquarianism and ceremonial.[22] This statement has been variously interpreted as an attack on Karl Harrer of the PAZ and his attempt to control the early DAP, or on the Strasser group in North Germany during the 1920s. In any case, the outburst clearly implies Hitler's contempt for conspiratorial circles and occult-racist studies and his preference for direct activism. Hitler was surely influenced by the millenarian and manichaean motifs of Ariosophy, but its descriptions of a prehistoric golden age, a gnostic priesthood, and a secret heritage in cultural relics and orders had no part in his political or cultural imagination. These ideas were of course wide-spread in the *völkisch* movement, but Hitler's achievement was the transformation of this nationalist feeling and nostalgia into a violently anti-Semitic movement concerned with national revolution and revival. By contrast, Heinrich Himmler always dwelt on the old Germanic roots of his utopian plans.

Ariosophy is a symptom rather than an influence in the way that it anticipated Nazism. Its origins lay in the conflict of German and Slav interests in the borderlands of nineteenth-century Austria. Guido von List's eulogy of the ancient Teutons fostered German folk identity in the ethnically mixed provinces and towns of the late Habsburg empire. He then assimilated theosophy and occultism for his fabulous prehistory, describing the ancient priest-kings, their suppression by anti-German interests, and an apocalyptic prophecy of a glorious new Pan-German empire. Lanz von Liebenfels also formed his political outlook in the Pan-German movement of Schönerer but graduated to a more universal type of racism. Having engrossed himself in Monism and Social Darwinism, he developed his own mystical pan-Aryan doctrine. He combined anthropology and zoology with the Scriptures in his account of the heroic Aryan god-men, their near extinction due to the wiles of racial inferiors, and the possibility of their resurrection through a racist-chivalrous cult. List and Lanz both clearly expressed a widespread sense of German insecurity in late imperial Austria.

Their doctrines advocated the rule of gnostic élites and orders; the stratification of society according to racial purity and occult initiation; the ruthless subjugation and ultimate destruction of non-German inferiors; and the foundation of a great pan-German empire with world-hegemony. Only extreme insecurity and anxiety among the

German nationalists of Austria can account for these narcissistic, paranoid, and grandiose fantasies. These ideas found enthusiastic acceptance among the anti-Semitic conventicles of Wilhelmian Germany and exercised a renewed appeal to *völkisch* groups after its military defeat. The noxious psychological atmosphere of the war and its confused aftermath fostered myths of plots and visions of a new Reich. Small groups and magazines devoted to Armanism, Ariosophy, and rune occultism conjured the image of a heroic and powerful Germany against the tribulations of the Weimar Republic. Ariosophy continued to find its votaries from its beginnings in Vienna around 1890 until the Nazi revolution of 1933. The fantasies were then realized in the great homecoming of the Third Reich with its creation of a new pan-German order in Central and Eastern Europe.

The appeal of Nazism was based on powerful fantasies designed to relieve acute feelings of anxiety, defeat, and demoralization. An anti-German conspiracy of Jews and their minions was supposed to be threatening the very survival of the German nation. The Socialists, the 'November criminals' (the signatories of the shameful 1918 armistice), the Bolsheviks, the Freemasons, and even modern artists were all seen as agents of a monstrous Jewish plot to destroy Germany.[23] Only the total destruction of the Jews could thus save the Germans and enable them to enter the promised land. The chiliastic promise of a Third Reich echoed medieval Joachite prophecy and remained a potent metaphor in the fantasy-world of so many Germans who bemoaned the lost war, the harsh terms of the peace settlement, and the misery and chaos of the early Weimar Republic. These myths of conspiracy and millennium were rekindled by the economic crash and depression in the period 1930–33.

Semi-religious beliefs in a race of Aryan god-men, the needful extermination of inferiors, and a wonderful millennial future of German world-dominion obsessed Hitler, Himmler, and many other high-ranking Nazi leaders.[24] When the endless columns of steel-helmeted legionaries marched beneath the swastika at the massive martial displays of the 1930s, Germany was effectively saluting the founder-emperor of a new One Thousand Year Reich. But all this optimism, exuberance, and expectation was matched by a hellish vision. The shining new order was sustained by the wretched slave-cities where the Jewish demons were immolated as a burnt sacrifice or holocaust. The Nazi crusade was indeed essentially religious in its adoption of apocalyptic beliefs and fantasies including a New Jerusalem (cf. Hitler's plans for a magnificent new capital at Berlin) and the destruction of the Satanic hosts in a lake of fire. Auschwitz, Sobibor, and Treblinka are the terrible museums of twentieth-century Nazi apocalyptic.

The Nazi dreams did not come true. The Great Hall of Berlin with its enormous dome was not completed in 1950; the Wewelsburg was not reconstructed as a gigantic SS vatican by the 1960s; the giant motorways and broad gauge railways as far as the Caucasus and the Urals were never laid; Western Russia was not transformed into a huge colonial territory for German soldier-peasants; nor did the SS *Lebensborn* stud-farms produce 150 million pure-blooded Germans for the New Order.[25] The glorious One Thousand Year Reich actually ended a mere twelve years after its proclamation with the military defeat of Nazi Germany in 1945. But even if these grandiose plans and megalomaniac visions had not gone beyond the stage of maps, memoranda and miniature models, the Third Reich had accomplished sufficient demolition of the old order in Europe for it to remain an outrage which still haunts literature, films, and the memory of survivors. Both Ariosophy and the Nazi fantasies offer important materials for a study of apocalyptic hysteria in the leadership of a modern state. With the growth of religious nationalism in the late twentieth century, an understanding of the preconditions for such apocalyptic remains a crucial factor in the maintenance of global security.

APPENDIX A

GENEALOGY OF ADOLF JOSEF LANZ
ALIAS JÖRG LANZ VON LIEBENFELS

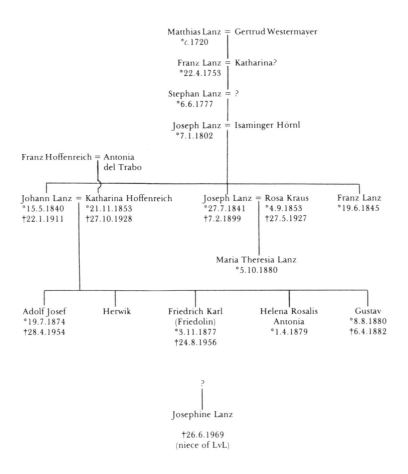

Source: Parish Registers at the Catholic Church of St Jakob,
Cumberland Strasse, Vienna-Penzing XIV.

APPENDIX B

GENEALOGY OF THE SEBOTTENDORFF FAMILY

(a) Von der Rose Line

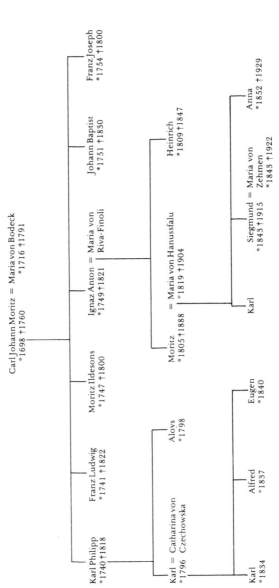

Sources: *Gothaische Genealogische Taschenbücher der freiherrlichen Häuser 7* (1857), 700–3; ibid., 38 (1888), 776f.

(b) Lortzendorff Line

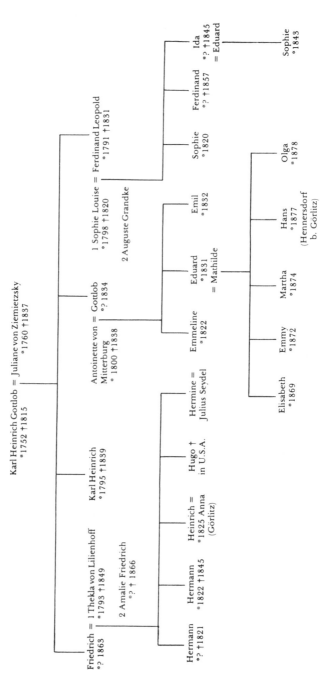

Source: *Genealogisches Taschenbuch der adligen Häuser* 12 (Brno, 1887), 440–2.

The History of Ariosophy

BETWEEN January 1929 and June 1930 a long essay by Lanz appeared in serial form in the *Zeitschrift für Geistes- und Wissenschaftsreform*. 'Die Geschichte der Ariosophie' claimed to trace the history of the ariosophical racial religion and its opponents from earliest times up until the present. This account provides a graphical account of Lanz's neo-manichaean conception of the world, inasmuch as he attempted to identify all historical agents as being within one or other of two eschatological camps, working respectively for good or evil, light and darkness, order and chaos.

According to Lanz, the earliest recorded ancestors of the present 'ario-heroic' race were the Atlanteans, who had lived on a continent situated in the northern part of the Atlantic Ocean.[1] They were supposedly descended from the original divine *Theozoa* with electromagnetic sensory organs and super-human powers. Catastrophic floods eventually submerged their continent in about 8000 BC and the Atlanteans migrated eastwards in two groups. The Northern Atlanteans streamed towards the British Isles, Scandinavia, and Northern Europe, while the Southern Atlanteans migrated across Western Africa to Egypt and Babylonia, where they founded the antique civilizations of the Near East. The ariosophical cult was thus introduced to Asia, where the idolatrous beast-cults of miscegenation had flourished.[2]

Lanz claimed that the racial religion had been actively preached and practised in the ancient world. He asserted that Moses, Orpheus, Pythagoras, Plato, and Alexander the Great had been its champions. The laws of Moses and Plato's esteem for the aristocratic principle, and his provision for a caste of priest-kings in *The Republic*, proved them Ariosophists. Lanz conflated the writings of these ancient thinkers into a monolithic ariosophical tradition, which focused on the famous library at Alexandria, which allegedly housed a magnificent collection of ariosophical scriptures. Scholars and priests from all over the world were said to have come here to study the old papyri of the Southern Atlanteans; here the Old Testament (a fundamental ariosophical text) was edited from scattered chronicles discovered in Palestine; a college of priest-kings attached to the library spread the racist gnosis through mission-aries as far as China. The entire Hellenistic world was thus supposed to be familiar with Ariosophy before the advent of Christ-Frauja. The coming of Frauja and his establishment of the Church unleashed—so it was maintained—a new wave of ariosophical missionary activity in the world.[3]

The Germans entered the ariosophical tradition as a result of the missionary activities of Wulfila (c. 311–83). Wulfila translated the Bible into the Gothic language and carried the gospel to the Germanic tribes which had settled on the Balkan peninsula and beyond the River Danube. He had also been a partisan of the Arian heresy (so named after the theologian Arius of Alexandria). Lanz claimed that Wulfilia had actually preached the Aryan racial religion to the Germanic tribes. The suppression of the Arian heresy was interpreted as a victory for those devoted to the beast-cults. Lanz angrily charged these pagans with the defacement of the famous codex of the Gothic Bible. Because most of its racist passages had been excised, the Germans were permitted to neglect those strict eugenic observances, which would have guaranteed their transformation into god-men.[4] Lanz wrote five *Luzerner Briefe* numbers about the supposedly suppressed writings of Wulfila, together with a lexicon which provided a key to the hidden meaning of his surviving text.[5]

Despite the suppression of the Arian heresy and the failure of the Goths to realize the racial parousia within their extensive sixth-century empire, Ariosophy was fostered by new historical agents. Lanz identified the revival of Ariosophy in the monastic tradition of medieval Europe. Lanz regarded the Benedictine Order as a revival of the old Aryan colleges of priest-kings, dedicated to the preaching of the racist gnosis and organized on hierarchical principles. He wrote five studies about the ariosophical inspiration of the Benedictines.[6] After identifying the reformed monastic orders as agents of Ariosophy Lanz traced this spiritual heritage to the Cistercian Order. Lanz celebrated this order and its famous leader St Bernard of Clairvaux (1090–1153) as the principal force behind Ariosophy in the Middle Ages.[7]

Because of their close links with the Cistercian Order, the military order of the Knights Templars was regarded by Lanz as the armed guard of Ariosophy. Its rule had been composed by St Bernard, who wrote a homily of praise, *De Laude novae militiae* (c. 1132), and preached the Second Crusade in 1146. According to Lanz, the Templars were attempting to stem the tide of inferior races in the Near East, and so provide a bulwark of racial purity on the eastern flank of Aryan Christendom. Their efforts were paralleled in the west by the military orders of Calatrava, Alcantara, and Aviz, which had been formed during the mid-twelfth century to fight the Moors in Spain.

Lanz invoked the struggle of the medieval military orders against the heathen powers as a legitimation of his own crusade against populism, democracy, and Bolshevism in the twentieth century. With graphical imagination Lanz conjured up an ideological map of the world from the eighth to the seventeenth century: within the ever tightening ring formed by the Islamic powers of Northern Africa, the Middle East and eventually the

Balkans, and the amorphous Mongol hordes of the steppes, lay the embattled 'ario-christian' domain. The constant offensive of peoples devoted to the beast-cults and the threatened destruction of European racial supremacy necessitated the crusades of the military orders. Thus medieval Christendom was envisaged as a martial monastery of aristocratic and racial virtue, from which armed knight-monks rode forth to break the vice-like encirclement of the aggressive inferiors. These images nourished Lanz's vision of a modern crusade against the political emancipation of the masses through parliamentary democracy and socialist revolution.

The Middle Ages represented the golden age of Ariosophy to Lanz. A world of bold knights, pious monks, magnificent castles, beautiful monasteries was underlaid by the racist-chivalrous cult of the religious and military orders. The religion of this period was *'keine weichliche Humanitäts-Religion, sondern eine extrem-aristokratische und ariokratische Rassenkultreligion und eine straffe, supranationale, alle arioheroischen Völker umfassende wissenschaftliche, politische und wirtschaftliche Organisation, welche rücksichtslos, bisweilen sogar mit Härte, das Untermenschentum ausrottete, oder im Sklaven- und Hörigentum oder in Judenghetti in Untermenschentum ausrottete, oder im Sklaven- und Hörigentum oder in Judenghetti in wohltätigen Schranken hielt!'* ['no insipid humanity-religion, but an extremely aristocratic and "ariocratic" racial cult religion and an austere scientific, political and economic organization embracing all ario-heroic peoples. This religion ruthlessly exterminated sub-humanity or else kept it charitably within the bounds of slavery and serfdom or in Jewish ghettoes!"] Lanz regarded the 'cosmic week' (a subdivision of the Platonic year) from 480 to orders. The culture of the period was described as *'die letzte herrliche, berückend schöne Blüte arisch-heldischer Religion, Kunst und Wissenschaft'* ['the last magnificent and fascinatingly beautiful blossoming of ario-heroic religion, art and science'].[8]

The suppression of the Templars in 1308 signalled the end of this era and the ascendancy of the racial inferiors. Henceforth Europe witnessed the slow decline of her racial, cultural, and political achievements. The growth of towns, the expansion of capitalism, and its creation of an industrial labouring class led to the breakdown of the aristocratic principle and the strict maintenance of racial purity. Christianity was perverted into a sentimental altruistic doctrine, which taught that all men were equal, and that man should love his neighbour, irrespective of his race. During the 'cosmic week' from 1210 to 1920 Europe was subject to a process of debasement, culminating in the enormities of Bolshevism and its open proclamation of rule by the masses.

Lanz was obliged to trace a typically Listian secret heritage for his account of the post-medieval Ariosophy tradition. He claimed that Ariosophy survived due to an underground culture of 'several spiritual orders and genial mystics'. The first link in this cryptic heritage was the Order of Christ, which had been founded in 1319 by the King of Portugal. This order was a successor organization to the Templars in Portugal and played an important role in the Portuguese voyages of discovery. Henry the Navigator (1394–1460), who sponsored the voyages which led to the discovery of the Azores, Madeira and northwestern Africa, was a grand master of the order. His ships sailed under the flag of the order, which bore the red heraldic cross of the Templars. The later colonization of Angola, the circumnavigation of the Cape of Good Hope, and the discovery of the passage to India were also associated with the patronage of the order, which had been partially secularized in 1496. The former military orders of the Reconquista, the Order of Aviz in Portugal, and the Orders of Calatrava and Alcantara in Spain, were also secularized in the early sixteenth century. They became royal orders of chivalry, conferred in respect of services to the Portuguese and Spanish crowns.

The survival of these medieval military orders and their involvement with the expansion of European interests appealed to Lanz in his quest for ariosophical agents. He claimed that their Cistercian origins and colonial achievements identified them as the secret instruments of a post-medieval, world-wide ariosophical crusade. Lanz ascribed all Portuguese and Spanish colonialism to the ships sailing under the red Templar cross: *'Die Flotten der Ritterorden entdeckten und eroberten eine ganze neue Welt . . . ein Universalreich unter Führung der Christus- und Calatrava-Ritter . . . stolz wehte die Christritter-Flagge auf alle Meeren, die Flagge mit dem roten Tempel-Ritterkreuz . . . Die Häuser der spanisch-portuguesischen Cisterzienser-Ritter zählten in den verschiedensten Ländern in die Tausende'* [The fleets of the chivalrous orders discovered and conquered a whole new world . . . a universal empire under the leadership of the Knights of Christ and the Knights of Calatrava . . . The flag of the Knights of Christ flew proudly over all the seas, the flag with the red chivalric cross of the Templars. There were thousands of houses belonging to the Spanish and Portuguese Cistercian knights in the most diverse countries']. Lanz also identified the two Habsburg houses of Spain and Austria as the cryptic agents of a new ariosophical empire, which embraced both the Spanish possessions in Central and South America and the core area of Central Europe under Emperors Frederick IV, Maximilian I, *'die letzten Ariosophen auf Kaiserthronen'* ['the last Ariosophists upon imperial thrones'], and Charles V in the early sixteenth century. After the Spanish had secured the New World it remained to expand Habsburg-ariosophical influence in the East. Lanz claimed that this was the real aim of Charles's plans for a new crusade against the Turks with the aid of the Spanish-Portuguese orders and the Maltese Knights of St John. He believed that this project fell victim to the demonic machinations of the Jews and the Lutherans, who wished to stifle the ariosophical renaissance.[9]

The mortality of all human institutions and empires frustrated Lanz's attempt to posit an enduring and visible ariosophical tradition in history. His spurious accounts of the monastic and military orders, the Portuguese voyages of discovery, and Spanish and Austrian imperialism, which sought to conflate distinct historical enterprises into a movement of unique inspiration and ambition, could not bear the scrutiny of informed criticism. Lanz turned to more marginal social elements in his quest for an irrefutable agent of the ariosophical gnosis down through the ages. He posited an underground ariosophical tradition of mystics, romantics, and occultists.

In the Middle Ages this 'ario-christian' mystical tradition included the following: Hildegard of Bingen (d. 1179), Gertrude the Great (d. 1303), Mechtilde of Magdeburg (d. 1282?), Meister Eckhart (d. 1327), Jan von Ruysbroeck (d. 1381) and Thomas à Kempis (d. 1471). In the early modern period, these mystics were succeeded by famous pietists, including: Jakob Boehme (d. 1624), Angelus Silesius (d. 1671), Nikolaus von Zinzendorf (d. 1760) and Emanuel Swedenborg (d. 1772). After the Enlightenment Lanz's roll of ariosophical initiates included romantic thinkers and occultists of the nineteenth century including: J. B. Kerning (1774–1851), the mystical Freemason; Carl von Reichenbach (1788–1869), the Viennese investigator of animal magnetism; the French occultists, Eliphas Lévi (1810–75), Josephin Péladan (1858–1918), Gérard Encausse (1865–1916), and Edouard Schuré (1841–1929); and the theosophists, Helena Petrovna Blavatsky (1831–91), Franz Hartmann (1838–1912), Annie Besant (1847–1933), and Charles Webster Leadbeater (1847–1934). The tradition finally led to Guido von List, Rudolf John Gorsleben, and the mythologists of an Aryan Atlantis, Karl Georg Zschaetzsch, and Hermann Wieland.[10]

This evident decline in the historical significance and intellectual calibre of ariosophical initiates was a logical corollary of Lanz's rejection of the modern age and its achievements. Because he could not identify with any cultural tradition of established status in the present, he could claim only a small group of sectarians as the sole representatives of the formerly universal religion. As List had discovered in his search for theological antecedents, it was relatively easier to recruit initiates in the distant past but the task was far more difficult in an age which was characterized as subject to darkness, evil and illusion. Like the Gnostics of antiquity, the Ariosophists could only claim to carry a spark of divinity in the midst of chaos.

New Templar Verse

Der Sang der Nibelungenstrom

Die Quellen, die aus Rhätiens Gletscherhallen
Seit ew'ger Zeit vom Inn zur Donau wallen,
Im Reich des Ostara als mächt'ger Strom
Dann grüssen Linz und seinen Dom.

Doch, wo Granit durchbrach der Wogendrang,
Wo einst der Nibelungen Horn erklang,
Wo jetzt der Strudel engt die Wellenpfade,
Ragt eine Burg auf schroffem Felsgestade.

Da grüsst im hellen Frühlingssonnenschein
Das Kreuzesbanner hoch von Werfenstein.
Die Donauwellen raunen alte Weisen
Vom Freundesbund der Edlen und Templeisen.

Der neue Bund, der Meister Werk zu krönen,
Dient Gott in Tat und weihevollen Tönen.
Vom Geist des Willens froh, vernimmt die Schar,
Was einst der Templeisen Sendung war.

Aus reinem Quell strömt auch für sie die Kraft,
Die niemals alternd, neues Leben schafft,
Und Burg und Bund, der Reinheit nur geweiht,
Stehn fest im Strudel und im Drang der Zeit.

Fr. Aemilius

[*Ostara* I, 88 *Templeisen-Brevier, ein Andachtsbuch für
wissende und innerliche Ariochristen, 2. Teil* (1916), p. 4.]

Burg und Hain von Werfenstein

Bruder, was dein Auge schaut,
Hier im heil'gen Haine,
Leg es in dein Herze traut
Als vom 'Werfensteine'.

Nicht des Daseins Alltagsbrauch
Wird den Menschen höher heben.
Nur wenn hehrer Geister Hauch
Ihn durchwehet, wird sein Leben

Würdevoll und edler Art,
Und sein inn'res Auge sehen,
Was von Gott gesetzt ihm ward
Als der Seele Auferstehen

Aus der Sünde düst'rem Tal
Zu der Gralsburg lichten Höhen.
Doch der Pfad zu ihr ist schmal,
Wen'ge werden ihn nur gehen.

Siehe dort im Tempelhain
Weissgekleidete Gestalten.
Brüder sind's von Werfenstein,
Frauja's Wille lenkt ihr Walten.

Einsam in der Menschenwelt,
Sind vom Herrn sie auserkoren,
Das zu tun, was Gott gefällt,
Reinheit haben sie geschworen.

Reinheit in des Leibes Blut,
Reinheit in des Geistes Streben.
Reinheit heisst ihr Edelgut,
Reinheit wird zu Gott sie heben.

Geh, und wahre dieses Wort:
Reinheit in des Herzens Schreine.
Mach Dein Herz zum Felsenhort,
Machs zur Burg vom Werfensteine!

Fr. Detlef

[*Ostara* I, 88 *Templeisen-Brevier, ein Andachtsbuch für wissende und innerliche Ariochristen, 2. Teil* (1916), p. 5.]

APPENDIX E

The Modern Mythology
of Nazi Occultism

IN this book we have recounted the ideas and the history of Ariosophy, including its links with the Nazi movement in Germany. However, there is a persistent idea, widely canvassed in a sensational genre of literature, that the Nazis were principally inspired and directed by occult agencies from 1920 to 1945. This mythology does not owe its origin to Ariosophy, but to a post-war fascination with Nazism. This fascination is perhaps evoked by the irrationality and macabre policies of Nazism and the short-lived continental dominion of the Third Reich. A small fanatical party is recalled to have seized power in a European country and then succeeded in extending its state power across a huge area from the Atlantic coast to. the Caucasus mountains, and in the course of all this made the extermination of the Jews one of its primary objectives. The immense significance of these events has set National Socialism quite apart from other topics in modern history. The enduring fascination with Nazism is well illustrated by the annual volume of new books devoted to Hitler and other Nazi leaders, the Second World War, the SS, the concentration camps and the holocaust. The total defeat of the Third Reich and the suicides and executions of its major figures have further mystified the image of Nazism. To a young observer, National Socialism frequently appears as an uncanny interlude in modern history.

This mysterious image of the movement accounts for that plethora of popular novels describing the adventures of fugitive war criminals, secret post-war Nazi organizations, and the discovery of Hitler many years after his supposed death. The appeal of this sensational literature lies in the uncanny intrusion of an extinct order, generally considered both monstrous and forbidden, upon the familiar world of liberal institutions.[1] Nor is this fascination with the macabre aspects of Nazism confined to literature. Insignia and mementoes from the Third Reich are often collected by psychopaths and sadists, while extreme right-wing groups and bizarre sects have adopted Nazi dress and ceremonial.[2] This literature of clandestine revivals, illicit initiations, and the persistence of evil ideas and agencies defines a realm of speculative history which has built on slender evidence and tenuous associations to suggest that National Socialism was linked with occultism.

Since 1960 a number of popular books have represented the Nazi phenomenon as the product of arcane and demonic influence. The remarkable story of the rise of Nazism is implicitly linked to the power of the supernatural. According to this mythology Nazism cannot have been the mere product of socio-economic factors. No empirical or purely sociological thesis could account for its nefarious projects and continued success. The occult historiography chooses to explain the Nazi phenomenon in terms of an ultimate and arcane power, which supported and controlled Hitler and his entourage. This hidden power is characterized either as a discarnate entity (e.g. 'black forces', 'invisible hierarchies', 'unknown superiors'), or as a magical élite in a remote age or distant location, with which the Nazis were in contact. Recurring themes in the tradition have been a Nazi link with hidden masters in the East, and the Thule Society and other occult lodges as channels of black initiation. All writers of this genre thus document a 'crypto-history', inasmuch as their final point of explanatory reference is an agent which has remained concealed to previous historians of National Socialism.

The myth of a Nazi link with the Orient has a complex pedigree of theosophical provenance. The notion of hidden sacred centres in the East had been initially popularized by Blavatsky in *The Secret Doctrine*, based on the 'Stanzas of Dzyan', which she claimed to have read in a secret Himalayan lamasery. Blavatsky maintained that there existed many similar centres of esoteric learning and initiation; magnificent libraries and fabulous monasteries were supposed to lie in mountain caves and underground labyrinths in the remote regions of Central Asia. Notable examples of these centres were the subterranean city of Agadi, thought to lie in Babylonia, and the fair oasis of Shamballah in the Gobi Desert, where the divine instructors of the Aryan race were said to have preserved their sacred lore.[3] This mythology was extended by a French author, Joseph Saint-Yves d'Alveydre (1842–1909), who described the secret city of Agartha as a theocracy that guided the course of world history. According to telepathic messages which he claimed to have received from the Dalai Lama of Tibet, this city lay beneath the Himalayas.[4] Ferdynand Ossendowski, who travelled through Siberia and Mongolia after the Russian Revolution, gave some credence to these fantasies with his account of local Buddhist beliefs, which referred to the subterranean kingdom of Agartha where the King of the World reigned. This utopian kingdom was credited with supernatural powers that could be unleashed to destroy mankind and transform the surface of the entire planet.[5]

These ideas of a secret theocracy in the East were supplemented by the power of *vril*. In his novel *The Coming Race* (1871) Sir Edward Bulwer-Lytton had attributed this power to a subterranean race of men, the Vril-ya, psychically far in advance of the human species. The powers of *vril* included telepathy and telekinesis. This fictional notion was subsequently exploited by Louis Jacolliot, French consul in Calcutta under the Second Empire, in his studies of oriental beliefs and sects, which Blavatsky had herself quarried while working on the text of *Isis Unveiled* (1877).[6] The *vril* was understood to be an enormous reservoir of energy in the human organism, inaccessible to non-initiates. It was believed that whoever became master of the *vril* force could, like Bulwer-Lytton's race of Vril-ya, enjoy total mastery over all nature. Willy Ley, who emigrated to the United States in 1935 after a short career as a rocket engineer in Germany, wrote a short account of the pseudo-scientific ideas which had found some official acceptance during the Third Reich. Besides the World Ice Theory and the Hollow Earth Doctrine, which both found Nazi patrons, Ley recalled a Berlin sect which had engaged in meditative practices designed to penetrate the secret of *vril*.[7]

Louis Pauwels and Jacques Bergier cited this article in their *Le matin des magiciens* (1960), the second part of which was devoted to the Third Reich under the suggestive title 'A few years in the absolute elsewhere'. They exaggerated the significance of this obscure Berlin sect, in order to claim that the Nazi leadership was determined to establish contact with an omnipotent subterranean theocracy and gain knowledge of its power. It was thought that this power would enable Germany to conquer the whole world and transform human life in accordance with a millenarian vision:

> Alliances could be formed with the Master of the World or the King of Fear who reigns over a city hidden somewhere in the East. Those who conclude a pact will change the surface of the Earth and endow the human adventure with a new meaning for many thousands of years ... The world will change: the Lords will emerge from the centre of the Earth. Unless we have made an alliance with them and become Lords ourselves, we shall find ourselves among the slaves, on the dungheap that will nourish the roots of the New Cities that will arise.[8]

Pauwels and Bergier claimed that Hitler and his entourage believed in such ideas. In their account the Berlin sect was known as the Vril Society or the Luminous Lodge (perhaps a garbled reference to the Lumenclub of Vienna) and credited with the status of an important Nazi organization. A French psychiatrist was quoted to the effect that 'Hitler's real aim was to perform an act of creation, a divine operation . . . a biological mutation which would result in an unprecedented exaltation of the human race and the "apparition of a new race of heroes and demi-gods and god-men"'.[9] In this way, racism was linked with the occult mythology of an Eastern theocracy and the *vril* force to evoke a millenarian image of the intended Nazi future.

This legendary account of Nazi inspiration and ambition was underpinned by a fanciful account of the Thule Society and certain of its members. Pauwels and Bergier singled out two particular individuals as Hitler's occult mentors at Munich during the early 1920s. Dietrich Eckart (1868–1923) was a *völkisch* playwright and journalist of violently anti-Semitic prejudice, and a prominent figure among the nationalist circles of Munich. He is also known to have attended meetings of the Thule Society. It is accepted by scholars that Eckart not only gave force and focus to Hitler's burgeoning anti-Semitism after the war, but that he also introduced the young party leader to moneyed and influential social circles.[10] The second individual was Karl Haushofer (1869–1946), who had served as a military attaché in Japan and became a lifelong admirer of oriental culture. After the First World War Haushofer embarked upon an academic career in the field of political geography, subsequently gaining the Chair of Geopolitics at the University of Munich, where Rudolf Hess was his student assistant. Hitler was supposedly impressed by Haushofer's theories, taken from Sir Halford Mackinder, that the 'heartland' of Eastern Europe and Russia ensured its rulers a wider dominance in the world.[11]

According to Pauwels and Bergier, the influence of these two men upon Hitler chiefly related to the communication of arcane knowledge which was derived from unknown powers, with which contact had been established through the Thule Society and other cults. Eckart's role as an occult counsellor was related explicitly to invisible hierarchies.

> Thule was thought to have been the magic centre of a vanished civilization. Eckardt [*sic*] and his friends believed that not all the secrets of Thule had perished. Beings intermediate between Man and other intelligent beings from Beyond, would place at the disposal of the Initiates [i.e. the members of the Thule Society] a reservoir of forces which could be drawn on to enable Germany to dominate the world . . . [its] leaders would be men who knew everything, deriving their strength from the very fountain-head of energy and guided by the Great Ones of the Ancient World. Such were the myths on which the Aryan doctrine of Eckardt and Rosenberg was founded and which these prophets . . . had instilled into the mediumistic mind of Hitler. [The Thule Society] was soon to become . . . an instrument changing the very nature of reality . . . under the influence of Karl Haushofer the group took on its true character as a society of Initiates in communion with the Invisible, and became the magic centre of the Nazi movement.[12]

This spurious account also maintained that Haushofer was a member of the Luminous Lodge, a secret Buddhist society in Japan, and the Thule Society. As an initiate of the Eastern mysteries, rather than as a geopolitician, Haushofer is supposed to have proclaimed the necessity of 'a return to the sources' of the human race in Central Asia. He advocated the Nazi colonization of this area, in order that Germany could have access to the hidden centres of power in the East.[13] The consequence of this link with 'unknown superiors' was that the Thule Society was thus revealed to be the secret directing agent of the Third Reich. This assertion and the other details are entirely fallacious. The Thule Society was dissolved around 1925 when support had dwindled. While Eckart and Rosenberg were never more than guests of the Thule during its heyday, there is no evidence at all to link Haushofer with the group.

This fictitious image of the Thule Society was developed further by Dietrich Bronder in his book *Bevor Hitler kam* (1964). Bronder claimed that Haushofer met George Ivanovitch Gurdjieff, the Caucasian thaumaturge, at least three times between 1903 and 1908 in Tibet. Gurdjieff was supposed to have initiated Haushofer into the Tibetan mysteries.[14] The Thule Society was alleged to have renewed German contact with the secret monastic orders of Tibet through a small colony of Tibetan Buddhists, which was established at Berlin in 1928; an SS expedition was said to have gone to Tibet with the express purpose of setting up an apparently vital radio link between the Third Reich and the lamas in 1939. The 'Stanzas of Dzyan' were allegedly used as a code for all messages between Berlin and Lhasa during the war. Bronder completed his account with a spurious membership roll of the Thule Society which included: Sebottendorff, Guido von List, Lanz von Liebenfels, Mussolini, Hitler, Hess, Goering, Himmler, Frank, and Haushofer.[15] This mythical account posited the existence of a sinister link of diabolical influence between Nazi Germany and a theosophically imagined Tibet. It may also be noted that Bronder's work was the first crypto-history to introduce the Ariosophists. Similar bizarre accounts of Nazi satanism, using the stock properties of the Vril Society, the much abused Haushofer, and the Thule Society were reiterated in Werner Gerson, *Le nazisme, société secrète* (1969), Elisabeth Antebi, *Ave Lucifer* (1970), Jean-Claude Frère, *Nazisme et sociétés secrètes* (1974), and J. H. Brennan, *Occult Reich* (1974).

While these mystifications may be traced to theosophical notions, there are other mythological sources for this crypto-history. Trevor Ravenscroft attached to Nazism a mythology that stems from anthroposophy. Several years after the Second World War, Ravenscroft met Walter Johannes Stein (1891–1957), an Austrian Jew who had emigrated from Germany to Britain in 1933. Before the establishment of the Third Reich, Stein had taught at the Waldorf School in Stuttgart, which was run according to the anthroposophical principles of Rudolf Steiner. During his time there, Stein wrote a curious and learned book, *Weltgeschichte im Lichte des Heiligen Gral* (1928), which was based upon an anthroposophical interpretation of medieval literature and history. Stein argued that the grail romance of Wolfram von Eschenbach's *Parzival* (c.1200) had been written against the historical background of the ninth century, and that the fabulous characters of the epic corresponded to real persons who had lived during the Carolingian Empire. For example, the grail king Anfortas was named as King Charles the Bald, the grandson of Charlemagne; Cundrie, the sorceress and messenger of the grail, was considered to have been Ricilda the Bad; Parzival himself was named as

Luitward of Vercelli, the chancellor to the Frankish court; and Klingsor, the evil magician and owner of the Castle of Wonders, was identified as Landulf II of Capua, a man of sinister reputation due to his pact with the heathen powers of Islam in Arab-occupied Sicily. The battle between the Christian knights and their evil adversaries was understood as an allegory of the enduring struggle for possession of the Holy Lance, supposed to have pierced the side of Christ at his Crucifixion.[16]

Ravenscroft based his occult account of Nazism on Stein's work. In *The Spear of Destiny* (1972) he related how the young student Stein had discovered a second-hand copy of *Parzival* in an occult bookshop in the old quarter of Vienna in August 1912. This volume contained numerous jottings in the form of a commentary on the text, which interpreted the epic as trials of initiation upon a prescribed path to the attainment of transcendent consciousness. This interpretation was supported by many quotations drawn from oriental religions, alchemy, astrology, and mysticism. Stein also noted that a strong theme of racial hatred and pan-German fanaticism ran through the entire commentary. The name written on the inside cover of the book indicated that its previous owner was Adolf Hitler. His curiosity aroused concerning the jottings, Stein returned to the bookshop to ask the proprietor if he could tell him anything about Hitler. Ernst Pretzsche informed Stein that Hitler was an assiduous student of the occult and gave him his address. Stein sought Hitler out. In the course of their frequent meetings, in late 1912 and early 1913, Stein learned that Hitler believed that the Holy Lance could grant its owner unlimited power to perform either good or evil. The succession of previous owners allegedly included Constantine the Great, Charles Martel, Henry the Fowler, Otto the Great, and the Hohenstauffen emperors. As the property of the Habsburg dynasty, the Lance now lay in the Hofburg at Vienna. Hitler was determined to gain possession of the Lance in order to secure his own bid for world domination. Ravenscroft also included the sensational story that Hitler had accelerated his occult development through the use of hallucinogenic peyote, to which he had been introduced by Pretzsche, who had worked until 1892 as an apothecary's assistant in the German colony at Mexico City.[17]

Ravenscroft described an equally fanciful social network of people supposedly involved with occult lore in Munich. Dietrich Eckart was described as an occult student who had travelled in Sicily to find the castle of Landulf II at Caltabellotta, where this putative model for Klingsor had performed satanic rituals of Arabian astrological magic that were said to have appalled the Christians of Southern Europe. Landulf was supposed to have invoked the spirits of darkness through the torture and sacrifice of human victims; Ravenscroft suggested that the Thule Society under the direction of Eckart, performed similar rituals on Jews and communists who had unaccountably disappeared in Munich during the early years of the

Republic. Ravenscroft even recruited for his Nazi mythology the person of Aleister Crowley (1875–1947), the English magician, who established his antinomian Abbey of Thelema at Celafu in 1921. Crowley was also alleged to have hunted for clues at Caltabellotta, while Eckart made a study of Crowley's gnostic sex-magic and its symbolical connections with Landulf's satanic practices. This jumble of links between twentieth-century occultism and ninth-century Sicily was crowned by the claim that Hitler believed himself to be the reincarnation of Klingsor-Landulf.[18] Ravenscroft concluded that Eckart and Haushofer initiated Hitler into black rituals designed to establish contact with evil powers:

> Dietrich Eckart contrived to develop and open the centres in the astral body of Adolf Hitler, giving him the possibility of vision into the macrocosm and means of communication with the powers of darkness . . . utilising his memories of a past incarnation as the Landulf of Capua in the ninth century . . . By divulging *The Secret Doctrine*, Haushofer expanded Hitler's time-consciousness . . . [and] awakened [him] to the real motives of the Luciferic Principality which possessed him so that he could become the conscious vehicle of its evil intent in the twentieth century.[19]

The centres of the astral body, vision into the macrocosm, the Luciferic Principality and its imminent manifestation as the Anti-Christ are all concepts derived from anthroposophy. Here it can be clearly seen how Ravenscroft adapted the materials of Rudolf Steiner and Walter Johannes Stein to the mythology of occult Nazism. Spiritualism also featured in his fantastic account of the Thule Society. Obscene seances with a naked medium were said to have been held by Eckart, Rosenberg, and Sebottendorff as a means of contacting the shades of the murdered Thule hostages. Both Prince von Thurn und Taxis and Heila von Westarp proclaimed from beyond the grave that Hitler would be the next claimant of the Holy Lance and lead Germany into a disastrous bid for global conquest.[20]

It was not long before the crypto-historians had discovered the Ariosophists. Their secret hierarchies and occult gnosis fulfilled all the requisite criteria for an arcane view of National Socialism. After Bronder's inclusion of List in the Thule Society, Ravenscroft was the next author to exploit List as Hitler's occult mentor. In the dingy office of Pretzsche's bookshop, Stein is said to have seen a group photograph which showed Pretzsche beside Guido von List. Stein recalled List as the infamous founder of an occult lodge, which had been exposed by the Vienna press as a 'blood brotherhood' for performing rituals involving sexual perversion and the practice of medieval black magic. On being exposed in 1909, List was compelled to flee from Vienna for fear of being lynched by outraged Catholics.[21] Ravenscroft inferred that both Ernst Pretzsche and Adolf Hitler were associated with List's lodge: 'According to Hitler, Pretzsche was himself present when Guido von List attempted to materialise "the Incubus" in a ritual designed to create a "Moon Child".'[22]

There is not a shred of evidence for such rituals. List was never obliged to leave Vienna and he enjoyed the patronage of prominent Vienna figures. The nature of the rituals Ravenscroft described indicate the inspiration of Aleister Crowley, especially with regard to the creation of a 'Moon Child'. It may be added that no one called Pretzsche was resident in Vienna between 1890 and 1920, nor did this name ever appear in the membership list of the List Society. The fictional nature of the whole episode surrounding the annotated copy of *Parzival* is suggested by the similarity of Pretzsche's obscure bookshop to the one described by Sir Edward Bulwer-Lytton in *Zanoni* (1842), which probably served Ravenscroft as a literary model.[23]

Lanz von Liebenfels made his début in this mythological history in Michel-Jean Angebert, *Les mystiques du soleil* (1971). In this account the young Hitler is supposed to have come under the influence of the Heiligenkreuz novice in 1898. The origins of this fantasy concern the choir school at Lambach monastery, which Hitler (*aet.* 8) attended for singing lessons from July 1897 to January 1899. In 1898 Lanz is alleged to have arrived at Lambach monastery, where he spent several weeks poring over the private library of Theoderich Hagn, its former abbot. The reason for his interest in these books lay in the nature of the abbot's studies. According to Angebert, the abbot had been a profound scholar of astrology and the occult sciences. Between 1856 and 1868 he was supposed to have travelled in the Middle East and the Caucasus in search of arcane lore. Angebert also attributed Hagn's choice of the swastika as his coat-of-arms to an oriental source of inspiration. This armorial swastika is in fact displayed in a relief above a gateway in the monastery. Frère repeated this story, stating that Lanz stayed long months in the library, 'rarely emerging save for a frugal meal, when he talked to no one and gave the impression of extreme agitation, as if labouring under the impact of an amazing discovery'.[24] The alleged contact between Lanz and Hitler was left unstated.

This episode is wholly imaginary. There is no evidence whatsoever for Hagn's extended travels; his blazon was traditionally borne by his family and derived from the name 'Hagn': *Haken* means hook and this swastika emblem is simply a hooked cross.[25] Nevertheless the myth of the Lambach swastika was already current during the Third Reich. A popular artist painted a tasteless pastiche of the famous picture of Saint Francis receiving the stigmata in which young Adolf was portrayed kneeling before the abbey gateway with rays of light falling from the heraldic swastika onto his out-stretched hands.[26] The painting was widely circulated in the form of little printed icons. These ideas of an early encounter between Lanz and Hitler, and Hitler's supposed veneration of the swastika in childhood, are evidence of the eagerness with which these crypto-historians seek to establish links with the occult in the early life of the future Führer.

Books written about Nazi occultism between 1960 and 1975 were typically sensational and under-researched. A complete ignorance of the primary sources was common to most authors and inaccuracies and wild claims were repeated by each newcomer to the genre until an abundant literature existed, based on wholly spurious 'facts' concerning the powerful Thule Society, the Nazi links with the East, and Hitler's occult initiation. But the modern mythology of Nazi occultism, however scurrilous and absurd, exercised a fascination beyond mere entertainment. Serious authors were tempted into an exciting field of intellectual history: Ellic Howe, *Urania's Children* (1967, reissued as *Astrology and the Third Reich*, 1984) dealt with the story of Hitler's alleged private astrologer, and James Webb devoted a chapter to 'The Magi of the North' in *The Occult Establishment* (1976). By focusing on the functional significance of occultism in political irrationalism, Webb rescued the study of Nazi occultism for the history of ideas.

Notes and References

INTRODUCTION

1 The term 'Ariosophy', meaning occult wisdom concerning the Aryans, was first coined by Lanz von Liebenfels in 1915 and became the label for his doctrine in the 1920s. List actually called his doctrine 'Armanism', while Lanz used the terms 'Theozoology' and 'Ario-Christianity' before the First World War. In this book 'Ariosophy' is used generically to describe the Aryan-racist-occult theories of both men and their followers.

2 George L. Mosse, *The Crisis of German Ideology* (New York, 1964), pp. 1–10.

3 The mobilization of German national feeling by means of monuments, choral, gymnastic, sharpshooters', and other public festivals is discussed in George L. Mosse, *The Nationalization of the Masses* (New York, 1975).

4 Fritz Stern, *The Politics of Cultural Despair* (Berkeley, Calif., 1961).

5 Peter G. J. Pulzer, *The Rise of Political Anti-Semitism in Germany and Austria* (New York, 1964).

1. THE PAN-GERMAN VISION

1 Robert A. Kann, *Das Nationalitätenproblem der Habsburgermonarchie*, second edition, 2 vols. (Graz and Cologne, 1964), II, 387–94. Population and nationality in the Austrian provinces, according to Kann, were distributed as follows:

> Lower Austria, including Vienna (pop. 3,500,000): Germans, 95 per cent; Czechs, 4 per cent. Upper Austria (pop. 850,000): Germans, 99.7 per cent. Salzburg (pop. 215,000): Germans, 99.7 per cent. Tyrol (pop. 950,000): Germans, 57 per cent; Italians, 42 per cent. Styria (pop. 1,440,000): Germans, 71 per cent; Slovenes, 29 per cent. Carinthia (pop. 400,000): Germans, 79 per cent; Slovenes, 21 per cent. Carniola (pop. 525,000): Germans, 5 per cent; Slovenes, 95 per cent. Bohemia and Moravia (pop. 9,400,000): Germans, 34 per cent; Czechs, 66 per cent. Silesia (pop. 760,000): Germans, 43.9 per cent; Poles, 32 per cent; Czechs, 24 per cent. Galicia (pop. 8,000,000): Germans, 1 per cent; Poles, 59 per cent; Ruthenes, 40 per cent. Bukovina (pop. 800,000): Germans, 21 per cent; Ruthenes, 38 per cent; Romanians, 34 per cent; Poles, 5 per cent; Magyars, 1 per cent. Dalmatia (pop. 650,000): Germans, 0.5 per cent; Serbo-Croats, 97 per cent; Italians, 3 per cent. Küstenland (Istria, Triest, Gorizia) (pop. 915,000): Germans, 4 per cent; Italians, 44 per cent; Serbo-Croats, 20 per cent; Slovenes, 32 per cent.

2 Eduard Pichl, *Georg Schönerer und die Entwicklung des Alldeutschtums in der Ostmark*, third edition, 6 vols. (Oldenburg and Berlin, 1938), VI, 168–72.

3 Andrew Gladding Whiteside, *The Socialism of Fools* (Berkeley, 1975), p. 269.

4 Whiteside, op. cit., pp. 43–63.

5 A full account of the disorders following the Badeni language decrees may be found in Whiteside, op. cit., pp. 160–87.

6 Whiteside, op. cit., p. 209. The background to such an anti-clerical reaction is described in William A. Jenks, *Austria under the Iron Ring 1879–1893* (Charlottesville, 1965).

7 *The Los von Rom* campaign is treated in detail in Whiteside, op. cit., pp. 243–62.

8 See below, pp. 68 ff.

9 *GLB* 2a (1911), pp. 25–7; and see below, p. 83.

10 *Ostara* III, 1 (1930), p. [v].

11 A. de Gobineau, *Essai sur l'Inégalité des Races* (Paris, 1853–5).

12 A detailed history of Social Darwinist publications and societies in Germany may be found in Hans-Günther Zmarzlik, 'Der Sozialdarwinismus in Deutschland als geschichtliches Problem', *Vierteljahreshefte für Zeitgeschichte* 11 (1963), 245–73.

13 The influence of Ernst Haeckel (1834–1919) and the Monist League in the dissemination of popular Social Darwinism is the subject of Daniel Gasman, *The Scientific Origins of National Socialism* (London, 1971).

14 William A. Jenks, *Vienna and the young Hitler* (New York, 1960), pp. 37–9.

15 ibid., p.118.

16 Adolf Hitler, *Mein Kampf* (Munich, 1934), pp. 59 ff.

17 Eugen Diederichs, the influential German publisher of Jena, had cultivated *völkisch* ideas since 1896 within a new religious mystique which drew on irrationalism, pantheism, gnosticism and theosophy. Gary D. Stark, *Entrepreneurs of Ideology* (Chapel Hill, 1981), pp. 69–76. Prominent Ariosophists in Germany before the First World War included Grävell (Heidelberg), Sebaldt and Stauff (Berlin). Over a third of the List Society members were resident in Germany at the time of its inauguration in 1908.

18 See below, Chapters 2 and 4.

19 Adolf Hitler, op. cit., p. 135.

2. THE MODERN GERMAN OCCULT REVIVAL 1880–1910

1 Richard Cavendish, *A History of Magic* (London, 1977), pp. 9f, 162f.

2 For the life of H. P. Blavatsky, see Vsevolod Soloviev, *A Modern Priestess of Isis* (London, 1895); Gertrude Marvin Williams, *Priestess of the Occult (Madame Blavatsky)* (New York, 1946); Howard Murphet, *When Daylight Comes* (Wheaton, Ill., 1975).

3 William Emmette Coleman, 'The source of Madame Blavatsky's writings', in Vsevolod Soloviev, *A Modern Priestess of Isis* (London, 1895), pp. 353–66.

NOTES AND REFERENCES

4 S. B. Liljegren, 'Quelques romans anglais. Source partielle d'une religion moderne', in *Mélanges d'histoire littéraire générale*, edited by Fernand Baldensperger, 2 vols. (Paris, 1930), II, 60–77, and *Bulwer-Lytton's Novels and Isis Unveiled* (Uppsala, 1957).

5 Coleman, op. cit., p. 358.

6 Helena Petrovna Blavatsky, *The Secret Doctrine*, second edition, 2 vols. (London, 1888), II, 6–12, 300f, 433–6. The myth of Lemurian miscegenation is discussed in ibid., II, 184, 266f, and may have inspired Lanz von Liebenfel's quasi-Gnostic concept of the Fall. See below p. 101f.

7 Alvin Boyd Kuhn, *Theosophy. A Modern Revival of Ancient Wisdom* (New York, 1930), pp. 206f, 232–52.

8 Blavatsky, op. cit., II, p. 318f.

9 Kuhn, op. cit., p. 199f.

10 George L. Mosse, 'The mystical origins of National Socialism', *Journal of the History of Ideas* 22 (1961), 81–96 (p. 81).

11 Janos Frecot, Johann Friedrich Geist and Diethart Kerbs, *FIDUS 1868–1948: Zur ästhetischen Praxis bürgerlicher Fluchtbewegungen* (Munich, 1972), pp. 15–58 and *passim*.

12 Details of Wilhelm Hübbe-Schleiden and this first theosophical venture in Germany may be found in Emil Bock, *Rudolf Steiner. Studien zu seinem Lebensgang und Lebenwerk*, second edition (Stuttgart, 1961), pp. 170–90.

13 Biographical details of Franz Hartmann may be found in Hugo Göring, *Dr Franz Hartmann, ein Vorkämpfer der Theosophie* (Brunswick, 1894) and Franz Hartmann, *Denkwürdige Erinnerungen* (Leipzig, 1898).

14 Walter Schönenberger, 'Monte Verità und die theosophischen Ideen', in *Monte Verità: Berg der Wahrheit*, edited by Harald Szeemann (Milan, 1980), pp. 65–79.

15 Schwabe, 'Protokoll über die 1. Nationalkonvention der "Theosophischen Gesellschaft" in Europa (Deutschland)', *Metaphysische Rundschau* 1 (1896), 279–83. The origins of American theosophy are documented in Emmett A. Greenwalt, *California Utopia: Point Loma 1897–1942* (San Diego, 1978).

16 Franz Hartmann, 'Ein Abenteuer unter den Rosenkreuzern', *Neue Metaphysische Rundschau* 1 (1898), 156–67, 232–43, 333–41, 386–9, 429–34; ibid. 2 (1899), 18–22, 46–51, 93–105, 241–54, 273–81, 305–14, 337–46. The first edition had appeared in English as *An Adventure among the Rosicrucians* (Boston, Mass., 1887).

17 Paul Zillmann, 'Die Wald-Loge und Akademie für okkulte Wissenschaften', *Neue Metaphysische Rundschau* 1 (1898), 226–8 and *Die Wald-Loge* (Gross-Lichterfelde, [1912]).

18 Paul Zillmann, 'Theosophische Bewegung', *Neue Metaphysische Rundschau* 4 (1901), 187–8.

19 Paul Zillmann, 'Unmassgebliches zum theosophischen Kongress 1902', *Neue Metaphysische Rundschau* 5 (1902), 168–72.

20 For a recent biography of Rudolf Steiner and an analysis of his thought see Geoffrey Ahern, *Sun at Midnight. The Rudolf Steiner Movement and the Western Esoteric Tradition* (Wellingborough, 1984).

21 Biographical details of Hugo Vollrath may be found in Ellic Howe, *Astrology and the Third Reich* [published originally as *Urania's Children*] (Wellingborough, 1984), p. 79f.

22 Elisabeth Kumpf-Rohm (Bopfingen) to author, letter dated 23 October 1979.

23 For a history of the New Thought movement in Germany, see Charles S. Braden, *Spirits in Rebellion* (Dallas, 1963), pp. 468–80.

24 See Bibliography for a list of these periodicals and book-series.

25 Friedrich Eckstein, *'Alte unnennbare Tage!'* (Vienna, 1936); cf. the account in Emil Bock, op. cit., pp. 58–61, 72–84.

26 The Association and its library are advertised in *Die Gnosis* 1 (September 1903).

27 Notices in *Zentralblatt für Okkultismus* 1 (1908), 385, 530.

28 Ellic Howe, op. cit., p. 81f.

29 Josef Greiner, *Das Ende des Hitler-Mythos* (Zurich, 1947), pp. 88f.

30 Paul Zillmann used the adjective 'metaphysical' to describe the entire range of disciplines in the modern occult revival. *Neue Metaphysische Rundschau* 1 (1898), ii.

31 Rudolf Steiner, *An Autobiography*, second edition (New York, 1980), pp. 141–4.

32 Carl E. Schorske, *Fin-de-Siècle Vienna* (Cambridge, 1981), pp. 5–10.

3. GUIDO VON LIST

1 Österreichisches Staatsarchiv (Allgemeines Verwaltungsarchiv), Vienna, Z1. 12.263/71.

2 The portrait is reproduced in Johannes Balzli, *Guido v. List. Der Wiederentdecker uralter arischer Weisheit* (Leipzig and Vienna, 1917), facing p. 5.

3 Guido List, *Deutsch-Mythologische Landschaftsbilder*, second edition, 2 vols. (Leipzig and Vienna, [1913]), II, 641 and plates, *passim*. This work is hereafter cited as *D-ML*.

4 Guido List, *D-ML*, II, 592.

5 Balzli, op. cit., pp. 15–17.

6 Balzli, op. cit., p. 18. Guido List, 'Neujahr 1870 in den Alpen', *Jahrbuch des Österreichischen Alpenvereins* 7 (1871).

7 Guido List, *D-ML*, II, 642.

8 ibid., I, 117–37.

9 ibid., II, 562–91.

10 ibid., II, 438.

11 ibid., I, 125.

12 ibid., II, 642f.

13 List may have given Lanz the impression that his mother had squandered her late husband's estate, in order to extenuate his own failure at business. According to Lanz, List lost his money through his mother and 'bad contracts, wills and women'. J. Lanz von Liebenfels, 'Guido von List', *Zeitschrift für Menschenkenntnis und Schicksalsforschung* 2 (1927), 74–89 (p. 76).

14 Guido List, *D-ML*, I, 328–45.

15 This essay was subsequently published in *D-ML*, II, 562–91.

16 ibid., II, 587.

17 The earliest reference to the Association dates from 1887, but it had no premises in Brno until 1891. For a history of the Association and a survey of its publications, see *Blätter vom Deutschen Hause*, 27 vols. (Brno, 1887–1913).

18 *Ostdeutsche Rundschau*, 1 October 1893, pp. 1–3; ibid., 31 October 1893, pp. 10–11.

19 *Ostdeutsche Rundschau*, 1894, *passim*.

20 *Ostdeutsche Rundschau*, 13 and 14 Feburary 1895, pp. 1–3.

21 *Ostdeutsche Rundschau*, 25 and 26 September 1895, pp. 1–2; ibid., 28 and 31 December 1895, pp. 1–3.

22 *Ostdeutsche Rundschau*, 12 February 1896, pp. 1–2.

23 See Bibliography for a survey of List's journalism.

24 The 1892 lecture is described in Balzli, op. cit., p. 30. The 1893 lecture is announced in *Ostdeutsche Rundschau*, 24 February 1893, p. 3 and published as an article, 'Von der deutschen Wuotanspriesterschaft', *Das Zwanzigste Jahrhundert* 4 (1893), 119–26, 242–51, 343–52, 442–51.

25 A report of the festival is printed in *Ostdeutsche Rundschau*, 3 and 4 December 1894, pp. 2–3, 5. The play was published as a pamphlet, Wolfgang Heinrich Collection (Linz). A second edition is printed in *Irminsul* 2 (1970), Heft 5.

26 The Guido List evening is announced in *Ostdeutsche Rundschau*, 9 April 1895, p. 3. Wiedener Sängerbund programmes, Wolfgang Heinrich Collection (Linz).

27 This incident is related in Balzli, op. cit., p. 33.

28 Österreichisches Staatsarchiv (Allgemeines Verwaltungsarchiv), Vienna, Zl., 12.263/71.

29 Herwig (pseudonym of Eduard Pichl), *Georg Schönerer und die Entwicklung des Alldeutschtumes in der Ostmark*, 4 vols. (Vienna, 1912–23) II, 426-8; Peter G. J. Pulzer, *The Rise of Political Anti-Semitism in Germany and Austria* (New York, 1964), p. 207.

30 The portrait is reproduced in Guido List, *D-ML*, I, plate facing p. 208.

31 Balzli, op. cit., p. 33.

32 Guido List, *Der Wiederaufbau von Carnuntum* (Vienna, 1900), pp. 16–31.

33 Balzli, op. cit., p. 35f; 'Die alten Götter—das alte Recht', *Irminsul* 10 (1978), Heft 5.

34 Guido List, 'Die Ursprache der Arier, deren Schrift und Heilszeichen', manuscript dated *c.* 1903, Bundesarchiv, Koblenz, NS26/1244. An account of the manuscript's

submission to the Academy and its reception is printed in the published edition. Guido List, *Die Ursprache der Ario-Germanen und ihre Mysteriensprache* (Leipzig and Vienna, [1914], pp. 1–8.

35 Balzli, op. cit., p. 11f. The old chronicle was Bucelinus, *Germania Topo-Chrono-Stemmato-Graphica* (Nuremberg, 1655–78).

36 W. H. Bruford, *The German Tradition of Self-Cultivation* (Cambridge, 1975) pp. 226–63.

37 The articles on heraldry appear in *Leipziger Illustrierte Zeitung*, 4 May 1905, p. 680f; 15 March 1906, p. 417f; and 31 January 1907, p. 188f.

38 Lanz von Liebenfels first met both List and Franz Kiessling at Gars am Kamp in *c.*1892. Sephine and Jörg Lanz von Liebenfels to Walther Gübitz, letters dated 12 and 20 August 1952, Rudolf Mund Archive (Vienna).

39 The text of the interpellation and its signatories is printed in *GLB* 6 [1914], pp. 2ff.

40 A list of signatories is printed in *GLB* 3 (1908), [p. 197f].

41 Membership lists are printed in *GLB* 2 (1908), pp. 71–4 and *GLB* 5 (1910), pp. 384–9. The articles of the List Society are printed in *GLB* 1, second edition (1912), pp. 68–78. Karl Herzog joined the Society *c.*1912. Karl Herzog to Philipp Stauff, letter dated 3 February 1912, Bundesarchiv, Koblenz, NS26/512a.

42 'Einige wenige Auszüge aus den Urteilen der Presse über die Guido-List-Bücherei', in *GLB* 2a (1911), pp. 269–85.

43 The lectures are described in *GLB* 2a (1911), pp. 239–41.

44 *GLB* 3 (1908), recto rear cover.

45 *GLB* 3 (1908), p. 191.

46 *GLB* 5 (1910), p. 13.

47 *GLB* 2a (1911), p. 242.

48 Balzli, op. cit., pp. 45f, 239–42.

49 Ellerbek (pseudonym for Gustav Leisner) wrote that the works of List and Tarnhari convinced him that 'AR selig lachend lebt', letter to List dated 25 October 1915, quoted in Balzli, op. cit., p. 155. Ellerbek's *Versailler Visionen* (1919), an apocalyptic critique of the peace settlement, was subtitled an 'occult-armanistic' confession, while his *völkisch* novel, *Sönne Sonnings Söhne auf Sonnen-See* (1920), contained four letters from Guido von List in an appendix. For later armanist usage see Carl Reinhold Petter, *Der Armanismus als Zukunfts-Religion* (Danzig-Langfuhr, 1919) and Kurt van Emsen, *Adolf Hitler und die Kommenden* (Berlin, 1932). Petter was the chairman of the Supranational Aryan League at Danzig.

50 Rudolf J. Mund, *Der Rasputin Himmlers* (Vienna, 1982).

51 The account of the pilgrimages and the photographs are in Guido List, *D-ML*, II, 591–602. The pilgrims were List and spouse, Wilhelm Koehne and spouse, Rudolf Janko and spouse, Friedrich Oskar Wannieck, Heinrich Winter, Eugen Mertens and Philipp Stauff. Heinrich Winter died on 18 July 1911, Wilhelm Koehne on 11 May 1912, and Friedrich Oskar Wannieck on 6 July 1912.

52 Balzli, op. cit., p. 68f. Participants at the HAO m. eting in April 1915 included: General Blasius von Schemua; Josef Neumayer, the retired Lord Mayor of Vienna; Franz Lang, Imperial Privy Councillor; Friedrich J. Bieber, the secretary of the List Society; Franz Zenkl; Emmerich Boyer von Berghof, the author; Baron Skal; A. Blamauer; Rudolf Janko; Heinrich Franz Lang; Walter Fellner; and Guido List.

53 Letters from soldiers and officers at the front to Guido List are printed in Balzli, op. cit., pp. 167–74.

54 Philipp Stauff, 'Guido von List gestorben', *Münchener Beobachter*, 24 May 1919, p. 4.

4. WOTANISM AND GERMANIC THEOSOPHY

1 K. V. Müllenhoff, *Deutsche Altertumskunde*, 5 vols. (Berlin, 1870–1900), IV, 585–7.

2 *GLB* 1 (1908), pp. 1–25.

3 George L. Mosse, *The Crisis of German Ideology* (New York, 1964), pp. 13f.

4 *'Wanidis'* was conceived as a three-volume work: I. Band. WAN, Das Wunschwähnen der Midgartmenschen (in three parts); II. Band. I, ein Ich; III. Band. DIS, Die arische 'Sexual-Religion' (in three parts). The first two volumes were never published but their contents may be inferred from a synopsis in the third. Maximilian Ferdinand, *'Wanidis'. Der Triumph des Wahnes*. III. Bd. DIS, Die arische 'Sexual-Religion' (Leipzig, 1897), pp. 5–8, 33–5.

5 [Guido List], 'Germanischer Lichtdienst', *Der Scherer* 1, Heft 4 (17 June 1899), p. 5. For details of this paper's political line see André Banuls, 'Das völkische Blatt "Der Scherer"', *Vierteljahreshefte für Zeitgeschichte* 18 (1970), 196–203.

6 Guido List, 'Die esoterische Bedeutung religiöser Symbole', *Die Gnosis* 1 (1903), 323–7. The two men were also personally acquainted, a fact made plain by a fly-leaf dedication to 'Guido von Lis☆, dem sinnenden Forscher, von Maximil. Sebald ☆, Sonnenwend 1906' in *Diaphetur* (1905). Ekkehard Hieronimus Archive (Hanover). The use of a ☆ for a 't' occurs often in List manuscripts.

7 *GLB* 3 (1908), pp. 15f, 19–23.

8 *GLB* 1 (1908), pp. 37f, 45, 66; *GLB* 2 (1908), p. 3; *GLB* 3 (1908), p. 190.

9 *GLB* 3 (1908), pp. 19f, 22n. Blavatsky had discussed these topics in *The Secret Doctrine* third edition, 2 vols. (London, 1893), II, 72f.

10 Guido List, *Die Religion der Ario-Germanen* (Zurich, 1910), pp. 91–3.

11 ibid., pp. 29–36.

12 *GLB* 5 (1910), p. 30.

13 *GLB* 5 (1910), pp. 22f, 55f, tables I, II and III. Table II is supplemented by references to texts about occult 'correspondences'. Agrippa von Nettesheim, *De occulta philosophia* (1533) and an obscure contemporary work, S. Schweinburg-Eibenschitz, *Studien eines Feldmarschalls über das Priester-Orakel der alten Hebräer* (Baden, 1895). The field marshal was Christoph Gottfried von Engelhardt (d. 1767), who was familiar with the theosophical and cabbalistic thought of the secret societies in the eighteenth century.

14 Franz Hartmann, 'Rundschau in der ausländischen theosophischen Literatur', *Neue Lotusblüten* 2 (1910), 370.

15 *GLB* 6 [1914], pp. 19–24, table I.

16 Friedrich Wannieck to Guido List, letter dated 12 December 1914, in Balzli, op. cit., pp. 183–6.

17 Willy Schrödter, *Die Geheimkünste der Rosenkreuzer* (Warpke-Billerbeck, 1954), p.121.

18 Friedrich Schwickert, *Das Lebenselixier in Bulwers Romanen* (Leipzig, 1918). Schwickert published several standard texts of astrological theory in the 1920s, which employed the deterministic method of the French astrologer, Morin de Villefranche (1583–1656), counsellor to Louis XIII, Louis XIV and Cardinal Richelieu.

19 Karl Heise wrote about sun-worship, reincarnation, the astral body and miracles. These themes were evidently consistent with the cult of Mazdaznan. This cult had been founded c.1900 in the United States by Otto Hanisch (1856–1936), a German immigrant from Poznán. Hanisch used the name Otoman Zar-Adusht Ha'nish and claimed to have been born in Tehran, supposedly in order to lend credence to the alleged Zoroastrian origins of his cult. The cult spread to Europe in the first decade of the century. Details of the cult in Ellic Howe, *Astrology and the Third Reich* (Wellingborough, 1984), p. 85, and James Webb, *The Occult Establishment* (La Salle, Ill., 1976), pp. 32, 74.

20 List first mentioned the 'Templeisen' in *GLB* 2 (1908), p. 64 f. He drew heavily on Lanz's racial dualism in *GLB* 2a (1911), pp. 66–71. The continent 'Arktogäa' was first mentioned in *GLB* 4 (1909), p. 2. A map, showing the location and coastline of 'Arktogäa', was published by Lanz in *Ostara* I, 50 (1911), p. 8, and used by List in *D-ML*, I, 119.

5. THE ARMANENSCHAFT

1 Cornelius Tacitus, 'Germania', in *Cornelii Taciti Opera Minora*, edited by M. Winterbottom and R. M. Ogilvie (Oxford, 1975), pp. 37–62 (p. 38).

2 *GLB* 2 (1908), p. 4.

3 *GLB* 1 (1908), p. 32.

4 *GLB* 2 (1908), p. 17.

5 *GLB* 2 (1908), p. 41; *GLB* 6 [1914], pp. 347–64.

6 *GLB* 2 (1908), p. 18f.

7 *GLB* 2 (1908), p. 4f.

8 *GLB* 2 (1908), p. 20.

9 The sacred legitimation (or sacralization) of social institutions confers upon them an ultimately valid ontological status. Peter L. Berger, *The Social Reality of Religion* (London, 1969), pp. 38–60.

10 J. M. Roberts, *The Mythology of the Secret Societies* (London, 1972), pp. 90–117. The sects of the eighteenth century are discussed at length in Auguste Viatte, *Les sources occultes du romantisme*, 2 vols. (Paris, 1928).

11 Frances Yates, *The Rosicrucian Enlightenment* (London, 1972), p. 40.

12 Klaus Epstein, *The Genesis of German Conservatism* (Princeton, 1966), pp. 84–111.

13 Christopher McIntosh, *The Rosy Cross Unveiled* (Wellingborough, 1980), pp. 72–100. Cf. Horst Möller, 'Die Bruderschaft der Gold- und Rosenkreuzer', in *Freimaurer und Geheimbünde im 18. Jahrhundert in Mitteleuropa*, ed. Helmut Reinalter (Frankfurt/Main, 1983), pp. 199–239.

14 The Rosicrucian Society in Germany and Hartmann's contact with Reuss are discussed in Ellic Howe and Helmut Möller, 'Theodor Reuss. Irregular Freemasonry in Germany, 1900–23', *Ars Quatuor Coronatorum* 91 (1978), 28–47.

15 'Geheime Figuren der Rosenkreuzer aus dem 16ten und 17ten Jahrhundert', *Neue Metaphysische Rundschau* [8] 12 (1905), 41–8, 92–8.

16 Norman Cohn documents the case in his study of European accusatory traditions. He argues that the charges of satanism fall within a stereotypical procedure, whereby social opponents are first vilified according to religious criteria, in order that they may be legitimately exterminated. This kind of thinking is also evident in List's vicious account of the Catholic Church. Norman Cohn, *Europe's Inner Demons* (London, 1975), pp. 75–98.

17 Roberts, op. cit., p. 99. For a comprehensive study of the occult Templar tradition, see Peter Partner, *The Murdered Magicians* (Oxford, 1982).

18 Josef von Hammer-Purgstall, 'Mysterium Baphometis revelatum', *Fundgruben des Orients* 6 (1818), 3–120, 5 tables.

19 Coleman, op. cit., pp. 357, 365.

20 Franz Hartmann and Karl Kellner (1851–1905), an industrial chemist with occult interests, collaborated in the production of ligno-sulphite, a by-product in paper manufacture, which Hartmann used to treat patients suffering from tuberculosis at his sanatorium in Hallein. Franz Hartmann, *Über eine neue Heilmethode zur Heilung von Lungentuberkulose* (Leipzig, 1893). Further details about Kellner and the OTO in Ellic Howe and Helmut Möller, 'Theodor Reuss. Irregular Freemasonry in Germany, 1900–23', *Ars 'Quatuor Coronatorum* 91 (1978), 28–47.

21 While Franz Hartmann's acquaintance with occult Templarism derived from a quasi-masonic background, Lanz von Liebenfels was inspired by the poetic and neo-romantic image of the Templars which was current at the turn of the century. List was indebted to both influences.

22 *GLB* 2 (1908), p. 65.

23 Guido List, 'Das Mittelalter im Armanentum', in *GLB* 2, second edition [1913], pp. 89–99 (p. 97).

24 *GLB* 5 (1910), p. 110; *GLB* 2a (1911), p. 4.

25 Guido List, 'Das Mittelalter im Armanentum', in *GLB* 2, second edition [1913], pp. 89–99 (pp. 90–6).

26 J. Lanz von Liebenfels, 'Guido von List', *Zeitschrift für Menschenkenntnis und Schicksalsforschung* 2 (1927), 74–89 (p. 76).

27 *GLB* 2a (1911), pp. 70 ff.

28 ibid., p. 86 f.

29 The Tree of Life is a complex cosmological model, which symbolizes the ten emanations of God, the ten aspects of the manifested universe and the ten modes of human awareness, in a sequence of increasing transcendence. The three highest *sefiroth*, as each of the ten stations are known, lie across 'a veil of the abyss', which denotes their special esoteric nature. The Tree forms the theological basis of the Jewish mystical tradition known as cabbalism, which began to enter the Western occult tradition during the sixteenth century and inspired the theosophical and Rosicrucian subcultures of the seventeenth and eighteenth centuries. The first application of the Tree to the grade scheme of an order is recorded in Magister Pianco (i.e. Hans Carl von Ecker und Eckhoffen), *Der Rosenkreuzer in seiner Blösse* (Amsterdam, 1781), which was subsequently used for the structure of the Rosicrucian Society in England (est. 1866) and the derivative Hermetic Order of the Golden Dawn. Ellic Howe, 'Fringe Masonry in England, 1870–85' *Ars Quatuor Coronatorum* 85 (1972), 242–80 (p. 251) and Ellic Howe, *The Magicians of the Golden Dawn* (London, 1972; reprinted 1985), pp. 22–5.

30 *GLB* 2a (1911), pp. 134–40.

31 Joachim Besser, 'Die Vorgeschichte des Nationalsozialismus in neuem Licht', *Die Pforte* 2 (1950), 763–84 (p. 772).

32 Letters from followers to Guido List are reprinted in Balzli, op. cit., pp. 148–97.

33 Bernhard Koerner's title is mentioned in Fritz Meier-Gostenhof to Johannes Hering, letter dated 11 December [1919?], Bundesarchiv, Koblenz, NS26/1244. List used his title at the end of his obituary to Friedrich Oskar Wannieck, *D-ML*, II, 650. The correspondence between these titles and the cabbalistic hierarchy of the *Armanenschaft* is set out in *GLB* 2a (1911), p. 138f.

34 A photograph of Winter's grave is printed in *D-ML*, II, plate facing p. 600. Wannieck's tumulus is illustrated in *GLB* 6 [1914], plate between pp. 420 and 421, and discussed in Friedrich Wannieck to Guido List, letter dated 12 December 1914, in Balzli, op. cit., pp. 183–6. Elsa Hauerstein's headstone is illustrated in *Imaginarium NT*, plate 165.

35 List discussed the occult interests of the Habsburg emperors Frederick IV, Maximilian and Rudolf II together with an esoteric interpretation of Frederick's imperial motto A.E.I.O.U. (usually held to stand for *Austria erit in orbe ultima*) and concluded that the Habsburgs must have been initiates of the *Armanenschaft* since the earliest days of the dynasty. Interestingly enough, Lanz von Liebenfels also celebrated Frederick IV and Maximilian as Ariosophists, see below p. 212. List described the reigning emperor, Franz Josef I (1848–1916) as the 'crowned sage', an explicit reference to the putative Armanism of contemporary Austrian royalty. *GLB* 5 (1910), p. 295f. A further indication of List's strong monarchical sentiment may be deduced from an episode when he and Captain Friedrich Kunitz, a List Society member serving with the army at Sarajevo in Austrian-occupied Bosnia, visited Schönbrunn Palace in May 1914. Kunitz saluted the window of the emperor, a gesture which filled List with emotion and reverence for the 'armanist' dedication of the officer class to the crown. Balzli, op. cit., p. 90f.

36 Ellic Howe, 'Fringe Masonry in England, 1870–85', *Ars Quatuor Coronatorum* 85 (1972), 242–80 (p. 267).

6. THE SECRET HERITAGE

1 Guido List, *Deutsch-Mythologische Landschaftsbilder*, first edition (Berlin, 1891), pp. 37–40; *D-ML*, I, 117–37.

2 Guido List, *D-ML*, I, 29, 35–9.

3 Guido List, *D-ML*, I, 215, 222, 260–75.

4 Guido List, *Deutsch-Mythologische Landschaftsbilder*, first edition (Berlin, 1891), pp. 183–93.

5 Guido List, *D-ML*, I, 67–72. List repeatedly quoted the letter of Pope Gregory the Great to Mellitus of Canterbury, which urged the assimilation and appropriation of pagan sanctuaries and rituals to communicate Christian doctrine, as prime evidence of a Wotanist background to any Christian institution. ibid., I, 140f.

6 Guido List, *D-ML*, I, 72–7.

7 See List's account of the legends surrounding the Agnesbründl near Vienna and his interpretation of the story of Ritter Georg and the dog-woman, related to him by an old lady at the Schalaburg in the 1860s. Guido List, *D-ML*, I, 84–116, 294–327.

8 *GLB* 3 (1908), *passim*.

9 According to List, the Armanist refugees in Iceland were the authors of the Edda. *GLB* 3 (1908), p. 38.

10 Guido List, 'Von der Wuotanspriesterschaft', *Das Zwanzigste Jahrhundert* 4 (1893), 119–26, 242–51, 343–52, 442–51 (p. 250).

11 The derivation of both terms remains obscure. List first used them in *GLB* 1 (1908). Although the 'sacred secret Eight' sounds like a hidden council of elders, List's usage indicates a language or some other means of storing, safeguarding and communicating information. *GLB* 2, second edition [1913], p. 53.

12 Guido List, 'Ursprung und Wesen der Wappen', in *Der Sammler* 13 (1891), 54–6, 65–7.

13 *GLB* 1 (1908), pp. 40–2 and diagram, facing p. 16.

14 *GLB* 5 (1910), pp. 152–4.

15 ibid., p. 159.

16 ibid., p. 255.

17 ibid., p. 113.

18 ibid., pp. 214, 216, 227ff, 257f, 267.

19 *GLB* 2a (1911), p. 45.

20 *GLB* 5 (1910), p. 304.

21 Details of these groups may be found in Philipp Stauff, *Das deutsche Wehrbuch* (Berlin, 1912), p. 152f, and Anon., *Deutschvölkischer Katechismus*, 2 vols. (Leipzig, 1929–31), II, 164–70.

22 Guido List, 'Die symbolischen Bildwerke am Riesenthore der Stefanskirche zu

Wien', *Laufers Allgemeine Kunstchronik* 12 (1889), 250–1, 283–4, 307–10 and 'Ursprung und Symbolik der Freimaurerei', in *GLB* 2a (1911), pp. 200–15. This article had been initially published in the Pan-German periodical *Der Scherer*, edited by Ottokar Stauf von der March.

23 *GLB* 1 (1908), diagram facing p. 16.

24 A recent example is Fulcanelli, *Le mystère des cathédrales* (London, 1971).

25 W. D. Robson-Scott, *The Literary Background of the Gothic Revival in Germany* (Oxford, 1965).

26 The chief representative of this sensational Gothic genre using the vehmgericht was Veit Weber (1762–1837). His works and his romantic image of the Middle Ages are discussed in Carl Müller-Fraureuth, *Die Ritter- und Räuberromane* (Halle, 1894), pp. 8–35 and in Walther Pantenius, 'Das Mittelalter in Leonhard Wächters (Veit Webers) Romanen' (unpublished D. Phil. thesis, University of Leipzig, 1904). J. W. Appell, *Die Ritter-, Räuber- and Schauerromantik* (Leipzig, 1859) gives a general survey of Gothic literature during the late eighteenth century in Germany.

27 Guido List, *Deutsch-Mythologische Landschaftsbilder*, first edition (Berlin, 1891), p. 96.

28 Guido List, 'Die Schalaburg', in *D-ML*, I, 294–327; *GLB* 1 (1908), p. 49.

29 Guido List, 'Der Einsiedel vom Hohenstein bei Rothenkreuz', in *D-ML*, 154–205. This story was first published in the *Deutscher Volkskalender des Bundes der Deutschen Nordmährens* (Olomouc, 1905). The league was founded in 1886 as a Pan-German organization for the German settlements in North Moravia. Hermann Brass, a List Society member, was its chairman in the period before the First World War. Details of the league may be found in Philipp Stauff, *Das deutsche Wehrbuch* (Berlin, 1912), p. 52).

7. THE GERMAN MILLENNIUM

1 Fritz Saxl, 'The revival of late antique astrology', in *Lectures*, 2 vols. (London, 1957), I, 73–84.

2 Guido List, *Deutsch-Mythologische Landschaftsbilder*, first edition (Berlin, 1891), *passim*.

3 H. R. Ellis Davidson, *Gods and Myths of Northern Europe* (Harmondsworth, 1964), p. 37 f. List discussed these myths in an apocalyptic context. *GLB* 2 (1908), pp. 46, 70 and *GLB* 4 (1909), pp. 4, 6.

4 This cameo is intended to delineate the typical motifs in the apocalypses of Daniel, Ezra, Baruch and the Book of Revelation. Details concerning the identity and nature of the evil spirit and the messiah, as well as the manner of their manifestation, vary among the authors of this long religious and literary tradition. The term 'millennium' derives from the Book of Revelation, which describes the establishment of a terrestrial kingdom of God lasting a thousand years before the eternal dispensation dawns. However, among historians and sociologists the word denotes the new age, irrespective of its duration. Although messianic beliefs and millenarianism often coincide historically, the two ideas do not necessarily imply one another. For surveys of apocalyptic literature and discussions, see *The Apocrypha and Pseudepigrapha of the Old Testament*, edited by R. H. Charles, 2 vols. (Oxford, 1913), *passim*; E. Hennecke, *New Testament Apocrypha*, 2 vols. (London,

1965), II, 582 ff; Norman Cohn, *The Pursuit of the Millennium* (London, 1957); Bryan R. Wilson, 'Millennialism in comparative perspective', in *Millennial Dreams in Action*, edited by Sylvia L. Thrupp, Comparative Studies in Society and History 2 (The Hague, 1962), pp. 93–114; Yonina Talmon, 'Pursuit of the Millennium: the relation between religious and social change', *Archives Européenes de Sociologie* 3 (1962), 125–48, and 'Millenarian movements', *Archives Européenes de Sociologie* 7 (1966), 159–200.

5 Norman Cohn, *The Pursuit of the Millennium*, third edition (New York, 1970), pp. 29–36, 53–70.

6 Yonina Talmon, 'Millenarian movements', *Archives Européenes de Sociologie* 7 (1966), 159–200 (p. 179 f).

7 *GLB* 2a (1911), pp. 25–7.

8 *GLB* 2a (1911), pp. 40–3.

9 Peter G. J. Pulzer, *The Rise of Political Anti-Semitism in Germany and Austria* (New York, 1964), p. 294.

10 *GLB* 2a (1911), p. 53.

11 Pulzer, op. cit., p. 177.

12 *GLB* 2a (1911), p. 48 f.

13 ibid., p. 16 f.

14 Guido List, *Die Religion der Ario-Germanen* (Zurich, 1910), p. 92 f. List was obviously familiar with this system of Hindu cosmology from Helena Petrovna Blavatsky, *Die Geheimlehre*, 2 vols. (Leipzig, 1897–1901). A Mahayuga, or complete cycle, lasted 4,320,000 years and was composed of four yugas of successively shorter duration. The shortest of these, the Kaliyuga, lasted 432,000 years and represented the most decadent phase of the Mahayuga. Within an apocalyptic scheme, the Kaliyuga could be regarded as the period of woes, provided that one ignored the cyclical nature of Hindu chronology, which denies ultimate salvation.

15 Guido List, 'Über die Möglichkeit eines ewigen Weltfriedens', *Prana* 7 (1917), in Balzli, op. cit., pp. 134–8 (p. 135).

16 Guido List, 'Neuzeitliche Einherier', *Österreichische Illustrierte Rundschau* 4 (1916), in Balzli, op. cit., pp. 116–24 (p. 117), and 'Wer ist der Starke von Oben?', *Prana* 7 (1917), in Balzli, op. cit., pp. 125–33 (p. 128).

17 The letter from Tarnhari was dated 11 November 1911, in Balzli, op. cit., p. 146. Tarnhari's real name was Ernst Lauterer. His speculations revolved around the derivation of his name from the three runes Laf-tar-ar (⌐-↑-⟩), which spelt the word 'Ulaftarhari', allegedly a cover-name for Wotan. Tarnhari also traced his ancestry to a sixteenth-century family Lautrer von Döfering zum Raidenstein, whose blazon showed a rampant lion. He claimed that the Laf-tar-ar runes were concealed in the body of this heraldic lion. Tarnhari, *Aus den Traditionen der Laf-tar-ar-Sippe der 'Lauterer'* (Diessen, [1915]). Tarnhari published another pamphlet, *An unsere Getreuen* (Diessen, [1914]). After the war he was associated with Alfred Bass in the Nationale Kanzlei at Leipzig which issued a *Hakenkreuz-Rundbrief* (1920) and also collaborated with Dietrich Eckart, the *völkisch* publicist at Munich.

18 *GLB* 2, second edition [1913], p. 98 f.

19 Friedrich Wannieck to Guido List, letter dated 12 December 1914, in Balzli, op. cit., pp. 183–6.

20 *GLB* 2a (1911), p. 81 f.

21 ibid., p. 107.

22 An extensive bibliography of conservative revolutionary literature may be consulted in Armin Mohler, *Die konservative Revolution in Deutschland 1918–1932* (Darmstadt, 1972).

23 This profuse pamphlet literature concerning 'spiritual' anti-Westernism in Germany during 1914 and 1915 is discussed by Fritz Ringer, *The Decline of the German Mandarins* (Cambridge, Mass., 1969), pp. 180–99 and Klemens von Klemperer, *Germany's New Conservatism* (Princeton, 1968), pp. 47–55. For the reactions of the cultural pessimists to the war, see Fritz Stern, *The Politics of Cultural Despair* (Berkeley, 1974), pp. 205–11.

24 Guido List, 'Ostarrede (21 April 1915)', in Balzli, op. cit., pp. 69–77.

25 These references may be found in Balzli, op. cit., pp. 149, 155, 143, 34.

26 Michael Barkun, *Disaster and the Millennium* (New Haven, 1974), p. 163.

27 Balzli, op. cit., p. 73.

28 Medieval German apocalyptic fantasies attaching to the figure of an emperor are discussed in Norman Cohn, *The Pursuit of the Millennium* (New York, 1970), pp. 30–3, 108–26.

29 *GLB* 2, second edition [1913], p. 97 f.

30 ibid., p. 95.

31 Guido List, *Deutsch-Mythologische Landschaftsbilder*, first edition (Berlin, 1891), p. 88.

32 The speculations about the reincarnated nationalist revolutionaries appear in the articles, 'Neuzeitliche Einherier' and 'Wer ist der Starke von Oben?', in Balzli, op. cit., pp. 116–24, 125–33.

8. JÖRG LANZ VON LIEBENFELS AND THEOZOOLOGY

1 Wilfried Daim, *Der Mann, der Hitler die Ideen gab* (Munich, 1958); Rudolf J. Mund, *Jörg Lanz v. Liebenfels und der Neue Templer Orden* (Stuttgart, 1976).

2 See Appendix A for the genealogy of Adolf Josef Lanz. It is interesting to note that his younger brother, Herwik Lanz, also indulged in similar fantasies. He claimed to have been born at San Giovanni on 10 June 1874 (pre-dated). *Kürschners Deutscher Literatur-Kalender* 36 (1914), p. 1003.

3 J. Lanz von Liebenfels, *Arithmosophikon* 19 (Thalwyl, [1949]), p. 725 f. Documentary evidence suggests that Lanz did not esteem the Templars until after 1905. See below p. 108, note 9.

4 For details of Lanz's monastic career, see Daim, op. cit., pp. 250, 252.

5 Fr. G . . ., O.C. [i.e. Lanz], 'Berthold v. Treun', *Berichte und Mittheilungen des Alterthums-*

Vereins zu Wien 30 (1894), 137–140; J. Lanz, 'Das Necrologium Sancrucense Modernum', *Archiv für Österreichische Geschichte* 89 (1900), 247–354.

6 Fr. G . . ., 'Berthold v. Treun', p. 138.

7 Georg Lanz to Heiligenkreuz Abbey authorities, letter dated 11 September 1899, Heiligenkreuz Abbey Archive; P. Hermann Watzl to the author, letter dated 19 November 1978.

8 Daim, op. cit., p. 252.

9 J. Lanz-Liebenfels, *Katholizismus wider Jesuitismus* (Frankfurt, 1903); *Das Breve 'Dominus ac redemptor noster'* (Frankfurt, [1904]); *Der Taxil-Schwindel* (Frankfurt, [1904]).

10 *Ostara* III, 1 (1930), p. [v].

11 The alleged marriage of Lanz is discussed by Theodor Czepl. Daim, op. cit., p. 44.

12 A description of these inventions and their evaluation by Professor G. Heinrich may be found in Daim, op. cit., p. 110f.

13 J. Lanz-Liebenfels, 'Die Urgeschichte der Künste', *Politisch-Anthropologische Revue* 2 (1903), 134–56. Although there is no record of a doctoral thesis submitted by Lanz at the University of Vienna, it is still possible that the degree was conferred by another Austrian university.

14 J. Lanz-Liebenfels, 'Anthropozoon biblicum', *Vierteljahrsschrift für Bibelkunde* 1 (1903), 307–16, 317–55, 429–69 (p. 321); ibid. 2 (1904), 26–60, 314–37, 395–412. This periodical is hereafter cited as *VfB*.

15 Lanz's sources for these archaeological finds were Sir Austen Henry Layard, *Nineveh and its Remains*, 2 vols. (London, 1849), *Inscriptions in the Cuneiform Character from Assyrian Monuments* (London, 1851), and Eberhard Schrader, *Keilinschriftliche Bibliothek*, 6 vols. (Berlin, 1889–1900). Both artefacts are in the British Museum, Department of Western Asiatic Antiquities, Nos. 124562 and 118885.

16 J. Lanz-Liebenfels, 'Antropozoon biblicum', *VfB* 1 (1903), 322–4.

17 ibid., 341–55.

18 ibid., 343–4.

19 J. Lanz-Liebenfels, *Theozoologie oder die Kunde von den Sodoms-Äfflingen und dem Götter-Elektron* (Vienna, 1905), p. 26f. This text is hereafter cited as *TZ*.

20 J. Lanz-Liebenfels, *TZ*, pp. 28–33.

21 ibid., pp. 35, 52, 56f.

22 Lanz's first mention of N-rays in 'Anthropozoon biblicum', *VfB* 1 (1903), p. 455n. His first mention of radium-rays in ibid., 2 (1904), p. 332. He discusses these theories in *TZ*, pp. 83–5.

23 J. Lanz-Liebenfels, *TZ*, pp. 79f, 85, 90f. Wilhelm Bölsche had suggested that the pineal gland represented the evolutionary residue of a magnetic third eye, which was more apparent in the prehistoric saurian reptiles. Quoted by J. Lanz-Liebenfels, 'Anthropozoon biblicum', *VfB* 1 (1903), p. 354. Bölsche, a popular scientific writer, probably took this idea from theosophy. Madame Blavatsky had

also mystified the gland as a magical third eye, a speculation which she may have borrowed from René Descartes, who sought the locus of the soul in the gland. *The Secret Doctrine*, second edition, 2 vols. (London, 1888), II, 299f.

24 J. Lanz-Liebenfels, *TZ*, pp. 114ff, 140, 120ff. The *Pistis Sophia* was the subject of learned discussion in the 1890s. *Encyclopaedia of Religion and Ethics*, edited by James Hastings, 13 vols. (Edinburgh, 1908–26), X, 45–8.

25 J. Lanz-Liebenfels, *TZ*, pp. 124–8.

26 ibid., p. 133.

27 ibid., pp. 142ff.

28 ibid., pp. 147–52.

29 For Himmler's eugenic policies see Clarissa Henry and Marc Hillel, *Children of the SS* (London, 1975) and Felix Kersten, *The Kersten Memoirs 1940–1945* (London, 1956), pp. 74–82, 176–83. Descriptions of his Eastern policies in Josef Ackermann, *Heinrich Himmler als Ideologe* (Göttingen, 1970), pp. 195–231 and Kersten, ibid., pp. 132–140.

30 ibid., p. 158f.

31 ibid., p. 160.

32 ibid., p. 112f.

33 Akademischer Verlag pamphlet, dated [1905].

34 Mund, op. cit., pp. 22ff, 210f.

35 *Ostara* I, 6 (July 1906), p. [21].

36 These codes had been edited by Sir William Jones, *Institutes of Hindu Law* (Calcutta, 1794) and translated into German by Johann Christoph Hüttner, *Hindu-Gesetzbuch* (Weimar, 1797). The codes had been examined in a racist context by F. Gernandt, 'Aus dem Hindu-Gesetzbuch des Manu', *Politisch-Anthropologische Revue* 3 (1904), 264–8, which may well have been Lanz's source of inspiration. The Sanskrit term *caṇḍāla (Tschandale)*, which denoted the lowest caste of untouchables, denoted to Lanz the mongrelized racial inferiors and lower social classes of modern times. *Ostara* I, 22 (April 1908), pp. 6, 16.

37 The first issue of *Ostara* was published at Graz, but the periodical was henceforth published at Rodaun until mid-1913, by which time sixty-six numbers had appeared. The periodical was then published at Mödling until 1917 (with No. 89), when the first series (*Ostara* I) was discontinued. A second abortive series (*Ostara* II) was begun at Magdeburg in 1922, but abandoned after several numbers, and the third series (*Ostara* III) was published in Vienna from 1927 to 1931 under the patronage of Johann Walthari Wölfl.

38 Harald Grävell van Jostenoode, *Ostara* I, 6 (July 1906), pp. 3, 10, 12f.

39 The works cited by Grävell were Annie Besant, *Der Stammbaum der Menschen* (Leipzig, 1907) and Rudolf Steiner, *Blut ist ein ganz besonderer Saft* (Berlin, 1907), both of which reflected the theosophical interest in racist ideas. Harald Grävell van Jostenoode, *Ostara* I, 25 (July 1908), p. 10f.

40 J. Lanz-Liebenfels, *Die Theosophie und die assyrischen 'Menschentiere'* (Berlin, 1907), p. 11, figures 4, 5. The maps were taken from Melchior Neumayr, *Erdgeschichte*, second edition, 2 vols. (Leipzig, 1895), and William Scott-Elliot, *Das untergangene Lemuria* (Leipzig, 1905).

41 J. Lanz-Liebenfels, *Die Theosophie und die assyrischen 'Menschentiere'* (Berlin, 1907), p. 22.

42 ibid., pp. 28–32.

43 The Monist League was founded at Jena in 1906 by Ernst Haeckel as an organization of Social Darwinists. Gasman notes that the League boasted a membership of some six thousand in over forty groups distributed throughout Germany and Austria. It is likely that Lanz became familiar with its doctrines through the Vienna branch. Gasman places Lanz 'on the lunatic fringe of the social Darwinist movement'. Daniel Gasman, *The Scientific Origins of National Socialism* (London, 1971), pp. 20 ff, 153 and *passim*. This is true insofar as many of Lanz's authorities, including Wilhelm Bölsche, Ludwig Woltmann, and Willibald Hentschel, were Social Darwinists.

44 *Ostara* I, 35 (1910), pp. 1–5.

45 *Ostara* I, 78 (1915), pp. 10 ff. Lanz subsequently extended this roll of ariosophical initiates to include numerous mystics, pietists, and occultists since antiquity. See Appendix C.

46 Ellic Howe, *Astrology and the Third Reich* (Wellingborough, 1984), pp. 78–103.

47 *Ostara* I, 78 (1915), recto rear cover.

48 *Ostara* I, 79 (1915), pp. 15–[18]. The titles included: Arthur Grobe-Wutischsky, *Der Weltkrieg 1914 in der Prophetie* (Leipzig, 1915); Karl Brandler-Pracht, *Häuser-Tabellen von 40°–56° geographischer Breite* (Leipzig, 1910); Albert Kniepf, *Die Weissagungen des altfranzösischen Sehers Michel Nostradamus und der heutige Krieg* (Hamburg, 1914). Other reviews covered G. W. Surya, *Moderne Rosenkreuzer*, second edition (Leipzig, 1914); Charles Leadbeater, *Der sichtbare und unsichtbare Mensch* (Leipzig, 1908). The following issue of *Ostara* reviewed the first German work of the German-American theosophist Max Heindel, who had studied under Rudolf Steiner at Berlin before emigrating. Max Heindel, *Die Weltanschauung der Rosenkreuzer* (Leipzig, 1913). Details of Heindel in Ellic Howe, op. cit., p. 84 f. Lanz also recommended the periodicals *Prana, Theosophie* and *Zum Licht. Ostara* I, 80 (1915), pp. 16–[18]. These references give a clear indication of how widespread was Lanz's interest in theosophical and occult literature.

49 *Ostara* I, 80 (1915), p. 8 f.

50 *Ostara* I, 81 (1915), pp. 12–18. The idea of the Church of the Holy Spirit derives from the apocalyptic thought of Joachim of Fiore (*c*.1135–1202), who described a temporal scheme of three ages, each of which corresponded to one of the persons of the Trinity. The first age was the Age of the Father, a dispensation characterized by a demand for strict obedience to the laws of God; the second age was the Age of the Son, a time of piety and faith in the gospel; the third age was the Age of the Holy Spirit which would witness the transformation of the whole world into a vast monastery of monks full of joy, love, and freedom. Marjorie Reeves, *Joachim of Fiore and the Prophetic Future* (London, 1976). On Joachite prophecy in relation to

millenarianism, Norman Cohn, *The Pursuit of the Millennium* (New York, 1970), pp. 108 ff. Lanz discussed such prophecy, implying that the *ordo futurus* of Joachim was the parousia of New Templarism. *Ostara* I, 78 (1915), p. 4 f. The site of Vienna as the origin of the millennium was consonant with Lanz's belief in the ariosophical mission of the Habsburg dynasty. He found some justification for this statement in an interpretation of two enigmatic Nostradamus references, according to which the intersection of the 48° latitude and the 'German mountains' (in Lanz's opinion, a certain ridge in the Wienerwald) defined a new spiritual source-point on the planet.

51 *Ostara* III, 4 (1928), pp. 2f, 13f.

52 Friedrich Heer has also suggested that the emotional inspiration of Hitler's adult dreams of world-dominion and Caesarism may have derived from his childhood experience of South German Catholic pomp and pageantry at Passau between 1892 and 1895. Friedrich Heer, *Der Glaube des Adolf Hitler* (Munich, 1968), pp. 19–21.

9. THE ORDER OF THE NEW TEMPLARS

1   See Appendix A for the genealogy of Adolf Josef Lanz.

2   The first traceable use of the name 'Liebenfels' by Lanz occurred in early 1903. Cf. Dr J. Lanz-Liebenfels, 'Die Urgeschichte der Künste', *Politisch-Anthropologische Revue* 2 (May 1903), 134–56 (p. 134). His earliest use of the title 'von' between the names dates from 1911. See letter-heads, Lanz to August Strindberg, letter dated 20 September 1911, Royal Library, Stockholm, and Lanz to Johannes Hering, letter dated 6 September 1911, Bundesarchiv, Koblenz, NS26/1229.

3   See the articles 'Lanz von Liebenfels' and 'Liebenfels' in *Historisches-Biographisches Lexikon der Schweiz*, 7 vols. (Neuenburg, 1927), IV, 606f, 677f; U. Dikenmann, 'Hans Lanz von Liebenfels, ein mittelalterlicher Emporkömmling', *Thurgauische Beiträge* 21 (1911), 34–48. Full genealogies in J. Kindler von Knobloch, *Oberbadisches Geschlechterbuch*, 3 vols. (Heidelberg, 1905), II, 461f, 504f, 508f.

4   C. von Lantz to August Näf, letters dated 5 July and 29 August 1878, Stadtbibliothek Vadiana, St Gallen, MS 145/169–70. This officer had received the Cross of the Franz Josef Order in 1874, Kriegsarchiv, Vienna, GASM 1874–40.

5   Hermann Hermann, *Genealogie und Heraldik bürgerlicher Familien Österreich-Ungarns*, 2 vols. (Vienna, 1899), I, 181.

6   Wilfried Daim, *Der Mann, der Hitler die Ideen gab* (Munich, 1958), p. 44. No positive evidence for a marriage has been found. Only a certain Moritz Felicetti von Liebenfels of Graz could be discovered in a contemporary Austrian directory of nobility. His family was of Italian origin and was first invested with the title 'von Liebenfels' in 1745. Since their blazon is quite different to that of the Swiss-Swabian family, which Lanz adopted, there is no reason to think that there was any relationship between the families. Karl Friedrich von Frank zu Döfering, *Alt-Österreichisches Adels-Lexikon*, 1 vol. (Vienna, 1928), I, 75 and Adelsarchiv, Vienna, Ministry of the Interior, Facs. 431 A.

7   Rudolf J. Mund, *Ahnennachweis von Joerg Lanz von Liebenfels Gründer des Ordo Novi Templi (ONT)*, Das andere Kreuz, 1 (Vienna, [1980]).

8 For a succinct analysis of this neo-romantic culture, see Jost Hermand, 'Gralsmotive um die Jahrhundertwende', *Vierteljahrsschrift für Literaturwissenschaft und Geistesgeschichte* 36 (1962), 521–43.

9 J. von Lanzenfels (i.e. Lanz), 'Der heilige Gral', *Stein der Weisen* 20 (1907), 218–26. Lanz had regarded the Templars negatively until as late as 1905. The allegations of blasphemy and sodomy, levelled against the Templars at their trial, led him to identify them as devotees of the beast-cults. J. Lanz-Liebenfels, 'Anthropozoon biblicum', *VfB* 1 (1903), p. 321; ibid. 2 (1904), p. 410 and *TZ*, pp. 21, 51.

10 J. von Lanzenfels, 'Der heilige Gral', *Stein der Weisen* 20 (1907), 218–26 (p. 226).

11 *Ostara* I, 69 (1913), pp. 12–16.

12 Although Lanz claimed to have first viewed Burg Werfenstein for the purposes of the ONT in 1896, accompanied by Amand von Schweiger-Lerchenfeld, author and editor of *Stein der Weisen*, and Alois Fischer, an official at court, and, furthermore, that he founded the ONT on Christmas Day 1900 with his two brothers, Herwik and Friedolin, these references must be treated with caution. J. Lanz von Liebenfels, *Arithmosophikon* 19 (Thalwyl, [1949]), pp. 726 ff; Georg Lanz von Liebenfels, *Regularium Fratrum Ordinis Novi Templi* (Werfenstein, 1921), p. 30. In the first place, Lanz was still denouncing the Templars in 1905, see above p.108, note 9. He cannot therefore have been wanting to emulate the order in 1896. Secondly, he stated that the party of 1896 had met August Strindberg at the Gasthof zum Werfenstein in Struden, while they were waiting for the castellan, but such a meeting is disproved by the contents of his own letter to Strindberg, dated 20 September 1911, Royal Library, Stockholm. An alternative explanation would be that the dates are authentic, but that he did not yet conceive of his chivalrous order in the *Templar* tradition.

13 J. Lanz-Liebenfels, 'Der Orden des neuen Tempels', *Ostara* I, 18 (December 1907), p. 15f.

14 *Ostara* III, 1 (1930), p. [iv].

15 Franz Herndl, *Die Trutzburg* (Leipzig, 1909), p. 251f. These fleur-de-lis, which recur in ONT heraldry, may derive from the blazon of the Muntprat family, which was associated with the Lanz von Liebenfels by two marriages in the sixteenth century. Gustav A. Seyler, *Abgestorbener Württemberger Adel* (Nuremberg 1911), p. 200 and plate 109.

16 See the personal seals on his letters to Johannes Hering, dated 22 September 1909, Bundesarchiv, Koblenz, NS26/1229, and to Philipp Stauff in late 1909, Bundesarchiv, Koblenz, NS26/512. He also used a chivalrous letter-head depicting a visored helm crowned with a cardinal's hat and an eagle wing. See his letters to August Strindberg, dated 20 September 1911, Royal Library, Stockholm, and to Johannes Hering, dated 6 September 1912, Bundesarchiv, Koblenz, NS26/1229. The ONT seal showed a mounted knight in armour decorated with swastikas, *Ostara* I, 35 (1910), recto front cover.

17 J. Lanz-Liebenfels, 'Geschichte der Burg Werfenstein', in Ludwig Commenda, *Neuer illustrierter Führer durch Grein und Umgebung* (Grein, 1910), pp. 84–95.

18 Herndl, op. cit., p. 257f.

19 Georg Lanz von Liebenfels, *Regularium Fratrum Ordinis Novi Templi* (Werfenstein, 1921), pp. 1–16. Hereafter cited as *Regularium*.

20 *Ostara* I, 26–31.

21 *Regularium*, pp. 4–6.

22 ibid., p. 8f.

23 ibid., p. 7f.

24 ibid., pp. 9–12.

25 *Ostara* I, 50 (1911), recto rear cover.

26 *Regularium*, p. 12. However, since this source claims an investiture for Amand von Schweiger-Lerchenfeld in August 1904, it may be considered unreliable in terms of chronology.

27 Lanz added the sigla PONT to his name in a letter to Johannes Hering, dated 6 September 1912, Bundesarchiv, Koblenz, NS26/1229.

28 Fra Erwin, 'Templeisenlehre', *Ostara* I, 69 (1913), p. 15f. Other order sigla in *Ostara* I, 79 (1915), pp. 15ff and *Ostara* I, 71, second edition (1918), verso rear cover.

29 *Ostara* I, 82 (1915), pp. 4–13; *Ostara* I, 88 (1916), pp. 8–13.

30 These paintings are illustrated in *Ostara* I, 82 (1915), p. 1 and *Ostara* I, 88 (1916), p. 1.

31 Fra Detlef, 'An St Bernhard v. Clairvaux', *Ostara* I, 78 (1915), p. 16; 'Templeisen-Andacht im Felde', *Ostara* I, 79 (1915), p. 17; 'Wir halten still', *Ostara* I, 80 (1915), p. 16; Fra Curt, 'Im Fieber', *Ostara* I, 79 (1915), p. 15.

32 Fra Aemilius, 'Der Sang vom Nibelungenstrom' and Fra Detlef, 'Burg und Hain von Werfenstein', *Ostara* I, 88 (1916), p. 4f. These poems are reprinted in Appendix D as examples of New Templar verse.

33 *Imaginarium NT*, plates 71, 73, 154, 112a and 164b. Lanz's exact relationship with Strindberg is controversial. The famous Swedish writer was for a time married to Frieda Uhl, whose family owned a small estate at Dornach in the Strudengau, which he visited between 1893 and 1896. The district is described in several of his works. Lanz wrote that he first met Strindberg at the inn in Struden in 1896. Together they walked up the Stillensteinklamm ravine behind Werfenstein and, on the following day, visited Baumgartenberg Abbey where they discovered a painting of the Portuguese Knights of Christ. Lanz claimed that their conversations on religious subjects helped restore Strindberg's faith. Lanz von Liebenfels, *Legendarium*, 15 May, pp. 470–2 and *Arithmosophikon* 19 (Thalwyl, [1949]), pp. 726–51. However, Strindberg ascribes his conversion to Swedenborgian visions in *Inferno* (1897). He actually describes a solitary walk up the Klamer Schlucht, another gorge about eight kilometres west of Werfenstein, while Lanz's letters to Strindberg assume no familiarity and even enquire whether Strindberg knows the Werfenstein area. Lanz to Strindberg, letter dated 20 September 1911, Royal Library, Stockholm.

34 Daim, op. cit., p. 114.

35 *Regularium*, p. 32. Cf. *Legendarium*, A 308, p. 171.

36 Jost Hermand, op. cit.

37 Detlef Schmude, 'Vorschlag zur Gründung von Siedlungs- und Arbeits-Freiwilligen-Korps aus Erwerblosen', leaflet dated May 1919. Schmude subsequently published two books about his experiences in post-war reconstruction.

38 *Regularium*, p. 16.

39 *Ostara* II, 1 (1922), p. 11. Schmude's letter to Lanz, dated *c.* November 1923, attributed the post-war disorder to an ignorance of eugenics amongst the leadership of Germany and appealed for a dictator in the form of a Listian 'Starke von Oben'. *Tabularium* 9 (December 1923), p. 31.

40 *Tabularium* 2 (May 1923), p. 6; *Tabularium* 9 (December 1923), p. 30. Hochberg used the order-name Frowin.

41 These details are recorded in *Tabularium* 15–17 (June-August 1924), pp. 56–9; *Tabularium* 18–21 (September–November 1924), pp. 63f, 68, 70; *Tabularium* 22, 23 (December 1924–January 1925), p. 76f; *Tabularium* 28, 29 (May–July 1925), p. 107.

42 *Tabularium* 13, 14 (May 1924), p. 47; *Tabularium* 28, 29 (May–July 1925) p. 107f.

43 *Tabularium* 35–7 (April–May 1926), p. 135; *Tabularium* 38–42 (June–December 1926), pp. [142, 147, 149].

44 *Imaginarium NT*, plates 171, 172. Jörg Weitbrecht (grandson of Konrad Weitbrecht) to the author, letter dated 25 January 1979.

45 Don Evrard Hauerstein (i.e. Georg Hauerstein Jr.), *Petena-Handschrift* 6, *Organum NT Vit.* (Petena, n.d.), p. 10f. Advertisement for 'Haus Ostara', *Zeitschrift für Menschenkenntnis und Schicksalsforschung* 2 (1927), p. 108.

46 *Tabularium* 38–42 (June–December 1926), p. [153f]; *Tabularium* 43 (January–April 1927), p. 8.

47 Hertesburg presbytery is illustrated in *Imaginarium NT*, plate 145. An account of its founding and mythical antecedents may be found in Don Evrard Hauerstein, op. cit., pp. 12ff.

48 Petena presbytery is illustrated in *Imaginarium NT*, plate 136. An account of its purchase and mythical antecedents is in Don Evrard Hauerstein, op. cit., pp. 15–23. Hauerstein subsequently started a schismatic order at Petena, the Vitalis New Templars, in November 1941.

49 *Tabularium* 15–17 (June–August 1924), pp. 53, 56.

50 *Tabularium* 30 (August–September 1925), p. 114f; *Tabularium* 35–7 (April–May 1926), pp. 131f, 140.

51 Lanz to Johann Walthari Wölfl, letter dated 1 May 1926, in *Ostara* III, 101 (1927), p. 2f. Franz Friedrich von Hochberg to Wölfl, letter dated 1 February 1927, in *Ostara* III, 101 (1927), supplement.

52 *Ostara-Rundschau* 1 (Whitsun 1931), p. 7f.

53 Daim, op. cit., p. 161f.

54 A short account of the nationalist associations may be found in C. A. Macartney, *October Fifteenth. A history of modern Hungary 1929–1945* (Edinburgh, 1956), pp. 28–30. Lanz's involvement is indicated in *Zeitschrift für Geistes- und Wissenschaftsreform* 7 (1932), p. 145n.

55 *Tabularium* 38–42 (June–December 1926), p. [150].

56 *Legendarium*, A 289, pp. 72–5. B. Raynald, *Emerich der Heilige* (Budapest, 1930).

57 Interviews with P. Miklos Kerper and Stephán Bodor (Balatoncsicso) and P. Miklos Szalai (Halimba), 9, 10 and 13 August 1978.

58 Marienkamp-Szent Balázs priory is illustrated in *Imaginarium NT*, plate 132. The heraldic devices and votive paintings in ibid., plates 1, 23, 24, 59, 77, 135.

59 Mag. Ortwinus, 'Bei Ihm zu Gast', *Zeitschrift für Geistes- und Wissenschaftsreform* 3 (1928), 218–19; *Legendarium*, A 289, pp. 75–7.

60 Szent Kereszt presbytery is illustrated in *Imaginarium NT*, plate 114.

10. THE GERMANENORDEN

1 See pp. 45, 64 f.

2 Uwe Lohalm, *Völkischer Radikalismus* (Hamburg, 1970), pp. 58–60.

3 Peter G. J. Pulzer, *The Rise of Political Anti-Semitism in Germany and Austria* (New York, 1964), pp. 88–117.

4 Richard and Eugen Haug, members of the Jungdeutscher Bund, established a Hammerbund at Stuttgart in 1906. Julius Rüttinger, the leader of the apprentice division of the DHV, founded a Hammer group at Nuremberg in 1912. Lohalm, op. cit., pp. 56–62. Both the *Jugendbünde* (youth organizations of the anti-Semitic parties) and the DHV had come into contact with members of the Austrian pan-German movement in the 1890s. This radical nationalist influence helps to explain the receptiveness of the successor Hammer groups to Listian ideas. Iris Hamel, *Völkischer Verband und nationale Gewerkschaft* (Frankfurt, 1967), pp. 72–82.

5 A blueprint for such a Germanic *Lebensreform* utopia was published by the Hammer-Verlag. Willibald Hentschel, *Mittgart* (Leipzig, 1904). See also Theodor Fritsch, 'Die Erneuerungs-Gemeinde', *Hammer* 7 (1908), 461–5 and 'Grundzüge der Erneuerungs-Gemeinde', *Hammer* 7 (1908), 678–81, 712–17.

6 Paul Förster, 'Ein deutsch-völkischer General-Stab', *Hammer* 3 (1904), 207–10.

7 Theodor Fritsch, 'Vom partei-politischen Antisemitismus', *Hammer* 11 (1912), 153–8.

8 Theodor Fritsch, 'Wenn ich der Kaiser wär!', *Hammer* 11 (1912), 309–11.

9 An unidentified newspaper photograph, evidently from 1935, with the caption 'Gründungstag des Reichshammerbundes', shows Theodor Fritsch, Julius Rüttinger, Hermann Pohl, Georg Hauerstein Sr., Karl August Hellwig and fifteen other persons, Bundesarchiv, Koblenz, NS26/887.

10 Karl August Hellwig, 'Verfassung des R.H.B.', Bundesarchiv, Koblenz, NS26/888; Theodor Fritsch, 'Richtlinien für den Reichshammerbund (R.H.B.)', Bundesarchiv, Koblenz, NS26/888.

11 Julius Rüttinger, 'Jahresbericht für 1912' and 'Kassenbericht für 1912', Bundesarchiv, Koblenz, NS26/888.

12 Theodor Fritsch had devoted a whole section of his *Antisemiten-Katechismus* (1887) to 'Jewish secret societies'. The origins of this notion may be sought in Sir John Retcliffe (pseudonym for Hermann Goedsche), *Biarritz*, 4 vols. (Berlin, 1868–70). The chapter entitled 'In the Jewish Cemetery in Prague' described, amid these uncanny surroundings, a secret nocturnal meeting of subversive Jewish agents, who discussed their progress in the undermining of European society. The chapter was frequently printed as an independent work and was one of the ingredients in the development of the Protocols of the Elders of Zion, for which see Norman Cohn, *Warrant for Genocide* (London, 1967), pp. 32–40 and *passim*.

13 Philipp Stauff to Heinrich Kraeger, letter dated 30 May 1910, Bundesarchiv, Koblenz, NS26/512.

14 Johannes Hering to Philipp Stauff, letter dated 18 January 1911, Bundesarchiv, Koblenz, NS26/512a.

15 Hermann Pohl, circular dated November 1911, Bundesarchiv, Koblenz, NS26/512a.

16 *Allgemeine Ordens-Nachrichten* 14 (September 1918), 3–4.

17 Hermann Pohl, 'Aufklärungschrift über Veranlassung, Zweck, Ziel, Ausbau der Treulogen', circular dated 12 January 1912, Bundesarchiv, Koblenz, NS26/512a.

18 Hermann Pohl, 'Vertrauliche Ordensnachrichten', circular dated July 1912, Bundesarchiv, Koblenz, NS26/492; *Vertrauliche Ordens-Nachrichten* 2 (December 1912).

19 *Vertrauliche Ordens-Nachrichten* 3 (May 1913).

20 Julius Rüttinger, 'Von 1904 bis 1937', typescript dated 30 January 1937, Bundesarchiv, Koblenz, NS26/887; Karl Mathes to Julius Rüttinger, letters dated 12 December 1912 and 19 October 1913; Julius Rüttinger to Karl Mathes, letters dated 21 and 24 November 1913, Bundesarchiv, Koblenz, NS26/885.

21 Arthur Strauss to Julius Rüttinger, letter dated 20 May 1914, Bundesarchiv, Koblenz, NS26/885.

22 Julius Rüttinger, 'Versuch zur Gewinnung einer Organisation der G. O. Gauloge Franken', typescript dated September 1915, Bundesarchiv, Koblenz, NS26/852.

23 'Germanen-Botschaft', undated leaflet, Bundesarchiv, Koblenz, NS26/852.

24 'Beitritts-Erklärung', form, Bundesarchiv, Koblenz, NS26/852.

25 'Anweisung zur Werbearbeit', undated leaflet, Bundesarchiv, Koblenz, NS26/852. The recommended *Ostara* numbers were *Ostara* I, 26 *Einführung in die Rassenkunde* (1908), *Ostara* I, 27 *Beschreibende Rassenkunde* (1908), and *Ostara* I, 65 *Rasse und Krankheit* (1913). It will be recalled that Lanz von Liebenfels had applied these racial typologies for the ordering of brothers in the Ordo Novi Templi; see above p. 110f.

26 *Allgemeine Ordens-Nachrichten* 13 (March 1918), 3–4.

27 *Allgemeine Ordens-Nachrichten* 9 (July 1916), front cover, and in successive numbers.

28 The correspondence between Haus Ecklöh and the List Society secretariat, dated 1917–19, Bundesarchiv, Koblenz, NS26/1244.

29 See below, p. 151.

30 Confidential invitation to initiation ceremony, dated 29 December 1913, Bundesarchiv, Koblenz, NS26/852. The 'plastometer' is illustrated in Robert Burger-Villingen, *Geheimnis der Menschenform*, fifth edition (Berlin, 1940), p. 81.

31 'An die Einführung in den Untergrad', manuscript dated *c.* 1912, Bundesarchiv, Koblenz, NS26/852. This particular lodge was probably located in Magdeburg or Breslau. Such a well-appointed lodge was described in these towns in *Vertrauliche Ordens-Nachrichten* 2 (December 1912).

32 Hermann Pohl to Julius Rüttinger, letter dated 22 November 1914, Bundesarchiv, Koblenz, NS26/886.

33 *Allgemeine Ordens-Nachrichten* 10 (Autumn 1917), p. 4f.

34 Töpfer to Julius Rüttinger, letters dated 24 September and 6 December 1915, Bundesarchiv, Koblenz, NS26/886.

35 *Allgemeine Ordens-Nachrichten* 9 (July 1916).

36 *Allgemeine Ordens-Nachrichten* 10 (Autumn 1917), p. 6; Alfons Steiger, *Der neudeutsche Heide im Kampf gegen Christen und Juden* (Berlin, 1924), p. 175.

37 Erwin von Heimerdinger, Dr Gensch, and Bernhard Koerner, circular dated 20 October 1916, Bundesarchiv, Koblenz, NS26/852; Steiger, op. cit., p. 175; Rudolf von Sebottendorff, *Bevor Hitler kam*, second edition (Munich, 1934), pp. 34, 245.

38 Ernst Böttger to Grand Ducal Court of Weimar, letter dated 6 July 1912, Bundesarchiv, Koblenz, NS26/510. According to Böttger, the *völkisch* lawyer acting for Stauff, the *Semi-Gotha* bore the full title *Weimarer historisch-genealogisches Taschenbuch des gesamten Adels jehudäischen Ursprunges* (Weimar, 1912). The edition had been confiscated by the court in June 1912. According to a later genealogical work by Stauff, *Semi-Imperator 1888–1918* (Munich, 1919), the *Semi-Alliancen* had been first published in 1912 and the *Semi-Gotha* ran to subsequent editions in 1913 and 1914. *Semi-Imperator 1888–1918* (Munich, 1919), p. 5f.

39 See the correspondence addressed to Philipp Stauff, Bundesarchiv, Koblenz, NS26/510.

40 Guido von List, 'Erklärungen und Bemerkungen zu den spiritistischen Sitzungs-Protokollen vom 14./16. und 19. Februar 1913 zu Berlin', *Zeitschrift für Geistes- und Wissenschaftsreform* 3 (1928), 59–68.

41 Stauff closed a letter to List, dated 6 September 1913, with the salute 'Armanengruss und Templeisensieg', which is redolent of both HAO and ONT usage, in Balzli, op. cit., p. 187 f. This hint of New Templarism is given further force by the fact that Lanz had corresponded with Stauff as early as 1909, letter of late 1909, Bundesarchiv, Koblenz, NS26/512.

42 Photograph of Koerner at the Western Front, in Balzli, op. cit., p. 43; Bernhard Koerner to Guido von List, letter dated 12 January 1917, in Balzli, op. cit., pp. 174–6.

43 Eberhard von Brockhusen to Erwin von Heimerdinger, letters dated 27 December

1918 and 28 February 1919, Bundesarchiv, Koblenz, NS26/852.

44 Dietwart (i.e. Philipp Stauff) to Brockhusen, letter dated 2 March 1919; Brockhusen to Koerner, letters dated 6 and 26 July 1919; Brockhusen to Heimerdinger, letters dated 5 and 15 September 1919, Bundesarchiv, Koblenz, NS26/852.

45 Irmin (i.e. Johann Albrecht zu Mecklenburg) to Heimerdinger, letters dated 7 October and 30 December 1919 and 14 January 1920; funerary notice decorated with swastikas, Bundesarchiv, Koblenz, NS26/852.

46 'Mihilathing', assembly minutes dated 29 September 1921, Bundesarchiv, Koblenz, NS26/852.

47 Gotthard Jasper, 'Aus den Akten der Prozesse gegen die Erzberger-Mörder', *Vierteljahreshefte für Zeitgeschichte* 10 (1962), 430–53, especially trial documents 5, 6, 9 and 10; Uwe Lohalm, op. cit., pp. 227–37.

11. RUDOLF VON SEBOTTENDORFF AND THE THULE SOCIETY

1 Birth certificate, Rat der Stadt Hoyerswerda.

2 Rudolf von Sebottendorff, *Der Talisman des Rosenkreuzers* (Pfullingen, 1925), p. 7. The character Erwin Torre represents Sebottendorff in the book. This work is hereafter cited as *TR*.

3 Ernst Tiede, *Astrologisches Lexikon* (Leipzig, 1922), p. 279; Sebottendorff, *TR*, p. 7 f.

4 Sebottendorf, *TR*, pp. 8–12; Ellic Howe, 'Rudolph Freiherr von Sebottendorff', unpublished typescript dated 1968, p. 9.

5 Sebottendorf, *TR*, pp. 15–20.

6 ibid., pp. 18–20; Lloyds Record Library, London.

7 Sebottendorf, *TR*, pp. 20–2. The Lloyds registry confirms that the S.S. Ems sailed from Naples for New York on 9 February 1900, while the S.S. Prinz Regent Luitpold arrived in Naples on 14 February. The Norddeutscher Lloyd agent at Gibralter, Marseilles or Genoa could have telegraphed to Naples with a request for an electrician. Howe, op. cit., p. 10.

8 Sebottendorf, *TR*, pp. 22–5.

9 Tiede, op. cit., p. 279; Sebottendorf, *TR*, pp. 30–7.

10 Sebottendorf, *TR*, pp. 31, 40–2, 46–58.

11 ibid., pp. 31f, 34–7.

12 ibid., pp. 53–7.

13 ibid., pp. 65–8.

14 Haupt-Liste für den In- Reichs- Aus-Länder No. 513699, Stadtarchiv, Munich.

15 Familienbogen Glauer, dated 19 November 1918, Stadtarchiv, Munich.

16 'Das Porträt eines hakenkreuzlerischen Hochstaplers', *Münchener Post*, 14 March 1923, p. 7. This account states that the incident occurred in 1909, which must be a misprint for 1908.

17 Rudolf von Sebottendorf, *Geschichte der Astrologie*, 1 vol. (Leipzig, 1923), I, 5.

18 Rudolf von Sebottendorf, 'Erwin Haller. Ein deutscher Kaufmann in der Türkei', *Münchener Beobachter*, 31 August 1918–10 May 1919.

19 The book on the Baktashi dervishes finally achieved publication after the war as *Die Praxis der alten türkischen Freimaurerei* (Leipzig, 1924). Two other works on mysticism were written by Sebottendorff at this time. *Deutsche Mystik*, written in Turkish (Stamboul, 1915), cited by Tiede, op. cit., p. 279, and *Tauler und Boehme*, written in Persian (n.p., n.d.), advertised in Sebottendorf, *TR*, p. 2. Neither of these works has been traced.

20 See above p. 59; Sebottendorf, *Die Praxis der alten türkischen Freimaurerei* (Leipzig, 1924), pp. 5ff, 19.

21 Rudolf von Sebottendorff, *Bevor Hitler kam*, second edition (Munich, 1934), pp. 169, 267. This work is hereafter cited as *BHK*. The Turkish Ministry of the Interior confirms that Sebottendorff became a Turkish citizen in 1911. Zeki Kuneralp (Ministry of Foreign Affairs, Ankara) to John Jardine (British Council, Ankara), letter dated 21 February 1969.

22 Familienbogen Glauer, op. cit.

23 'Reichsfreiherr Siegmund von Sebottendorff von der Rose, k.u.k. Hofkämmerer und Major a.D.† 21 Oktober 1915 in Wiesbaden', *Wiesbadener Zeitung*, 23 October 1915, p. 6.

24 *Gothaische genealogische Taschenbücher der freiherrlichen Häuser* 7 (1857), 700–3; ibid. 38 (1888), 776f; *Genealogisches Taschenbuch der adligen Häuser* 12 (1887), 440–2. See Appendix B for these genealogies.

25 Sebottendorf, *TR*, p. 80f.

26 Notes on the tank of Friedrich Göbel are in *Technik-Geschichte* 23 (1934), 102ff.

27 Irmgard Uhlig (Kleinzschachwitz) to author, letter dated 20 April 1980.

28 Familienbogen Glauer, op. cit. Sebottendorff, *BHK*, pp. 168, 226. Sebottendorff vengefully lampooned Alsberg and Heindl as transvestites, Sebottendorf, *TR*, p. 86.

29 Sebottendorf, *TR*, pp. 86–8.

30 ibid., pp. 90–5.

31 ibid., pp. 95–8.

32 ibid., p. 98f and *BHK*, p. 40. This new lodge in Berlin is identical with the lodge in the Köthener Strasse near Potsdamer Platz, headed by G. W. Freese, see above, p. 131.

33 This biographical account is taken from 'Zum Gedächtnis an Walter Nauhaus', *Deutscher Roland* 13 (1920), Sonderdruck, Bundesarchiv, Koblenz, NS26/1229.

34 Walter Nauhaus to Guido von List Gesellschaft, letter dated January 1917, in Balzli, op. cit., p. 176f.

35 Sebottendorf, *TR*, p. 99 and *BHK*, p. 53.

36 Sebottendorf, *TR*, p. 99; Johannes Hering, 'Beiträge zur Geschichte der Thule-Gesellschaft', typescript dated 21 June 1939, Bundesarchiv, Koblenz, NS26/865.

37 Sebottendorff, *BHK*, pp. 57–60.

38 *GLB* 1 (1908), p. 13f.

39 *GLB* 5 (1910), table I.

40 'Aus der Geschichte der Thule Gesellschaft', *Thule-Bote* 1 (1933), 1–2.

41 Sebottendorff, *BHK*, p. 3f.

42 The ensuing account draws heavily upon Reginald H. Phelps, '"Before Hitler came": Thule Society and Germanen Orden', *Journal of Modern History* 25 (1963), 245–61.

43 Sebottendorff, *BHK*, p. 43f.

44 ibid., p. 194f.

45 ibid., pp. 63–70.

46 The executed Thulists were: Walter Nauhaus, Baron Teuchert, Walter Deicke, Friedrich Wilhelm von Seydlitz, Countess Heila von Westarp, Prince Gustav von Thurn und Taxis, and Anton Daumelang. 'Shooting of Hostages . . . Munich Savagery' was the headline in *The Times*, 5 May 1919, p. 1.

47 Sebottendorff, *BHK*, pp. 62, 237, 240, 248, 264. Eckart, Hitler's most important Munich mentor, lectured in the Thule on 30 May 1919. Johannes Hering, 'Beiträge zur Geschichte der Thule-Gesellschaft', typescript dated 21 June 1939, Bundesarchiv, Koblenz, NS26/865.

48 List of members in Sebottendorff, *BHK*, pp. 225–74.

49 ibid., p. 74. Details of Karl Harrer on p. 247.

50 Politische Arbeiter-Zirkel meeting minutes, Bundesarchiv, Koblenz, NS26/76.

51 Anton Drexler, 'Lebenslauf', typescript dated 12 March 1935, supplied by Dr Reginald Phelps with the permission of Drexler's daughter, Frau Anni Widmaier. Michael Lotter, 'Der Beginn meines politischen Denkens', typescript of lecture delivered on 19 October 1935, Bundesarchiv, Koblenz, NS26/78.

52 Reginald H. Phelps, 'Hitler and the Deutsche Arbeiterpartei', *American Historical Review* 68 (1963), 974–86.

53 Georg Franz-Willing, *Ursprung der Hitlerbewegung*, second edition (Preussisch Oldendorf, 1974), pp. 115, 123–6. Franz-Willing based this account upon interviews and correspondence with Friedrich Krohn, Josef Feuss, Karolina Gahr, Erna Hanfstängl and others.

54 Ernst Tiede to Guido von List, letter dated 25 February 1917, in Balzli, op. cit., pp. 214–16.

55 Baron v.d. Launitz, Duke of Gothien to SS-Obersturmbahnführer Theodor Christensen, letter dated 13 October 1936, Bundesarchiv, Koblenz, EAP 173-b-20-16/19a.

56 SA warning cards on Rudolf von Sebottendorff, dated 29 January and 2 March 1934, Berlin Document Center, Zehlendorf.

57 Herbert Rittlinger to Ellic Howe, letter dated 20 June 1968.

12. THE HOLY RUNES AND THE EDDA SOCIETY

1 Armin Mohler, *Die konservative Revolution in Deutschland 1918–1932* (Darmstadt, 1972), gives a comprehensive survey and bibliography of these various right-wing movements after the war.

2 'Lebenslauf Rudolf John Gorsleben', *Zeitschrift für Geistes- und Wissenschaftsreform* 3 (1928), 115–16; Rudolf John Gorsleben, 'Fahrt durch Syrien', *Zeitschrift für Geistes- und Wissenschaftsreform* 3 (1928), 323-8, 368–73.

3 Rudolf John Gorsleben, 'Als Rätegeisel', *Zeitschrift für Geistes- und Wissenschaftsreform* 3 (1928), 118–19.

4 Johannes Hering, 'Beiträge zur Geschichte der Thule-Gesellschaft', typescript dated 21 June 1939, Bundesarchiv, Koblenz, NS26/865.

5 Uwe Lohalm, *Völkische Radikalismus* (Hamburg, 1970), pp. 260–3, 309f, 420. Lohalm notes that the fragmentation of the league favoured the growth of the Nazi Party in late 1922 and early 1923.

6 Rudolf John Gorsleben, *Hoch-Zeit der Menschheit* (Leipzig, 1930), pp. 16–21.

7 ibid., p. 251.   8 ibid., pp. 251–80.   9 ibid., pp. 294–307.

10 ibid., pp. 656–77.   11 ibid., p. 109.   12 ibid., p. 328f.

13 Bacchos-Dionysos (i.e. Martin Brücher), *Ich befehle! Die befreiende Sendung Deutschlands im metaphysischen Geheimnis der deutschen Ursprache* (Oberursel, [1920]).

14 Further members were Otto Dickel, Ernst Hauck, Hans von Joeden, Kurt Prinz zur Lippe, Mathilde Merck, Hans Georg Müller, Erich Riedl-Riedenstein, Arnold Rüge, Tassiso Scheffer, Alfred Schmidt, Graf Tassilo Strachwitz, Kaspar Stuhl, Karl Weinländer, Arnold Wagemann, Edmund von Wecus, and Richard Anders. Frater Georg Nikolaus (ONT), 'Lexikon der Ariosophie', undated manuscript, Rudolf Mund Archive (Vienna).

15 'Ziele und Satzungen der EDDA-GESELLSCHAFT', *Hag All All Hag* 10 (1933), Heft 6, 16–17. It is also recorded that Bülow received a modest grant from Reichsführer-SS Heinrich Himmler towards the costs of publishing the periodical.

16 'Gleichschaltung', *Hag All All Hag* 10 (1933), Heft 4, 3–5; 'Die Heimkehr der Ostmark ins Reich', *Hagal* 15 (1938), Heft 5, 69; 'Böhmen und Mähren', *Hagal* 16 (1939), Heft 3, 34–5.

17 Werner von Bülow, 'Mimirs Quelle', *Hagal* 11 (1934), Heft 7, 4–7 and 'Denkmäler: Die Geheimsprache der Denkmäler', *Hagal* 11 (1934), Heft 11, 1–3.

18 Biographical data in Friedrich Bernhard Marby, *Sonne und Planeten im Tierkreis* (Stuttgart, 1975), p. 255 and jacket.

19 Friedrich Bernhard Marby, 'Von den Geheimnissen alter Türme und Kirchen', in *Der Weg zu den Müttern* (Stuttgart, 1957), pp. 65–80.

20 Siegfried Adolf Kummer, *Runen-Magie* (Dresden, 1933) and *Heilige Runenmacht* (Hamburg, 1932).

21 Weisthor (i.e. Wiligut) to Himmler, letter dated 2 May 1934, Bundesarchiv, Koblenz, Himmler Nachlass 19.

NOTES AND REFERENCES

13. HERBERT REICHSTEIN AND ARIOSOPHY

1 The earliest traceable mention of the word 'Ariosophy' occurs in *Ostara* I, 82 (1915), p. 3.

2 Jörg Lanz von Liebenfels, 'Grundriss der ariosophischen Geheimlehre', *Zeitschrift für Menschenkenntnis und Menschenschicksal* 1 (1925–6), 4–11.

3 A survey of the periodical literature may be found in Ingeborg Besser, 'Die Presse des neueren Okkultismus in Deutschland von 1875 bis 1933' (unpublished Ph.D. thesis, University of Leipzig, 1945).

4 Wilhelm Th. H. Wulff, *Tierkreis und Hakenkreuz* (Gütersloh, 1968).

5 Ernst Issberner-Haldane, 'Frodi Ingolfson Wehrmann', *Zeitschrift für Geistes- und Wissenschaftsreform* 3 (1928), 163–4. Although he did not personally meet List, Wehrmann corresponded regularly with him before 1919. Frodi Ingolfson Wehrmann, 'Zum Gedenken an Guido von List's zehnten Sterbetag', *Zeitschrift für Geistes- und Wissenschaftsreform* 4 (1929), 157–8 and Gerhard Kurtz (Stuttgart) to author, letter dated 17 March 1979.

6 Arnulf, 'Unsere Bildbeilage', *Zeitschrift für Geistes- und Wissenschaftsreform* 3 (1928), 58.

7 Herbert Reichstein, 'Wie sich ein "Genie" bekannt macht', *Zeitschrift für Geistes- und Wissenschaftsreform* 5 (1930), 162–4. The English text was Eleanor Kirk, *The Influence of the Zodiac upon Human Life* (London, 1915).

8 Frodi Ingolfson Wehrmann, *Die Tragik der Germanen* (Düsseldorf, 1926) represented a typically Listian reinterpretation of historical and cultural materials. His second text was *Die Sendung der Germanen* (Düsseldorf, 1926).

9 Ernst Issberner-Haldane, *Der Chiromant* (Bad Oldesloe, 1925), *passim*. According to this autobiography, Issberner-Haldane again met Mr Hewalt in Berlin after the war. At this time Hewalt is portrayed as a mystic with clairvoyant powers, who is fighting to safeguard Aryan purity by advising young women vigorously against racial *mésalliances*. He is proposing to withdraw shortly to his private monastery in Colombia, ibid., pp. 305–18. Although many episodes in the autobiography may owe their inspiration to the post-war theosophical-occult subculture, the encounters with such guru figures are recounted in detail, as they might describe authentic influences upon Issberner-Haldane before 1914.

10 ibid., pp. 182–7, 190–8.   11 ibid., pp. 222–33.

12 Notice in *Zeitschrift für Menschenkenntnis und Schicksalsforschung* 1 (1926), 167.

13 The first issue of *Die Chiromantie* in Reichstein's periodical appeared in October 1929. Here Issberner-Haldane described the person of Mr Hewalt and his clairvoyant characterological powers, mentioning their two encounters. Ernst Issberner-Haldane, 'Meister-Charakterologen', *Zeitschrift für Geistes- und Wissenschaftsreform* 4 (1929), 292–4. Issberner-Haldane is first mentioned as a Novice, Fra Yvo NNT, in April 1927. *Tabularium* 43 (January–April 1927), p. 8. An advertisement for the 'Svastika-Heim' appears in *Zeitschrift für Geistes- und Wissenschaftsreform* 7 (1932), 135. One of Ellic Howe's German contacts told him in the 1960s that Issberner-Haldane remarried late in life 'in order to procreate a Christ Child'. He died in 1966.

14 *Zeitschrift für Geistes- und Wissenschaftsreform* 7 (1932), 163. With the exception of the abortive second *Ostara* series begun by Schmude at Magdeburg in 1922, Lanz had found no outlet for his writings on a regular basis since the conclusion of the first *Ostara* series.

15 Herbert Reichstein, 'Geleitworte', *Zeitschrift für Menschenkenntnis und Menschenschicksal* 1 (1925–6), 1–4; cf. 'Was wir wollen', ibid., verso front cover.

16 ibid., verso front cover.

17 J. Lanz von Liebenfels, *Grundriss der ariosophischen Geheimlehre* (Düsseldorf, 1925), verso rear cover.

18 *Zeitschrift für Menschenkenntnis und Schicksalsforschung* 1 (1926), verso front cover of Heft 8/9; cf. announcements in J. Lanz von Liebenfels, *Jakob Lorber. Das Grösste ariosophische Medium der Neuzeit*. III. Teil (Düsseldorf, 1926), p. 18, and *Jakob Lorber. Das grösste ariosophische Medium der Neuzeit*. IV. Teil (Düsseldorf, 1926), verso rear cover.

19 Joseph Fischer-Hartinger, 'Der Dichter Gregor Bostunitsch. Ein kleines Lebensbild', *Zeitschrift für Geistes- und Wissenschaftsreform* 4 (1929), 333–8.

20 Norman Cohn had described how this originally Russian forgery of a plan for Jewish world-conquest, composed *c.*1895, enjoyed renewed popularity among the Whites after the October revolution. Norman Cohn, *Warrant for Genocide* (London, 1967), pp. 117–19.

21 Gregor Schwartz-Bostunitsch, *Doktor Steiner—ein Schwindler wie keiner* (Munich, 1930), p. 3; James Webb, *The Occult Establishment* (La Salle, Ill., 1976), pp. 186, 266f; James Webb, *The Harmonious Circle* (London, 1980), pp. 185–7.

22 *Zeitschrift für Geistes- und Wissenschaftsreform* 3 (1928), pp. 73, 250–6.

23 Correspondence between Schwartz-Bostunitsch, Himmler and other senior SS officers, Bundesarchiv, Koblenz, NS19/870. Further biographical details in Walter Laqueur, *Russia and Germany* (London, 1965), pp. 122–5.

24 *Zeitschrift für Geistes- und Wissenschaftsreform* 3 (1928), 14–19, 31–2, 45–7, 47–9, 55–7, 196–9.

25 Herbert Reichstein, 'Rudolf John Gorsleben †', *Zeitschrift für Geistes- und Wissenschaftsreform* 5 (1930), 281.

26 *Imaginarium NT*, plate 102.

27 Frodi Ingolfson Wehrmann and Herbert Reichstein, 'Aufruf!', *Zeitschrift für Geistes- und Wissenschaftsreform* 3 (1928), 250–6.

28 Lanz von Liebenfels appears to have been the first to develop this mantic system. J. Lanz von Liebenfels, Meister Amalarich and Meister Archibald, *Die ariosophische Kabbalistik von Name und Örtlichkeit* (Düsseldorf, 1926). Herbert Reichstein published his own *Praktisches Lehrbuch der ariosophischen Kabbalistik* in serial form in his periodical between May 1930 and June 1931.

29 J. Lanz von Liebenfels, 'Guido von List', *Zeitschrift für Menschenkenntnis und Schicksalsforschung* 2 (1927), 74–89; 'Benito Mussolini', *Zeitschrift für Geistes- und Wissenschaftsreform* 3 (1928), 77–94; 'Ernst Issberner-Haldane', *Zeitschrift für Geistes-*

und Wissenschaftsreform 3 (1928), 145–50. 'Die Geschichte der Ariosophie' appeared in the periodical between January 1929 and June 1930. See Appendix C for its analysis.

30 'Mitteilungen der "Neuen Kalandsgesellschaft"', *Zeitschrift für Geistes- und Wissenschaftsreform* 4 (1929), 26.

31 'Mitteilungen der "Neuen Kalandsgesellschaft"', *Zeitschrift für Geistes- und Wissenschaftsreform* 4 (1929), 91.

32 Herbert Reichstein, 'Charakter- und Schicksalsdeutung aus den Namen eines Menschen', *Zeitschrift für Geistes- und Wissenschaftsreform* 4 (1929), 213–19. The lecture tour is announced in 'Mitteilungen der "Neuen Kalandsgesellschaft"', ibid., 296.

33 'Mitteilungen der "Neuen Kalandsgesellschaft"', *Zeitschrift für Geistes- und Wissenschaftsreform* 4 (1929), 296. Cf. *Zeitschrift für Geistes- und Wissenschaftsreform* 5 (1930), 279.

34 'Mitteilungen der "Neuen Kalandsgesellschaft"', *Zeitschrift für Geistes- und Wissenschaftsreform* 4 (1929), 56–7, 229–30.

35 Notices in *Zeitschrift für Geistes- und Wissenschaftsreform* 5 (1930), pp. 101, 105.

36 Gerhard Kurtz (Stuttgart) to author, letters dated 17 March 1979 and 23 October 1980.

37 'Mitteilungen der "Ariosophischen Kulturzentrale"', *Zeitschrift für Geistes- und Wissenschaftsreform* 6 (1931), 199–201, 260.

38 A brief description of the birthday celebrations appeared in 'Mitteilungen der "Ariosophischen Kulturzentrale"', *Zeitschrift für Geistes- und Wissenschaftsreform* 7 (1932), 208. Lanz himself was not present, but sent a letter of gratitude from Biberach, ibid., p. 207.

39 Ingeborg Besser, op. cit., p. 58.

40 Herbert Reichstein, 'Totgeschwiegene Forscher', *Zeitschrift für Geistes- und Wissenschaftsreform* 5 (1930), 201–6.

41 *Zeitschrift für Geistes- und Wissenschaftsreform* 6 (1931), Heft 11.

42 *Ostara* III, 28 (1931), recto rear cover. The founder of the Hollow Earth Doctrine was Cyrus Romulus Reed Teed (1839–1908). Teed claimed to have undergone a spiritual illumination in 1870, when he received by revelation the tenets of this doctrine, which he called Koreshianity (Koresh is the Hebrew for Cyrus). In 1903 he established a sectarian community at Estero, Florida. The doctrine was introduced to Germany by Peter Bender, who read the sect periodical *The Flaming Sword*, while a prisoner of war in France. Karl E. Neupert wrote several books on the subject. Elmer T. Clark, *The Small Sects in America* (New York, 1949), pp. 147–50 and J. Gordon Melton, *The Encyclopedia of American Religions* (Wilmington, Ind., 1978), II, 37f.

43 Herbert Reichstein, 'Kabbalistische Horoskope', *Zeitschrift für Geistes- und Wissenschaftsreform* 5 (1930), 85–9.

44 Herbert Reichstein, 'Adolf Hitler—ein Werkzeug Gottes', *Zeitschrift für Geistes- und Wissenschaftsreform* 7 (1932), 105–6.

45 Ernst Lachmann, 'Deutschlands bevorstehende Schicksalsjahre im Lichte astrologischer und historionomischer Prophetie', *Zeitschrift für Geistes- und Wissenschaftsreform* 5 (1930), 89–91. '1931—das deutsche Wende-und Schicksalsjahr', *Zeitschrift für Geistes- und Wissenschaftsreform* 6 (1931), 85–7. '1932—Auftakt zur deutschen Revolutionsperiode', *Zeitschrift für Geistes- und Wissenschaftsreform* 7 (1932), 61–3.

46 Notice in *Zeitschrift für Geistes- und Wissenschaftsreform* 8 (1933), Heft 4.

47 Interview with Arthur Lorber (Donzdorf), 22 August 1979.

48 Rudolf Olden, *Das Wunderbare oder die Verzauberten* (Berlin, 1932).

49 Sefton Delmer, *Weimar Germany* (London, 1972), p. 95.

50 Statements of faith in *Zeitschrift für Geistes- und Wissenschaftsreform* 7 (1932), pp. 157–64.

14. KARL MARIA WILIGUT: THE PRIVATE MAGUS OF HEINRICH HIMMLER

1 Joachim C. Fest, *The Face of the Third Reich* (London, 1970), pp. 111–24; Bradley F. Smith, *Heinrich Himmler: a Nazi in the making 1900–26* (Stanford, Calif., 1971); Josef Ackermann, *Heinrich Himmler als Ideologe* (Göttingen, 1970).

2 Michael H. Kater, *Das 'Ahnenerbe' der SS 1935–1945* (Stuttgart, 1974).

3 For most information on Wiligut I am indebted to Rudolf J. Mund, *Der Rasputin Himmlers* (Vienna, 1982). Further details were gleaned from the Wiligut-Weisthor SS file, Berlin Document Center.

4 Details of wartime military service in Mund, op. cit., pp. 18–22.

5 K. M. Wiligut-Weisthor, 'Lebenslauf', typescript dated 16 May 1937, Wiligut-Weisthor SS file, Berlin Document Center.

6 According to Frau B., another Mund source, Adolf Hitler is supposed to have frequented this group between 1908 and 1913. Mund, op. cit., p. 25.

7 Theodor Czepl, 'Gedächtnisprotokoll und Bericht Czepls an den ONT aus dem Jahre 1921', in Mund, op. cit., pp. 27–34.

8 Wiligut's chronology is described fully in Mund, op. cit., pp. 153–75. The centrality of Goslar in his account may derive from his familiarity with Ernst Betha, *Die Erde und unsere Ahnen* (Berlin, 1913), which identified Goslar as the chief shrine of ancient Germany.

9 Wiligut's account of his family in the medieval period is contained in his own 'Lebenslauf', dated 16 May 1937, Wiligut-Weisthor SS file, Berlin Document Center.

10 A full description of the case and the report of the court in Mund, op. cit., pp. 35–51.

11 'Uraltes Familien-Siegel des Hauses Wiligut', *Hag All All Hag* 10 (1933), Heft 2/3, 290–3.

12 Jarl Widar, 'Gotos Raunen—Runenwissen!', 'Runen raunen . . . ', 'Die Vierheiten', *Hagal* 11 (1934), Heft 7, 7–15; 'Die Zahl: Runen raunen, Zahlen reden . . . ', *Hagal* 11 (1934), Heft 8, 1–4; 'Die Schöpfungsspirale, das "Weltenei"!', *Hagal* 11 (1934), Heft 9, 4–7.

NOTES AND REFERENCES

13 Erik Gustafson, 'Einleitung', *Hagal* 11 (1934), Heft 7, 1–4.

14 Surviving items are a draft of his first Hagal article 'Gotos Raunen—Runenwissen!' (July 1934) with a handwritten dedication 'in Armans-Treue!'; 'Harumar' (4 May 1934), a seven-verse mythological poem; 'Die neun Gebote Gôts' (summer 1935); 'Darstellung der Menschheitsentwicklung' (17 June 1936); 'O mani batme hum!', a mythological idyll; several letters dated 1935–6; and 'Ur-Vatar-unsar!' (14 August 1934), the Irminist paternoster reproduced here:

> *Vatar unsar der Du bist der Aithar*
> *Gibor ist Hagal des Aithars und der Irda!*
> *Gib uns Deinen Geist und Deine Kraft im Stoffe*
> *Und forme unsere Skould also gleich dem Werdandi.*
> *Dein Geist sei unser auch in Urd*
> *Von Ewigkeit zu Ewigkeit—Om! (:Amen:)*

Bundesarchiv, Koblenz, Nachlass Himmler 19.

15 Kirchhoff to Weisthor, letter dated 24 June 1934, Bundesarchiv, Koblenz, NS21/31.

16 Weisthor to Himmler, letter dated 17 August 1934, Bundesarchiv, Koblenz, NS21/31.

17 Weisthor to Himmler and Darré, letter dated 2 September 1934, Bundesarchiv, Koblenz, NS21/31.

18 Günther Kirchhoff, 'Rotbart von Kyffhäuser' (1 September 1934) and letter to Weisthor dated 27 August 1934, Bundesarchiv, Koblenz, NS21/31. Other Kirchhoff items in this folder, NS21/299 and NS19/neu 747.

19 K. M. Weisthor, 'Bericht über die Dienstreise von SS-Oberführer Weisthor nach Gaggenau/Baden und Umgebung vom 16.–24. Juni 1936' and 'Bericht über die Auffindung des Irminkreuzes als Ortung im südlichen Niedersachsen, also die 5. Irminskreuzortung' (2–24 July 1936) and accompanying letter to Reichsbauernführer R. Walther Darré dated 31 August 1936, Bundesarchiv, Koblenz, Nachlass Darré AD26. The article describing the 'turning eye' *(Draugh)* was 'Gotos Raunen—Runenwissen!', *Hagal* 11 (1934), Heft 7, 7–14.

20 Theodor Weigel, 'Bericht über den Stein von Baden-Baden und andere Entdeckungen des Herrn G. Kirchhoff, Gaggenau' (15 April 1937), Bundesarchiv, Koblenz, NS21/31.

21 Otto Plassmann, 'Stellungnahme zu dem Schreiben des Günther Kirchhoff in Gaggenau vom 17. März 1938' (25 March 1938) and Löffler to Siewers, letter dated 19 June 1939, Bundesarchiv, Koblenz, NS21/31.

22 Kirchhoff had first met Tarnhari at the List Society in Berlin during the 1920s. He addressed his letter concerning the Raidenstein complex and its associations with the Lauterer-Tarnhari family to Walther Wüst, letter dated 18 July 1938. Evidence for Himmler's positive attitude towards Kirchhoff despite the objections of the Ahnenerbe is contained in Brandt to Kirchhoff, letter dated 14 June 1939, Siewers to Schleif, letter dated 2 August 1939 and Brandt to Wüst, letter dated 26 March 1941, Bundesarchiv, Koblenz, NS21/31.

23 Kirchhoff to Hitler, letter dated 11 November 1944, Bundesarchiv, Koblenz, NS19/neu 747.

24 Karl Hüser, *Wewelsburg 1933–1945* (Paderborn, 1982) gives a comprehensive account of the castle as an SS institution.

25 Mund, op. cit., p. 115.

26 Ferdinand Freilingrath (1810–76), 'Am Birkenbaum', in Werner Ilberg (ed.), *Freilingraths Werke in einem Band*, third edition (Berlin and Weimar, 1976), pp. 145–51. The poem achieved its final form in 1850.

27 Hüser, op. cit., p. 24f.

28 Hüser, op. cit., pp. 33f, 212. The stick and its use is described in Mund, op. cit., p. 127.

29 Knobelsdorff to Weisthor, letter dated 16 October 1934, Walther Müller SS file, Berlin Document Center.

30 Wiligut used similar runes in his design for a wooden bowl to be used in the ceremony of bread and salt at SS weddings. Ulrich Hunger, 'Die Runenkunde im Dritten Reich' (unpublished Dr. phil. dissertation, University of Göttingen, 1983), p. 158.

31 Hüser, op. cit., pp. 66f, 326ff, and J. Ackermann, *Heinrich Himmler als Ideologe* (Göttingen, 1970), p. 72.

32 Hüser, op. cit., pp. 294–8.

33 A description of Weisthor's life at Berlin appears in Mund, op. cit., pp. 98–103.

34 K. M. Weisthor, 'Zur Herstellung des "Urglaubens"', undated typescript, Bundesarchiv, Koblenz, Nachlass Himmler 19.

35 Details of Rahn's career appear in Rahn SS file, Berlin Document Center.

36 Rahn to Weisthor, letter dated 27 September 1935, Bundesarchiv, Koblenz, Nachlass Himmler 19.

37 Correspondence relating to the SS interest in Evola, Bundesarchiv, Koblenz, NS19/1848.

38 Mund, op. cit., p. 123f. Wolff to Pancke, letter dated 5 February 1939; Wolff to Schmitt, letter dated 22 August 1939, Wiligut-Weisthor SS file, Berlin Document Center.

39 The last period of Wiligut's life is described in Mund, op. cit., pp. 124–7.

15. ARIOSOPHY AND ADOLF HITLER

1 Lanz to Frater Aemilius, letter dated 22 February 1932 in Wilfried Daim, *Der Mann, der Hitler die Ideen gab* (Munich, 1958), p. 12.

2 A survey of the unreliable and sensational literature relating to Nazi occultism appears in Appendix E.

3 Friedrich Heer, *Der Glaube des Adolf Hitler* (Vienna, 1968), pp. 15–22.

4 Billy F. Price (ed.), *Adolf Hitler als Maler und Zeichner. Ein Werkkatalog der Ölgemalde, Aquarelle, Zeichnungen und Architekturskizzen* (Zug, 1983).

5 Heer, op. cit., pp. 22–33.

6 Adolf Hitler, *Mein Kampf* (Munich, 1934), pp. 21, 59f.

7 Daim, op. cit., pp. 14–17, 20–7.

8 Daim, op. cit., pp. 27–34.

9 A detailed analysis of the discrepancies between the account of Greiner and that provided by reliable sources is in Robert G. L. Waite, *The Psychopathic God: Adolf Hitler* (New York, 1977), pp. 427–32.

10 Franz Jetzinger, *Hitler's Youth* (Westport, Conn., 1976), pp. 136, 182f; Reinhold Hanisch, 'I was Hitler's buddy', *New Republic* 98 (1939), 239–42, 270–2, 297–300.

11 Hermann Rauschning, *Hitler Speaks* (London, 1939), p. 227.

12 Daim, op. cit., pp. 16, 162f.

13 Reginald H. Phelps, 'Die Hitler-Bibliothek', *Deutsche Rundschau* 80 (1954), 923–31.

14 Inge Kunz, 'Herrenmenschentum, Neugermanen und Okkultismus. Eine soziologische Bearbeitung der Schriften von Guido List' (unpublished Dr. phil. thesis, University of Vienna, 1961), pp. 4–6. Schmidt-Falk must have been referring to Friedrich Oskar Wannieck, who died on 6 July 1912.

15 Phelps, op. cit., p. 925.

16 August Kubizek, *Young Hitler* (Maidstone, 1973), p. 110f.

17 Kunz, op. cit., pp. 4, 9, 11.

18 Kubizek, op. cit., p. 135.

19 Price, op. cit., pp. 165–183. There are in this volume numerous illustrations of Hitler paintings which were forged by Konrad Kujau, also notorious as the author of the *Stern* Hitler Diaries. Many of the dubious items are located in the D1 collection of Fritz Stiefel at Waiblingen.

20 Edouard Calic, *Ohne Maske*. Hitler-Breiting Geheimgespräche 1931 (Frankfurt, 1968), p. 60.

21 Johannes Hering, 'Beiträge zur Geschichte der Thule-Gesellschaft', typescript dated 21 June 1939, Bundesarchiv, Koblenz, NS26/865.

22 Adolf Hitler, *Mein Kampf* (Munich, 1934), pp. 325–8.

23 The importance of the Protocols of the Elders of Zion for the growth of this postwar demonology in Germany is fully documented in Norman Cohn, *Warrant for Genocide* (London, 1967), pp. 126–215.

24 James M. Rhodes, *The Hitler Movement* (Stanford, 1980) draws on the writings and speeches of Hitler, Goebbels, Rosenberg, Strasser, and other Nazi leaders to highlight their apocalyptic consciousness.

25 These grandiose projects are documented in the following works: Albert Speer, *Inside the Third Reich* (London, 1970) and *The Spandau Diaries* (London, 1976); Karl

Hüser, *Wewelsburg 1933–1945* (Paderborn, 1982); Anton Joachimsthaler, *Die Breitspurbahn Hitlers* (Freiburg, 1981); Felix Kersten, *The Kersten Memoirs 1940–1945* (London, 1956); Josef Ackermann, *Heinrich Himmler als Ideologe* (Göttingen, 1970); Clarissa Henry and Marc Hillel, *Children of the SS* (London, 1975).

APPENDIX C: THE HISTORY OF ARIOSOPHY

1 Lanz took the idea of a proto-Aryan settled continent of Atlantis from two post-war *völkisch* mythologists: Karl Georg Zschaetzsch, *Atlantis, die Urheimat der Arier* (Berlin, 1922) and Hermann Wieland, *Atlantis, Edda und Bibel* (Weissenburg, 1925).

2 J. Lanz v. Liebenfels, 'Die Geschichte der Ariosophie', *Zeitschrift für Geistes- und Wissenschaftsreform* 4 (1929), 34 f.

3 ibid., 35.   4 ibid., 100.

5 J. Lanz v. Liebenfels, *Die unterschlagene esoterische Lehre des Ulfilas* (Szt. Balázs, 1930); *Ulfilas und das Schlüsselwörterbuch zur Esoterik des Altertums und Mittelalters*, 4 vols. (Szt. Balázs, 1930).

6 J. Lanz v. Liebenfels, *Das Leben St. Benedikts von Nursia* (Szt. Balázs, 1930); *Der Tod St. Benedikt von Nursia und seine Ordensregel, I. Teil* (Szt. Balázs, 1930); *Die Ordensregel St. Benedikts von Nursia, II. Teil* (Szt. Balázs, 1930); *Die Priesterschaft Benedikts von Nursia, I. Teil: Ursprünge und Vorläufer* (Szt. Balázs, 1930); *Die Priesterschaft Benedikts von Nursia, II. Teil: Die Einwirkung auf die Menschheitsentwicklung* (Szt. Balázs, 1930).

7 J. Lanz v. Liebenfels, *Die Priesterschaft St. Bernhards von Clairvaux*, 2 vols. (Szt. Balázs, 1930).

8 J. Lanz v. Liebenfels, 'Die Geschichte der Ariosophie', *Zeitschrift für Geistes- und Wissenschaftsreform* 4 (1929), 179.

9 ibid., 237–40.

10 A full list of ariosophical mystics from antiquity up until the present is given in J. Lanz v. Liebenfels, *Praktische Einführung in die arisch-christliche Mystik. VI. Teil: Praxis, Geschichte und Literatur der Mystik* (n.p., 1934), pp. 4–16.

APPENDIX E: THE MODERN MYTHOLOGY OF NAZI OCCULTISM

1 A sample of such works might include the following: Nazi-hunting in the German expatriate communities of South America, including the search for the allegedly fugitive Martin Bormann, are represented by Ladislas Farago, *Aftermath. Martin Bormann and the Fourth Reich* (London, 1974), and Erich Erdstein with Barbara Bean, *Inside the Fourth Reich* (London, 1978). Robert Ludlum, *The Holcroft Covenant* (St Albans, 1978) describes a Nazi revival against the background of high finance. Michael Sinclair, *A Long Time Sleeping* (London, 1975) tells how Hitler survived until 1967 in the United States with contacts among the old guard in high political office throughout the world. W. Mattern, *UFOs. Letzte Geheimwaffe des Dritten Reiches* (Toronto, n.d.) suggests that the flying saucers are directed by a clique of Nazi survivors bent upon the successful resumption of world conquest.

2 Right-wing political groups of explicit Nazi inspiration in Great Britain and the United States are described in Angelo del Boca and Mario Giovana, *Fascism Today* (London, 1970), pp. 261–70, 323–66. Nazi chants and salutes are used in the Church of Satan, a sect devoted to devil-worship and unbridled sensual

gratification, which was founded in 1966 in San Francisco. Anton Szandor LaVey, *The Satanic Rituals* (New York, 1972).

3 Helena Petrovna Blavatsky, *The Secret Doctrine*, second edition, 2 vols. (London, 1888), I, xxiii–xxv.

4 Joseph Saint-Yves d'Alveydre, *La Mission de l'Inde en Europe* (Paris, 1910), p. 27.

5 Ferdynand Ossendowski, *Beasts, Men and Gods* (London, 1923), pp. 299–316.

6 Louis Jacolliot, *Les fils de Dieu* (Paris, 1873) referred to the *vril* in connection with the magical practices of the Jainists in India. For Blavatsky's debt to Jacolliot, see Coleman, op. cit., pp. 357–366.

7 Willy Ley, 'Pseudoscience in Naziland', *Astounding Science Fiction* 39 (1947), 90–8.

8 Louis Pauwels and Jacques Bergier, *The Morning of the Magicians* (St Albans, 1971), p. 146 f.

9 ibid., p. 148 n.

10 For an objective account of Eckart's influence on Hitler, see John Toland, *Adolf Hitler* (New York, 1976), pp. 99–101 and Robert G. L. Waite, *The Psychopathic God: Adolf Hitler* (New York, 1977), pp. 116–18.

11 The limited extent of Hitler's contact with Karl Haushofer may be deduced from Hans-Adolf Jacobsen, *Karl Haushofer. Leben und Werk Bd. 1*, Schriften des Bundesarchivs 24/1 (Boppard, 1979), pp. 224–258.

12 Pauwels and Bergier, op. cit., p. 193.

13 ibid., pp. 195–8.

14 The presence of Gurdjieff himself in Tibet is a matter of contention and mystification. James Webb, *The Harmonious Circle* (London, 1980), pp. 48–74.

15 Dietrich Bronder, *Bevor Hitler kam* (Hanover, 1964), pp. 239–44.

16 Walter Johannes Stein, *Weltgeschichte im Lichte des heiligen Gral*, 1 vol. (Stuttgart, 1928), I, 6–8, 381–94.

17 Trevor Ravenscroft, *The Spear of Destiny* (London, 1972), pp. 67–88. The repatriation of the Habsburg imperial regalia to Germany formed the subject of *Ostara* I, 6 (July 1906). Hitler actually had the regalia transferred to Nuremberg after 1938.

18 ibid., pp. 167–70, 186.

19 ibid., p. 230.   20 ibid., pp. 103–5.

21 ibid., p. 59.   22 ibid., p. 76.

23 The conjuring of a 'Moon Child' is redolent of myths surrounding Aleister Crowley. Somerset W. Maugham wrote a caustic satire about Crowley, in which a certain 'Oliver Haddo' engaged in evil alchemical experiments at his Staffordshire mansion to create a homunculus with the life-force of his poor wife. Somerset W. Maugham, *The Magician* (London, 1908). Crowley also wrote a novel about the magical creation of familiar spirits and discarnate entities. Aleister Crowley, *Moonchild* (London, 1929). The fictional status of both Ernst Pretzsche and his

bookshop is discussed in Christoph Lindenberg, 'The Spear of Destiny [review]', *Die Drei*, December 1974, 631–5.

24 Jean-Claude Frère, *Nazisme et sociétés secrètes* (Paris, 1974), pp. 142–4.

25 Franz Trefflinger, 'Beiträge zu einer Biographie des Abtes Theoderich Hagn von Lambach (1816–1872)' (unpublished Ph.D. thesis, University of Vienna, 1967).

26 Franz Jetzinger, *Hitler's Youth* (Westport, Conn., 1976), p. 58f.

Bibliography

A. PRIMARY SOURCES

I. Theosophical and Astrological Publications

(a) Periodicals

Astrologische Rundschau. Monthly. Theosophical
Publishing House: Leipzig, October 1910–
36. Edited by Karl Brandler-Pracht, 1910–
14, Ernst Tiede, 1914–20, Rudolf von
Sebottendorff, 1920–4.
Die Gnosis. Fortnightly. W. Opetz: Vienna,
1903–4. Edited by Philipp Maschlufsky.
Isis. Monthly. E. Fiedler: Leipzig, 1908–9.
Edited by Casimir Zawadzki. Continued
as *Theosophie.*
Lotusblüthen. Monthly. W. Friedrich: Leipzig,
1892–1900. Edited by Franz Hartmann.
Metaphysische Rundschau. Monthly. Paul Zill-
mann: Gross-Lichterfelde, 1896–7. Edited
by Paul Zillmann. Continued as *Neue
Metaphysische Rundschau.*
Neue Lotusblüten. Fortnightly. Jaeger'sche
Buchhandlung: Leipzig, 1908–15. Edited
by Franz Hartmann, 1908–12, Harald
Arjuna Grävell van Jostenoode, 1913,
Reich-Gutzeit, 1914–15.
Neue Metaphysische Rundschau. Monthly. Paul
Zillmann: Gross-Lichterfelde, 1898–1918.
Edited by Paul Zillmann.
Prana. Monthly. Theosophical Publishing
House: Leipzig, October 1909–September
1919. Edited by Karl Brandler-Pracht,
1909–14, Johannes Walter, 1915, Johannes
Balzli, 1916–19.
Die Sphinx. Monthly. Theodor Grieben: Leipzig,
1886, Theodor Hoffmann: Gera, 1887–8,
C. A. Schwetschke: Brunswick, 1888–95.
Edited by Wilhelm Hübbe-Schleiden.
Theosophie. Monthly. Theosophical Publishing

House: Leipzig, April 1910–1930s. Edited
by members of the Theosophical Society,
1910, Hugo Vollrath, 1911–20.
Theosophisches Leben. Monthly. Paul Raatz:
Berlin, 1898–1920. Edited by Paul Raatz.
Der theosophische Wegweiser. Monthly. Verlag des
theosophischen Wegweisers: Leipzig,
October 1898–September 1907. Edited by
Arthur Weber.
Der Wanderer. Monthly. Theosophical Publish-
ing House: Leipzig, July 1906–June 1908.
Edited by Arthur Weber.
Zentralblatt für Okkultismus. Monthly. Max Alt-
mann: Leipzig, July 1907–33. Edited by
D. Georgiewitz-Weitzer.

(b) Book-Series

    Astrologische Bibliothek. 18 vols. Theo-
    sophical Publishing House: Leipzig,
    1910–23.

1 Brandler-Pracht, Kleines astrologisches
   Lehrbuch (1910).
2 Brandler-Pracht,   Astrologische
   Aphorismen (1910).
   Brandler-Pracht, Häuser-Tabellen von
   40°-50° geographischer Breite
   (1910).
4 Brandler-Pracht, Das Solarhoroskop—
   Jahreshoroskop (1910).
5 Brandler-Pracht, Die Lehre von den
   astrologischen Direktionen (1910)
6 Brandler-Pracht, Die Stunden-Astrologie (1912).
7 Pöllner, Mundan-Astrologie (1914).

8 Pöllner, Schicksal und Sterne (1914).

9 Feerhow, Die medizinische Astrologie (1914).

10 Mörbitz, Berechnungstabellen für die astrologische Praxis (1919).

11 Pöllner, Tafeln für die schiefe Aufsteigung für die Polhöhe von 1° bis 60° [1922].

12 Heindel, Vereinfachte wissenschaftliche Astrologie (1920).

13 Heindel, Die Botschaft der Sterne (1921).

14 Tiede, Astrologisches Lexikon [1922].

15 Sebottendorff, Geschichte der Astrologie. Bd. 1 (1923).

16 Sebottendorff, Sterntafeln (Ephemeriden) von 1838–1922 [1922].

17 Sebottendorff, Praktischer Lehrgang zur Horoskopie (1922).

18 Sebottendorff, Sonnen- und Mondorte [1923].

second edition:

1 Pöllner, Astrologisches Lehrbuch (1920).

2 Feerhow, Astrologische Dienstregeln (1920).

4 Sebottendorff, Die Hilfshoroskopie [1921].

5 Grimm, Die Lehre von den astroloischen Direktionen (1920).

6 Sebottendorff, Stunden- und Frage-Horoskopie (1921).

Hartmann, Die Religionslehre der Buddhisten (1898).

2 Sankaracharya, Das Palladium der Weisheit (Viveka Chudamani) (1898).

3/4 Hartmann, Die Geheimlehre der christlichen Religion nach den Erklärungen von Meister Eckhart (1898).

5 Leiningen-Billigheim, Was ist Mystik? (1898).

7/8 Besant, Die sieben Prinzipien oder Grundteile des Menschen (1899).

7/8 Besant, Reinkarnation oder Wiederverkörperungslehre (1900).

9 Hartmann, Tao-Teh-King (Der Weg, die Wahrheit und das Licht) (1900).

10 Leadbeater, Unsere unsichtbaren Helfer (1900).

11/12 Hartmann, Die Erkenntnislehre der Bhagavad Gita im Lichte der Geheimlehre betrachtet (1900).

Geheime Wissenschaften. 21 vols. H. Barsdorf: Berlin, 1913–20.

1 Enth. die Johann Valentin Andreä zugeschriebenen vier Hauptschriften der alten Rosenkreuzer. 1. Chymische Hochzeit: Christian Rosencreutz. anno. 1459. Nach der zu Strassburg bei Lazari Zetzners seel. Erben im J. 1616 erschienenen Ausgabe originalgetreu neugedruckt. 2–4. Allgemeine und General Reformation der gantzen weiten Welt. Beneben der Fama und Confession fraternitatis des löblichen Ordens des Rosen Creutzes, an alle Gelehrte, und Häupter Europae geschrieben. Mit Einleitung von Ferdinand Maack (1913).

2 Die Elemente der Kabbalah. 1. Teil. Theoretische Kabbalah. Das Buch Jezirah. Sohar-Auszüge. Erl. von Erich Bischoff (1913).

3 Die Elemente der Kabbalah. 2. Teil. Praktische Kabbalah. Magische Wissenschaft, magische Künste (1914).

4 Elias artista redivivus, oder Das Buch von Salz und Raum. Hrsg. von Ferdinand Maack (1913).

5–8 Hermetisches A.B.C., derer ächten Weisen alter und neuer Zeiten von Stein der Weisen. Aus gegeben von einem wahren Gott- und Menschenfreunde. 4. Teile. Berlin 1778, 1779 bey Christian Ulrich Ringmacher. Originalgetreuer Facs. -Ausgabe (1915).

9 Des Hermes Trismegist's wahrer alter Naturweg zur Bereitung der grossen Universaltinctur. (Wahrer alter Naturweg oder: Geheimnis wie die grosse Universaltinctur ohne Gläser, auf Menschen und Metalle zu bereiten). Hrsg. von einem ächten Freimaurer I.C.H. Originalgetreuer Facs. -Ausgabe (1915).

10–14 Heinrich Cornelius Agrippa's von Nettesheim, Magische Werke sammt den geheimnisvollen Schriften des Petrus van Abano, Pictorius von Villingen, Gerhard von Cremona, Abt Tritheim von Spanheim, dem Buche Arbatel, der sogenannten Hl. Geist-Kunst und verschiedenen anderen. 5 vols (1916).

15 Ernst Tiede, Ur-Arische Gotteserkenntnis. Ihr neues Erwachen im Sonnenrecht und die Erschliessung der kleinen und grossen Mysterien (1917).

16 Seraphinische Blumen-Gärtlein. Auslese aus den mystisch-religiösen Schriften Jakob Böhmes. Nach der Amsterdam Orig. -Ausgabe von 1700 neu hrsg. von Antonius van der Linden (1918).

17 Franz Freudenberg, Paracelsus und Fludd. Die beiden grossen Okkultisten und Ärzte der 15. und 16. Jahrhunderte (1918).

18 Erich Bischoff, Das Jenseits der Seele. Zur Mystik des Lebens nach dem Tode <Unsterblichkeit, ewige Wiederkunft, Auferstehung, Seelenwanderung> (1919).

19 Franz Freudenberg, Der Blick in die Zukunft. Die Wahrsagerkunst im Spiegel der Zeit und der Völkergeschichte (1919).

20 Erich Bischoff, Die Mystik und Magie der Zahlen. <Arithmetische Kabbalah>. Zahlenmystik des Himmels, der Musik, der Natur, des menschlichen Lebenslaufes, der Geschichte und des Geisteslebens. Die Magie der Zahlen und Zahlenfiguren, ihre Bedeutung für Verständnis und Berechnungen von Vergangenheit und Zukunft. Berechnungen der Geburtsplaneten und wichtigen Lebensdaten. Systematische Symbolik der Zahlen von 1–4,320,000 (1920).

21 Compass der Weisen. [Verfasser: Adam Michael Birkholz]. Hrsg. von Ketmia Vere (i.e.) Baron Proek. Berlin und Leipzig bey Christian Ulrich Ringmacher, 1779 (1920).

Geheimwissenschaftliche Vorträge. 27 vols. Theosophische Centralbuchh: Leipzig, 1902–7.

1 Rudolf, Keine Religion ist höher als die Wahrheit (1902).

2 Rudolf, Die 'Theosophische Gesellschaft' (1902).

3 Rudolf, Das Christentum, vom Standpunkte der occulten Philosophie aus betrachtet (1902).

4 Rudolf, Warum vertritt die 'Theosophische Gesellschaft' das Prinzip der Toleranz? (1902).

5 Rudolf, Karma, das Gesetz der Wiedervergeltung und Harmonie im Weltall (1904).

6 Rudolf, Der verlorene Sohn (Ev. Lucae 15, 11–32) (1904).

7 Rudolf, Die Lebendigen und die Toten (1904).

15 Hartmann, Der wissenschaftliche Beweis der Unsterblichkeit und die occulte Philosophie (1905).

16 Böhme, Die 'Internationale theosophische Verbrüderung' und die 'Theosophischen Gesellschaften' (1905).

17 Rudolf, Der Patriotismus und die theosophische Verbrüderung der Menschheit (1905).

18–20 Hartmann, Über den Verkehr mit der Geisterwelt (1905).

21–23 Böhme, Das Gedankenleben und seine Beherrschung (1905).

24 Rudolf, Die Ehe und die Geheimlehre (1905).

25 Rudolph, Kunst und Religion (1907).

26 Hartmann, Chemie und Alchemie (1907).

27 Weber, Eine Betrachtung einiger Lehren der Upanishaden (1907).

Geisteswissenschaftliche Vorträge. 25 vols. Theosophical Publishing House: Leipzig, 1909, 1914.

1 Besant, Die Aufgabe der theosophischen Gesellschaft (1909).

2 Besant and Leadbeater, Der Äther im Weltenraume (1909).

3 Besant, Der Zeitgeist (1909).

4 Leadbeater, Unsichtbare Helfer (1909).

5 Besant, Der Vegetarismus im Lichte der Theosophie (1909).

6 Scott-Elliott, Das Gesetz des Opfers (1909).

7/8 Chatterji, Der Pfad der Vervollkommnung. Das göttliche Schauen der Weisen Indiens (1909).

9 Besant, Die Notwendigkeit der Wiederverkörperung (1909).

10 Besant, Die Aufgabe der Politik im Leben der Völker (1909).

11 Besant, Das Geheimnis der Entwicklung (1909).

12 Besant, Die Hüter der Menschheit (1909).

13 Besant, Hâtha-Yoga und Râga-Yoga oder geistige Entwicklung nach altindischer Methode (1909).

14 Besant, Das Suchen nach Glück (1909).

15 Böhme, Was ist Toleranz? (1909).

16/17 Blavatsky, Die Jüngerschaft. Aussprüche (1909).

18 Leadbeater, Naturgeister (1909).

19 Besant, Geistige Dunkelheit (1909).

20 Besant, Die Gesetze des höheren Lebens (1909).

21 Besant, Betrachtungen über Christus (1914).

22 Schneider, Theosophische Gesellschaft (1914).

23 Feerhow, Die geistige Hierarchie (1914).

24 Besant, Die Mysterien (1914).

25 Grävell, Die Grunderfordnisse zum Studium der Geisterwissenschaft (1914).

Theosophische Flugschriften. 9 vols. Theosophical Publishing House: Leipzig, 1907.

1 Böhme, Was ist Theosophie? (1907).

2 Hartmann, Die theosophische Verbrüderung der Menschheit (1907).

3 Hartmann, Philotheosophie (1907).

4 Hartmann, Der Socialismus vom Standpunkte der occulten Wissenschaft aus betrachtet (1907).

5 Rudolph, Gibt es eine Weiterbildung der Religion? (1907).

6 Böhme, Der Weg (1907).

7 Böhme, Gott, Welt und Mensch (1907).

8 Blavatsky, Die Urgeschichte der Menschheit (Runden und Rassen) (1907).

9 Rudolph, Unser Sonnensystem (1907).

Theosophische Schriften. 30 vols. C. A. Schwetschke: Brunswick, 1894–6.

1 Besant, Die Sphinx der Theosophie (1894).

2 Hübbe-Schleiden, Karma (1894).

3 Chakravarta, Der Weltberuf der Theosophischen Gesellschaft (1894).

4 Hübbe-Schleiden, Karma im Christentum (1894).

5 Hübbe-Schleiden, Die Lehre der Wiederverkörperung im Christentum (1894).

6 Göring, Dr Franz Hartmann; Hartmann, Wiederverkörperung (1894).

7 Ewald, Theosophie gegen Anarchie (1894).

8 Krecke, Wie die Theosophie dem sittlichen und sozialen Elend entgegenwirkt (1894).

9 Besant, Theosophie und soziale Fragen (1894).

10 Hübbe-Schleiden, Die geistige und geschichtliche Bedeutung der theosophischen Bewegung (1894).

11 Mead, Yoga, die Wissenschaft der Seele (1895).

12/13 Hartmann, Mystik und Weltende (1895).

14/15 Besant, Interview über Theosophie (1895).

16/17 Koeber, Der Gedanke der Wiederverkörperung in Hellas und Rom (1895).

18 Hartmann, Gedanken über die Theosophie und die 'Theosophische Gesellschaft' (1895).

19 Friedrichsort, Hübbe-Schleidens Weltanschauung (1895).

20 Hartmann, Die Feuerbestattung (1895).

21 Tolstoy, Religion und Moral (1895).

22/23 Besant, Symbolik (1895).

24 Krecke, Weltverbesserung (1895).

25 Diestel, Karma; Anderson, Bestimmung des Geschlechtes bei der Wiederverkörperung (1895).

26 Diestel, Buddhismus und Christentum (1895).

27 Göring, Erziehung zu religiösem Leben (1895).

28 Wolf, Mensch, Tier und Vivisektion (1895).

29/30 Besant, Die Mahâtmas, ihre thatsächliche Existenz und das von ihnen verkörperte Ideal (1896).

Theosophische Strahlen. 18 vols. Paul Raatz: Berlin, 1901–4.

1 Raatz, Die Notwendigkeit der Reinkarnation (1901).

2 Corvinus, Die theosophische Lehre der Kreisläufe (Cyclen) (1901).

3/4 Raatz, Die siebenfache Konstitution des Menschen (1901).

5 Raatz, Allgemeine Brüderschaft (1901).

6 John, Der wahre Wert des Lebens (1901).

7/8 Judge, Das Entwickeln der Konzentration. –Okkulte Kräfte und deren Anneigung (1902).

9 Raatz, Die Karma- Lehre und ihre praktische Anwendung (1902).

10 Vogel, Kampf der Wahrheit mit der Lüge. Eine Allegorie (1902).

11 Boldt, Karma, oder Was wir säen, das ernten wir (1902).

BIBLIOGRAPHY

12 Raatz, Die theosophische Bedeutung der Geburt Jesu (1902).

13 Green, Theosophie und Naturwissenschaft oder die Grundlage der esoterischen Philosophie (1903).

14 'Meister der Weisheit', Einige Worte fürs tägliche Leben (1904).

15/16 Judge, Aus H. P. Blavatskys Leben (1904).

17/18 Raatz, Die esoterische Erklärung des Gleichnisses vom verlorenen Sohn (1904).

(c) Books

Annie Besant
  Der Stammbaum der Menschen (Leipzig, 1907).

Helena Petrovna Blavatsky
  Isis Unveiled, 2 vols. (London, 1877).
  The Secret Doctrine, second edition, 2 vols. (London, 1888).
  Die Geheimlehre, translated by Robert Froebe, 2 vols. (Leipzig, 1897–1901).

Edwin Böhme
  Giebt es ein Weiterleben und Wiedersehen nach dem Tode? (Leipzig, 1900).
  Die 'Internationale theosophische Verbrüderung' und die 'Theosophischen Gesellschaften' (Leipzig, 1905).
  Das Gedankenleben und seine Beherrschung (Leipzig, 1905).
  Gott, Welt und Mensch (Leipzig, 1907).
  Was ist Theosophie? (Leipzig, 1907).

Karl Brandler-Pracht
  Mathematisch-instruktives Lehrbuch der Astrologie (Leipzig, 1905).
  Lehrbuch der Entwicklung der okkulten Kräfte im Menschen (Leipzig, 1907).
  Kleines astrologisches Lehrbuch (Leipzig, 1910).
  Astrologische Aphorismen (Leipzig, 1910).
  Häuser-Tabellen von 40°–56° geographischer Breite (Leipzig, 1910).
  Das Solarhoroskop—Jahreshoroskop (Leipzig, 1910).
  Die Lehre von den astrologischen Direktionen (Leipzig, 1910).
  Die Tatwas und ihre Bedeutung für das praktische Leben (Leipzig, 1911).
  Unterrichtsbriefe zur Entwickelung der Willenkraft, 10 vols. (Leipzig, 1911–13).
  Die Neugedankenlehre (Leipzig, 1912).
  Die Stunden-Astrologie (Leipzig, 1912).
  Der Heilmagnetismus von okkultem Standpunkt (Berlin-Charlottenburg, 1914).

Wladimir von Egloffstein
  Die Periodicität in der Kirchengeschichte (Altenburg, 1911).

Hugo Göring
  Dr Franz Hartmann, ein Vorkämpfer der Theosophie (Brunswick, 1894).

Harald Arjuna Grävell van Jostenoode
  Christlich-Germanisch, third edition (Leipzig, 1899).
  Der neue Kurs im Unterrichtswesen, second edition of 'Klassisch v. volkstümlich?' (Leipzig, 1899).
  Arische Gesinnung und deutsches Schildesamt (Leipzig, 1900).
  Die Volkspoesie im Unterricht (Leipzig, 1901).
  Die 10 Gebote der Germanen (Brunswick, 1901).
  Aryavarta (Vienna, 1905).
  Die neue Bildung (Stuttgart, 1905).
  Die Reichskleinodien zurück nach dem Reich!, Ostara I, 6 (Rodaun, 1906).
  Das Ariertum und seine Feinde, Ostara, I, 25 (Rodaun, 1908).
  Die arische Bewegung (Leipzig, 1909).

Arthur Grobe-Wutischky
  Impfung und Impfgesetz (Berlin-Charlottenburg, 1914).
  Der Weltkrieg 1914 in der Prophetie (Leipzig, 1915).

Franz Hartmann
  Report of Observations made during a nine months' stay at the Headquarters of the Theosophical Society at Adyar (Madras), India (Madras, 1884).
  White and Black Magic (Boston and Madras, 1885).
  An Adventure among the Rosicrucians (Boston, 1887).
  The Life of Philippus Theophrastus Bombast (London, 1887).
  Cosmology (Boston, 1888).
  The Life of Jehoshua, the prophet of Nazareth (London, 1888).
  The Principles of Astrological Geomancy (London, 1889).
  In the Pronaos of the Temple of Wisdom (London, 1890).
  The Talking Image of Urur (New York, [1890])
  The Life and Doctrines of Jacob Boehme (London, 1891).
  Die Bhagavad Gita, translated by Dr F. Hartmann (Leipzig, 1892).
  Über eine neue Heilmethode zur Heilung von Lungentuberkulose (Leipzig, 1893).
  Die weisse und schwarze Magie (Leipzig, [1894])
  Selbsterkenntnis und Wiederverkörperung (Brunswick, 1894).

Mystik und Weltende (Brunswick, 1895).

Gedanken über die Theosophie und die 'Theosophische Gesellschaft' (Brunswick, 1895).

Die Feuerbestattung (Brunswick, 1895).

Among the Gnomes. An occult tale of adventure in the Untersberg (London, 1895).

Atma Bodha, translated by F. Hartmann (Leipzig, [1895]).

Tattwa Bodha, translated by F. Hartmann (Leipzig, [1895]).

Die Geheimlehre in der christlichen Religion nach den Erklärungen von Meister Eckart (Leipzig, 1895).

Unter den Gnomen im Untersberg. Eine sonderbare Geschichte (Leipzig, [1896]).

Lebendig begraben. Eine Untersuchung der Natur und Ursachen des Scheintodes (Leipzig, 1896).

Karma, oder Wissen, Wirken und Werden (Leipzig, [1897]).

Jehoshua der Prophet von Nazareth (Leipzig, [1897]).

Die Erkenntnislehre der Bhagavad Gita, im Lichte der Geheimlehre betrachtet (Leipzig, 1897).

Theosophie in China, Betrachtungen über den Tao-Teh-King (Leipzig, 1897).

Die Religionslehre der Buddhisten (Leipzig, 1898).

Die Reinkarnation oder Wiederverkörperung (Leipzig, 1898).

Grundriss der Lehren des Theophrastus Paracelsus von Hohenheim (Leipzig, [1898]).

Denkwürdige Erinnerungen (Leipzig, [1898]).

Die Medizin des Theophrastus Paracelsus von Hohenheim (Leipzig, [1899]).

Kurzgefasste Grundriss der Geheimlehre (Leipzig, [1899]).

Populäre Vorträge über Geheimwissenschaft (Leipzig, 1899).

Tao-Teh-King (Leipzig, 1900).

Betrachtungen über die Mystik in Goethes 'Faust' (Leipzig, [1900]).

Unter den Adepten. Vertrauliche Mittheilungen aus den Kreisen der indischen Adepten und christlichen Mystiker (Leipzig, 1901).

Mysterien, Symbole und magisch wirkende Kräfte (Leipzig, 1902).

Was ist Theosophie? (Leipzig, 1903).

Sechs Zeugen für die Wahrheit der Lehre von der Wiederverkörperung (Berlin, 1906).

Der wissenschaftliche Beweis der Unsterblichkeit und die occulte Philosophie (Leipzig, 1905).

Über den Verkehr mit der Geisterwelt (Leipzig, 1905).

Chemie und Alchemie (Leipzig, 1907).

Die theosophische Verbrüderung der Menschheit (Leipzig, 1907).

Philotheosophie (Leipzig, 1907).

Der Socialismus vom Standpunkte der occulten Wissenschaft aus betrachtet (Leipzig, 1907).

Hermetische Kindergeschichten (Leipzig, 1909).

With the Adepts. An Adventure among the Rosicrucians, second edition (London, 1910).

Unter den Adepten und Rosenkreuzern, second edition (Leipzig, [1912]).

Max Heindel

Die Weltanschauung der Rosenkreuzer oder Mysterisches Christentum, translated by S. v. d. Wiesen (Leipzig, 1913).

Die Esoterik in Wagners 'Tannhäuser', translated by Arminius (Leipzig, [1918]).

Vereinfachte wissenschaftliche Astrologie, translated by Richard Voss (Leipzig, 1920).

Die Rosenkreuzer-Mysterien (Leipzig, [1920]).

Die Botschaft der Sterne, translated by Rudolf von Sebottendorff (Leipzig, 1921).

Rosenkreuzer-Philosophie in Frage und Antwort (Leipzig, [1923]).

Karl Heise

Passionslegende und Osterbotschaft im Lichte der occulten Forschung (Leipzig, 1907).

Lourdes (Lorch, 1908).

Vom Pfad zum unermesslichen Lichte. Eine Studie über den Buddhismus (Lorch, 1909).

Karma, das universale Moralgesetz der Welt (Lorch, n.d.).

Seelenwanderung (Lorch, n.d.).

Das Alter der Welt im Lichte der okkulten Wissenschaft (Leipzig, 1910).

Die astrale Konstitution des Menschen (Leipzig, 1911).

Geschichte des Weltkrieges und zum Verständnis der wahren Freimaurerei (Basle, 1919).

Die englisch-amerikanische Weltlüge (mit einer Geheimakte aus englischen Freimaurerlogen (Constance, 1919).

Lazar Hellenbach

Mr Slade's Aufenthalt in Wien (Leipzig, 1878).

Ist Hansen ein Schwindler? Eine Studie über den 'animalischen Magnetismus' (Leipzig, 1887).

Geburt und Tod als Wechsel der Anschauungsform oder die Doppel-Natur des Menschen (Leipzig, 1897).

Die Magie der Zahlen als Grundlage aller Mannigfaltigkeit, second edition (Leipzig, 1898).

Franz Herndl

Das Wörtherkreuz. Mystisch-socialer Roman (Vienna, 1901).

Die Trutzburg. Autobiographische Skizzen des Einsiedlers auf der Insel Wörth. Sozial-reformatorischer Roman (Leipzig, 1909).

Wilhelm Hübbe-Schleiden

Jesus, ein Buddhist? Eine unkirchliche Betrachtung (Brunswick, 1890).

Das Dasein als Lust, Leid und Liebe. Die altindische Weltanschauung in neuzeitlicher Darstellung (Brunswick, 1891).

Hellenbach, der Vorkämpfer für Wahrheit und Menschlichkeit (Leipzig, 1891).

Karma, die theosophische Begründung der Ethik (Brunswick, 1894).

Die Lehre der Wiederverkörperung im Christentum (Brunswick, 1894).

Die geistige und die geschichtliche Bedeutung der theosophischen Bewegung (Brunswick, 1894).

Indien und die Indier (Hamburg, 1898).

Das Streben nach Vollendung und dessen Voraussetzung (Hamburg, 1900).

Warum Weltmacht? Der Sinn unserer Kolonialpolitik (Hamburg, 1906).

Die Botschaft des Friedens (Leipzig, 1912).

Das Morgenrot der Zukunft (Leipzig, 1912).

Das Suchen des Meisters (Lorch, 1916).

Karl Kiesewetter

Geschichte des neueren Occultismus. I. Teil. Geheimwissenschaftliche Systeme von Agrippa von Nettesheym bis zu Carl du Prel (Leipzig, 1891).

John Dee, ein Spiritist des 16. Jahrhunderts (Leipzig, 1893).

Franz Anton Mesmer's Leben und Lehre (Leipzig, 1893).

Geschichte des neueren Occultismus II. Teil. Die Geheimwissenschaften (Leipzig, 1895).

Albert Kniepf

Die Weissagungen des altfranzösischen Sehers Michel Nostradamus und der heutige Krieg (Hamburg, 1914).

Ferdinand Maack

Zur Einführung in das Studium des Hypnotismus und thierischen Magnetismus (Neuwied, 1888).

Über Phosphoreszenz-Strahlen. Ein Beitrag zum Neo-Okkultismus (Berlin, 1897).

Die Weisheit von der Welt-Kraft. Eine Dynamosophie (Leipzig, 1897).

Das sichtbare Newton'sche Spektrum als Ausgangspunkt für dynamosophische Betrachtungen (Gross-Lichterfelde, 1897).

Okkultismus, Was ist er? Was will er? Wie erreicht er sein Ziel? (Berlin-Zehlendorf, 1898).

Die goldene Kette Homers. Ein zum Studium und zum Verständnis der gesamten hermetischen Litteratur unentbehrliches Hilfsbuch (Lorch, 1905).

Das Schachraumspiel (Potsdam, 1908).

Carl du Prel

Das weltliche Kloster. Eine Vision (Leipzig, 1887).

Die monistische Seelenlehre (Leipzig, 1888).

Die Mystik der alten Griechen (Leipzig, 1888).

Das hypnotische Verbrechen und seine Entdeckung (Munich, 1889).

Studien aus dem Gebiete der Geheimwissenschaften (Leipzig, 1890).

Das Sprechen in fremden Zungen (Leipzig, 1892).

Justinus Kerner und die Seherin von Prevorst (Leipzig, 1893).

Die Entdeckung der Seele durch die Geheimwissenschaften, 2 vols. (Leipzig, 1894).

Der Tod, das Jenseits, das Leben im Jenseits (Munich, 1899).

Die vorgeburtliche Erziehung als Weg zur Menschenzüchtung (Jena, 1899).

Die Magie als Naturwissenschaft, 2 vols. (Jena, 1899).

Hermann Rudolph

Die Constitution der Materie und der Zusammenhang zwischen ponderabler und imponderabler Materie (Berlin, 1898).

Keine Religion ist höher als die Wahrheit (Leipzig, 1902).

Die 'Theosophische Gesellschaft' (Leipzig, 1902).

Das Christentum, vom Standpunkte der occulten Philosophie aus betrachtet (Leipzig, 1902).

Warum vertritt die 'Theosophische Gesellschaft' das Prinzip der Toleranz? (Leipzig, 1902).

Karma, das Gesetz der Wiedervergeltung und Harmonie im Weltall (Leipzig, 1904).

Der verlorene Sohn (Ev. Lucae 15, 11–32) (Leipzig, 1904).

Die Lebendigen und die Toten (Leipzig, 1904).

Der Patriotismus und die theosophische Verbrüderung der Menschheit (Leipzig, 1905).

Die Ehe und die Geheimlehre (Leipzig, 1905).

Kunst und Religion (Leipzig, 1907).

Gibt es eine Weiterbildung der Religion? (Leipzig, 1907).

Unser Sonnensystem (Leipzig, 1907).

Die Seelenlosen (Leipzig, 1909).

Die deutschen Märchen als Zeugen einer uralten Religion (Leipzig, 1909).

Die internationale theosophische Verbrüderung und die kommende Rasse (Leipzig, 1912).

William Scott-Elliot
Atlantis nach okkulten Quellen, translated by F. P. (Leipzig, [1903]).
Das untergangene Lemuria, translated by A. von Ulrich (Leipzig, 1905).

Max Ferdinand Sebaldt von Werth (also wrote under the pseudonyms Maximilian Ferdinand and G. Herman)
Das 'Angewandte' Christentum. 'Ernste Gedanken' über die Fragen der Zeit, with Moritz von Egidy (Berlin, 1891).

Maximilian Ferdinand
D.I.S. 'Sexualreligion'. Enthüllungen, 3 vols., Sexual-Mystik, Sexual-Moral, Sexual-Magie (Leipzig, 1897).
'Wanidis'. Der Triumph des Wahnes. D.I.S. Die arische 'Sexualreligion' als Volks-Veredelung in Zeugen, Leben und Sterben. Mit einem Anhang über Menschenzüchtung von Carl du Prel (Leipzig, 1897).

G. Herman
'Genesis', das Gesetz der Zeugung, 5 vols. (Leipzig, 1898–1903).
Naturgeschichte der Geschlechtsliebe (Leipzig, 1899).
Analogien der Iggdrasil, second edition of 'Sexual-Moral' (Leipzig, 1905).
Mythologie des Diaphetur, second edition of 'Sexual-Mystik' (Leipzig, 1905).
Xenologie des Saeming, second edition of 'Sexual-Magie' (Leipzig, 1905).
'Nackte Wahrheit'. Aktenmässige Darstellung des Verhältnisses zwischen Schönheits-Abenden und Nackt-Logen (Berlin, 1909).

Max Seiling
Mailänder, ein neuer Messias (Munich, 1888).
Meine Erfahrungen auf dem Gebite des Spiritismus (Leipzig, 1898).
Goethe und der Okkultismus (Leipzig, 1901).
Ernst Haeckel und der 'Spiritismus' (Leipzig, 1901).
Pessimistische Weisheitskörner (Munich, 1901).
Goethe und der Materialismus (Leipzig, 1904).
Die Kardinalfrage der Menschheit (Leipzig, 1906).

Peryt Shou
Der Weltentag oder die grosse Periode des Lichtes (Manvantara) (Leipzig, 1910).
Das Mysterium der Zentralsonne (Leipzig, 1910).
Die Esoterik der Atlantier in ihrer Beziehung zur aegyptischen, babylonischen und jüdischen Geheimlehre (Leipzig, 1913).
Die Heilkräfte des Logos (Berlin-Steglitz, 1913).
Der Verkehr mit Wesen höherer Welten (Berlin-Steglitz, 1914).

Praktische Esoterik oder die Gesetze höherer Welten (Leipzig, 1914).

G. W. Surya (pseudonym for Demeter Georgiewitz-Weitzer)
Moderne Rosenkreuzer oder die Renaissance der Geheimwissenschaften. Ein okkultwissenschaftlicher Roman (Leipzig, 1907).
Die Sonne, das Licht und die Heilkraft des Lichtes (Leipzig, 1907).
Der Triumph der Alchemie (Die Transmutation der Metalle) (Leipzig, 1908).
Okkulte Medizin (Leipzig, 1909).
Okkulte Astrophysik (Leipzig, 1910).
Schlangenbiss und Tollwut (Leipzig, 1913).
Rationelle Krebs- und Lupuskuren (Lorch, 1913).
Moderne Rosenkreuzer, second edition (Leipzig, 1914).

Ernst Tiede
Die Stimme im Verborgenen (Lorch, 1906).
Der Dämon des deutschen Volkes (Lorch, 1907).
Astrologische Mutmassungen über den Krieg der Deutschen 1914 (Leipzig, 1914).
Ur-Arische Gotteserkenntnis. Ihr neues Erwachen im Sonnenrecht und die Erschliessung der kleinen und grossen Mysterien (Berlin, 1917).
Astrologisches Lexikon (Leipzig, [1922]).

Arthur Weber
Über die Unsterblichkeit der menschlichen Seele (Lorch, 1903).
Die Bewusstseinreiche im Weltall (Leipzig, 1904).
Die sieben Grundkräfte oder Schwingungszustände in der Konstitution des Menschen (Leipzig, 1906).
Die Zitronenkur (Leipzig, 1910).

Paul Zillmann
Die neue Hochschule für animalischen (Heil-) Magnetismus in Deutschland (Gross-Lichterfelde, 1898).
Zur Metaphysik des Klavierspieles (Gross-Lichterfelde, 1908).
Die Wald-Loge. Die okkulte Gemeinde Deutschlands (Gross-Lichterfelde, [1912]).

II. Guido (von) List

(a) Newspaper Journalism

Articles in *Ostdeutsche Rundschau*. Wiener Wochenschrift für Politik, Volkswirtschaft, Kunst und Literatur, edited by K. H. Wolf.

'Götterdämmerung', *OR*, 1 October 1893, pp. 1–3.

'Allerseelen und der vorchristliche Todtenkult des deutschen Volkes, *OR*, 31 October 1893, pp. 10–11.

'Der Weinkellerschlüssel. Eine Humoreske aus der Cäsarenzeit', *OR,* 3 November 1893, p.7; *OR*, 4 November 1893, p. 12; *OR*, 6 November 1893, p. 5; *OR*, 7 November 1893, p. 7; *OR*, 8 November 1893, p. 7; *OR*, 9 November 1893, p. 7; *OR*, 10 November 1893, p. 7; *OR*, 11 November 1893, p. 12; *OR*, 13 November 1893, p. 5; *OR*, 14 November 1893, p. 12; *OR*, 16 November 1893, p. 7; *OR*, 17 November 1893, p. 7; *OR*, 18 November 1893, p. 12; *OR*, 20 November 1893, p. 5; *OR*, 21 November 1893, p. 7; *OR*, 22 November 1893, p. 7.

'Die Zwölften', *OR*, 30 December 1893, pp. 9–12.

'Die deutsche Mythologie im Rahmen eines Kalenderjahres', *OR*, 14 January 1894, pp. 9–10; *OR*, 23 March 1894, pp. 1–2; *OR*, 24 March 1894, pp. 1–3; *OR*, 25 April 1894, pp. 1–2; *OR*, 27 April 1894, pp. 1–2; *OR*, 29 May 1894, pp. 1–2; *OR*, 1 June 1894, pp. 1–3; *OR*, 13 July 1894, pp. 1–2; *OR*, 14 July 1894, pp. 1–2; *OR*, 27 July 1894, pp. 1–3; *OR*, 28 July 1894, pp. 1–2; *OR*, 28 August 1894, pp. 1–2; *OR*, 29 August 1894, pp. 1–2; *OR*, 27 September 1894, pp. 1–4; *OR*, 27 October 1894, pp. 1–2; *OR*, 30 October 1894, pp. 1–2; *OR*, 30 November 1894, pp. 1–3; *OR*, 30 December 1894, pp. 1–3.

'Die Blütezeit des deutschen Handwerkes im Mittelalter', *OR*, 13 February 1895, pp. 1–3; *OR*, 14 February 1895, pp. 1–3.

'Donau-Delawaren (eine Humoreske aus dem Donauruderleben)', *OR*, 26 February 1895, pp. 1–3.

'Das Marcus Curtiusloch in Wien', *OR*, 3 May 1895, pp. 1–3.

'Ein Idyll aus dem alten Wien', *OR*, 30 May 1895, pp. 1–3.

'Ludwig Ritter von Mertens', *OR*, 28 June 1895, pp. 1–2.

'Was eine verregnete Raxbesteigung alles verschulden kann', *OR*, 14 July 1895, pp. 1–3.

'Chremisa. Ein Festgruss zum neunhundertjährigen Jubiläum der Stadt Krems a.d. Donau', *OR*, 10 August 1895, pp. 1–2.

'Die alten Höfe Wiens', *OR*, 28 August 1895, pp. 1–2.

'Der deutsche Zauberglaube im Bauwesen', *OR*, 25 September 1895, pp. 1–2; *OR*, 26 September 1895, pp. 1–2.

'Die Gründung des Klosters Cotwich. Historische Novelle aus dem elften Jahrhundert', *OR*, 29 September 1895, p. 7; *OR*, 1 October 1895, p. 5; *OR*, 2 October 1895, p. 6; *OR* 3 October 1895, p. 5; *OR*, 4 October 1895, p. 7; *OR*, 5 October 1895, p. 7; *OR* 6 October 1895, p. 10; *OR*, 8 October 1895, p. 5; *OR*, 10 October 1895, p. 5; *OR*, 11 October 1895, p. 7; *OR*, 13 October 1895, p. 7; *OR*, 15 October 1895, p. 5.

'Mephistopheles', *OR*, 28 December 1895, pp. 1–2; *OR*, 31 December 1895, pp. 1–3.

'Die Juden als Staat und Nation', *OR*, 12 February 1896, pp. 1–2.

'Die alte Schule zu St. Anna in Wien', *OR*, 26 February 1896, pp. 1–2; *OR*, 28 February 1896, pp. 1–2.

'Die Liebe in der deutschen Mythologie', *OR*, 16 April 1896, pp. 1–2.

'Ostara's Einzug', *OR*, 22 May 1896, pp. 1–3.

'Schöne Frauen', *OR*, 29 August 1896, pp. 1–3.

'Die Michaelskirche in Heiligenstadt in Wien', *OR*, 15 November 1896, pp. 9–10.

'Vom Jubiläumstheater in Währing', *OR*, 12 April 1896, pp. 5–6; *OR*, 21 April 1896, pp. 1–2; *OR*, 28 April 1896, pp. 1–2; *OR*, 10 May 1896, pp. 1–3; *OR*, 31 May 1896, pp. 1–4; *OR*, 15 October 1896, pp. 1–3; *OR*, 22 December 1896, pp. 1–2.

Articles in *Leipziger Illustrierte Zeitung.*

'Die Hieroglyphik der Germanen', *LIZ*, 4 May 1905, pp. 680–1.

'Mistel und Weihnachtsbaum', *LIZ*, 21 December 1905, p. 950.

'Die Hieroglyphik der Germanen. II. Weitere Hieroglyphen der Heraldik', *LIZ*, 15 March 1906, pp. 417–18.

'Die Kunst des Feuerzündens und die Erfindung des Rades und des Wagens', *LIZ*, 16 August 1906, pp. 278–9.

'Die Hieroglyphik der Germanen. III. Der Einfluss der Kala auf die Entwicklung der heraldischen Hieroglyphen', *LIZ*, 31 January 1907, pp. 188–9.

(b) Periodical Articles

'Die symbolischen Bildwerke am Riesenthore der Stefanskirche zu Wien', *Laufers Allgemeine Kunst-Chronik* 12 (1889), 250–1, 283–4, 307–10.

'Ursprung und Wesen der Wappen', *Der Sammler* 13 (1891), 54–6, 65–7.

'Von den Wuotanspriesterschaft', *Das Zwanzigste Jahrhundert* 4 (1893), 119–26, 242–51, 343–52, 442–51.

'Die esoterische Bedeutung religiöser Symbole', *Die Gnosis* 1 (1903), 323–7.

'Vom Wuotanstum zum Christentum', *Der Deutsche* 1 (1904), 403–12.

'Das Geheimnis der Runen', *Neue Metaphysische Rundschau* [9] 13 (1906), 23–4, 75–87, 104–26.

'Von der Armanenschaft der Arier', *Neue Metaphysische Rundschau* [9] 13 (1906), 162–75, 214–26.

'Ursprung und Symbolik der Freimaurerei', *Die Nornen* 1 (18 October 1912), 5–8.

'Neuzeitliche Einherier', *Österreichische Illustrierte Rundschau* 4 (1916), reprinted in Balzli, op. cit., pp. 116–24.

'Wer ist der Starke von Oben?', *Prana* 7 (1917), reprinted in Balzli, op. cit., pp. 125–33.

'Über die Möglichkeit eines ewigen Weltfriedens', *Prana* 7 (1917), reprinted in Balzli, op. cit., pp. 134–8.

(c) Books

Carnuntum. Historischer Roman aus dem 4. Jahrhundert n. Chr., 2 vols. (Berlin, 1888).

Deutsch-Mythologische Landschaftsbilder (Berlin, 1891).

Tauf-, Hochzeits- und Bestattungs-Gebräuche und deren Ursprung (Salzburg, 1892).

Litteraria sodalitas Danubiana (Vienna, 1893).

Jung Diether's Heimkehr. Eine Sonnwend-Geschichte aus dem Jahre 488 n. Chr. (Brno, 1894).

Der Wala Erweckung (Vienna, 1894).

Walküren-Weihe. Epische Dichtung (Brno, 1895).

Pipara. Die Germanin im Cäsarenpurpur. Historischer Roman aus dem 3. Jahrhundert n. Chr., 2 vols. (Leipzig, 1895).

Niederösterreichisches Winzerbüchlein (Vienna, 1898).

Der Unbesiegbare. Ein Grundzug germanischer Weltanschauung (Vienna, 1898).

König Vannius. Ein deutsches Königsdrama (Brno, 1899).

Der Wiederaufbau von Carnuntum (Vienna, 1900).

Sommer-Sonnwend-Feuerzauber. Skaldisches Weihespiel (Vienna, 1901).

Alraunen-Mären. Kulturhistorische Novellen und Dichtungen aus germanischer Vorzeit (Vienna, 1903).

Das Goldstück. Ein Liebesdrama in fünf Aufzügen (Vienna, 1903).

Das Geheimnis der Runen [GLB 1] (Gross-Lichterfelde, 1908).

Die Armanenschaft der Ario-Germanen [GLB 2] (Leipzig and Vienna, 1908).

Die Rita der Ario-Germanen [GLB 3] (Leipzig and Vienna, 1908).

Die Namen der Völkerstämme Germaniens und deren Deutung [GLB 4] (Leipzig and Vienna, 1909).

Die Religion der Ario-Germanen in ihrer Esoterik und Exoterik (Zurich, 1909 or 1910).

Die Bilderschrift der Ario-Germanen (Ario-Germanische Hieroglyphik) [GLB 5] (Leipzig and Vienna, 1910).

Die Armanenschaft der Ario-Germanen. Zweiter Teil [GLB 2a] (Leipzig and Vienna, 1911).

Der Übergang vom Wuotanstum zum Christentum (Zurich, 1911).

Die Armanenschaft der Ario-Germanen. Erster Teil, second edition (Vienna, [1913]).

Deutsch-Mythologische Landschaftsbilder, second edition, 2 vols. (Vienna, [1913]).

Die Ursprache der Ario-Germanen und ihre Mysteriensprache [GLB 6] (Leipzig and Vienna, [1914]).

(d) Biographical and Literary Studies

Johannes Balzli, *Guido v. List. Der Wiederentdecker uralter arischer Weisheit* (Leipzig and Vienna, 1917).

E. H., 'Guido List (Lebensbild eines Wiener Poeten)', *Randglossen zur deutschen Literaturgeschichte* 11 (1905), 1–58.

August Horneffer, 'Guido von List, der völkische Philosoph und Prophet', *Am rauhen Stein* 29 (1932), 35–45.

Inge Kunz, 'Herrenmenschentum, Neugermanen und Okkultismus. Eine soziologische Bearbeitung der Schriften von Guido List' (unpublished Dr. phil. thesis, University of Vienna, 1961).

[J. Lanz-Liebenfels], *Guido von List, ein moderner Skalde* (Gross-Lichterfelde, [1907]).

J. Lanz von Liebenfels, 'Guido von List. Eine ariomantische Studie', *Zeitschrift für Menschenkenntnis und Schicksalsforschung* 2 (1927), 74–89.

Philipp Stauff, 'Guido von List gestorben', *Münchener Beobachter*, 24 May 1919, p. 4.

Philipp Stauff, 'Von unseres Meisters letzter Zeit', in Guido von List, *Die Rita der Ario-Germanen*, third edition (Berlin, 1920), appendix pp. I–VIII.

Franz Wastian, 'Guido v. List, ein deutscher Erzieher', *Südmark-Kalender* 13 (1910), 119–23.

Arthur Wolf-Wolfsberg, 'Guido von List, Der Skalde, Seher und Forscher', *Zeitschrift für Menschenkenntnis und Schicksalsforschung* 2 (1927), 93–6.

III. Adolf Josef Lanz alias Jörg Lanz von Liebenfels

(a) Periodical Articles

'Berthold v. Treun. Eine Studie von Fr. G . . ., O.C.', *Mittheilungen des Alterthums-Vereins zu Wien* 30 (1894), 137–40.

'Das Necrologium Sancrucense Modernum', *Archiv für Österreichische Geschichte* 89 (1900), 247–354.

'Anthropozoon biblicum', *Vierteljahrsschrift für Bibelkunde* 1 (1903), 307–16, 317–55, 429–69; *Vierteljahrsschrift für Bibelkunde* 2 (1904), 26–60, 314–34, 395–412.

'Zur Theologie der gotischen Bibel', *Vierteljahrsschrift für Bibelkunde* 1 (1903), 497–8.

'Die Armee des schwarzen Papstes', *Das freie Wort* 2 (1903), 394–402, 451–9, 721–9.

'Die Urgeschichte der Künste', *Politisch-Anthropologische Revue* 2 (1903), 134–56.

'Deutschland und die Jesuiten', *Politisch-Anthropologische Revue* 3 (1904), 389–91.

'Der grosse Kampf des Jesuitismus gegen den Katholizismus', *Das freie Wort* 3 (1904), 49–56.

'Leo XIII., der "Friedenspapst"', *Das freie Wort* 3 (1904), 338–46.

'Politische Anthropologie', *Das freie Wort* 3 (1904), 778–95.

'Die Jesuiten vor "Pilatus"', *Das freie Wort* 4 (1905), 63–9, 118–23.

'Menschenveredelung', *Das freie Wort* 4 (1905), 189–92.

'Die Deutschen als Wirtschaftsgrossmacht in Österreich. Ein freies Wort zum österreichischen Problem', *Das freie Wort* 4 (1905), 582–90.

'Zur Anthropologie des Genies', *Das freie Wort* 4 (1905), 887–94.

'Eine neue Schule', *Hammer* 4 (1905), 369–71.

'Germanischer Advent', *Hammer* 5 (1906), 97–9.

'Ungarns wirtschaftlicher Bankerott', *Hammer* 5 (1906), 395–7.

'Der heilige Gral', *Stein der Weisen* 20 (1907), 218–26.

'Die Babenberger' and 'Klöster und heilige Stätten in Osterreich', in *Osterreichs Hort. Geschichts- und Kulturbilder aus den Habsburgischen Erbländern*, edited by Albin von Teuffenbach zu Tiefenbach und Massweg (Vienna, 1910), pp. 22–49, 276–90.

(b) Books

Katholizimus wider Jesuitismus (Frankfurt, 1903).

Das Breve 'Dominus ac redemptor noster' (Frankfurt, [1904]).

Der Taxil-Schwindel. Ein welthistorischer Ulk (Frankfurt, [1904]).

Theozoologie oder Die Kunde von den Sodoms-Äfflingen und dem Götter-Elektron. Eine Einführung in die älteste und neueste Weltanschauung und eine Rechtfertigung des Fürstentums und des Adels (Vienna, [1905]).

Der Affenmensch der Bibel (Bibeldokumente 1) (Gross-Lichterfelde, n.d.).

Die Theosophie und die assyrischen 'Menschentiere' in ihrem Verhältnis zu den neuesten Resultaten der anthropologischen Forschung (Bibeldokumente 2) (Gross-Lichterfelde, 1907).

Die Archäologie und Anthropologie und die assyrichen Menschenthiere (Bibeldokumente 3) (Gross-Lichterfelde, n.d.).

Die griechischen Bibelversionen (Septauginta und Hexapla), Vol. i. (Orbis antiquitatum Pars II, Tom. 1, Vol. i) (Vienna, 1908).

Die lateinischen Bibelversionen (Itala und Vulgata), Vol. i. (Orbis antiquitatum Pars II, Tom. 2, Vol. i.) (Vienna, 1909).

'Geschichte der Burg Werfenstein', in Ludwig Commenda, *Neuer illustrierter Führer durch Grein und Umgebung* (Grein, 1910), pp. 84–95.

Weltende und Weltwende. Der Zusammenbruch der europäischen Kulturwelt (Lorch, 1923).

Praktisch-empirisches Handbuch der ariosophischen Astrologie. Bd. 1 Die Berechnung von Geburtshoroskopen (Düsseldorf-Unterrath, 1923).

Praktisch-empirisches Handbuch der ariosophischen Astrologie. Bd. 2 Die Deutung von Geburtshoroskopen (Astromantie) (Berlin, 1933).

Das Buch der Psalmen teutsch, das Gebetbuch der Ariosophen, Rassenmystiker und Antisimiten. Bd. 1 Text (Düsseldorf-Unterrath, 1926).

Grundriss der ariosophischen Geheimlehre (Oestrich, 1925).

Ariosophische Rassenphrenologie (Düsseldorf-Unterrath, 1926).

Jakob Lorber, das grösste ariosophische Medium der Neuzeit.

    I. Teil Lebensgang und die Mysterien der irdischen Welt.

    II. Teil Die Mysterien der planetarischen Welt.

    III. Teil Die Mysterien der makrokosmischen Welt.

IV. Teil Die Mysterien der mikrokos-mischenmischen Welt.

(Düsseldorf-Unterrath, 1926).

Das Sakrament der Ehe im Lichte der ariosophischen Theologie (Düsseldorf-Unterrath, 1926).

Die ariosophische Kabbalistik von Name und Örtlich-keit, with Meister Archibald and Meister Amalarich (Düsseldorf-Unterrath, 1926).

Abriss der ariosophischen Rassenphysiognomik (Pforzheim, 1927).

Ariosophische Urgeschichte der Handwerke und Künste (Pforzheim, 1928).

Ariosophisches Wappenbuch (Pforzheim, 1928).

(c) Pamphlet-Series

Ostara. First Series. Graz, 1905, Rodaun, 1906–13, Mödling, 1913–16. All titles written by Lanz von Liebenfels unless another author is indicated.

1 Die österreichischen Deutschen und die Wahlreform (Graz, 1905).

2 Wahlreform, Gewerbereform, Rechts-reform. Von sc (Rodaun, March 1906).

3 Revolution oder Evolution? Eine frei-konservative Osterpredigt für das Herrentum europäischer Rasse (April 1906).

4 Ungarns wirtschaftlicher Bankerott und wie machen wir Ungarn kirre? (May 1906).

5 Landgraf werde hart, eine altdeutsche Volkssage neuzeittümlich erzält von Adolf Hagen (June 1906).

6 Die Reichskleinodien zurück nach dem Reich! Völkische Richtlinien für unsere Zukunft von Harald Arjuna Grävell van Jostenoode (July 1906).

7 Ostara, die Auferstehung des Menschen. Eine Festschrift von Dr. phil. Adolf. Harpf (August 1906).

8 Die deutsch-österreichischen Alpen-länder als Fleisch- und Milch-produzenten. Eine volkswirtschaft-liche Studie von Ingenieur L. von Bernuth (August 1906).

9 Der völkische Gedanke, das aristokrat-ische Prinzip unserer Zeit, von Dr. phil. Adolf Harpf (September 1906).

10/13 Anthropogonika – Urmensch und Rasse im Schrifttum der Alten, aus-gewählte rassengeschichtliche Urkunden (October 1906).

11/12 Das Weibwesen, eine Kulturstudie, von Dr. phil. Adolf Harpf (January 1907).

14 Triumph Israels, von R. Freydank

(March 1907).

Das Ganze voran! (Spring 1907).

15 Weibliche Erwerbsfähigkeit und Prosti-tution, von Dr. Eduard Ritter von Liszt (April 1907).

16 Juda's Geldmonopol im Aufgang und Zenith, zwei Zeitgedichte, von Dr. Adolf Wahrmund (June 1907).

17 Die Titelfrage der Techniker (July 1907).

18 Rasse und Wohlfahrtspflege, ein Aufruf zum Streik der wahllosen Wohltätig-keit (December 1907).

19/20 Die Zeit des ewigen Friedens, eine Apologie des Krieges als Kultur-und Rassenauffrischer, von Dr. Adolf Harpf (January 1908).

21 Rasse und Weib und seine Vorliebe für den Mann der niederen Artung (March 1908).

22/23 Das Gesetzbuch des Manu und die Rassenpflege bei den alten Indo-Ariern (April 1908).

24 Über Patentrecht und Rechtlosigkeit des geistigen Arbeiters. Von sc (May 1908).

25 Das Ariertum und seine Feinde, von Dr. Harald Grävell van Jostenoode (July 1908).

26 Einführung in die Rassenkunde.

27 Beschreibende Rassenkunde.

28 Antlitz und Rasse, ein Abriss der rassenkundlichen Physiognomik.

29 Allgemeine rassenkundliche Somato-logie.

30 Besondere rassenkundliche Somato-logie I.

31 Besondere rassenkundliche Somato-logie II.

32 Vom Steuer-eintreibenden zum Divi-denden-zahlenden Staat (1909).

33 Die Gefahren des Frauenrechtes und die Notwendigkeit der mannesrecht-lichen Herrenmoral (1909).

34 Die rassenwirtschaftliche Lösung des sexuellen Problems (1909).

35 Neue physikalische und mathematische Beweise für das Dasein der Seele (1910).

36 Das Sinnes- und Geistesleben der Blonden und Dunklen (1910).

37 Charakterbeurteilung nach der Schädel-form, eine gemeinverständliche Rassen-Phrenologie (1910).

38 Das Geschlechts- und Liebesleben der Blonden und Dunklen I. Anthro-pologischer Teil (1910).

39 Das Geschlechts- und Liebesleben der Blonden und Dunklen II. Kulturgeschichtlicher Teil (1910).

40 Rassenpsychologie des Erwerbslebens I. Die Verarmung der Blonden und der Reichtum der Dunklen (1910).

41 Rassenpsychologie des Erwerbslebens II. Die maskierte Dieberei als Erwerbsprinzip der Dunklen. Eine Auflärung für Blonde (1910).

42 Die Blonden und Dunklen im politischen Leben der Gegenwart (1910).

43 Einführung in die Sexual-Physik oder die Liebe als odische Energie (1911).

44 Die Komik der Frauenrechtlerei, eine heitere Chronik der Weiberwirtschaft (1911).

45 Die Tragik der Frauenrechtlerei, eine ernste Chronik der Weiberwirtschaft (1911).

46 Moses als Darwinist, eine Einführung in die anthropologische Religion (1911).

47 Die Kunst schön zu lieben und glücklich zu heiraten, ein rassen-hygienisches Brevier für Liebesleute (1911).

48 Genesis oder Moses als Antisimit, d.i. Bekämpfer der Affenmenschen und Dunkelrassen (1911).

49 Die Kunst der glücklichen Ehe, ein rassenhygienisches Brevier für Ehe-Rekruten und Ehe-Veteranen (1911).

50 Urheimat und Urgeschichte der blonden heroischen Rasse (1911).

51 Kallipädie, oder die Kunst der bewussten Kinderzeugung, ein rassenhygienisches Brevier für Väter und Mütter (1911).

52 Die Blonden als Schöpfer der Sprachen, ein Abriss der Ursprachenschöpfung (Protolinguistik).

53 Das Mannesrecht als Retter aus der Geschlechtsnot der Weiberwirtschaft (1912).

54 Exodus, oder Moses als Prediger der Rassenauslese und Rassenmoral (1912).

55 Die soziale, politische und sexuelle Weiberwirtschaft unserer Zeit (1912).

56 Die rassentümliche Erziehung und die Befreiung der Blonden aus der Schreckenherrschaft der Tschandala-Schule (1912).

57 Die rassentümliche Wirtschaftsordnung und die Befreiung der Blonden aus der Schreckenherrschaft der tschandalistischen Ausbeuter (1912).

58 Die entsittlichende und verbrecherische Weiberwirtschaft unserer Zeit (1912).

59 Das arische Christentum als Rassenkultreligion der Blonden, eine Einführung in die Hl. Schrift des Neuen Testamentes (1912).

60 Rassenbewusstlose und rassenbewusste Lebens- und Liebeskunst, ein Brevier für die reife, blonde Jugend (1912).

61 Rassenmischung und Rassenentmischung (1912).

62 Die Blonden und Dunklen als Heer- und Truppenführer (1913).

63 Die Blonden und Dunklen als Truppen (1913).

64 Viel oder wenig Kinder (1913).

65 Rasse und Krankheit, ein Abriss der allgemeinen und theoretischen Rassenpathologie (1913).

66 Nackt- und Rassenkultur im Kampf gegen Mucker- und Tschandalenkultur (1913).

67 Die Beziehungen der Dunklen und Blonden zur Krankheit, ein Abriss der besonderen und praktischen Rassenpathologie (Vienna, 1913).

68 Der Wiederaufstieg der Blonden zu Reichtum und Macht, eine Einführung in die Rassensoziologie (Vienna, 1913).

69 Der Gral als das Mysterium der arisch-christlichen Rassenkultreligion (1913).

70 Die Blonden als Schöpfer der technischen Kultur (Mödling, 1913).

71 Rasse und Adel (1913).

72 Rasse und äussere Politik (1913).

73 Die Blonden als Musik-Schöpfer (1913).

74 Rassenmetaphysik oder die Unsterblichkeit des höheren Menschen (1914).

75 Die Blonden als Träger und Opfer der technischen Kultur (1914).

76 Die Prostitution in frauen- und mannesrechtlichen Beurteilung (1914).

77 Rassen und Baukunst im Altertum und Mittelalter (1914).

78 Rassenmystik, eine Einführung in die ariochristliche Geheimlehre (1915).

79 Rassenphysik des Krieges 1914/15 (1915).

80 Einführung in die praktische Rassenmetaphysik (1915).

81 Rassenmetaphysik des Krieges 1914/15 (1915).

82 Templeisen-Brevier, ein Andachtsbuch für wissende und innerliche Ariochristen 1. Teil (1915).

83 Rasse und Dichtkunst (1916).

84 Rasse und Philosophie (1916).

85 Rasse und Baukunst in der Neuzeit (1916).

86 Rasse und Malerei (1916).

87 Rasse und innere Politik (1916).

88 Templeisen-Brevier, ein Andachtsbuch für wissende und innerliche Ariochristen 2. Teil (1916).

89 Rassenphysik der Heiligen (1917).

Ostara. Second Series. Magdeburg, 1922.

1 Die Ostara und das Reich der Blonden (1922).

Ostara. Third series. Vienna, 1927–31.

1 Die Ostara und das Reich der Blonden (1927).

2 Der Weltkrieg als Rassenkampf der Dunklen gegen die Blonden (1927).

3 Die Weltrevolution als Grab der Blonden (1928).

4 Der Weltfriede als Werk und Sieg der Blonden (1928).

5 Theozoologie oder Naturgeschichte der Götter I. Der 'alte Bund' und alte Gott (1928).

6/7 Theozoologie oder Naturgeschichte der Götter II. Die Sodomssteine und Sodomswässer (1928).

8/9 Theozoologie oder Naturgeschichte der Götter III. Die Sodomsfeuer und Sodomslüfte (1928).

10 Anthropogonika, Urmensch und Rasse im Schrifttum der Alten (1931).

11 Der wirtschaftliche Wiederaufbau durch die Blonden, eine Einführung in die privatwirtschaftliche Rassenökonomie (1929).

12 Die Diktatur des blonden Patriziates, eine Einführung in die staatswirtschaftliche Rassenökonomie (1929).

13/14 Der zoologische und talmudische Ursprung des Bolschewismus (1930).

15 Theozoologie oder Naturgeschichte der Götter IV. Der neue Bund und neue Gott (1929).

16/17 Theozoologie V. Der Götter-Vater und Götter-Geist oder die Unsterblichkeit in Materie und Geist (1929).

18 Theozoologie oder Naturgeschichte der Götter VI. Der Göttersohn und die Unsterblichkeit in Keim und Rasse (1930).

19 Theozoologie VII. Die unsterbliche Götterkirche (1930).

20 Rasse und Wohfahrtspflege, ein Aufruf zum Streik der wahllosen Wohltätigkeit (1930).

21 Rasse und Weib und seine Vorliebe für den Mann der minderen Artung (1929).

22/23 Rasse und Recht und das Gesetzbuch des Manu (1929).

26 Einführung in die Rassenkunde (1930).

27 Beschreibende Rassenkunde (1930).

28 Antlitz und Rasse, ein Abriss der rassenkundlichen Physiognomik (1931).

29 Allgemeine rassenkundliche Somatologie (1931).

33 Die Gefahren des Frauenrechts und die Notwendigkeit des Mannesrechts (1929).

34 Die rassenwirtschaftliche Lösung des sexuellen Problems (1928).

35 Neue physikalische und mathematische Beweise für das Dasein der Seele (1929).

36 Das Sinnes- und Geistesleben der Blonden und Dunklen (1929).

38 Das Geschlechts- und Liebesleben der Blonden und Dunklen I. Anthropologischer Teil (1929).

43 Einführung in die Sexual-Physik oder die Liebe als odische Energie (1931).

47 Die Kunst, schön zu lieben und glücklich zu heiraten; ein rassenhygienisches Brevier für Liebesleute (1928).

49 Die Kunst der glücklichen Ehe, ein rassenhygienisches Brevier für Ehe-Rekruten und Ehe-Veteranen (1929).

51 Kallipädie oder die Kunst der bewussten Kinderzeugung, ein rassenhygienisches Brevier für Väter und Mütter (1931).

61 Rassenmischung und Rassenentmischung (1930).

78 Rassenmystik, eine Einführung in die ariochristliche Geheimlehre (1929).

90 Des hl. Abtes Bernhard von Clairvaux Lobpreis auf die neue Tempelritterschaft und mystische Kreuzfahrt ins hl. Land (1929).

91/93 Die Heiligen als Kultur- und rassengeschichtliche Hieroglyphen (1930).

94 Rasse und Bildhauerei I. Rassenanthropologischer Teil (1931).

95 Rasse und Bildhauerei II. Rassengeschichtlicher Teil (1931).

101 Johann Walthari Wölfl, Lanz-Liebenfels und sein Werk 1. Teil: Einführung in die Theorie (1927).

Ariomantische Bücherei. Lucerne, 1933–*c.*37. The series appeared under the various titles *Ariomantische Briefe an meine Freunde, Briefe an meine Freunde, Luzerner Briefe an meine Freunde* and was not issued through the book-trade, but as a private edition. After No. 24 the dating of these pamphlets is unreliable.

1 Blondheit und Rasse. Eine Einführung in die Ariomantik (1933).

2 Die arioheroische Rasse und das Wirtschaftsleben oder: Wie wird der Blonde reich? (1934).

3 Der elektrische Urgott und sein grosses Heiligtum in der Vorzeit (1933).

4 Das wiederentdeckte Vineta-Rethra und die arisch-christliche Urreligion der Elektrizität und Rasse (1934).

5 Praktische Einführung in die arisch-christliche Mystik I. Teil: Wesen und Zweck der Mystik (1934).

6 Praktische Einführung in die arisch-christliche Mystik II. Teil: Naturwissenschaftliche Begründung (1934).

7 Praktische Einführung in die arisch-christliche Mystik III. Teil: Die mystische Vorbereitung (Praeambulum).

8 Praktische Einführung in die arisch-christliche Mystik IV. Teil: Läuterung (purgatio) und Beschauung (contemplatio) (1934).

9 Praktische Einführung in die arisch-christliche Mystik V. Teil: Die mystische Verzückung u. Hochzeit (Ecstasis u. Unio) (1934).

10 Praktische Einführung in die arisch-christliche Mystik VI. Teil: Praxis, Geschichte und Literatur der Mystik (1934).

11 Über den Umgang mit Tschandalen, ein neuer 'Knigge'. I. Teil (1934).

12 Über den Umgang mit Tschandalen, ein neuer 'Knigge', II. Teil [1934].

13 Über den Umgang mit Tschandalen, ein neuer 'Knigge', III. Teil [1934].

14 Ariomantische Boden- und Lebenspflege I. Teil [1935].

15 Ariomantische Boden- und Lebenspflege II. Teil [1935].

16 Ariomantische Boden- und Lebenspflege III. Teil [1935].

20 Die Theorie der natur- und artgemässen Ernährungs- u. Lebensweise (1935).

21 Ariomantischer Brief über Praxis und Kochkunst der naturgemässen Ernährungsweise.

22 Ariomantischer Brief an Sephin über Mode und Menschenkunde [1935].

23 Ariomantischer Brief an Peppo über Praxis der naturgemässen Landwirtschaft [1935].

24 Ariomantischer Brief an Roderich über die Urreligion der Engel und Walküren im biblischen und nordischen Schrifttum [1935].

25 Ariomantischer Brief an Peppo über Garten und Küche als Grundlage der Gesundheit [1934].

26 Ariomantischer Brief an Walter über die Priesterschaft des Orpheus und Musaeus-Moses [1929].

27 Über Duft, Licht und Geist als Lebensnahrung [1930].

28 Über die Priesterschaft des Pythagoras und Brahma [1929].

29 Ueber die Priesterschaft des Apollonius von Tyana und Frauja [1930].

30 Ueber die Priesterschaft des Ulfilas und die gotische Bibel [1930].

31 Die unterschlagene esoterische Lehre des Ulfilas [1930].

32 Ulfilas und das Schlüsselwörterbuch zur Esoterik des Altertums und Mittelalters. I. Teil: A-C. [1930].

33 Ulfilas und das Schlüsselwörterbuch zur Esoterik des Altertums und Mittelalters. II. Teil: D-J. [1930].

34 Ulfilas und das Schlüsselwörterbuch zur Esoterik des Altertums und Mittelalters. III. Teil: K-S. [1930].

35 Ulfilas und das Schlüsselwörterbuch zur Esoterik des Altertums und Mittelalters. IV. Teil: S-Z. [1930].

36 Jakob Lorber, der grosse Seher der vergangenen und kommenden Zeiten, I. Teil: Lorbers Leben.

37 Jakob Lorber, der grosse Seher vergangener und kommender Zeiten, II. Teil: Die Mysterien der irdischen Welt und des Mondes [1926].

38 Jakob Lorber, der grosse Seher ver-

gangener und kommender Zeiten, III. Teil: Die Wunderwelt der Planeten Merkur, Mars und Jupiter.

39 Jakob Lorber, der grosse Seher vergangener und kommender Zeiten, IV. Teil: Die Wunderwelt der Planeten Saturn, Uranus und Neptun [1926].

40 Das Leben St. Benedikts von Nursia [1930].

41 Der Tod St. Benedikts von Nursia und seine Ordensregel I. Teil [1930].

42 Die Ordensregel St. Benedikts v. Nursia, II. Teil [1930].

43 Die Priesterschaft Benedikts v. Nursia, I. Teil: Ursprünge und Vorläufer [1930].

44 Elektrotheologie von Ritus und Liturgie, I. Teil [1930].

45 Elektrotheologie von Ritus und Liturgie, II. Teil [1908].

46 Elektrotheologie des Sakraments der Taufe [1908].

47 Elektrotheologie der Sakramente der Firmung, Busse und Krankenölung [1908].

Elektrotheologische Handschriften. Burg Werfenstein, 1908, Manserie Szt. Balázs, 1930. The dating and place of publication is unreliable, since these pamphlets continue the themes of the late numbers of the *Ariomantische Bücherei*.

E1 Elektrotheologie des Sakraments der Eucharistie, Messe u. Gralsfeier I. Teil: Name und Einsetzung [1908].

E2 Elektrotheologie des Sakraments der Eucharistie, Messe und Gralsfeier II. Teil: Geschichte und Wesen [1908].

E3 Elektrotheologie des Sakraments der Ehe und Priesterweihe [1908].

E4 Die Priesterschaft Benedikts von Nursia, II. Teil: Die Einwirkung auf die Menschheitsentwicklung [1930].

E5 Die Priesterschaft St. Bernhards v. Clairvaux I. Teil [1930].

E6 Die Priesterschaft St. Bernhards v. Clairvaux II. Teil [1930].

(d) **Ritual Books.** Privately published.

Regularium Fratrum Ordinis Novi Templi (Werfenstein, 1921).

Tabularium ONT, 43 vols. (April 1923–April 1927).

*Librarium ONT, c.*15 vols. (1925–6).

Examinatorium ONT, 7 vols. (1925).

Festivarium NT oder Gedenk-und Festtagslesungen des Neutempleisen-Breviers. I. Buch: Legendarium. Templeisengeschichtliche- und templeisenwissenschaftliche Lesungen für die Matutin (Szt. Balázs, n.d.).

Festivarium II. Buch: Evangelarium. Templeisenmoralische Lesungen für die Prim.

Festivarium. III. Buch: Visionarium. Templeisenmetaphysische Lesungen für das Completorium.

Hebdomadarium

Cantuarium

Rituarium

Imaginarium NT, Alt- und Neutempleisentum in Bildern (Werfenstein, Szt. Balázs, Staufen, n.d.).

Bibliomystikon oder Die Geheimbibel der Eingeweihten, 10 vols. (Pforzheim, then Untertullnerbach near Vienna, then Berlin, finally Szt. Balázs?, 1930–c.38).

Das Buch der Psalmen teutsch, das Gebetbuch der Ariosophen, Rassenmystiker und Antisimiten 1. Bd: Text (Düsseldorf, 1926).

Geschichte der Mystik, 7 instalments (Thalwyl, post-1945).

Arithmosophikon. Ein modern-wissenschaftliches Lehrbuch der Kabbala und der Geistersprache der Zahlen, Buchstaben, Worte, Personen- und Ortsnamen, 19 instalments (Thalwyl, c.1949).

(e) **Biographical Studies**

Wilfried Daim, *Der Mann, der Hitler die Ideen gab* (Munich, 1958).

F. Dietrich, 'Georg Lanz von Liebenfels†', *Die Arve,* Heft 23 (May 1955), 1–5.

Rudolf J. Mund, *Jörg Lanz v. Liebenfels und der Neue Templer Orden* (Stuttgart, 1976).

IV. The Armanists

Ellegaard Ellerbek (i.e. Gustav Leisner)
Auf heldischer Heerfahrt im heiligen Jahr (Hanover, 1915).
Aus deutscher Mutternacht (Hanover, 1915).
PPPRRResident Bluff. Amerika-Skizzen (Hanover, 1916).
Versailler Visionen. Ein okkult-armanisches Bekenntnis zu Pauli Wort: 'Wisset Ihr nicht, dass Ihr Götter seid?' (Berlin, 1919).
Sönne Sonnings Söhne auf Sonnensee (Berlin, 1920).

Wallfahrt zu Gott. Ein Spiel aus deutschem Streben ins Licht (Berlin, 1922).

Georg Hauerstein Sr.
Die Sippensiedlung (Isernhagen b. Hanover, 1914).

Franz Herndl
Das Wörtherkreuz (Vienna, 1901).
Die Trutzburg. Autobiographische Skizzen des Einsiedlers auf der Insel Wörth (Leipzig, 1909).

Franz X. Kiessling
Denkstätten deutscher Vorzeit im niederösterreichischen Waldviertel (Vienna, 1891).
Die drei Thayaburgen Buchenstein, Eibenstein, Unter-Thürnau, nebst der Örtlichkeiten Lehstein und einem kurzen, geschichtlichheraldischen Abrisse über das Geschlecht der Herren von Tirna (Vienna, 1895).
Deutscher Turnerbund oder deutsche Turnerschaft? (Vienna, 1895).
Verwälschtes und verlorenes deutsches Blut. Eine Mahnung zur Pflege alldeutscher Gesinnung (Vienna, 1897).
Eine Wanderung im Poigreiche. Landschaftliche, vorgeschichtliche, müthologische und volksgeschichtliche Betrachtungen über die Örtlichkeiten Horn, Rosenburg, Altenburg, Drei-Eichen, Messern, Rondorf, Haselberg und andere, sowie deren Umgebungen mit besonderer Berücksichtigung der deutschen Vorzeit und auf Grundlage von Müthe, Meinung und Sage des Volkes (Horn, 1898).
Über Besiedlungsverhältnisse, sowie völkische und glaubensthümliche Zustände in der Vorzeit Niederösterreichs, mit besonderer Berücksichtigung von Vindobona (Vindomina) – Wien und dessen Umgebung (Vienna, 1899).
Das deutsche Weihnachtsfest in Beziehung zur germanischen Müthe (Vienna, 1902).
Das deutsche Fest der Sommersonnwende, beleuchtet in Müthe, Meinung und Sage des Volkes (Vienna, 1903).

Bernhard Koerner
Genealogisches Handbuch bürgerlicher Familien. Deutsches Geschlechterbuch, vols. 6–119, edited by Bernh. Koerner (Görlitz, 1899–1944).

Josef Ludwig Reimer
Ein pangermanisches Deutschland (Leipzig, 1905).
Grundzüge deutscher Wiedergeburt (Leipzig, 1906).

Rudolf von Sebottendorff
Metoula-Führer: Türkisch (Berlin, 1913).
'Erwin Haller. Ein deutscher Kaufmann in der Türkei', *Münchener Beobachter,* 31 August 1918–10 May 1919.
Die Symbole des Tierkreises. Zur Symbolik jedes Grads nach alten Quellen gesammelt (Leipzig, [1921]).
Die Hilfshoroskopie (Leipzig, [1921]).
Stunden- und Frage- Horoskopie. Mit Berücksichtigung der Perioden, Zyklen, Tattwas, kabbalistische Horoskopie (Leipzig, 1921).
Sterntafeln (Ephemeriden) von 1838–1922 (Leipzig, [1922]).
Praktischer Lehrgang zur Horoskopie (Leipzig, 1922).
Sonnen- und Mondorte. Sternzeit. Die Frage der Häuserberechnung (Leipzig, [1923]).
Geschichte der Astrologie. Band 1. Urzeit und Altertum (Leipzig, 1923).
Die Praxis der alten türkischen Freimaurerei. Der Schlüssel zum Verständnis der Alchimie. Eine Darstellung des Rituals, der Lehre, der Erkennungszeichen orientalischer Freimaurer (Leipzig, [1924]).
Der Talisman des Rosenkreuzers. Roman (Pfullingen, [1925]).
'Die Levitation der Mewlewi', *Die weisse Fahne* 6 (1925), 390–3.
Astrologisches Lehrbuch (Leipzig, 1927).
Bevor Hitler kam. Urkundliches aus der Frühzeit der national-sozialistischen Bewegung, second edition (Munich, 1934).

Philipp Stauff
Wegweiser und Wegwarte. Deutschvölkische Vorzeitung, 7 vols. (1907–14).
Der Krieg und die Friedensbestrebungen unserer Zeit. Gedankengänge (Enzisweiler a. Bodensee, 1907).
Das deutsche Wehrbuch (Berlin, 1912).
Runenhäuser (Berlin, 1912).
Semi-Gotha. Weimarer historisch-genealogisches Taschenbuch des gesamten Adels jehudäischen Ursprunges (Weimar, 1912).
Semi-Alliancen (Berlin, 1912).
Semi-Kürschner oder Literarisches Lexikon der Schriftsteller, Dichter, Bankiers, Geldleute, Ärzte, Schauspieler, Künstler, Musiker, Offiziere, Rechtsanwälte, Revolutionäre, Frauenrechtlerinnen, Sozialdemokraten usw., jüdischer Rasse und Versippung (Berlin, 1913).

Märchendeutungen. Sinn und Deutung der
deutschen Volksmärchen (Berlin,
1914).

Semi-Imperator, 1888–1918 (Munich, 1919).

Meine geistig-seelische Welt (Berlin-Lichterfelde, 1922).

Tarnhari (i.e. Ernst Lauterer)

An unsere Getreuen. Mahn- und Freundes-
worte an die Einsamen im Hause
(Diessen, [1914]).

*Aus den Traditionen der Laf-tar-ar-Sippe der
der 'Lauterer'.* Eine Weihegabe an alle
Treubefundene (Diessen, [1915]).

An alle Deutschvölkischen! (Leipzig, 1920).

1. Hakenkreuz-Rundbrief der Nationalen Kanzlei
(Leipzig, [1920]).

V. The Ariosophists

(a) Periodicals

*Zeitschrift für Menschenkenntnis und Menschen-
schicksal,* 1 issue (Oestrich im Rheingau,
October 1925). Continued as *Zeitschrift für
Menschenkenntnis und Schicksalsforschung.*

*Zeitschrift für Menschenkenntnis und Schicksals-
forschung.* Monthly. Düsseldorf-Unterrath,
1926-27. Edited by Herbert Reichstein.

Zeitschrift für Geistes- und Wissenschaftsreform.
Monthly. Pforzheim, then Pressbaum b.
Vienna, then Berlin, 1928-33. Edited by
Herbert Reichstein.

Der Wehrmann. Organ der 'Deutschen Wehr-
mann-Gesellschaft'. Monthly. Pforzheim,
1931-32. Edited by F. I. Wehrmann.

Sig-Run (Pan-arische Jugendzeitschrift).
Monthly. Pasing b. Munich, 1932. Edited
by Wilhelm von Arbter.

Die neue Flagge. Monthly. Dresden, 1931-33.
Edited by Georg Richter.

Arische Rundschau. Weekly. Berlin, 1933-? Edited
by Herbert Reichstein and Karl Kern.

(b) Book-Series

Ariosophische Bibliothek. 23 vols. Herbert
Reichstein: Oestrich, then Düsseldorf-Unterrath, then Pforzheim,
1925-29.

1 Lanz v. Liebenfels, Grundriss der ariosophischen Geheimlehre (1925).

2 Wehrmann, Die Tragik der Germanen.
Gottgeschöpf Weib und sein Fall
(1926).

3 Lanz v. Liebenfels, Ariosophische
Rassenphrenologie (1926).

4 Wehrmann, Die Sendung der Germanen. Gottgeschöpf Weib und
sein Aufstieg (1926).

5 Reichstein, Warum Ariosophie? (1926).

6 Schmude, Ariosophische Gedichte
und Sprüche (1926).

Lanz v. Liebenfels, Jakob Lorber, das
grösste ariosophische Medium der
Neuzeit.

7 I. Teil: Lebensgang und die Mysterien
der irdischen Welt (1926).

8 II. Teil: Die Mysterien der planet-
arischen Welt (1926).

9 III. Teil: Die Mysterien der makro-
kosmischen Welt (1926).

10 IV. Teil: Die Mysterien der mikro-
kosmischen Welt (1926).

11 Dietrich, Weisse und schwarze Magie
(1926).

12 Lanz v. Liebenfels, Das Sakrament der
Ehe im Lichte der ariosophischen
Theologie (1926).

13 Tordai v. Szügy, Die Materie, eine grosse
Illusion (1926).

14 Stromer-Reichenbach, Was wird?
Vorausberechnung der deutschen
Revolutions-Entwicklung (1926).

15 Lanz v. Liebenfels, Meister Archibald
u. Meister Amalarich, Die ariosophische Kabbalistik von Name
und Örtlichkeit (1926).

16/17 Lanz v. Liebenfels, Ariosophische
Rassenphysiognomik (1927).

18 Die ariosophische Runen-Magie von
Ihm . . . selbst durch den heiligen
ariosophischen Geist der Gegenwart
(1928).

19 Lanz v. Liebenfels, Ariosophische
Urgeschichte der Handwerke und
Künste (1928).

20/21 Lanz v. Liebenfels, Ariosophisches
Wappenbuch (1928).

22 Richter, Heilmagnetismus und
Gedankenkräfte (1929).

23 Rüdiger, Tyrkreis und Tattwas im
Lichte wissenschaftlicher Forschung
(1929).

Das Weistum des Volkes. 5 vols. Herbert
Reichstein: Berlin, 1934–35.

1 Reichstein, Das religiöse und rassische
Weltgeschehen von Urbeginn bis
heute (1934).

2 Reichstein, Gelöste Rätsel ältester

Geschichte – von Atlantis, Edda und der Bibel (1934).

3 Reichstein, Enthält die Bibel arisches Weistum? (1935).

4 Reichstein, Die Religion des Blutes (1935).

5 Reichstein, Nationalsozialismus und positives Christentum (1935).

(c) **Books**

Friedbert Asboga

Handbuch der Astromagie. Ein Lehrgang für Suchende und Lebensreformer, 8 parts (Pfullingen, 1925–28).

Astromedizin, Astropharmazie und Astrodiätetik (Memmingen, 1931).

Robert H. Brotz

Grosses Lehr- und Handbuch der ariosophischen Graphologie, 19 instalments (Pforzheim, 1927).

Die Graphologie als Hilfsmittel zur Krankheitserkennung, second edition (Zeulenroda, 1932).

Fra Dietrich (pseudonym for Theodor Czepl)

Weisse und schwarze Magie (Düsseldorf-Unterrath, 1926).

'"Adveniat regnum tuum . . . "', *Die Arve*, Heft 15 (December 1951), 11–13.

'Sparta, das grosse Beispiel', *Die Arve*, Heft 18 (November 1952), 8–12.

Georg Hauerstein Jr.

Petena-Handschrift 5. Bildersammlung NT Vit. (Imaginarium NT II. Band) zur Templeisengeschichte (Petena, n.d.).

Petena-Handschrift 6. Organum NT Vit. Gründung, Regel und Geschichte des Vitaleisentums (Petena, n.d.).

Ernst Issberner-Haldane

Der Chiromant. Werdegang, Erinnerungen von Reisen und aus der Praxis eines Chirosophen, mit Vorträgen und Betrachtung für eine höhere Weltanschauung (Bad Oldesloe, 1925).

Wissenschaftliche Handlesekunst, 2 vols. (Berlin, 1921–2).

Menschen und Leute (Berlin, 1927).

Handschriftdeutung (Leipzig, 1928).

Yogha-Schulung für westliche Verhältnisse (Pforzheim, [1928]).

Praktische Anleitung zur Handschriftendeutung (Wolfenbüttel, 1929).

Charakterologische Tatsachen und deren Merkmale (Lorch, 1929).

Karl Kern

Rassen-Schutz (Stuttgart, 1927).

Mensch und Charakter von Johann Praetorius, edited by Karl Kern, c.5 instalments (Pressbaum, 1931–2).

Handbuch der Ariosophie Bd. 1 (Pressbaum, 1932).

B. Raynald

Emerich der Heilige. Der erste Christusritter und der Tempelherren-Orden in Ungarn (Budapest, 1930).

Herbert Reichstein

Warum Ariosophie? (Düsseldorf-Unterrath, 1926).

Praktisches Lehrbuch der ariosophischen Kabbalistik, c.12 instalments (Pressbaum, 1931).

Das Weistum des Volkes. Schriften über Rasse, Religion und Volkstum, 5 vols. (Berlin, 1934–35).

Alfred Richter

Die urewige Weisheitssprache der Menschenformen (Leipzig, 1932).

Unsere Führer im Lichte der Rassenfrage und Charakterologie (Leipzig, 1933).

Der Heilgruss. Seine Art und Bedeutung (Dresden, 1933).

Georg Richter

Warum lebe ich auf Erden? Ein Wegweiser für suchende Seelen (Niedersedlitz, 1927).

Warum praktische Menschenkenntnis? (Niedersedlitz, 1929).

Heilmagnetismus und Gedankenkräfte (Pforzheim, 1929).

AEIOU. Kraft-Welle—Mensch (Dresden, 1931).

Erwachtes Germanien (Dresden, 1933).

Reichstag 1975. Vision (oder Wirklichkeit) (Dresden, 1933).

Frenzolf Schmid

Die Ur-Strahlen. Eine wissenschaftliche Entdeckung (Munich, 1928).

Das neue Strahlen-Heilverfahren. Die Therapie der Zukunft (Halle, 1929).

Urtexte der Ersten Göttlichen Offenbarung. Attalantische Urbibel (Pforzheim, 1931).

Detlef Schmude

Vom Schwingen und Klingen und göttlichen Dingen (Quedlingburg, [1919]).

Das Gebot der Stunde. Über die Arbeit zur Siedlung (Berlin, 1920).

Durch Arbeit zur Siedlung (Berlin, 1922).

Ariosophische Gedichte und Sprüche (Pforzheim, 1927).

Gregor Schwartz-Bostunitsch (formerly Grigorij Bostunič)

Masonstvo i russkaya revoljucija (Novi Sad, 1922).

Des Henkers Tod. Drama in einem Akt (Graz, 1926).

Die Freimaurerei, ihr Ursprung, ihre Geheimnisse, ihr Wirken (Weimar, 1928).

Die Bolschewisierung der Welt (Munich, 1929).

Ein bulgarischer Faust (Pforzheim, 1930).

Doktor Steiner – ein Schwindler wie keiner. Ein Kapital über Anthroposophie und die geistige Arbeit der 'Falschen Propheten' (Munich, 1930).

Der Zarenmord und die rätselhaften Zeichen am Tatort des Mordes (Munich, 1931).

Jüdischer Imperialismus (Landsberg, 1935).

Friedrich Schwickert (also used the pseudonym Sindbad)

Das Lebeselixier in Bulwers Romanen und in den Schriften wirklicher Adepten (Leipzig, 1918).

Sindbad and Adolf Weiss

Die astrologische Synthese eine Kombinationslehre (Munich, 1925).

Bausteine der Astrologie, 5 vols. (Munich, 1926–27).

Frodi Ingolfson Wehrmann

Die Wirkung der Sonne in den zwölf Tierkreisen (Berlin, 1923).

Die Tragik der Germanen. Gottgeschöpf Weib und sein Fall (Düsseldorf-Unterrath, 1926).

Die Sendung der Germanen. Gottgeschöpf Weib und sein Aufstieg (Düsseldorf-Unterrath, 1926).

Sonne und Mensch (Stuttgart, 1927).

Das Garma der Germanen (Berlin-Niederschönhausen, 1927).

Dein Schicksal (Pforzheim, 1929).

Hermann Wieland

Atlantis, Edda und Bibel. Das entdeckte Geheimnis der Heiligen Schrift des deutschen Volkes Rettung aus Not und Tod (Nuremberg, 1922).

VI. The Rune Occultists

(a) Periodicals

Deutsche Freiheit. Monthly. Munich, then Dinkelsbühl, 1919–26. Edited by R. J. Gorsleben. Continued as *Arische Freiheit.*

Arische Freiheit. Monthly. Dinkelsbühl, 1927. Edited by R. J. Gorsleben. Absorbed by *Zeitschrift für Geistes- und Wissenschaftsreform* in 1928, then continued as *Hag All All Hag.*

Hag All All Hag. Monthly. Dinkelsbühl, then Mittenwald, 1929–1934. Edited by R. J. Gorsleben, then Werner von Bülow. Continued as *Hagal* in July 1934.

Hagal. Monthly. Munich, then Mittenwald, July 1934–1939. Edited by Werner von Bülow.

(b) Books

Werner von Bülow

Märchendeutungen durch Runen (Dresden, 1925).

Der Ewigkeitsgehalt der eddischen Runen und Zahlen. Grundriss arischer Weisheit und Jungbrunnen des deutschen Volkstums (Munich, 1925).

Rudolf John Gorsleben

Allgemeine Flugblätter deutscher Nation, 5 issues, edited by R. John v. Gorsleben (Munich, 1914).

Der Rastaguär. Eine ernsthafte Komödie (Leipzig, 1913).

Die Überwindung des Judentums in uns und ausser uns (Munich, 1920).

Die Edda [ältere Edda]. (Götterlieder) (Pasing, 1922).

Die Edda, ihre Bedeutung für Gegenwart und Zukunft (Pasing, 1923).

Das Blendwerk der Götter <Gylfaginning>. (Pasing, 1923).

Das Geheimnis von Dinkelsbühl. Eine tiefgründliche und doch kurzweilige Abhandlung über den Ursprung der Stadt Dinkelsbühl (Dinkelsbühl, 1928).

Hoch-Zeit der Menschheit. Das Welt-Gesetz der Drei oder Entstehen – Sein – Vergehen in Ursprache – Urschrift – Urglaube. Aus den Runen geschöpft (Leipzig, 1930).

Siegfried Adolf Kummer

Heilige Runenmacht. Wiedergeburt des Armanentums durch Runenübungen und Tänze (Hamburg, 1932).

Runen-Magie (Dresden, 1933).

Walhall. Hand- und Bilderschrift für Runenkunde, Mystik und Vorgeschichte. Briefe 1, 2. (Obersteina b. Radeberg, 1934).

Runen-Raunen. Eine Sammlung eingesandter Berichte nach der Runenkunde (Obersteina b. Radeberg, 1934).

Georg Lomer

Hakenkreuz und Soujetstern (Bad Schmiedeberg, 1925).

Die Götter der Heimat. Grundzüge einer germanischer Astrologie (Bad Schmiedeberg, 1927).

Wir und die Juden im Lichte der Astrologie (Hanover, 1928).

Die Evangelien als Himmelsbotschaft (Hanover, 1930).

Friedrich Bernhard Marby
 'Die Kreuzesform in Fleisch und Blut'. Arisch-christliches Bühnenspiel (Stuttgart, 1924).
 Runenschrift, Runenwort, Runengymnastik (Stuttgart, 1931).
 Marby-Runen-Gymnastik (Stuttgart, 1932).
 Runen raunen richtig Rat! Runen-Übungen als Notwende und Heilsweg (Stuttgart, 1934).
 Rassische Gymnastik als Aufrassungsweg (Stuttgart, 1935).
 Der Weg zu den Müttern inmitten der Kette der Wiedergeburten. Mit dem Anhang: Von den Geheimnissen alter Türme und Kirchen (Stuttgart, 1957).
 Sonne und Planeten im Tierkreis (Stuttgart, 1975).

VII. SS Ariosophists

Günther Kirchhoff
 'Politische Notwendigkeiten', typescript dated 11 August 1934, Bundesarchiv, Koblenz, NS21/31.
 'Rotbart von Kyffhäuser', typescript dated 1 September 1934, Bundesarchiv, Koblenz, NS21/31.
 'Die FAMA von Christian Rosenkreuz', typescript dated May 1936, Bundesarchiv, Koblenz, NS21/31.
 'Heimat-Geschichte des Ufgaues!', undated typescript, Bundesarchiv, Koblenz, NS21/31.
 'Das politische Rätsel Asien aus Ortung erschlossen', in: Rudolf J. Mund, *Der Rasputin Himmlers* (Vienna, 1982), pp. 260–9.

Otto Rahn
 Kreuzzug gegen den Gral (Freiburg, 1933).
 Luzifers Hofgesind. Eine Reise zu Europas guten Geistern (Leipzig, 1937).

Karl Maria Wiligut (alias Karl Maria Weisthor and Jarl Widar)
 Seyfrieds Runen (Rabensteinsage) (Vienna, 1903).
 'Uraltes Familien-Siegel des Hauses Wiligut', *Hag All All Hag* 10 (1933), Heft 2/3, 290–3.
 'Gotos Raunen – Runenwissen!', 'Runen raunen . . .' and 'Die Vierheiten', *Hagal* 11 (1934), Heft 7, 7–15.
 'Die Zahl: Runen raunen, Zahlen reden . . .', *Hagal* 11 (1934), Heft 8, 1–4.

'Die Schöpfungsspirale, das "Weltenei"!', *Hagal* 11 (1934), Heft 9, 4–7.
'Bericht über die Dienstreise von SS-Oberführer Weisthor nach Gaggenau/Baden und Umgebung vom 16.–24. Juni 1936', typescript, Bundesarchiv, Koblenz, Nachlass Darré AD26.
'Bericht über die Auffindung des Irminkreuzes als Ortung im südlichen Niedersachsen, also die 5. Irminskreuzortung', typescript dated July 1936, Bundesarchiv, Koblenz, Nachlass Darré AD26.

(b) Biographical Studies

Rudolf J. Mund, *Der Rasputin Himmlers.* Die Wiligut-Saga (Vienna, 1982).
——, *Eine notwendige Erklärung,* Das andere Kreuz (Vienna, 1983).

B. SECONDARY SOURCES

Ackermann, Josef. *Heinrich Himmler als Ideologe* (Göttingen, 1970).
Appell, J. W. *Die Ritter-, Räuber- und Schauerromantik* (Leipzig, 1859).
Besser, Joachim. 'Die Vorgeschichte des Nationalsozialismus in neuem Licht', *Die Pforte* 2 (1950), 763–84.
Butler, Rohan d'O. *The Roots of National Socialism 1783–1933.* (London, 1941).
Cohn, Norman. *The Pursuit of the Millennium,* third edition (New York, 1970).
——, *Warrant for Genocide.* The myth of the Jewish world-conspiracy and the Protocols of the Elders of Zion (London, 1967).
——, *Europe's Inner Demons.* An enquiry inspired by the Great Witch-Hunt (London, 1975).
Coleman, William Emmette. 'The source of Madame Blavatsky's writings', in Vsevolod Soloviev, *A Modern Priestess of Isis* (London, 1895), pp. 353–66.
Dikenmann, U. 'Hans Lanz von Liebenfels, ein mittelalterlicher Emporkömmling', *Thurgauische Beiträge* 21 (1911), 34–48.
Eckstein, Friedrich. *'Alte unnennbare Tage!'* Erinnerungen aus siebzig Lehr- und Wanderjahren (Vienna, 1936).
Epstein, Klaus. *The Genesis of German Conservatism* (Princeton, 1966).
Fest, Joachim. *Hitler,* translated by Richard and Clara Winston (London, 1974).
Field, Geoffrey G. *Evangelist of Race.* The Germanic vision of Houston' Stewart Chamberlain (New York, 1981).

Franz-Willing, Georg. *Ursprung der Hitler-bewegung 1919–1922*, second edition (Preussisch Oldendorf, 1974).

Frecot, Janos, Geist, Johann Friedrich and Kerbs, Diethart. *FIDUS 1868–1948: Zur ästhetischen Praxis bürgerlicher Fluchtbewegungen* (Munich, 1972).

Gasman, Daniel. *The Scientific Origins of National Socialism*. Social Darwinism in Ernst Haeckel and the German Monist League (London, 1971).

Greiner, Josef. *Das Ende des Hitler-Mythos* (Zurich, 1947).

Hamel, Iris. *Völkischer Verband und nationale Gewerkschaft*. Der Deutschnationale Handlungsgehilfen-Verband 1893–1933 (Frankfurt, 1967).

Heer, Friedrich. *Der Glaube des Adolf Hitler*. Anatomie einer politischen Religiosität (Munich, 1968).

Henry, Clarissa and Hillel, Marc. *Children of the SS* (London, 1975).

Hermand, Jost. 'Gralsmotive um die Jahrhundertwende', *Vierteljahresschrift für Literaturwissenschaft und Geistesgeschichte* 36 (1962), 521–43.

Herwig. (i.e. Eduard Pichl). *Georg Schönerer und die Entwicklung des Alldeutschtumes in der Ostmark*, 4 vols. (Vienna, 1912–23).

Howe, Ellic. *Urania's Children*. The strange world of the astrologers (London, 1967).
———, 'Rudolph Freiherr von Sebottendorff' (unpublished typescript, 1968).
———, *The Magicians of the Golden Dawn*. A documentary history of a magical order 1887–1923 (London, 1972).
———, 'Fringe Masonry in England, 1870–85', *Ars Quatuor Coronatorum* 85 (1972), 242–80.

Howe, Ellic and Möller, Helmut. 'Theodor Reuss. Irregular Freemasonry in Germany, 1900–23', *Ars Quatuor Coronatorum* 91 (1978), 28–47.

Hunger, Ulrich. *Die Runenkunde im Dritten Reich*. Ein Beitrag zur Wissenschafts- und Ideologiegeschichte des Nationalsozialismus (Frankfurt, 1984).

Hüser, Karl. *Wewelsburg 1933–1945*. Kult- und Terrorstätte der SS (Paderborn, 1982).

Jasper, Gotthard. 'Aus den Akten der Prozesse gegen die Erzberger-Mörder', *Vierteljahreshefte für Zeitgeschichte* 10 (1962), 430–53.

Jenks, William A. *Vienna and the young Hitler* (New York, 1960).
———, *Austria under the Iron Ring 1879–1893* (Charlottesville, 1965).

Jetzinger, Franz. *Hitler's Youth*, translated by Lawrence Wilson (Westport, Conn., 1976).

Joachimsthaler, Anton. *Die Breitspurbahn Hitlers*. Eine Dokumentation über die geplante transkontinentale 3-Meter-Breitspureisenbahn der Jahre 1942–1945 (Freiburg, 1981).

Jones, J. Sydney. *Hitler in Vienna 1907–13*. Clues to the future (London, 1983).

Kater, Michael H. *Das 'Ahnenerbe' der SS 1935–1945*. Ein Beitrag zur Kulturpolitik des Dritten Reiches (Stuttgart, 1974).

Kersten, Felix. *The Kersten Memoirs 1940–1945*, translated by Constantine Fitzgibbon and James Oliver (London, 1956).

Klemperer, Klemens von. *Germany's New Conservatism*. Its history and dilemma in the twentieth century (Princeton, 1968).

Kubizek, August. *Young Hitler*. The story of our friendship, translated by E. V. Anderson (Maidstone, 1973).

Kuhn, Alvin Boyd. *Theosophy. A modern revival of ancient wisdom* (New York, 1930).

Laqueur, Walter Z. *Young Germany*. A history of the German youth movement (London, 1962).
———, *Russia and Germany*. A century of conflict (London, 1965).

Lebovics, Herman. *Social Conservatism and the Middle Classes in Germany 1914–1933* (Princeton, 1969).

Liljegren, S. B. 'Quelques romans anglais. Source partielle d'une religion moderne', in *Mélanges d'histoire littéraire générale*, edited by Fernand Baldensperger, 2 vols. (Paris, 1930), II, 60–77.
———, *Bulwer-Lytton's Novels and Isis Unveiled* (Uppsala, 1957).

Lohalm, Uwe. *Völkischer Radikalismus*. Die Geschichte des Deutschvölkischen Schutz- und Trutz-Bundes 1919–1923 (Hamburg, 1970).

McIntosh, Christopher. *The Rosy Cross Unveiled* (Wellingborough, 1980).

Mohler, Armin. *Die konservative Revolution in Deutschland 1918–1932*. Ein Handbuch (Darmstadt, 1972).

Mosse, George L. 'The mystical origins of National Socialism', *Journal of the History of Ideas* 22 (1961), 81–96.
———, *The Crisis of German Ideology*. Intellectual origins of the Third Reich (New York, 1964).
———, *The Nationalization of the Masses* (New York, 1975).

Müller-Fraureuth, Carl. *Die Ritter- und Räuberromane* (Halle, 1894).

Müllern-Schönhausen, Johannes von. *Die Lösung des Rätsel's Adolf Hitler.* Der Versuch einer Deutung der geheimnisvollsten Erscheinung der Weltgeschichte (Vienna, [1959]).

Murphet, Howard. *Hammer on the Mountain.* The Life of Henry Steel Olcott (1832–1907) (Wheaton, Ill., 1972).

——, *When Daylight Comes.* A biography of Helena Petrovna Blavatsky (Wheaton, Ill., 1975).

Phelps, Reginald H. 'Die Hitler-Bibliothek', *Deutsche Rundschau* 80 (1954), 923–31.

——, 'Theodor Fritsch und der Antisemitismus', *Deutsche Rundschau* 87 (1961), 442–9.

——, 'Anton Drexler – Der Gründer der NSDAP', *Deutsche Rundschau* 87 (1961), 1134–43.

——, '"Before Hitler came": Thule Society and Germanen Orden', *Journal of Modern History* 25 (1963), 245–61.

——, 'Hitler and the Deutsche Arbeiterpartei', *American Historical Review* 68 (1963), 974–86.

Poliakov, Léon. *The Aryan Myth.* A history of racist and nationalist ideas in Europe (London, 1974).

Pulzer, Peter G. J. *The Rise of Political Anti-Semitism in Germany and Austria* (New York, 1964).

Ravenscroft, Trevor. *The Spear of Destiny.* The occult power behind the spear which pierced the side of Christ (London, 1972).

Rhodes, James M. *The Hitler Movement.* A modern millenarian revolution (Stamford, Calif., 1980).

Ringer, Fritz, K. *The Decline of the German Mandarins.* The German academic community 1890–1933 (Cambridge, Mass., 1969).

Roberts, J. M. *The Mythology of the Secret Societies* (London, 1972).

Rogalla von Bieberstein, Johannes. *Die These von der Verschwörung 1776–1945.* Philosophen, Freimaurer, Juden, Liberale und Sozialisten als Verschwörer gegen die Sozialordnung (Frankfurt, 1978).

Soloviev, Vsevolod. *A Modern Priestess of Isis* (London, 1895).

Speer, Albert. *Inside the Third Reich* (London, 1970).

——, *The Spandau Diaries* (London, 1976).

Stark, Gary D. *Entrepreneurs of Ideology.* Neoconservative publishers in Germany 1890–1933 (Chapel Hill, 1981).

Stern, Fritz. *The Politics of Cultural Despair.* A study in the rise of the Germanic Ideology (Berkeley, 1974).

Viatte, Auguste. *Les sources occultes du romantisme,* 2 vols. (Paris, 1928).

Waite, Robert G. L. *Vanguard of Nazism.* The Free Corps movement in postwar Germany 1918–1923 (Cambridge, Mass., 1970).

Waite, Robert G. L. *The Psychopathic God: Adolf Hitler* (New York, 1977).

Webb, James. *The Flight from Reason.* Volume 1 of the Age of the Irrational (London, 1971).

——, *The Occult Establishment* (La Salle, Ill., 1976).

——, *The Harmonious Circle.* The lives and work of G. I. Gurdjieff, P. D. Ouspensky, and their followers (London, 1980).

Whiteside, Andrew Gladding. *Austrian National Socialism before 1918* (The Hague, 1962).

——, *The Socialism of Fools.* Georg Ritter von Schönerer and Austrian Pan-Germanism (Berkeley, 1975).

Williams, Gertrude Marvin. *Priestess of the Occult (Madame Blavatsky)* (New York, 1946).

Wilson, Bryan R. 'Millennialism in comparative perspective', in *Millennial Dreams in Action,* edited by Sylvia L. Thrupp, Comparative Studies in Society and History 2 (The Hague, 1962), pp. 93–114.

——, *Religion in Secular Society* (London, 1966).

Wulff, Wilhelm Th.H. *Tierkreis und Hakenkreuz.* Als Astrologe am Himmlers Hof (Gütersloh, 1968).

Yates, Frances A. *The Rosicrucian Enlightenment* (London, 1972).

Zmarzlik, Hans-Günther. 'Der Sozialdarwinismus in Deutschland als geschichtliches Problem', *Vierteljahreshefte für Zeitgeschichte* 11 (1963), 245–73.

Index

INDEX